1,000,000 Books

are available to read at

www.ForgottenBooks.com

Read online
Download PDF
Purchase in print

ISBN 978-1-333-53728-9
PIBN 10516979

This book is a reproduction of an important historical work. Forgotten Books uses
state-of-the-art technology to digitally reconstruct the work, preserving the original format
whilst repairing imperfections present in the aged copy. In rare cases, an imperfection in
the original, such as a blemish or missing page, may be replicated in our edition. We do,
however, repair the vast majority of imperfections successfully; any imperfections that
remain are intentionally left to preserve the state of such historical works.

Forgotten Books is a registered trademark of FB &c Ltd.
Copyright © 2018 FB &c Ltd.
FB &c Ltd, Dalton House, 60 Windsor Avenue, London, SW19 2RR.
Company number 08720141. Registered in England and Wales.

For support please visit www.forgottenbooks.com

1 MONTH OF
FREE
READING

at

www.ForgottenBooks.com

By purchasing this book you are eligible for one month membership to ForgottenBooks.com, giving you unlimited access to our entire collection of over 1,000,000 titles via our web site and mobile apps.

To claim your free month visit:

www.forgottenbooks.com/free516979

* Offer is valid for 45 days from date of purchase. Terms and conditions apply.

English
Français
Deutsche
Italiano
Español
Português

www.forgottenbooks.com

Mythology Photography **Fiction**
Fishing Christianity **Art** Cooking
Essays Buddhism Freemasonry
Medicine **Biology** Music **Ancient
Egypt** Evolution Carpentry Physics
Dance Geology **Mathematics** Fitness
Shakespeare **Folklore** Yoga Marketing
Confidence Immortality Biographies
Poetry **Psychology** Witchcraft
Electronics Chemistry History **Law**
Accounting **Philosophy** Anthropology
Alchemy Drama Quantum Mechanics
Atheism Sexual Health **Ancient History**
Entrepreneurship Languages Sport
Paleontology Needlework Islam
Metaphysics Investment Archaeology
Parenting Statistics Criminology
Motivational

FIVE PROBLEMS
OF STATE AND RELIGION.

BY REV. WILL C. WOOD, A. M.

379 Pages. Price, $1.50.

CONTENTS:

THE STATE AND THE SABBATH. 1. The Sabbath a Benefactor to the State. 2. The God of the Sabbath a Benefactor to the State.

THE STATE AND TEMPLES. Taxing God's House.

THE STATE AND THE CHURCH. Their Separation discussed from first Principles. Our Connections with Rome. The English Established Church.

THE STATE SCHOOLS AND RELIGION. 1. Recognition of God in Public Education by the Bible. 2. God in the Nation, therefore God in Public Education. 3. Mother and Child; Bible and School. 4. Free America born of the Bible. 5. Bible in the Schools and Religionists. 6. State Schools and Church Schools. 7. The English and the Douai Versions. 8. The Imperial Exile. 9. The Bible and the Manual of Morals.

THE STATE INSTITUTIONS AND RELIGION. Divine Service; History of Chaplaincies; One Chaplain, only one Chaplain.

FOR SALE BY THE TRADE EVERYWHERE.

Mailed, prepaid, by Publisher,

HENRY HOYT . . . . . . No. 9 Cornhill, Boston.

" I congratulate you on the favorable notices your keen and timely book on the ' Five Problems' is receiving." — *Joseph Cook.*

" A volume adapted to do good and only good. It answers each of the problems as the Gospel requires and the public needs that it should be answered. Its easy, familiar style and its affluence of illustrations will give it a welcome and insure for it a holding ground in many quarters in which an abstract discussion would be of no avail. I should rejoice to have such a book go wherever there are readers that can understand its reasonableness." — *A. P. Peabody, D. D.*

" I take pleasure in saying that I regard it as a valuable and timely contribution to the discussion of a question which is coming up in new aspects. ... His view of what religion has to do with the State and of the mutual independence of State and Church is worthy of most careful attention; and such attention the book, with its vividness of style and illustration, is well suited to command and reward." — *Leonard Bacon, D. D.*

" I take pleasure in commending to the public the volume ' Five Problems.' The subjects are vitally connected with the prosperity of our free institutions, the treatment of them is vigorous, and the sentiments cannot fail to commend themselves to the patriot and Christian." — *Mark Hopkins, D. D.*

" An able and thoughtful discussion of important topics." — *S. C. Bartlett, D. D.*

"The merit and value of the Fourth Discussion seem to me extraordinary. Its candor, its breadth of view, the justness of its thought, the pertinence of its illustrative citations and allusions, and the philosophic serenity and victorious strength of its argumentation, are traits which qualify this treatise to make an enduring mark upon the history of our race." — *Myron A. Munson, A. M.*

"One of the most marked excellences of the book is its readableness. Opened almost anywhere, it catches even a listless mind by some allusion or citation and carries it along to the end of the chapter." — *Prof. J. Henry Thayer.*

"Our friend, the late pastor at Wenham, has done good service. These several propositions are supported with much clearness of argument, ingenuity of illustration, wealth of quotation, and fairness of spirit. The discussion is successfully relieved from heaviness by its peculiar structure and lively method, and at points is enriched with the results of careful research. The comparison of the common English and Douai versions of the Bible is extremely interesting. Mr Wood has made a good and useful book, one worth not only reading, but owning." — *Congregationalist.*

"Abounds in valuable thoughts on a question of extreme importance. Many of the authorities quoted are of particular interest and value to the discussion." — *Advance.*

"The discussion of these five topics is the fruit of various reading, and proves, what we have known before, that Mr. Wood possesses an active, sprightly, and energetic mind, which he disciplines by earnest and diligent labor." — *Bibliotheca Sacra.*

"A thesaurus, from which the preacher, who wishes to present to his people any one of these topics, may both gather material and find stimulus in his work. We hope the facts relative to Sabbath observance may be heralded through the land. . . . In showing the vast superiority of our authorized English version of the Scriptures over the Douai version, with his array of the opinions of some of the ablest writers on the subject, both American and European, Mr. Wood has done good service. Indeed, we thank him for the entire volume. It is stimulating and will provoke inquiry." — *Congregational Quarterly, Christopher Cushing, D. D.*

"An interesting chapter is that on the comparative authoritative value of the English and Douai versions of the Bible, and is worth more to the reader than several times the cost of the book. The volume throughout is scholarly, vigorous, always in advocacy of the right, and one of the best productions of this year of grace, 1877." — *Central Methodist.*

"We find in these essays an attempt, and we think a successful attempt, to consider these questions from a point of view which has the advantage of being sustained by the moral sentiment of the people as *citizens.* If our author has succeeded in indicating a common method of studying or discussing these subjects, he has done a great and good work." — *S. W. Presbyterian.*

"An admirable book, and we rejoice that so much of truth on these important questions, and in such an interesting style, is given to the public." — *Christian Press, Cincinnati.*

"These essays are strong, and their power will be recognized even by those who disagree with their conclusions." — *New Haven Palladium.*

"Vigorous reasoning." — *Boston Advertiser.*

ie extraordi-
ght, the per-
philosophic
raits which
story of our

eadableness.
me allusion
of. *J. Henry*

od service.
ess of argu-
ess of spirit.
its peculiar
e results of
Douai vi r-
ade a good
– *Congrega-*

mportance
value to the

ading, and
an active,
nd diligent

sent to his
d *stimulus*
ce may be
of our au-
n, with his
ject, both
ndeed, we
rovoke in-

tive value
ore to the
ughout is
f the best

l attempt,
advantage
s. If our
ng or dis-
W. Pres-

the se im-
the pub-

even by
um.

FIVE PROBLEMS OF STATE AND RELIGION.

FIVE PROBLEMS

OF

STATE AND RELIGION.

BY

WILL C. WOOD, A.M.,

LATE PASTOR AT WENHAM, MASS.

———

BOSTON:

HENRY HOYT, PUBLISHER.

1877.

III. .71292

C.10248.77.5

HARVARD COLLEGE

SEP 10 1906

LIBRARY.

COPYRIGHT,

1877,

BY HENRY HOYT.

Stereotyped and Printed by
Rand, Avery, and Company,
117 Franklin Street,
Boston.

"Our fathers' God, from out whose hand
The centuries fall like grains of sand!
We meet to-day, united, free,
And loyal to our land and thee,
To thank thee for the era done,
And trust thee for the opening one.

Oh! make thou us, through centuries long,
In peace secure, and justice strong;
Around our gifts of freedom draw
The safeguard of thy righteous law;
And, cast in some diviner mould,
Let the new cycle shame the old."

WHITTIER'S CENTENNIAL HYMN.

" The American State recognizes only the catholic religion. It eschews all sectarianism. The State conforms to what each holds that is catholic, that is always and everywhere religion; and whatever is not catholic it leaves as outside of its province, to live or die, according to its own inherent vitality, or want of vitality. The State conscience is catholic, not sectarian."—O. A. BROWNSON.

" If ever our liberties perish, it will be by the explosion of the volcanic power of the European and American populace, and foreign influence, and American demagogues in bad alliance, who will ride in the whirlwind, and direct the storm. This, I am aware, is strong language: but strong language is needed; for this giant nation sleepeth, and must be awaked." " It is said again, ' The conspiracy, if real, to overthrow our republic by immigration and a foreign religion, is impotent and chimerical, — a thing which cannot be done.' Indeed! Is our republic, then, so mature, and solid, and strong, as to bid defiance to peril? Our wisest men have regarded its preservation, when formed of native citizens only, as an experiment, urged on by high hopes indeed and strenuous efforts, but amid stupendous difficulties, and not yet consummated; and, though hitherto our ship has weathered every storm, has it been accomplished with such ease and safety as to justify the proud contempt of greater dangers?" — LYMAN BEECHER, 1835.

PREFATORY.

THESE essays, which have appeared in various public prints,[1] are now, for the first time, published in a collected form. It is believed the discussions are timely, and needful to the republic. Whatever merit these essays may have will be found to consist in this, — that they are, so far as is known to the writer, the first discussion of these subjects on the basis of *natural religion*, on which alone, in a mixed and free State, any satisfactory results can be gained. It has been the fault of even excellent works on this subject, that they start with some assumption unwarranted or challenged in a free mixed State; as, that "This is a Protestant country;" or, "The Bible is the word of God." Starting with such assumptions, the discussion, however valuable in portions, must needs be, as a whole, unsatisfactory. By such unsuccessful arguments, men's inner sense, that there is valid ground for a religious service in the schools, has been disappointed. In the whole course of the present argument it is assumed that we live in a *free mixed State;* and the Bible is not here referred to as the book *of* God, but only (which can by none be denied) that it is a book *about* God, and, to the European and American mind, the *best* book *about* God. The reader will be in a better state to appreciate the force of the argument throughout, if he will bear in mind that *religion*, as used in these essays, means *natural religion*, and *not revealed religion*, and if he observes that the Scriptures and Scripture personages, even he who is called Lord, are referred to only as *natural religion* may properly take account of them. On this plane alone, it is believed, can a just and permanent settlement of these important and vexed questions be reached, in our country, among what is confessedly a free people, each of whom is protected in the full exercise of his *personal religion*.

[1] Church Union, Congregationalist, Watchman.

vii

As the writer has been told that this argument strengthens as it advances, he begs suspension of judgment till the final pages on the part of any who may commence to read in the spirit of dissent. 'Tis a summary but superficial way to dispose of the Fourth Discussion —the main one, perhaps — in this volume by exclaiming, "Intolerance, sectarianism!" Deep subjects are not settled by shallow clamors. This discussion, though doubtless not faultless, is the fruit of patient thought. The first four essays in that discussion comprise the positive grounds for reading the Scriptures in public schools ; the next three essays meet opposing lines of thought ; the next essay surveys the results of withdrawing the Bible ; and the final essay is recapitulatory, corroboratory, and also expository of the Manual of Morals. The writer will be gratified if the remark of a Boston editor on one of these essays shall, to the candid and thoughtful, seem to apply to the whole, — " It *subsoils* the subject."

Our theme — not the connection of State and Church, but of the State and Religion — finds fit emblem in the design so skilfully set by the artist on our cover, — morning beam of our whole argument, — the Crown and the Sceptre, national authority possessed and national power wielded — reposing, for enlightenment and glory, under the full radiance of Heaven.

" *Laus Deo*," after the fashion of Handel, would we write in our margin, if this volume might prove a *Campus Martius* (*not* martial camp, good reader), — a place of meeting and agreement of the citizens of the republic. We trust that the motive of our heart has been to bring all good men speedily upon common ground on these questions which threaten to disturb our peace, to "dwell together in unity ; " "that we may lead a quiet and peaceable life, in all godliness and honesty, for this is good and acceptable in the sight of God our Saviour."

With these words, these discussions, with all their faults, are by the writer given to his countrymen, especially to thoughtful men, leaders of public opinion, with the hope that they may commend themselves to their candid judgment as the just and sound and safe basis on which — with the union and approbation of all good men, of whatever religious name — the American State may build itself up for a thousand years, harmoniously, righteously, in the favor of God. " *Sicut patribus, sit Deus nobis*."   WILL C. WOOD.

WEST ROXBURY, Sept. 1, 1877.

CONTENTS.

THE STATE AND THE SABBATH.

THE SABBATH THE BENEFACTOR
OF THE STATE.

[Unofficial.]

INTERNATIONAL EXHIBITION, PHILADELPHIA,
May 26, 1876.

REV. WILL C. WOOD.

Dear Sir, — The original vote of the United-States Centennial Commission, referring to the Sunday question, was taken two years ago, and was to
this effect : —

The Exhibition shall be open from nine o'clock in the morning until six
o'clock in the evening, daily, except Sunday.

Subsequently, about three months ago, the Executive Committee of the
Commission affirmed the first vote. Still later, in April last, the Commission
voted squarely on the question, " Shall the Exhibition be open on Sunday ? "
and decided in the negative by a vote of 29 to 9. The last vote was by
States, each State having one vote.

Yours very respectfully,

E. LEWIS MOORE.

Monday, May 15, the following resolutions were passed by
the evangelical ministers of Boston and vicinity, numbering
nearly four hundred : —

" *Resolved*, That we most heartily approve the action of the Centennial
Commissioners in closing the Exhibition and grounds on the Lord's Day,
and that we fervently hope they will maintain the American idea of the
Christian Sabbath by adhering most firmly to their wise decision.

" *Resolved*, That the secretary of the meeting transmit by telegraph the
above resolution to Gen. Hawley, Chairman of the Commissioners, as the
unanimous expression, by rising vote, of the Evangelical Ministers' Association of Boston and vicinity, in large attendance, this day at noon."

The action of these men is sound. It is fitting that this

commission of men in a religious land, it is fitting that these ministers of public virtue and patriotic spirit, should speak and act so decidedly in regard to Sabbath observance at our nation's Centennial.

Immortal are those words of Gen. Joseph Russell Hawley, worthy to be recalled with distinguished honor a hundred years hence, and not only to shine in letters of transient glory amid the coruscations of the pyrotechnic display, but to be carved in the enduring marble pedestal of the statue of the President of the First Centennial Exhibition of the Republic, to show the generations to come that the heroes of the early age were fearless in the field, yet God-fearing, and wise in counsel: " BEFORE GOD, I AM AFRAID TO OPEN THE EXHIBITION-GATES ON THE SABBATH." The noble words of Corliss, also, will go down with equal honor to posterity with the memory of his magnificent engine: " My opinion on that point is very decided, and I am very free to express it. All the good that would be accomplished by this grand Exhibition will be neutralized if it is opened on Sunday, and it would better never have been. I am ready to run at night, or at any hour, for the benefit of those who do not find it convenient to attend during the day, and I would favor a reduction in the rates of admission for such ; but under no circumstances would I consent to have it run on Sunday." [1]

Montalembert said, in his report to the French Parliament in 1850, " We need not hesitate to place in the front rank of our dangers and our faults the public profanation of the Sabbath." In this Centennial time of hope, we desire to avoid the dangers of our second century by laying still broader our foundations as state and nation on principles which are divine and eternal. That desire is the occasion of this fresh presentation of the Sabbath question in an unaccustomed form, — *an appeal to the State.* The argument in its whole course applies so powerfully to the individual, that we trust it may not be overlooked that the drift of the argument which follows is the demonstration of the obligations of the corporate *State* to the day of rest.

---

[1] Commissioner Corliss of Rhode Island.

AN ingenious writer, with whom we used to walk under the noble elms of Harvard, has lately enriched the world by a discourse on "Duty considered as Due-ty." He sets forth his germ idea thus: "Duty is nothing else than due-ty; that which is due; that which one being owes to another for something that has been received."[1]

In this thought of benefits received we will consider the fact that the STATE (the *State* as well as the *individual*) has a "duety" to the Sabbath, — a duty as imperative in its obligation, and as fruitful of good in its observance, as the duty of the individual, since whatever blesses her citizens blesses her, and becomes a reason — even where they are oblivious of the good received or possible — that she, in her sovereignty over them, should honor, cherish, and defend the Benefactor, even against all recusants, and thus not only discharge an obligation, but, perchance, give wider scope and channel to those benefactions in time to come.

The first of these essays will consider the "due-ty" of the State to the *Sabbath:* the second will consider the "due-ty" of the State to the *God* of the Sabbath. The first will consider the Sabbath without reference to its origin, as an impersonal thing, an institution: the second will meditate on the Sabbath as a benefit which can be traced to a personal Benefactor. The first paper is, "The Sabbath the Benefactor of the State;" the second, "The God of the Sabbath the Benefactor of the State."

THE SABBATH THE BENEFACTOR OF THE STATE.

This title contains several elementary ideas. The STATE, it is conceived, and not merely the individual, has a "due-ty" to the Sabbath.

States, as well as individuals, may have benefactors.

"In August, 1824, Lafayette came to the United States as the guest of the nation whose independence he had assisted in gaining with his blood and his fortune. He visited each of the twenty-four States, and was everywhere received with enthusiastic greetings of gratitude and joy. He remained in the country a

---

[1] Rev. Myron A. Munson.

little more than a year ; and, when ready to return, the President placed at his disposal a frigate, named, in compliment to him, 'The Brandywine,' to carry him back to France. Congress still further manifested their appreciation of his services by voting him a township and two hundred thousand dollars." The *State* considered this man a benefactor, and with good reason ; for, in 1777, Lafayette, a wealthy nobleman, not yet twenty years old, giving up the ease and elegance of his home, fitted out a vessel at his own expense, and crossed the ocean to offer his services to the Americans in their struggle for independence, asking only to serve as a volunteer, and without pay. The same national gratitude was felt toward De Kalb the Prussian, and Pulaski and Kosciusko the Poles.

States, then, may have benefactors, and may be grateful to them.

In the title, also, is contained the thought, that

The State may regard as a benefactor not only a person, but a beneficent institution; a day which, like the Sabbath, constantly recurs, bringing the boon of rest.

Suppose that that were done by a man which is done by the Sabbath : would he not be deemed a benefactor ? The shops are shut ; the wharves are silent ; the coal-miner is allowed to spend a day with his family in fresh green fields, under blue sky; the merchant's brain is set free from the cares of trade ; the cotter rejoices in his "Saturday night;" the hall of legislation is closed, and the court-room : all men give up toil and moil ; and myriad places are thrown open, where the soul is refreshed with glimpses

"Through open vistas into heaven."

This is done not one day, but two and fifty times a year. This day, this instituted day, constantly abiding in our civilization, and established in it like Jacob's well in Samaria's fields, welling forth as pure waters as in bygone millenniums, — is not this *day* a benefactor ? Is it difficult to personify it ?

The old Greeks would have apotheosized it. The old Greek sculptors would have delighted to carve the figure which should fitly represent *Sabbath Benefactor.* It should be of purest Parian marble, that it might emblem the serenity of the holy day of rest. It should be lofty, and loftily placed, like Minerva's statue, that it might look in benediction on all the city roofs and country fields.   It should be with benignant yet holy countenance, as of a divine friend.   It should be in "station," as if "new lighted" "from above, pure, peaceable, full of good fruits, without partiality;" yet it should stand as if come to abide.   Its drapery should be moved by the airs of heaven.   One hand should be extended as in act to shed abroad a holy calm over land and sea, giving repose to all labor; while the other should point upward and forward as if to bespeak the Creator's benediction which she came to bring to his creatures, and to remind that her most gracious service is to usher man into God's presence and rest.   So imaged in white marble, the Sabbath might engage our thought, even if it did not, as it might to the Greek, bow the knee.   But, even without the marble image of the sculptor, is it difficult for the imagination to behold the benignant and divine figure of *Sabbath Benefactor?*

The idea is also wrapped up in the title, that *the Sabbath is a benefactor independently of its origin.*   No matter whence it came: if this day has brought mental and physical repose and prosperity to whole peoples, it is a benefactor.   It may have come from China, like the silk manufacture; it may have had its origin from Central Asia, like the horse; it may have come from Europe, like the apple; it may have been derived from Greece, like our culture of the beautiful; or from Israel, like the sacred books of the Occident; or from Great Britain, like Magna Charta: whencesoever sprung, it is a benefactor, if it can be shown to be unspeakable in the value and extent of its beneficent influences.   If it be "earth-born," it is a benefactor; if it be "heaven-descended," it is a benefactor.   Its lofty place as benefactor does not depend on its origin.   If it can be shown that it does for man, for mankind, for a *nation,* what nothing else can do for them, then the State may well feel that she has a duty to perform, — to preserve to the day its integrity and sanctity, by virtue of which it has been and will be perennial in its benefactions to nations as well as to individuals.

This paper will aim to set forth the benefactions of the Sabbath to the State and her citizens, wherever her benignant mission has been accepted.

A preliminary word needs to be spoken in answer to a question which naturally suggests itself as to the necessity, the essential value, of the supposed benefactions of the Sabbath. Are these benefits so essential, when Greece and Rome could do without them?

The inquiry may arise in a reflecting mind, How is it, if the Sabbath be so necessary, and even essential to the well-being of man, his rest of body and mind, that the ancients could have dispensed with it, and yet have displayed such remarkable vigor both of body and mind? The facts in connection with this subject may, perhaps, be of great interest.

It may be said, to begin with, that it is difficult to compare a present state of things, in which there are undoubted improvements, with a past state, obscured by the gathered mists of many years, in which those improvements did not exist: it is much easier to compare what *we* are with the improvements with what *we* should be without them. The amelioration of mankind by laws and institutions is not always striking, even where a thoughtful mind must estimate it as considerable, and even unspeakable. The closing of stores on Saturday afternoon brings great refreshment. But does not the question always recur at these innovations, " Did not they get along well enough in the days before us?" So with the stage-coach: as you read history up to the year 1825, does it often strike one that their locomotion was limited in facilities? Occasionally only we are struck with the failure, from slow travelling, of some personage to reach a dying friend. So, before the days of steamboats, a casual glance does not reveal but that their travel by water was satisfactorily rapid. The same principle applies in the matter of stoves in dwellings, and furnaces in churches. Only occasionally, when we hear of the communion-wine frozen in the chalice, do we estimate the difference between then and now. Very evident is it, that our modern system of medicine is unspeakable in its benefits ; yet what superficial reader often thinks but that people in the past lived just as long, were just as well, and recovered from sickness just as soon, as we? How few of us, by historical or traditionary comparison, without research, could say that the sick did not fare as well before as since the discovery of ether? The right way to argue these cases, it is evident, is, not to compare ourselves with the benefits and a dimly known past without them, but to compare ourselves with them and ourselves without them.

So with the Sabbath. Even though we had no evidence that the Greeks and Romans were inferior in health and spiritual culture without the day, even though it were not known that they had imperfect substitutes for it, still, by comparison of ourselves with it, and ourselves without it, we are prepared to say confidently, that they must have lost much in having no Sabbath, both in health and morals. This is all which need be said to prevent any objection from this quarter.

But now, on the positive side, the evidence is ample and exceedingly interesting, that the Greeks and Romans did, by the movings of tired and restless nature, contrive some poor substitutes for the septenary day of rest. Many of the ancient and modern pagan nations have a day more or less devoted to rest and worship. The Saracens and Mohammedans keep Friday; the inhabitants of Guinea, Tuesday. The Chinese, it is said, once kept the seventh day.

But their great substitute for the Sabbath was the festivals. These were frequent. Lucius Accius informs us that the Greeks in town and country celebrated the Saturnalia. "The manner in which all public *feriæ* were kept," says one of the best writers on Greek and Roman antiquities, "bears great analogy to our Sunday. The most serious and solemn seem to have been the *feriæ imperativæ;* but all the others were generally attended by rejoicings and feastings. All kinds of business, especially lawsuits, were suspended during the public *feriæ,* as they were considered to pollute the sacred season." Such was the ancient groping for God's gift of the sacred day of rest.

The most thoughtful among the Greeks and Romans perceived the important effect of these days of rest. They eulogized them. They even go so far as to call them the gift of the gods. "Seneca applauds the holidays of heathendom as a wise appointment of legislators for the necessary attempering of human labor." Cicero commends festival days. Plato, in a remarkable passage, extols festivals as the "*gift of the gods for the relief of toil-doomed man.*"

But it may be thought that these festivals must have recurred so seldom, as in no way to compensate for lack of the Sabbath, and in no way to show the demand for it.

Under the auspices of the Genevan Société d'Utilité Publique, a valuable little volume was issued, entitled " Le Repos Hebdomadaire."[1] In the Appendix, Rabaud makes some interesting statements as to the number of the ancient festivals. He reminds us of the days of the Grecian games, — Olympic, Pythian, Isthmian, and Nemean, — and then adds this remarkable statement, that, in the Roman calendar, the fixed and regular festivals alone numbered *forty-seven.*[2] Claudius reduced the number to *thirty-seven.* Observe that there were seven in the month of February. This unequal distribution is sufficient to condemn their system in comparison with our regular appointment of time for labor and holy rest. Yet the great number of the days shows that man's nature craves a large number of days of rest, inasmuch as the Romans had as many regular festival days, within five, as we have Sabbaths in the year.[8]

The argument for the necessity of the Sabbath is therefore advanced, and not retarded, by the consideration that the Greeks and Romans were without it, but that they had a poor yet somewhat satisfactory substitute for it, on which they set such value as to call it "*the gift of the gods for the relief of toil-burdened man.*"

The main argument, then, can advance unimpeded, nay, with

---

[1] Camille and Edouard Rabaud, 1870.

[2] " Three in January, seven in February, five in March, five in April, five in May, five in June, five in July, three in August, three in September, two in October, two in November, two in December: total, forty-seven." " Most of these festivals lasted several days, as high as fifteen; and they certainly offered a full equivalent for our fifty-two dominical seasons."

[8] See also Graecia Feriata, in six books, Johannes Meursius; also the chapter, Weekly Repose among Ancient Nations other than the Hebrews, in another volume, Repos Hebdomadaire, by Lucien Jottrand, also issued by the Genevan Society of Public Utility.

an impetus forward, from the preceding considerations, to evince the benefactions of the Sabbath.

I. — THE SABBATH IS A BENEFACTOR TO THE STATE IN BESTOWING PHYSICAL REST UPON HER CITIZENS.

In 1832 the British House of Commons appointed a committee to investigate the effects of laboring seven days in a week, compared with those of laboring only six, and resting one. That committee consisted of Sir Andrew Agnew, Sir Robert Peel, Sir Robert Inglis, Sir Thomas Baring, Sir George Murray, Fowell Buxton, Lord Morpeth, Lord Ashley, Lord Viscount Sandon, and twenty other members of Parliament. They examined a great number of witnesses, of various professions and employments. Among them was John Richard Farre, M.D., of London, of whom they speak as "an acute and experienced physician." The following is his testimony : —

"I have practised as a physician between thirty and forty years ; and during the early part of my life, as the physician of a public medical institution, I had charge of the poor in one of the most populous districts of London. I have had occasion to observe the effect of the observance and non-observance of the seventh day of rest during the time. I have been in the habit, during a great many years, of considering the *uses* of the Sabbath, and of observing its *abuses*. The abuses are chiefly manifested in labor and dissipation. Its use, medically speaking, is that of a day of rest.

"As a day of rest, I view it as a day of *compensation* for the inadequate restorative power of the body under continued labor and excitement. A physician always has respect to the preservation of the restorative power, because, if once this be lost, his healing office is at an end. A physician is anxious to preserve the balance of circulation as necessary to the restorative power of the body. The ordinary exertions of man *run down* the circulation every day of his life ; and the first general law of nature by which God (who is not only the giver, but also the preserver and sustainer, of life) prevents man from destroying himself is the alternating of day and night, that repose may succeed action. But although the night apparently equalizes the circulation, yet it does not sufficiently restore its balance for the attainment of a long life. Hence one day in seven, by the bounty of Providence, is thrown in as a day of compensation, to perfect by its repose the animal system.

"Take that fine animal the horse, and work him to the full extent of his powers every day in the week, or give him rest one day in seven, and you will soon perceive, by the superior vigor with which he performs his functions on the other six days, that this is necessary to his well-being. Man, possessing a superior nature, is borne along by the very vigor of his mind, so that the injury of continued diurnal exertion and excitement on his animal system is not so immediately apparent as it is in the brute ; but in the long-run he breaks down more suddenly. It abridges the length of his life, and that vigor of his old age, which, as to mere animal power, ought to be the object of his preservation.

"I consider, therefore, that, in the bountiful provision of Providence for the preservation of human life, the sabbatical appointment is not, as it has been sometimes theologically viewed, simply a precept partaking of the nature of a political institution, but that it is to be numbered amongst the natural duties, if the preservation of life be admitted to be a duty, and the premature destruction of it a suicidal act. This is simply said as a physician, and without reference at all to the theological question. But, if you consider further the proper effect of real Christianity, — namely, peace of mind, confiding trust in God, and good-will to men, — you will perceive in this source of renewed vigor to the mind, and through the mind to the body, an additional spring of life imparted from this higher use of the Sabbath as a holy rest."

Dr. Farre's testimony was *unanimously* indorsed by the New-Haven Medical Association.

" At a regular meeting of the New-Haven Medical Association, composed of twenty-five physicians, among whom were the professors of the medical college, the following questions were considered : —

"1. Is the position taken by Dr. Farre in his testimony before the committee of the British House of Commons, in your view, correct?

"2. Will men who labor but six days in a week be more healthy, and live longer, other things being equal, than those who labor seven?

"3. Will they do more work, and do it in a better manner?

"The vote on the above was *unanimously in the affirmative.*

"(Signed)   "ELI IVES, *Chairman.*

"PLINY A. JEWETT, *Clerk.*"

Dr. Rush of Philadelphia says, "If there were no hereafter, individuals and societies would be great gainers by attending public worship. Rest from labor in the house of God winds up the machine of the soul and body better than any thing else, and thereby invigorates it for the labors and duties of another week."

Ebenezer Alden, M.D., of Massachusetts, asserts, "Unnecessary labor on the Sabbath is a *physical sin*, the transgressing of a *physical law*, — a law to which a penalty is attached, a penalty which cannot be evaded. Such is my opinion; and such, I apprehend, will be found to be substantially the opinion of every reflecting and well-educated physician."

In 1839 a committee was appointed in the legislature of Pennsylvania, who made a report with regard to the employment of laborers on their canals. In that report they say, in reference to those who had petitioned against the employment of the workmen on the Sabbath, "They assert, as the result of their experience, that both man and beast can do more work by resting one day in seven than by working the whole seven."

They then add, "Your committee feel free to confess that *their own experience*, as business-men, farmers, or legislators, corresponds with this assertion."

"A gentleman from Vermont, who was in the habit of driving his horses twelve miles a day, seven days in the week, afterwards changed his practice, and drove them but six days, allowing them to rest one. He then found, that, with the same keeping, he could drive them fifteen miles a day, and preserve them in as good order as before; so that a man may rest on the Sabbath, and let his horses rest, yet promote the benefit of both, and be in all respects the gainer." This is doubtless the universal result of this experiment on man and beast. "A number of men started from Ohio with droves of cattle for Philadelphia. They had often been before, and had been accustomed to drive on the Sabbath as on other days. One had now changed his views as to the propriety of travelling on that day. On Saturday he inquired for pastures. His associates wondered that so shrewd a man should think of consuming so great a portion of his profits by stopping with such a drove the whole day. He stopped, however, and kept the Sabbath. They, thinking that they could not afford to do so, went on. On Monday he started again. In the course of the week he passed them, arrived first in the market, and sold his cattle to great advantage. So impressed were the others with the benefits of thus keeping the Sabbath, that they afterwards followed his example."

"Two neighbors in the State of New York, each with a drove of sheep, started on the same day for a distant market. One started several hours before the other, and travelled uniformly every day. The other rested every Sabbath; yet he arrived at the market first, with his flock in a better condition than that of the other. In giving an account of it, he said that he drove his sheep on Monday about seventeen miles, on Tuesday not over sixteen, and so lessening each day, till on Saturday he drove them only about eleven miles; but on Monday, after resting on the Sabbath, they would travel again seventeen miles; and so on each week. But his neighbor's sheep, which were not allowed to rest on the Sabbath, before they arrived at the market could not travel, without injury, more than six or eight miles a day."

"The experiment was tried on a hundred and twenty horses. They were employed, for years, seven days in a week; but they became unhealthy, and finally died so fast, that the owner thought it too expensive, and put them on a six-days' arrangement. After this he was not obliged to replenish them one-fourth part as often as before. Instead of sinking continually, his horses came up again, and lived years longer than they could have done on the other plan."

A livery-stable keeper who had kept no Sabbath proposed to make a change. "I had advertisements struck off and posted up, saying that my stable would not be opened on the Sabbath. At first some fell off, but others liked it. I began to fill up; and my business, on the whole, was quite as profitable as before. One thing was very remarkable: I had been at an expense before, upon an average, for a number of years, of from three to four hundred dollars, on account of the lameness and sickness of horses; but afterwards these expenses were not ten dollars a year."

"In a large flouring establishment, the men worked, for a number of years, seven days in a week. The superintendent was then changed. He ordered the men to stop the works at eleven o'clock on Saturday night, and not to start them until one o'clock on Monday morning; thus allowing a full Sabbath every week. And the same men during the year actually ground fifty thousand bushels more than had ever been ground in a single year in that establishment. The men—having been permitted to cleanse themselves, put on their best apparel, rest from worldly business, go with their families to the house of God, and devote the Sabbath to its appropriate duties — were more healthy, moral, punctual, and diligent. They lost less time in drinking, dissipation, and quarrels. They were more clear-headed and whole-hearted, knew better how to do things, and were more disposed to do them in the right way."

"Two thousand men in England were employed, for years, seven days a week. To render them contented in giving up their right to the Sabbath as a day of rest, *that birthright of the human family*, they paid them double wages on that day, — eight days' wages for seven days' work. But they could not keep them healthy, nor make them moral. Things went badly; and they changed their course, — employed the workmen only six days a week, and allowed them to rest on the Sabbath. The consequence was, that they did more work than ever before. This, the superintendent said, was owing to two causes, —*the demoralization of the people* under the first system, and *their exhaustion of bodily strength,* which was visible to the most casual observer."

Henry R. Schoolcraft gives an account of an expedition which he made with twenty men to examine the Upper Mississippi in the summer of 1830. He went on another tour in 1832. He says, "No Sabbath Day was employed in travelling. It was laid down as a principle to rest on that day; and wherever it overtook us, whether on the land or on the water, the men knew that their labor would cease, and that the day would be given them for rest. It may perhaps be thought that the giving up of one-seventh part of the whole time employed on a public expedition in a very remote region, and with many men to subsist, must have, in this ratio, increased the time devoted to the route. But the result was far otherwise. The time devoted to recruit the men not only gave the surgeon of the party an opportunity to heal up the bruises and chafings they complained of, but it replenished them with strength. They commenced the weekly labor with renewed rest; and this rest was, in a measure, kept up by reflection that the ensuing Sabbath would be a day of rest. It was found by computing the whole route, and comparing the time employed with that which had been devoted on similar routes in that part of the world, that an equal space had been gone over in less time than it had ever been known to be performed by loaded canoes or (as the fact is) by light canoes before."

"No fewer than six hundred and forty-one medical men of London, including Dr. Farre, subscribed a petition to Parliament against the opening of the Crystal Palace for profit on Sundays, containing the following sentence : 'Your petitioners, from their acquaintance with the laboring-classes and with the laws which regulate the human economy, are convinced that a seventh day of rest, instituted by God, and coeval with the existence of man, is essential to the bodily health and mental vigor of man in every station of life.'" "Many men on the other side of the Atlantic," says Gilfillan, "of whom we name only Drs. Warren of Boston, Smith of New York, Harrison and

Mussey of the Ohio Medical College, and Alden of Massachusetts, are equally decided in entertaining the same views. We
must content ourselves with the striking words of Dr. Mussey,
professor of surgery in the above-mentioned institution, who
affirms, that, 'under the due observance of the Sabbath, life
would, on the average, be prolonged more than *one-seventh* of its
whole period ; that is, *more than seven years in fifty.*'"

Thoughtless people have admired the Parisian Sabbath.

" A Paris Sunday," says Russell S. Cook, Corresponding
Secretary New-York Sabbath Committee, " has become proverbial for its godlessness. Passing along its clean and beautiful streets, you find the *cafés* and restaurants crowded with
men, taking their morning meal, and reading the newspapers of
the day. Cries of fruit-dealers and street venders are everywhere heard ; though the needless abomination of crying newspapers is not tolerated, even in Paris. Paviors, masons, roof-
ers, painters, all kinds of mechanics, are engaged in their
usual avocations. Places of business are universally open till
mid-day, as on other days. The whirl of cabs and omnibuses is
even more constant than during the six days of the week. I
had the curiosity to count the vehicles passing the Industrial
Palace, Champs Élysées, mostly going to or returning from the
Bois de Boulogne, in the afternoon of the second Sabbath in
August, — the grand *fête* day at Cherbourg, when Paris was
emptied of the *élite* of its fashionable society, — and found the
average to be one hundred and forty a minute, or one thousand
six hundred and eighty an hour. The grand water-works at
St. Cloud and Versailles play only on Sunday. As the day
advances, the gardens of the Tuileries and the Champs Élysées
present a scene of unrivalled gayety and folly. Bands of music
execute lively military and operatic airs. Gaudy booths are
surrounded with crowds of men, women, and children, absorbed
by childish sports. Automata, too silly for the amusement of
infants, serve to delight other groups of soldiers and stragglers.
Goat-carriages, and whirligigs of wooden horses or mimic ships,
divert the children and nurses. As evening sets in, the out-
door concert and drinking-saloons flaunt their attractions ;

brilliant mirrors reflect the fanciful gas-jets; singing men and singing women, accompanied by orchestras below, amuse the multitude with comic, and sometimes immoral songs. Every conceivable device for drawing away the people from home and from God is employed. The Cirque de l'Impératrice furnïshes its equestrian attractions and its mirth-inspiring exhibitions. Adjacent public gardens are thronged with dancers. Operatic and theatrical amusements add their seductive performances. The whole line of the Boulevards is filled with people, seated in front of the *cafés*, sipping their brandied coffee, playing dominoes, or gazing at the promenaders along the broad pavements. Houses and homes (if there be such a thing, without the name, in France) seem to be emptied into the streets and places of amusement; and the city is converted into a pandemonium of folly, and of genteel or gross dissipation.

"Since the accession of the reigning dynasty, Sunday labor has been suspended on the public works in France. But I observed that the stupendous preparations for the emperor's *fête* day fireworks in the Place de la Concorde were in full progress on the second Sabbath in August, the *fête* occurring on the succeeding Sunday; but on Monday the Sunday workmeh were not there, because either dissipation or over-exertion compelled a day of rest. Such, without more of detail, is a Paris Sunday."

This seems to the frivolous a feast of delights; but it is a Damocles feast, with the *sword* suspended by a hair above it. This is the city which has no word for "home;" which knows the terrors of the commune; which, during 1874, had the bodies of one thousand suicides lying in her morgue.

Chambers' "Journal" says, "The Paris workman has no grandchildren. Were it not for the constant influx from the provinces, the Parisian artisan would soon be extinct." A letter from Paris, 1870, says, "The consequence of this feverish activity is this: there is not an old stone-mason, or an old carpenter, or an old shoemaker, or an old printer, or any other old artisan, in Paris."

Yet, in face of all these evils, the individual, left to himself, can hardly withstand the temptation of an open Sabbath;

and only the State can secure, by her arm that reaches all, that suspension of labor which insures to her citizens the blessings of the Sabbath. " If," says " The London Times," " the sacred character of the day be once obscured, there would not remain behind any influence strong enough to keep a thrifty tradesman from his counter for twelve hours together. A man who would observe the day as a Sabbath would retrench it as a holiday; and thus competition and imitation would at length bring all to the common level of universal profaneness and continuous toil."

The STATE, then, receives from the Sabbath *ten years of additional work in the lives of her industrious and laboring classes,* while the whole life is more healthful, restful, cheerful, and contented. She receives less sickness to burden friends and fill asylums, and sickness which is sooner healed. These blessings, scattered in every town and village in the land among her citizens, should lead the State to pronounce the Sabbath a great benefactor to her.

II. — EQUALLY EVIDENT IS THE AMPLE BENEFACTION WHICH THE STATE IN THE GENERAL WELFARE OF HER CITIZENS RECEIVES IN INTELLECTUAL HEALTH, CHEERFULNESS, AND POWER.

" A steamer on the Thames having been blown up, the foreman and stokers laid the blame on Sabbath work, which stupefied and imbittered them, made them blunder, and heedless what havoc they might occasion."

" A mechanic in Massachusetts, whose business required special skill and care, was accustomed at times, when pressed with business, to pursue it on the Sabbath, after having followed it during six days of the week; but he so often *made mistakes,* by which he lost more than he gained, that he abandoned the practice as one which he could not afford to continue. Mind is no more made to work vigorously and continuously in one course of effort seven days in a week than the body, and it cannot do it to advantage."

Jorgenson, in his " Travels through France," says, " The moroseness occasioned by the want of a Sabbath in France has an effect upon the cleanliness of the young men engaged in manual labor. They pursue their daily drudgery in their dirty working-dresses ; and habit renders them, at length, averse to a change of linen and clothes."

A prize essay on the Sabbath has the title, " Heaven's Antidote to the Curse of Labor."

Three excellent little books, published by the American Sunday School Union, are commended for the reading of youth, — "The Last Day of the Week," "The First Day of the Week," "The Week Completed."

Some old lines, once familiar, now so almost forgotten that we could not find any one who could repeat them entire, deserve to be brought to the front in the thought of both young and old : —

> " A Sabbath well spent
> Brings a week of content,
>   And strength for the toils of the morrow ;
> But a Sabbath profaned,
> Whatsoever be gained,
>   Is a certain forerunner of sorrow."
>
> *Golden Maxim of Sir Matthew Hale.*

" I feel," says Coleridge, "as if God had, by the Sabbath, given fifty-two springs in the year."

" I am prepared to affirm," writes Isaac Taylor, " that to the studious especially, and whether younger or older, a Sabbath well spent, — spent in happy exercises of the heart, devotional and domestic, — a Sunday given to the soul, is the best of all means of refreshment to the mere intellect."

" Dr. Carpenter, and he is himself a host, writing to a friend in 1852, said, ' My own experience is very strong as to the importance of the complete rest and change of thought once in the week.' The evidence of J. R. Farre, M.D., has obtained considerable currency and fame. ' All men of whatever class,' he says, ' who must necessarily be employed six days in the week, should abstain on the seventh, and in the course of life would assuredly gain by giving to their bodies the repose, and to their mind the change of ideas, suited to the day, for which it was appointed by unerring wisdom. I have frequently observed the premature death of medical men from continued exertion. I have advised the clergyman, in lieu of his Sabbath, to rest one day in the week: it forms a continual prescription of mine. I have seen many destroyed by their duties on that day; and, to preserve others, I have frequently suspended them, for a season, from the discharge of those duties. The working of the mind in one continued train of thought is destructive of life in the most distinguished class of society; and senators' themselves stand in need of reform in that particular. I have observed many of them destroyed by neglecting this economy of life.' "

Henry Ward Beecher says in his "Yale Lectures on Preaching," " Saturday should be a play-day. I make it a day, not of laziness, but of general, social, pleasurable exhilaration. I go up street and see pleasant people. I go and look at pictures. I love to see horses. I like to go to Tiffany's. After I get home, I enjoy myself quietly in the evening; and, when Sunday comes, I am impleted."[1] " Saturday and Monday ought to be inclined planes, — the former a very inclined plane up to Sunday, and the latter a very inclined plane away from it."

Rev. Charles F. Deems explains how he keeps himself able to work hard without any results of weariness or ill health. He says, "I keep a Sabbath: few ministers do so. Many years I did not. On Friday night I go to bed, and say, 'Now I lay me down to sleep;' and no one must wake me until Sunday morning, even if 'The Sunday Magazine' should suspend, or the Church of the Strangers should burn down. I never yet have slept that long, as I generally rise on Saturday afternoon to boil for an hour in the Russian bath. Generally on Saturday night I cannot recollect what the texts for Sunday are, having put the preparation all safely away. Such a regimen enables me to begin fresh on Sunday, and work till Friday night like a house afire and the wind blowing."

Sir David Wilkie, the celebrated painter, remarked, that " those artists who wrought on Sunday were soon disqualified from working at all."

[1] Yale Lectures, p. 200.

Dr. Johnson, on his death-bed, made three requests of Sir Joshua Reynolds : the first was, " that he would never paint on a Sunday." " The editor of ' The Standard,' some years ago, recorded this result of many years' observation in these words : 'We never knew a man work seven days a week who did not kill himself, or kill his mind.' ' I have found it necessary to my own well-being,' says Dr. Farre, ' to abridge my labors on the Sabbath to what is actually necessary.' "

Says Beecher, " Through the week we go down into the valleys of care and shadows : our Sabbaths should be hills of light and joy in God's presence."

" A distinguished financier, charged with an immense amount of property during the great pecuniary pressure of 1836 and 1837, said, ' I should have been a dead man had it not been for the Sabbath. Obliged to work from morning till night through the whole week, I felt on Saturday, especially Saturday afternoon, as if I *must* have *rest*. It was like going into a dense fog. Every thing looked dark and gloomy, as if nothing could be saved. I dismissed all, and kept the Sabbath in the good old way. On Monday it was all bright and sunshine. I could see through, and I got through. But, had it not been for the Sabbath, I have no doubt I should have been in the grave.' "

These testimonies are numerous and interesting. " Rev. Dr. Wilson of Philadelphia, once a lawyer, was accustomed, when pressed with business, to make out his briefs, and prepare for his Monday pleading, on the Sabbath. But he so uniformly failed in carrying out his Sunday plans, that it arrested his attention. As a philosopher, he inquired into the cause of his uniform failure, and came to the conclusion that it might be, and probably was, on account of his violation of the Sabbath by employing it in secular business. He therefore, from that time, abandoned the practice of doing any thing for his clients on that day. The difficulty ceased : his efforts on Monday were as successful as on other days."

" A lawyer of distinguished talents, on his death-bed, said to his friend, ' *Charge every young lawyer not to do any thing in the business of his profession on the Sabbath. It will injure him, and lessen the prospect of his success.* I have tried it. I do not know why it is ; but there is something about it very striking. My Sabbath efforts have almost always failed. I found unexpectedly that my clients had deceived me, and that the evidence was very different from what I expected ; some of my witnesses would be absent ; my own efforts would fail ; the judge would go against me, or the jury could not agree. *Tell all the young lawyers, that, if they would succeed, they must not take the Sabbath for business. It is the way to fail.*'"

Sir Matthew Hale writes, " Though my hands and my mind have been as full of secular business, both before and after I was judge, as, it may be, any man's in England, yet I never wanted time in six days to ripen and fit myself for the business and employments I had to do, though I borrowed not one minute from the Lord's Day to prepare for it by study or otherwise. But, on the other hand, if I had at any time borrowed from the day any time for my secular employment, I found it did further me less than if I had let it alone ; and therefore, when some years' experience, upon a most attentive and vigilant observation, had given me this instruction, I grew peremptorily resolved never in this kind to make a breach upon the Lord's Day, which I have now strictly observed for more than thirty years." " He also declared that it had become almost proverbial with him, when any one importuned him to attend to secular business on the Sabbath, to tell them, if they expected it to 'succeed amiss,' they might desire him to undertake it on that day ; that he feared even to *think* of secular business on the Sabbath, because the resolution then taken would be disappointed or unsuccessful ; and that, the more faithfully he applied himself to the duties of the Lord's Day, the more happy and successful was his business during the week."

" A distinguished merchant, who for twenty years did a vast amount of business, said, ' Had it not been for the Sabbath, I have no doubt I should have been a maniac long ago.' This was mentioned in a company of merchants ; when one remarked, ' That is exactly the case with Mr. ——. He used to say that the Sabbath was the best day in the week to plan successful voyages, showing that his mind had no Sabbath. He has been in the insane-asylum for years, and will probably die there.'"

Romilly, though urged, would not give up his Sunday consultations. He lost his reason, and terminated his own life. Castlereagh, also, walked the same path to the grave, — *Sabbath-work, loss of reason, self-destruction.*

Wilberforce wrote to a friend, "I am strongly impressed by the recollection of your endeavor to prevail upon the lawyers to give up Sunday consultations, in which poor Romilly would not concur." This was Sir Samuel Romilly, solicitor-general of England under Fox's administration, who terminated his life Nov. 2, 1818. On Castlereagh's suicide, Wilberforce, reminded of Romilly, wrote, "If he had suffered his mind to enjoy such occasional remission, it is highly probable that the strings of life would never have snapped from over-tension. Alas, alas, poor fellow!"

"Wilberforce ascribes his own continuance for so long a time, under such a pressure of cares and labors, in no small degree to his conscientious and habitual observance of the Sabbath. 'Oh, what a blessed day,' said he, 'is the Sabbath, which allows us a precious interval wherein to pause, to come out from the thickets of worldly concerns, and give ourselves up to heavenly and spiritual things!'"

How much bad legislation has been due to men whose minds were jaded and perturbed by Sabbath work, it would be difficult to estimate. It is a curious speculation, *whether, had our statesmen been devout Sabbath-observers, the Rebellion had not been prevented.*

Observing these things, the increase of vigor in all minds by the Sabbath, the preservation of valuable minds of great power and activity under great labors, and how the freshness of each mind affects the whole, and considering how much of good legislation must be due to rested minds, is not the claim just, that the Sabbath is the benefactor to the *State?*

In some way connecting itself with the Centennial display of inventions and products of labor, it comes in place to observe, that, —

III. — THE STATE IS GREATLY INDEBTED TO THE SABBATH FOR
ITS PROSPERITY IN LABOR AND BUSINESS.

If it preserves fresh and vigorous mind and body, as all the
facts show, this must be the case. The stokers on the Thames
said that the *steamboat* blew up because they were worn out and
disturbed in mind by Sabbath work, which made them reckless.
This shows how abuse of the Sabbath destroys property. Lord
Macaulay says, "If the Sunday had not been observed as a day
of rest, but the axe, the spade, the anvil, and the loom had been
at work every day during the past three centuries, I have not
the smallest doubt that we should have been at this moment
a poorer people, and a less civilized people, than we are. Of
course, I do not mean that a man will not produce more in a
week by working seven days than by working six days: but I
very much doubt, whether, at the end of a year, he will generally
have produced more by working seven days a week than by
working six days a week; and I firmly believe, that, at the end
of twenty years, he will have produced less by working seven
days a week than by working six days a week."

As to his remuneration for labor, John Stuart Mill makes the
striking statement, "OPERATIVES ARE PERFECTLY RIGHT IN
THINKING, THAT, IF ALL WORKED ON SUNDAY, SEVEN DAYS' WORK
WOULD HAVE TO BE GIVEN FOR SIX DAYS' WAGES." Why do not
the intelligent poor open their eyes to this, that however Sunday
work and Sunday amusements may, *at first, seem* to advantage
and recreate *them*, the eventual effect must be, in the nature of
things, and is by actual fact, to subject them and their time
more absolutely to the *rich?* The process as to work is this:
first, your Sunday labor is *extra*, and you exult; then *expected*,
then *exacted*, and you are discharged if it is not rendered. The
process as to amusements is, first, the poor have a nearly equal
share: but the pleasures of the rich encroach upon the time of
the poor; and the stabler, for instance, who might in independence have had his Sabbath at home, must give his day to furnish
horses to please the rich. Every one should remember that
every extra hour he gives of labor to the rich for a "considera-

tion" will subject the workman of another generation to an hour's labor for *nought.* For example, should actors accommodatingly give two hours for a Sunday rehearsal, the actors of ten years hence will *have* to attend Sunday-night rehearsal, or receive discharge. Mill's remark should be impressed on all working-men, "SEVEN DAYS' WORK WOULD HAVE TO BE GIVEN FOR SIX DAYS' WAGES." Resist demand on you for a single minute of Sunday work. What you do now accommodatingly you will do hereafter by *compulsion.* 'Tis a yoke, even if velvet-lined.

Sabbath work must impoverish the State both in the quantity and quality of the labor. Mr. Bagnall, an extensive iron-master, discontinued the working of the blast-furnaces on the Lord's Day ; and in 1841, about two years after the change had been adopted, stated to a committee of the House of Lords, "We have made rather more iron since we stopped on Sundays than before." After a seven-years' trial of the plan, Mr. Bagnall wrote thus : "We have made a larger quantity of iron than ever, and gone on, in all our six iron-works, much more free from accidents and interruptions than during any preceding seven years of our lives." "Such facts as these prepare us for the statement that the amount of productive labor in France was diminished by the change from a seventh to a tenth day's rest." It is well known, that in September, 1792, the "fierce democracy" of France thought to "change times and seasons," abolished the Christian year, gave new names to the months, worshipped a noted figurante from the opera as the Goddess of Reason in Notre Dame, and, putting away the Christian week and Sabbath, invented a week of ten days, — the *décadi.* But the revolutionists found it true, that "men who work against God's commandments work against the providence of God, and the providence of God will be too strong for them."

That was a noble and morally helpful wife, who, when her husband informed her that he had been requested to go with the cars on the Sabbath, quietly replied, "I take it for granted that you do not intend to go." He urged the necessity of gaining a livelihood. Her reply was, — a sentence which ought to be written in letters of gold, —"*If a man cannot support a family by keeping the Sabbath, he certainly cannot support them by breaking it.*" — "I am very glad," said the man, "that you think so: I think so myself. That was what I wanted, — to see whether we think alike." He did not lose his place.

A distinguished merchant once observed, "There is no need of breaking the Sabbath, and no benefit from it. We have not had a vessel leave the harbor on the Sabbath for more than twenty years. It is about thirty years since I came to this city; and every man through this whole range, who came down to his store or suffered his counting-room to be opened on the Sabbath, has lost his property."

Sabbath husbandry does not prosper.

The people of Israel found no lack, but blessing on basket and store, while they observed the command, "*In earing time*" [*aro*, to plough] "*and in harvest thou shalt rest.*" Many a Gentile farmer has found it for his interest not to disregard that saying.

There would seem to be a Divine Providence, which sometimes sets its mark of disapprobation on the wanton disregard of this time.

"A man in the State of New York remarked that he intended to cheat the Lord out of the next Sabbath by going to a neighboring town to visit his friends. He could not afford to take one of his own days, and therefore resolved to cheat the Lord out of his. On Saturday he went with his team into a forest to get some wood. By the fall of a tree he was placed in such a situation, that he did not attempt to carry his intended fraud into execution: he was willing to stay at home.

"But another man in the same State, who had spent the Sabbath in getting in his grain, said that he *had* fairly cheated the Almighty out of one day. He boasted of it as a mark of his superiority. On Tuesday the lightning struck his barn. He gained nothing by working on the Sabbath."

"'Those views,' said a man, 'are all superstition. The idea that it is not profitable or safe to work on the Sabbath as on other days is *false*. I will prove that it is false.' So he at-

tempted it. He ploughed his field, and sowed his grain, on the
Sabbath. It came up, and grew finely. Often, during the season, he pointed to it in proof that Sabbath-day labor is safe and
profitable. He reaped it, and stacked it up in the field. His boys
took the gun, and went out into the woods. It was a dry time,
and they set the leaves on fire. The wind took the fire : it swept
over the field, and nought but the blackness of ashes marked
the place where the grain stood. He could not prove, though
he tried long and hard, that it is safe or profitable to work on
the Sabbath."

" Though this is not a state of full retribution, yet Jehovah is
' a God who judgeth *in the earth ;* ' and sometimes, even here, he
visits certain sins with his curse.'"

" It is said that those who manufacture salt by boiling must
violate the Sabbath, because it will not do to let the kettles cool
down as often as once a week. But a gentleman tried the experiment, who said, that, if he could not keep the Sabbath, he
would not make salt. He had thirty-two kettles. He allowed
the fires to go out, and all the works to stop, from Saturday till
Monday. His men attended worship on the Sabbath. In the
season they boiled seventy-eight days, and made an average of
two hundred bushels of salt a day, at a breakage expense of six
cents. His neighbors could hardly believe it. Not a man with
his dimensions of kettles had made as much salt as he, and
their expenses for breakage and repairs had been much greater."

" A gentleman belonging to a fishing town which sends out
more than two hundred vessels in a year writes, ' Those vessels
which have not fished on the Sabbath have, taken together, met
with *more than ordinary success.* The vessel whose earnings
were the highest the last year and the year before was one on
board which the Sabbath was religiously kept. There is one
firm which has had eight vessels in its employ this season. Seven
have fished on the Sabbath, and one has not. That one has
earned seven hundred dollars more than the most successful of
the seven. There are two other firms employing each three vessels. Two out of the three in each case have kept the Sabbath,
and in each case have earned *more than two-thirds of the profits.*' "

These incidents and many like them, which Edwards has set forth in his excellent "Sabbath Manual," in regard to the keeping of this day in travelling, manufacturing, haying, harvesting, and other avocations, are so wonderful, that even an irreligious mind cannot fail to be impresed by them, and feel inclined to believe that a Divine Providence watches over this day, to stamp its infraction with his displeasure, and its keeping with his great reward.

Take the testimony of whale-fishers, which is certainly marvellous. It would seem, on the one hand, as if sometimes, to test man's faith in a Divine Providence in the most trying way, God sent his leviathans that day alone, week after week, to disport themselves before the wistful eyes of men, which from mast-top had searched the whole expanse of ocean for months in vain ; while, on the other hand, it would seem as if, when the trial of faith was over, God himself became the rewarder, and led his sea-monsters, as by a hook in the nose, to lay their lives at the feet of man, then most lord of creation when most obedient to his Maker.

"Capt. Scoresby of the British navy, afterwards commander of a whale-ship in the northern seas, says in his journal, that he does not recollect a case in which they saw whales on the Sabbath, and did not attempt to take them, where they were not remarkably successful during the subsequent week." Capt. Green of England, and a Massachusetts captain of a whale-ship, record a similar experience. "Capt. John Stetson, our consular agent at the Sandwich Islands, gives a singularly striking account of a converted captain, who called his ship's company together, and informed them of his views. They agreed to give up whaling on the Sabbath. The next Sabbath, a man on deck cried out, ' There she blows ! ' They did not lower the boats, though the whale passed near the ship. The week passed away without seeing another whale. The Sabbath came, and a whale was again seen. Another week passed away, and no whales. The third Sabbath came, and again they saw whales. The crew became almost mutinous ; but the captain assured them they were in the path of duty, and went on with his religious services

This was the last trial. They soon obtained all the oil they wanted, and returned in much less time than many who took whales on the Sabbath."

William E. Dodge of New York, more than twenty-five years connected with travelling corporations, says, "*The desecration of the Sabbath by railroads is an absolute loss to those companies.*" "You go on a Monday morning, and see a poor, haggard-looking engineer, all dirty, kept up all day Sunday, and all night, and worn out, perhaps. He steps upon the engine: if you are a railroad man, you feel intense anxiety all the time." And then he takes up the extremest case. "Within the last fortnight the engineer came to us and said, 'I know your principles; but we are placed under circumstances in which it becomes absolutely necessary for us to work on the Sabbath.' — 'What is the matter?' — 'We have a bridge that is unsafe. We have forty or fifty trains running over it a day; and we see no other way in the world to repair it but to start all our force Saturday night, and get it done Monday morning.' — 'Is there any thing that cannot be done on any other day?' — 'We shall have to stop the trains.' — 'Then it is only a matter of dollars and cents. Just give notice to the connecting railroads that there will be no trains, and take time and do the work.' Said the engineer, 'I guess you are right. I often think that I have worked my men all day Sunday to get a job on the road done, and on Monday and Tuesday they were not worth a cent. I made up my mind I never got ahead one inch by working Sunday.'"

It is a serious question, *how far the great tornado of strikes which has just spent its fury was due, directly or indirectly, to disregard of what our Anglo-Saxon forefathers called Rest Day, its repose and instructions, by railroad and mining corporations, and by miners and railroad employees themselves.*

The question put to railroad corporations received reply from *eighteen*, that they found Sunday trains profitable; from *thirty-eight*, unprofitable. The St. Paul corporation answered, "What shall it profit a man if he gain the whole world, and lose his own soul?" Some of the replies of these superintendents would be worth quoting, had we space.

The North-western Railroad Company in England, in 1849, issued the following circular: "It is commended to the attention of the stockholders and directors of railroads in this country, as the judgment of railway authorities of experience and position, that the business shall be suspended on Sundays, except for such restricted conveyance of passengers as seems called for on the ground of public necessity; and the directors, to whom is hereby confided the duty of devising the extent of such restrictions, shall take as their guide in discharging their duty the consideration of the public good, and not the private interests of the company."

Some of the railroad companies take a noble stand in this matter. But there yet remains much noble work to· be done by these corporations. Few of them are aware how annoying Sunday travel and freighting is to thousands of people *who tolerate it.* "The railroad interest has become one of the most important in the financial and commercial world." "The moral influence of the railroad system is a matter of immense moment." "It is believed that the tendency of the railroads of the country, under proper regulations, would be greatly to diminish the amount of intemperance, Sabbath-breaking, and kindred vices." Thousands read with pleasure such items as this, from the "Journal of Commerce:" —

"DEL., LACK., AND W. R.R. CO.,
NEW YORK, May 31, 1876.

"The gauge of this company's railroad was altered on Saturday, not Sunday last, as stated in error in your 'Journal.' Please make the correction, as we believe in the observance — by rest from labor at least — of the Christian as well as the 'American Sabbath,' and that railroad management should be exemplary in the proper obligations to the community.

"Yours truly,

"SAMUEL SLOAN, *President.*"

"If there is any city in the world," says Boardman, "which requires a general delivery of letters on Sunday, it must be the financial centre of the world, London. It is preposterous to claim, in behalf of any community, an extent of post-office accommodations beyond that which satisfies the two millions of that great capital."

Twenty-five years ago, London presented a memorial to the government against Sabbath mails. The subscription is headed by the great name of the *Barings*.

DECLARATION.

" LONDON, January, 1850.

" We the undersigned, being strongly impressed with a belief that there exists no greater necessity to justify the transaction of the ordinary business of receiving and delivering letters on the Sabbath Day in any of the post-offices of the United Kingdom than in those of the metropolis, do hereby earnestly request her Majesty's government to take into immediate consideration the expediency and propriety of causing the same to be discontinued, by ordering the post-offices in the country to be altogether closed on that day. This belief is grounded on the following facts : —

" 1. That the metropolis, containing a population of two million two hundred thousand, has never experienced any necessity for the opening of the metropolitan post-offices on Sundays.

" 2. That the great acceleration which has recently taken place in the postal communications throughout the empire must necessarily diminish, to a very great extent, any inconvenience which it might otherwise be supposed would arise from closing the provincial post-offices on Sunday.

"And believing that the effectual preservation of a seventh day of rest from their ordinary labor is a principle of vital importance to the physical and social well-being of the poorer classes of society, whilst the due observance of the Lord's Day is a duty of solemn obligation upon all classes of the community, we agree to take such measures as may appear best calculated to press the foregoing considerations on the attention of the government and the legislature.

BARING BROTHERS.	BARCLAY, BEVAN, TRITTON, & CO.
WILLIAMS, DEACON, & CO.	JONES, LLOYD, & CO.
HANKEYS & CO.	MASTERMAN, PETERS, & CO."

And twenty-nine other banking firms of the metropolis of the world.

Similar *declarations* were signed by the leading mercantile firms, the principal surgeons and solicitors, and the aldermen of London.

Even in war, Sunday battles have been observed to be generally disastrous to the beginner of them. Big Bethel, Bull Run, Ball's Bluff, were our Sunday battles before McClellan's noble Sabbath order ; Mill Springs, which lost the Rebels Kentucky ; Winchester, which lost them the Virginia Valley ; and Pittsburg, which cost them the Mississippi Valley. " Almost without exception, the assailing party in Sunday warfare, whether Union or Confederate, was defeated."

"Nor are these isolated historical facts. History is full of them. The British forces assailed us on Lake Champlain and at New Orleans on Sunday, and were defeated. We assailed them at Quebec: our army was repulsed, and its leader slain. Napoleon began the battle of Waterloo on Sunday, and lost his army and his empire."

Exceptions of course there are, since instant and obvious and entire retribution is not the invariable rule on earth, — it is said that our pious ancestors commenced the great Narragansett fight on the Sabbath, — but the examples are sufficiently numerous to be suggestive to an assailing general on the Sabbath who is whipped.

The Sabbath orders of Washington, Lincoln, McClellan, and Foote, make a fair page of our history. *McClellan's noble order* was dated Sept. 6, 1861: "The general commanding regards this as no idle form: one day's rest in seven is necessary to men and animals: more than that, the observance of the holy day of the God of mercy and of battles is our sacred duty."

Commodore Foote's order was dated Dec. 17, 1861: "The voice of Washington thus echoed such utterances of revelation to the army of the Revolution, and now to the army of Restoration: 'We can have little hope of the blessing of Heaven on our arms if we insult it by our impiety and folly.'"

That of *Lincoln* speaks thus: —

"EXECUTIVE MANSION, WASHINGTON,
Nov. 15, 1862.

"The President, commander-in-chief of the army and navy, desires and enjoins the orderly observance of the Sabbath by the officers and men in the military and naval service. The importance for man and beast of the prescribed weekly rest, the sacred rights of Christian soldiers and sailors, a becoming deference to the best sentiment of a Christian people, and a due regard for the Divine Will, demand that Sunday labor in the army and navy be reduced to the measure of strict necessity. The discipline and character of the national forces should not suffer, nor the cause they defend be imperilled, by the profanation of the day or name of the Most High.

"'At the time of public distress,' adopting the words of Washington in 1776, 'men may find enough to do in the service of God and their country, without abandoning themselves to vice and immorality.' The first general order issued by the Father of his Country indicates the spirit in which our institutions were founded, and should ever be defended: 'The general hopes and trusts that every officer and man will endeavor to live and act as becomes a Christian soldier defending the dearest rights and liberties of his country.' — ABRAHAM LINCOLN."

These last examples — railroads, post-offices, and warfare — are extreme examples. Come back to the routine of life. "There is not," says a working-man, "a neighborhood, village, or township, that is notable for its profanation of the sacred day of rest, but is proverbial for its poverty and its crime." J. S. Thomas, superintendent of police in England, says, "I know from experience that persons who are in the habit of attending a place of worship are more careful in their pecuniary transactions, they are more careful in their language, they are more economical in their arrangements at home, they are more affectionate and humane, and in every respect superior beings by far, than persons of contrary habits. Those who neglect a place of worship generally become idle, neglectful of their person, filthy in their habits, careless as to their children, and equally careless in their pecuniary transactions." Were there no other considerations in the same direction, these would be sufficient to stamp the Centennial Commissioners in their action as wise men, considerate of the present and permanent good of their country, as well as reverent men, regardful of the command of the Almighty.

IV. — FOR MUCH OF HER MORAL VIRTUE, AND TONE OF CHAR-
ACTER, THE STATE IS INDEBTED TO THE SABBATH.

Blackstone says, "A corruption of morals usually follows a profanation of the Sabbath." Montalembert writes, "There is no religion without worship, and no worship without the Sabbath." John Foster speaks thus, that this day is "a remarkable appointment for raising the general tenor of moral existence." "It prevents strong temptation to intemperance," says Gilfillan, "by giving rest, instead of unnatural stimulant to further activity." Baron Gurney, when passing sentence of death on two boatmen at the Stafford assizes, said, "There is no body of men so destitute of all moral culture as boatmen: they know no Sabbath, and are possessed of no means of religious instruction." Mr. Edge of Manchester observes respecting the London bakers, that "the low mental and moral condition of the trade generally in London, at the present time, is notorious." Mr. Henry Ellis, a master-baker, says of them, "Those good and moral impressions which they first receive in their early days are entirely lost from the continual practice of working on the Sabbath." The chaplain of the Model Prison, London, says, "We are called to minister to few but Sabbath-breakers." The chaplain of Clerkenwell affirms, "I do not recollect a single case of capital offence where the party has not been a Sabbath-breaker. Indeed, I may say, in reference to prisoners of all classes, that, in nineteen cases out of twenty, they are persons who have not only neglected the Sabbath, but all religious ordinances."

A distinguished merchant, long accustomed to observe men, and who had gained an uncommon knowledge of them, said, "When I see one of my apprentices or clerks riding out on the Sabbath, on Monday I dismiss him. Such a one cannot be trusted."

One does well to be a little shy, in matters which concern himself, of any man who he knows deliberately breaks *any* command laid upon his conscience; since, if temptation were to come to him in a form which involved disregarding his fellows' rights, the same habit of sacrificing duty to interest would be likely to prevail. A ship-captain discharged a crew who would not work for him on the Sabbath. Meeting an old sailor, he sought to hire him. The answer was, "No." — "Why not?" — "Because," answered the sailor, "the man who will rob the Almighty of his day, I should be afraid would, if he could, rob me of my wages."

"A father, whose son was addicted to riding out for pleasure on the Sabbath, was told, that, if he did not stop it, his son would be ruined. He did not stop it, but sometimes set the example of riding out for pleasure himself. His son became a man; was placed in a responsible situation, and intrusted with a large amount of property. Soon he was a defaulter, and absconded. In a different part of the country he obtained another responsible situation, and was again intrusted with a large amount of property. Of that he defrauded the owner, and fled again. He was apprehended, tried, convicted, and sent to the state-prison. After years spent in solitude and labor, he wrote a letter to his father; and, after recounting his course of crime, he added, '*That was the effect of breaking the Sabbath when I was a boy.*'"

"I once defended a man," says Daniel Webster, "charged with the awful crime of murder. At the conclusion of the trial, I asked him what could have induced him to stain his hands with the blood of a fellow-being. Turning his bloodshot eyes full upon me, he said, 'Mr. Webster, in my youth I spent the holy Sabbath in evil amusements, instead of frequenting the house of prayer and praise.'" Webster's words in regard to the Sabbath school are weighty: "The Sabbath school is one of the great institutions of the day. It leads our youth to the path of truth and morality, and makes them good men and useful citizens. As a school of religious instruction, it is of inestimable value; as a civil institution, it is priceless. It has done more to preserve our liberties than grave statesmen and armed soldiers. Let it, then, be fostered and protected until the end of time."[1]

Gilfillan calls our attention to the fact that "*the family flourishes where the Sabbath is really observed,* and nowhere more than in Great Britain and America." The connection it would not be difficult to trace. To the family, the Sabbath, in a less pronounced form, is a kind of Thanksgiving Day and family festival. The "Cotter's Saturday Night" has in prospect the cheer of the family gathering of the next day, around

"The ingle blinking bonnily,"

and the walk to the "kirk" together, each seeing the others in their neatest garb and most cheerful mood. Gilfillan quotes Madame de Staël: "Nowhere can be seen such faithful protec-

---

[1] Letter to Prof. Pease, June 15, 1852; quoted by Hon. S. Benson: sent to Christian Union by J. S. C. Abbott.

tion on the one side, and such tender and pious devotedness on the other, as in married life in England. Nowhere do the wives share with so much courage and simplicity the troubles and dangers of the husbands wherever the duties of their profession may call them." Baron d'Haussez observes, "All things considered, *cæteris paribus*, thanks to the influence of their manners, the married state in England is happier than in any other country." In equally laudatory terms do M. de Tocqueville and M. Michel Chevalier write of the marriage-tie and conjugal happiness as they exist in America. Of Scotland Dr. Currie remarks, "A striking particular of the character of the Scotch peasantry is the one which it is hoped will not be lost, — the strength of their domestic affections."

Henry Ward Beecher says, "The one great poem of New England is her Sunday. Through that she has escaped materialism. That has been her crystal dome overhead, through which imagination has been kept alive. New England's imagination is to be found, not in art or literature, but in her inventions, her social organism, and, above all, in her religious life. The Sabbath has been the nurse of that. When she ceases to have a Sunday, she will be as this landscape is now, — growing dark, all its lines blurred, its distances and gradations fast merging into sheeted darkness and night."

Webster says, "The longer I live, the more highly do I estimate the Christian Sabbath, and the more grateful do I feel toward those who impress its importance on the community." Robespierre, who said good things and did bloody things, in a report for the Committee of Public Safety affirms that it is desirable that there should be in the citizen "a rapid instinct for moral things." Proudhon remarks, that "this 'rapid instinct,' this second conscience, the Sabbath created in the Israelite, and the Sunday, in a greater degree, in a Christian." "How many heroic devotions," he exclaims, "how many sacrifices, were consummated in the heart in the inexpressible monologues of the holy days! What high thoughts, magnificent conceptions, descended into the soul of philosopher and poet! What generous resolutions were taken! Hercules, at the close of his youth, offered a sacrifice to Minerva. Standing before the altar, after making the libations and singing hymns to the goddess, he awaited in silence the flame to consume the holocaust. Suddenly two goddesses appeared, Pleasure and Virtue, who displayed their charms, and each demanded his homage. Pleasure spread out her seductions: Virtue offered labors an1 perils with glory incorruptible. The young hero chose Virtue." This vision, this choice, comes to youth in the day and place of worship. Statesmen are made who are incorruptible, and all society is toned up in virtue. On the other hand, Prideaux remarks, " It is not to be doubted, that, if the public teaching of religion on the Sabbath were once dropped among us, the generality of the people, whatever else might be done to obviate it, would, in seven years, relapse into as bad a state of barbarity as was ever in practice among the worst of our Saxon or Danish ancestors."

V. — ONE VIEW, NOT OFTEN TAKEN, DISCLOSES THE SABBATH AS BENEFACTOR TO THE STATE IN BESTOWING AND SECURING LIB-ERTY, REPUBLICAN LIBERTY, AND THE BLESSINGS WHICH COME IN ITS TRAIN.

The connection of this day's observance with republican institutions is apparent when it is remembered that it is a day of concourse of citizens and neighbors; a day of reflection and cheerful rest; a day of profound speculation oftentimes; a day of imploring God's favor; a day of reading that book, which, in its inner principles, sets forth

" A church without a bishop, and a state without a king."

But we prefer to call witnesses. A wise observer (Russell S. Cook) has entitled his report on the Sabbath in Europe, "The Holy Day of Freedom, and the Holiday of Despotism." He says, "Nothing can be clearer to the intelligent observer of European life than that a holiday Sabbath is a frightful cause of physical, political, and moral degradation to the masses of the people. A day of worldly pleasure for the rich makes a day of toil for the dependent classes." " A holiday Sabbath is thus the *ally of despotism.* It is a memorable fact, that the only free countries in the world are those in which popular conviction and legal enactment recognize and conserve the sacred character of the Sabbath. One of our most eminent writers, who has 'made the French and Continental mode of keeping Sunday a matter of calm, dispassionate inquiry and observation,' has said, 'There is not a single nation, possessed of a popular form of government, which has not our theory of the Sabbath. Protestant Switzerland, England, Scotland, and America cover the whole ground of popular freedom ; and, in all these, this idea of the Sabbath prevails with a distinctness about equal to the degree of liberty. Nor do I think this result an accidental one.' How should it be accidental, when there is the best evidence that Continental rulers encourage Sabbath profanations as a means of unfitting their subjects for the assertion and exercise of their political rights ? The historian Hallam reveals a pregnant fact when he states that all European despots 'have for many years perceived and acted on the principle, that it is the policy of government to encourage a love of pastime and recreation in the people, both because it keeps them from speculating on religious and political matters, and because it renders them more cheerful, and less sensible of the evils of their condition.' But the very life of a free people depends, under God, on such a perpetual speculation on religious and political matters as the Bible and the Sabbath and a free gospel prompt. If we would cling to our institutions, we must cherish the holy day of freedom and religion, and frown on the holiday of despots."

This opinion does not stand uncorroborated. Another writer says, " It was in logical harmony with the whole genius of the Stuart dynasty that James I., and after him Charles I., should attempt to break down the Sabbath by imposing the 'Book of Sports' upon the British people." " A nation that moils for six days, and frolics the seventh, is about as fit material for a tyrant as could be desired. But a tyrant could do nothing with a people who had free access to the Bible. Such a people would have too much intelligence to wear the yoke of the oppressor.

They would understand their rights, and have the courage to assert them. Neither crown nor mitre could terrify them into a servile submission to wrong, nor put off their demand for their proper franchises with a sop of ' beggarly amusements.' "

Thus is verified what Adam Smith said long ago in a more general way, " The Sabbath as a political institution is of inestimable value, independently of its claims to divine authority ; " and what the dispassionate Blackstone wrote, " The keeping of one day in seven holy as a time of relaxation and refreshment, as well as for public worship, is of admirable service to the State, considered merely as a civil institution. It humanizes, by the help of conversation and society, the manners of the lower classes, which would otherwise degenerate into a sordid ferocity and savage selfishness of spirit. It enables the industrious workman to pursue his occupation in the ensuing week with health and cheerfulness. It imprints on the minds of the people that sense of their duty to God so necessary to make them good citizens, but yet which would be worn out and defaced by an unremitted continuance of labor without any stated times of calling them to the worship of their Maker."

In 1850, Montalembert, in the name of a commission, reported to the French Parliament on Sabbath observance. After remarking that the Almighty conferred success on human labor in proportion as nations respect the Lord's Day, he refers in proof to England and the United States, and says, —

" Witness that city London, the capital and focus of most of the commerce of the world, where Sunday is observed with the most scrupulous care, and where two and a half millions of people are kept in order by three battalions of infantry and some troops of guards, while Paris requires the presence of fifty thousand men."

The writer already quoted says of the Sabbaths of Italy, " They are skilfully adapted for the diversion of a people sporting with their chains. We need to seek no further for an adequate cause for that enervation of character which renders self-government impossible. *He* who made the Sabbath for *man* has ordained the connection between the sacred day and that *manliness* of character which can brook no bonds."

Montalembert's whole report before a hostile Parliament which constantly interrupted him is full of spirit, yet of a pro found view of the Sabbath: " Wĕ need not hesitate to place in the first rank of our dangers and our faults the public profanation of the Sabbath." " To suppress the Sabbath is, for most working-men, to suppress instruction." " The State which tranquilly assists at the undermining of the fundamental principle of all society becomes the *accomplice* of that mining before becoming its *victim.*"

One hundred of the New-York clergy issued a weighty document, which has these words : "*Man needs the Sabbath physically as a season when labor may wipe off its grime, and breathe more freely after the week's exhaustion. Man needs it morally to rise by its aid out of engrossing secularities. Toil needs it to rescue its share of rest and its season of devotion from the absorbing despotism of capital; and capital needs it to shield its own accumulations from the recklessness and anarchy of an imbruted and desperate proletaire, and to keep its own humanity and conscience alive. The State needs it as a safeguard of the public order, quiet, and virtue; human laws becoming, however wise in form, effete in practical exercise, except as they are based upon conscience and upon the sanctions of eternity as recognized by a free people, and God's day cultivating the one, and reminding us of the other. And in a republic more especially, whose liberties, under God, inhere in its virtues, the recognition freely and devoutly by an instructed nation of God's paramount rights is the moral underpinning requisite to sustain the superstructure of man's rights; and without the support of religion, not as nationally established, but as personally and freely accepted, all human freedom finally moulders, and totters into irretrievable ruin.*"

Pres. Mark Hopkins of Williams College, in a discourse in 1863 on " The Sabbath and Free Institutions," maintained three propositions : —

" *First,* A religious observance of the Sabbath, or the *religious Sabbath,* would secure the permanence of free institutions.

" *Second,* Without the Sabbath religiously observed, the permanence of free institutions cannot be secured.

"*Third,* The civil as based on the religious Sabbath is an institution to which society has a natural right, precisely as it has to property." He says, "In my own belief, the comprehensive reason for this" (Proposition II.) "is, that God will not permit it. The Sabbath is his; and he will not suffer that the highest result of moral forces should be reached, except in obedience to him." "History shows, that, where both have been in question, the enemies of freedom and of the Sabbath have been the same. Here Pilate and Herod have become friends. Here infidelity and formalism, despotism and anarchy, join hands."

A writer in 1833 said, "Why are the French people incapable of sustaining free institutions? Because they have no Sabbath. I cannot prevent myself from perceiving that our political superiority has its principal source in the exact observance of the day of rest." Another writer from Paris, in 1870, pens this: "The Paris commune is the ripe fruit of the Paris Sunday. Sunday toil on the one hand, and Sunday dissipation on the other, are, in no small measure, both cause and consequence of the social and moral degeneracy which has brought on France such fearful disaster."

Not without reason did Mirabeau exclaim, "God is as necessary as liberty to the French people." Long ago, Jefferson remarked to Webster, on a quiet Sabbath at Monticello, "The Sunday schools present the only legitimate means under the Constitution of avoiding the rock on which the French Republic was wrecked." "Raikes has done more for our country than the present generation will acknowledge. Perhaps, when I am cold, he will obtain his reward. He is *clarum et venerabile no-men.*" Webster says of the Sabbath school, "As a civil institution it is priceless. It has done more to preserve our liberties than grave statesmen and armed soldiers."

Pierre Duval, a French Catholic, after a visit to the United States, wrote of our Sabbath thus: "When I bethink me that this medley of men have withdrawn themselves for prayer and meditation, I confess that I feel myself impressed. I become earnest, religiously disposed. I understand why this people is a great people. I know why for a century it has been free, yea, the freest people which is found." " As to France, I understand why this people, so gifted, so great in the past, still so rich in the present, suffers and complains. I understand why this people, so in love with liberty, is not yet free, and will not easily become so. 'Woe to America' (says a church historian) 'if it ever ceases to keep holy the Lord's Day!' Yes, woe to America, and woe, then, to liberty!"

Thus the State is indebted to the Sabbath, in behalf of her multitudinous population, for this fivefold blessing bestowed upon them and her. Her children individually reap these blessings: the State also, in her corporate life, reaps the same blessings. It is not only a benefit to *each man* that he enjoy physical rest, mental relaxation, business prosperity, moral culture, and freedom, but it is as needful that the STATE, for its continued existence and vigor, should have in its citizens and statesmen physical rest, mental rest, business prosperity, moral culture, and liberty. These five are gifts of the Sabbath. The State, as such, can take cognizance of these benefits and this benefactor, and may not only advise her children to observe so wholesome a day for the good of each, but in her sovereign capacity she may compel such an observance as shall gratefully recognize the benefactor, and as shall not impair the benefits which the Sabbath brings to her as a corporate State.

This has been the view of great legal and judicial minds who have not been kept, by the fact that the Sabbath is a religious day, from observing that the Sabbath is also a *civil institution*, of which the State may take cognizance. Pres. Hopkins says, " The precise points to which the friends of the Sabbath and free institutions should direct their efforts at all times, and with special energy in the present hour of peril, are three : They must (1) be themselves careful to keep the Sabbath holy. This is indispensable. (2) They must do what they can by *moral* means to promote the intelligence, the morality, and especially the personal religion, of individuals. Only religious men will keep the Sabbath religiously. (3) They must maintain and defend the civil Sabbath as they would any other natural right."

Attorney-Gen. Bates (under Pres. Lincoln) remarks, "The religious character of an institution so ancient, so sacred, so lawful, and so necessary to the peace and comfort and the respectability of society, ought alone to suffice for its protection ; but, that failing, surely the laws of the land made for its account ought to be as strictly enforced as the laws for the protection of person and property. Vice and crime are always progressive and cumulative. If the Sunday laws be neglected or despised, the laws of person and property will soon share their fate, and be equally disregarded."

Thus the State, without transcending its sphere, nay, in the performance of its bounden duty and its imperative obligations, is to protect and cherish the "civil Sabbath." In the words of Judge Allen, "As a civil and political institution, the establishment and regulation of the Sabbath is within the just power of the civil government." "All interests require national conformity in the day observed, and that its observance should be so far compulsory as to protect those who desire and are entitled to the day."

"Blue Laws" we do not desire on Sabbath-keeping. The State is to be wise, considerate, and gracious in what she allows as well as in what she forbids. Legislators who are statesmen know how to enact laws which are strong, and effective of good results, and at the same time are considerate.

The statutes wisely provide, "Whoever conscientiously believes the seventh day of the week ought to be observed as the Sabbath, and actually refrains from secular business, travel, and labor on that day, shall not be liable to the penalties of this chapter for performing secular business, travel, or labor on the Lord's Day, or first day of the week, *provided* that he disturbs no other person." We would even go so far as to allow these persons conscientiously holding the seventh day as commanded of God to buy and sell to each other, provided that the store be not opened to the front.

The children of such parents should be treated most generously in regard to absence from school on the seventh day, and their class-standing should not be affected by their absence.

But, on the other hand, we believe the just laws of the land should be faithfully and strictly and impartially executed as to the keeping, by corporations and individuals, of the civil Sabbath, which, under the laws of the State, is designated as the Lord's Day. Excepting only apothecaries' stores, strictly so called, and, for a few hours in the morning, bakers' stores, all shops and stores should be made to close on the Sabbath. The selling and crying of Sunday papers should be made to cease. All shows, exhibitions for making money, all concerts, — excepting *sacred concerts*, in the *honest* sense of the words, in the *legal* sense of the words, where a *majority of the time is employed in sacred music*, — should be abolished, as they are now by law forbidden. Public parks and gardens should be open on the Sabbath for purposes of rest to the people ; but all exhibitions, menageries, shows, and so forth, in them, should be closed. The reading-rooms of Christian Associations — a kind of Christian home to many — should be open. All public halls and libraries — since the necessary attendants must be deprived of the Sabbath, while the occupation is really, as a matter of fact, in the nature of mental labor or amusement, and not of hallowed rest — should be closed. Railroad companies, except within a score of miles of large cities, for purposes of church attendance, travel for visiting hospitals, prisons, &c., should be compelled to desist from travel and freighting ; also steamboat companies. Harbor and picnic excursions, should be prohibited. Whatever corporation or company discharges an official or a workman for refusing to perform Sabbath labor should be liable for damages in law.

Has not the proof been most ample, in all the views taken, that the Sabbath is the benefactor of the State ? Is it not right to speak of the "due-ty" of the State to the Sabbath ? Is it not for the State — finding through commissions of her appointment, and by the recorded wisdom of profound observers, the value of the day of rest, its varied blessings to her citizens, its necessity to secure republican institutions — to overrule with strong hand the lawlessness and ignorance and the cupidity of those who advocate the European Sunday, and decree that this benefactor shall be continued in her sphere, and be allowed to continue her benign ministrations to the State? Can we not conceive the whole nation, become truly thoughtful on this subject, — from the miner of California and Nevada, the coal-worker of Pennsylvania, the careworn merchant of New York, the farmer of the West, the planter of the South, and the manufacturer and mechanic of New England, — rising in solemn gratitude to the sentiment, *"The Sabbath, the Nation's Benefactor"*? And when the Republic and the State decree in the words of Webster, "Let it be fostered and protected until the end of time," will not the people, like the voice of many waters, say "Amen"?

THE GOD OF THE SABBATH A BENE-
FACTOR TO THE STATE.

" Deus nobis hæc otia fecit."

THE Sabbath itself has been rightly considered as a benefactor to the State. The blessings of the Sabbath have been found to be in five principal directions : I. Physical rest ; II. Mental rest ; III. Prosperity in business ; IV. Moral culture and worship ; V. Freedom, individual and national. It has been fully shown that the STATE, as well as the individual, is indebted to the Sabbath. Nothing, we believe, need be added to strengthen the impression of the *benefits received* by the State from the weekly day of rest, which have been recounted.

The previous paper considered the "due-ty" of the State to the Sabbath : we now consider the "due-ty" of the State to the *Lord* of the Sabbath. It has been observed, also, that these blessings from the *sacred day* are great, even if we inquire not into its origin. What is designed now, in tracing these benefits one step farther back, is to show, first, that they have their origin in the will of the Creator and Preserver, and hence that the duty of State as well as of individual is to preserve and observe the day according to the intent of the Personal Founder. The point to be established is, that the Sabbath is not "earth born," but "heaven-descended." For some of these suggestions we are indebted to Gilfillan. Observe that the argument is entirely from nature ; and in no respect do we here draw it from revelation. **45**

I. — THE EXTREMELY EARLY INSTITUTION OF THIS DAY IS AN EVIDENCE THAT IT CAME, LIKE MAN, FRESH FROM THE HAND OF THE MAKER.

The septenary division of time is ancient and wide-spread. "Laplace assigns to the week a high antiquity; and its existence among successive generations is held to be a high proof of their common origin."

"The week is, perhaps, the most ancient and incontestable monument of human knowledge." "The septenary arrangement of days," says Scaliger, "was in use among the Orientals from the remotest antiquity." "We have reason to believe," observes Pres. Goguet, "that the institution of that short period of seven days called a *week* was the first step taken by mankind in dividing and measuring their time. We find, from time immemorial, the use of this period among all the nations, without any variation in the form of it." "Pres. Goguet observes, further, that the Israelites, Assyrians, Egyptians, Indians, Arabians, and, in a word, all the nations of the East, have, in all ages, made use of a week consisting of seven days. We find the same custom among the ancient Romans, Gauls, Britons, Germans, the nations of the North and of America." Humboldt makes a similar observation. "We add a sentence from Humboldt, venturing, however, to premise that the Peruvian ninth day of rest seems to prove a former notation of time by weeks even in America. 'It appears,' he remarks, 'that no nation of the new continent was acquainted with the week, or cycle of seven days, which we find among the Hindoos, the Chinese, the Assyrians, and the Egyptians, and which, as Le Gentil has very justly remarked, is followed by the greater part of the nations of the Old World.'" Proudhon affirms the same universality of the Rest Day: "Especially among the Chinese, as appears from this passage of the annals of Sec-Masico, 'The emperor offered sacrifices to the Supreme Unity, Tog-y, every seven days;' and from this still more significant sentence of Cheri-King, 'All the ancient emperors on the seventh day, called the "Great Day," caused the doors of houses to be closed. No business was done that day, and the magistrates judged no case.'" Proudhon is profoundly moved on dwelling upon the universality and solidarity of Sabbath-keeping in all lands and ages: "This hebdomadal rest, going back to an epoch so remote, perpetuated from age to age until our days, appears to us as the profound indication of an act of nature, of a providential will. It is not in our power to remain indifferent to the thought of the throng of generations which have successively made use of this day, in circumstances so diverse, and during so many centuries."

"Many vain conjectures," says Goguet, "have been formed concerning the reasons and motives which determined all mankind to agree in this primitive division of their time. Nothing but tradition concerning the time employed in the creation of the world could give rise to this universal, immemorial practice." We know of no man to whom even tradition has ascribed this admirable arrangement of week and rest day. No one could ascribe a measure so wise, and peculiarly and greatly adapted to affect the human race, to a caprice of primitive man in the childhood of his being, or to any thing less than the wisdom of the Creator.

II. — ANOTHER EVIDENCE THAT THE SABBATH IS A DIVINE INSTITUTION IS THE PERFECT ADAPTATION OF THE DAY TO THE PURPOSES OF REST, OF SACRED REST.

As we have seen at great length, the day is wonderfully adapted to serve the combined purposes, twined together like a thread of silver with a thread of gold, of *rest* and *worship*. It recuperates body of man and beast, and refreshes the mind ; and it "restores the soul, leading it in green pastures and by still waters."

No primitive man, no philosopher, could have devised this cessation from labor. Proudhon says it is "an institution of which our modern genius, with all its theories of civil and political rights, has never reached the height." "Montesquieu," he says, "spoke not of it, because he did not comprehend it." "No people without a Sabbath have ever of their own impulse introduced it."

"That a seventh day of sacred rest renders the labor of six days more remunerative than would be that of seven under a system of unremitting toil, and that it interposes a barrier against the enslaving of mankind, are proofs of the profound wisdom of the institution, which it was reserved for recent times to bring into clearer view, if not entirely to discover. It is one thing, moreover, to see and unfold the merits of a discovery, and altogether another to make it. To the origination, in short, of an institution proved to be adapted to the whole constitution and circumstances of mankind, there was indispensable so large a measure of knowledge, that the claim, by the Author of the Sabbath, to omniscience itself, would be no arrogance, and his exercise of the attribute no difficulty."

Some one has followed out the well-known argument of Paley in regard to sleep, applying it to the Sabbath. "Paley has deduced an argument for this world being the work of an Intelligent Cause from the relation of sleep to night. He says, 'It appears to me to be a relation which was expressly intended. Two points are manifest: *first*, that the animal frame requires sleep; *secondly*, that night brings with it a silence, and a cessation of activity, which allows of sleep being taken without interruption and without loss.' But what the rest of sleep is to the body the repose of the Sabbath is to both body and soul."

III. — ANOTHER PROOF THAT GOD IS THE AUTHOR OF THE
    SABBATH IS, THAT IT IS SUCH A DAY AS GOD, AND NOT
    MAN, WOULD MAKE.

"The sanctity of the Sabbath is a further evidence of its divine original. The ordinance is far too sacred for human beings to desire, or even to think of." "The Sabbath was evidently made for man, but not by man. Its Author must have been divinely holy, as well as divinely benignant, intelligent, and wise." Dr. Croly says, "The divine origin of the Sabbath might be almost proved from its opposition to the lower propensities of mankind. In no age of the world, since labor was known, would any master of the serf, the slave, or the cattle, have *spontaneously* given up a seventh part of their toil. No human legislator would have proposed such a law of property; or, if he had, no nation would have endured it. The Sabbath in its whole character is so strongly opposed to the avarice, the heartlessness, and the irreligion of man, that, except in the days of Moses and Joshua, it has never been observed with due reverence by any nation in the world." "If," says "The London Times," "the sacred character of the day be once obscured, there would not remain behind any influence strong enough to keep a thrifty tradesman from his counter for twelve hours together. A man who would observe the day as a Sabbath would retrench it as a holiday; and thus competition and imitation would at length bring all to the common level of universal profaneness and continuous toil." J. Stuart Mill says, "Operatives are perfectly right in thinking, that, if all worked on Sunday, seven days' work would have to be given for six days' wages."

IV. — ANOTHER INDICATION THAT THE SABBATH IS THE GIFT OF GOD IS, THAT IT IS FOUND FLOURISHING IN GREATEST VIGOR IN ISRAEL.

Israel, to say the least, *appears* and *claims* to have been a *nation divinely led.* The oracles of this nation ascribe the Sabbath to God; *first*, as a memorial of his cessation from creation, in which, as an example to his creatures to be made in his image, he seems to have first acted and then spoken anthropomorphically; and, *second*, as the commencement of the exodus. The clearer the type, the nearer the foundry. Israel's clear commands and careful Sabbath-keeping show the origin of the day in Israel's God,

V. — ONE MORE EVIDENCE THAT GOD MADE THE SABBATH IS THE EXACTNESS OF THE ADAPTATION OF THE REST DAY TO GIVE THE NEEDED REFRESHMENT.

How fared France while she worshipped the Goddess of Reason, and kept her tenth-days, her *décadis?* Not well. They came back to the old seventh day ordained by a higher Reason, who "sees the end from the beginning."

Proudhon exclaims, "What statistician could have first dis-

covered, that, in ordinary times, the period of labor ought to be.
to the period of rest in the ratio of six to one ?" He expounds
Pythagoras' *doctrine of crises*, who, as he says, first brought calculation into the study of man ; then he says, "Moses, then,
having to regulate in a nation the labors and the days, the rests
and the festivals, the toils of the body and the exercises of the
soul, the interests of hygiene and of morals, political economy
and personal subsistence, had recourse to a science of numbers,
to a *transcendental harmony*, which embraced all space, duration,
movement, spirits, bodies, the sacred and the profane. The
certainty of the science is demonstrated by the result. Diminish
the week by a single day, the labor is insufficient relatively to
the repose ; augment it in the same quantity, it becomes excessive. Establish every three days and a half a half-day of relaxation, you multiply, by the breaking of the day, the loss of time ;
and, in shattering the natural unity of the day, you break the
numerical equilibrium of things. Accord, on the contrary, forty-
eight hours of repose after twelve consecutive days of labor, you
kill the man by inertia, after having exhausted him by fatigue."
And he says pithily, that one might as philosophically ascribe
such an invention to primitive man as believe "the fable of the
sow writing the Iliad with her snout." [1]

With this discovery, that the day of rest is of divine appointment, what new duty imposes itself upon individuals, and upon
the STATE acting wisely for her citizens ?

Even were the Sabbath only a chance, or, as the Pantheist
might dream, some exquisite flowering of the All, still it would
be a benefactor, and as such, in the words of Webster, to be
"fostered and protected until the end of time." In that case
we are left to our own experiment and reason to devise the
best means to make the benefactions of the day most available.

But with the discovery that there is a Personal Founder of the
Sabbath, and that this rest day is a gift from him to the human
race, two things follow as to the keeping of the day both by individuals and by *States*.

[1] Proudhon, Pierre Joseph: Du Dimanche: Hygiène, Morale, Famille, Cité.

First, Gratitude would lead us to observe his wishes and intent in giving the day. If a benevolent man has madé a wise will, the recipient of his favors, unless there are powerful reasons to the contrary, should use the bequests according to his intent who gave them.

Second, Prudence would lead us to observe his wishes and intent in giving the day. We were not wise enough to devise the Sabbath: we are not wise enough to use the Sabbath. We need some God to tell us. There is some machine constructed which only one supreme genius, some James Watt, could have designed. We need the same genius to explain to us how to work his machine. The nearer we get to the mind of God, the more we, state or individuals, shall receive "his favor, which is life," in observing it, and the more wisely shall we use the Sabbath, as states and individuals, to gain all the benefits which the Divine Inventor intended.

In this paper, as in the preceding, it is not to be overlooked that the argument is aimed at the duty of the STATE as a corporate body, a "moral personality," in relation to the *Lord* of the Sabbath. It is true, we may well believe, that each individual has a religious duty to the Sabbath and its Divine Founder. It is true, moreover, that each citizen has a personal duty to the Sabbath, as one of a community, and of that community, the State. It is well for the Sabbath-breaking citizen to reflect, in the light of all the foregoing considerations, that it is indeed hardly figures of speech to say, that, whenever he takes the reins for a Sabbath pleasure-drive, he, like Phaëthon, snatches the reins which guide our nation in a safe course; whenever he patronizes a cigar-store on that day, he puffs into smoke part of the Magna Charta of our liberties; whenever he rushes in car or steamship over land or sea, he is, so far as he is concerned, just so fast rushing this nation to destruction; that, when he is attending a so-called "Sunday concert," what he hears is not music, but the clinking of some future American's chain. The citizen, then, has his personal duties to the State as one of her children in connection with the observance of the Sabbath. Yet our argument is mainly insisting, let it be distinctly observed, on the duty of the STATE, the corporate body, which, as truly as individuals, has eyes and discernment and duties, to secure the observance of the *civil Sabbath* within her bounds, by compulsory and protective measures if need be, lest, in offending her Divine Benefactor, and breaking the laws he has imposed upon nature, she drop from the firmament like a lost star.

Nothing can be more truly rational, then, than for the States, as well as individuals, to become little children, and discern profoundly, and obey carefully, the spirit and intent of the decree and statute of the Great King, which reads thus in the nature of things as well as in a certain revered book : —

"REMEMBER THE SABBATH DAY TO KEEP IT HOLY. SIX DAYS SHALT THOU LABOR, AND DO ALL THY WORK; BUT THE SEVENTH DAY IS THE SABBATH OF THE LORD THY GOD: in it thou shalt not do any work, thou, nor thy son, nor thy daughter, thy man-servant, nor thy maid-servant, nor thy cattle, nor thy stranger that is within thy gates. For in six days the Lord made heaven and earth, the sea, and all that in them is, and rested the seventh day: wherefore the Lord blessed the Sabbath Day, and hallowed it."

"SIX DAYS SHALL WORK BE DONE; BUT THE SEVENTH DAY IS THE SABBATH OF REST, A HOLY CONVOCATION: IT IS THE SABBATH OF THE LORD IN ALL YOUR DWELLINGS."

Let us not forget, because we are growing to be a giant nation, with thirty-eight stars instead of thirteen in our sky in our Centennial year, that a medal of our early history had the motto, *"Non sine Diis animosus infans."* Let us not imagine, because we rest securely between the two oceans, and lay our hands on the Alleghanies and the Sierras, that we are too great a nation to obey the Almighty Father. Babylon and the empires in ruins may become the prototypes of our "decline and fall." That gloomy and heart-shattering word may be written on our palace-walls as on Babylon's, — *"Tekel:* Weighed, Wanting."

For He still lives who turned them to destruction ; and to States as well as to men his word applies, "Them that honor me I will honor; but they that despise me shall be lightly esteemed."

For in the olden time, for three-quarters of a century, the lonely sun looked down on a land bereft of her brave sons and fair daughters, who by the waters of Babylon were singing to the plaintive music of their exiled harps, — a land without wheat-field or vineyard-terrace as of yore, but over whose lichened orchards, and weed-grown acres, and dilapidated landmarks, moved a voice as of One that is mighty, in words as of divine sarcasm, *"As long as she lay desolate, the land kept Sabbath threescore years and ten."* Yet once before, and once afterward, that people "sat under their own vine and fig-tree," and "called the Sabbath a delight."

"THE LORD *rested* the seventh day," "*blessed* the Sabbath Day, and *hallowed* it." What will the STATE do with the Sabbath Day?

"I SAT DOWN UNDER HIS SHADOW — WITH GREAT DELIGHT."

THE STATE AND TEMPLES.

TAXING GOD'S HOUSE.

This essay appeared in "The Congregationalist," Feb. 18, 1875. A year later, in "The New-York Herald," March 7, 1876, appeared Gen. Dix's spirited and powerful letter; extracts from which having fallen under the eye of the writer, an interchange of papers and a pleasant correspondence took place, from which I take the liberty to make extracts, as also from the noble words of his public letter.

New York, 10 April, 1876.

Reverend and dear Sir, — I have read with great satisfaction your article in "The Congregationalist," which you had the kindness to send me, on "Taxing God's House." The coincidence of the currents of thought in your article and mine is certainly remarkable, the more so as I thought our side of the question had never been presented before. . . .

Very truly yours,   John A. Dix.

There is great danger, as has already become apparent, that the matter of taxing places of worship should be put upon false ground, or at least low ground; far below that upon which it ought to be argued; far below where it can be argued with most safety and cogency, and least friction of dissent; far below the plane where every religious mind — and all minds, we are told, are religious — would feel that the matter rests.

The subject is debated under this title, "The Taxation of *Churches.*" The arguments here, indeed, in favor of immunity from taxes to churches, vastly preponderate. But who that listens to argument on this subject from the benefits to society has not had a secret dissatisfaction, and the feeling that there *must* be higher ground than this, which accounts for our strong repugnance to entertaining the idea of taxing our temples ? [1]

This ground has, perhaps, been dimly seen ; but some have not pressed forward to hold it, partly from the pitiful dread of appealing to the common moral sentiments of mankind.

Let us restate the question in its true form ; not, " Shall we tax *churches ?*" but, "Shall we tax *God's house ?*" Edifices consecrated to the Supreme Being — is it comely to subject them to the levying of tax to pay the expenses of human government? Shall men take that gift which they have placed above their heads at the feet of the Supreme, and make it pay tribute? Let six of the most accomplished debaters of the land argue this question strictly, "Is it right to tax *God's house ?*" [2] and the whole subject would lie in so clear light in all minds, that this crepuscule of thought upon it would have vanished utterly.

The principle at root is, that what is rightfully given up to a higher Power is beyond our plane or level. Is it not the same principle, that it would be uncomely for the State to tax the Navy-Yard, or the Springfield Armory, or any other property formally committed to a *higher Power ?* United-States property is high above all transactions of levying and collection for State expenses. So our church-edifices are more than "meeting-houses : " they are "houses of God," formally consecrated to a higher Power. "Render therefore to God the things that are God's."

It was, of course, competent to the States out of which the District of Columbia was formed to cede or to retain that territory ; but, once ceded, that tract of land belonged to the General

---

[1] " The politico-economical side of the question had been exhausted by Pres. Eliot of Harvard University, and by Mr. Andrews, one of our city assessors, in a series of able articles in the New-York Times; and I thought it due to the importance of the subject to present the religious side. I thought, too, that the prevailing disregard of the sacred character of houses of worship justified stronger language than I am accustomed to use in the discussion of ordinary questions of policy or principle." — JOHN A. DIX, *Correspondence.*

[2] " In manifold instances, both in the Old and New Testaments, a house of worship is called the house of God ; and it is always named with appropriate expressions of reverence. The universal heart responds to this designation : and, no matter how humble the edifice consecrated to his service, all men, when within its hallowed walls, feel more sensibly than they do amid the turmoil of the outer world that they are in the presence of the Omnipotent Being by whom the great forces of the universe are moved and controlled; and that, by ignoring him, they renounce all hope of a higher state of existence." — JOHN A. DIX: *Letter to New York Herald,* March 7, 1876.

Government. It is competent to the State to say how much land, and how much of wealth and worth, shall be allowed to a house of worship; but, once *dedicated* to God, it should be beyond taxation. It is also competent to the State to limit, as should be done, the dedication to the *mere house of worship*, and to forbid the withholding from taxation of church-lands or other property; as also, if she choose, to tax the separate pews as the property of the individual owners.

The State might draw a legal distinction, if it be not drawn already, between *dedication* and *consecration*, allowing only those religious edifices to be *dedicated* which are to be legally exempt from taxation, and considering as merely *consecrated* all such religious property as men have given up, so far as they are concerned, to a higher use, but which the State does not consider beyond taxation. Thus *church edifices only*, and such buildings as are actually employed for Sabbath instruction in the things of God, should be allowed to be *dedicated* in the legal sense. We all pray to be delivered from such a state of things as has existed in all countries of large monastic endowments; for example, in France at the time of the Revolution, as described by Geffcken: "Add to this a vast host of ecclesiastical sinecures, without reckoning, indeed, the numerous and often very opulent monastic foundations, which were in a frightful state of decay. The crown had confiscated many of these as royal demesnes, but had granted them as benefices, exempt from all obligations; and they had offered to youthful ecclesiastics belonging to noble families an income adequate to their rank, until a suitable bishopric should fall vacant. Bestowed as they were by those who were powerful at court, it is easy to imagine the crowd of elegant abbés that surrounded a Madame de Pompadour. The whole enormous aggregate of ecclesiastical property — the revenue of which was estimated at a hundred million livres derived from tithes, and from sixty million to seventy million livres derived from landed possessions — was absolutely exempt from taxation. The clergy gave to the State a few millions as a gratuity (*don gratuit*), but resisted with the bitterest indignation any attempt to subject their estates to the universal obligation of taxation; and as late as 1788, when the financial embarassments of the nation and the misery of the lower orders had reached their climax, their reply to a demand of that kind, returned not in a synod, but in an assembly convoked for secular purposes, was this : 'Ces biens sont voués, consacrés à Dieu.   Notre conscience et notre honneur ne nous permettent pas de consentir à changer en tribut nécessaire ce qui ne peut être que l'offrande de notre amour.' 'This property is devoted, consecrated to God.   Our conscience and our honor do not permit us to consent to make an obligatory tribute that which can be only the offering of our love.' "[1]

This enormous evil, of large church properties exempted, can be prevented by allowing legal *dedication* only to church edifices, temples for the *worship of God.*

But it may be said, if the house is dedicated to God, then the protection of it belongs to him.   The State should not be taxed for care of it; just as the United States, after the ceding of the Navy-Yard, requires no further care for it from Massachusetts.

The answer is simple, that the State may properly, in consideration of the supreme majesty of the God to whom all temples are consecrated, give guard and protection, without compensation, to all his temples.   Were there an extensive, raging fire at the Charlestown Navy-Yard, the state' or the cities *might*, if they chose, properly *give* the service of their fire departments for its extinguishment.   Had " The Brandywine " been donated to the illustrious Lafayette, the State might properly freely have given the whole of her police force to guard it, without exacting any tax in return from the distinguished stranger.   The claim is not valid, then, that, because in some sort ceded to God, the temple should not, therefore, receive the State's protection without compensation or tax.

Even 'Rome regarded all worship.[2]   Dionysius of Halicarnassus says, " Men of a thousand nations come to the city, and must worship the gods of their country according to the laws at

---

[1] Geffcken: Church and State, ii. 472.

[2] " From that day to this, during the lapse of nearly sixteen hundred years, no government has undertaken to make church edifices pay tribute for the privilege of worshipping God.   Even the pagans, through the veneration in which they held the temples dedicated to their idols, manifest more reverence than the promoters of this raid upon religious worship." — *Letter to Herald.*

home." There were many *religiones licitæ* and *dei publice adsciti.* Their houses of worship were not taxed.

From his own religious point of view, *mutatis mutandis*, this principle, it is believed, will strike every man as according to the universal feeling of reverence.

This will be the natural view of the Christian and the Israelite. Imagine the taxation of the Holy of Holies to support Solomon's fish-ponds! It is not comely for governmental exactors to cross the threshold of the "Father's house."[1] Christ did not deem it a thing to be borne, that money transactions should go on in God's temple, even when auxiliary to an offering *to* God : how much more had government-officers, exacting *from* God to the State, entered there !

But atheists, pantheists, and idolaters, it is thought, would not allow this principle. How unduly afraid we are to trust to the religious nature in man which we are constantly asserting to be there ! If to that which any man reveres as the Supreme, be it to a known or an "unknown god," he build an altar, pillar, temple, joss-house, pagoda, mosque, pantheon, or whatever, that structure, consecrated to his Supreme, every man's religious sense tells him should not be subjected to profane mingling with barter, trade, or taxes. Let Mr. Emerson erect an altar to the "Over-Soul," and his fellows assemble for prayer, the "highest meditation," the Chinaman his joss-house, the German atheist his hall formally consecrated to Aletheia or Humanitas : exempt those edifices, exempt the chapel of the Parsee and of the serpent worshipper.

"But," said one to me, "the steamer of the Japanese in which they perform river-worship — would you exempt that?" Certainly, if publicly and permanently consecrated to their Supreme. "Render to God that which is God's," to Cæsar only that which is Cæsar's. The main principle in the matter is, not that the joss-house, or the sacred vessel, or the church, is

---

[1] "The Divine Founder of our faith gave an impressive proof of his conception of the sacred character of edifices consecrated to the service of God by driving the money-changers out of the temple, — the only act of violence in his meek and compassionate life; and I trust we shall have courage and reverence enough to imitate his example, and prevent the money-changers from getting a foothold in our houses of worship, and converting them into dens of thieves." — *Letter to Herald.*

of *advantage to society*, but rather, that, by common reverence of men, the house consecrated to worship of the Supreme is above taxation to support government among beings who are atoms in presence of the Supreme and Holy One.

Imagine such a picture as Nast might draw of the exactors of the king assessing the furniture of the Most Holy Place, — even the cherubim on the mercy-seat, — Jehovah's house paying taxes to King Solomon !

We have only restated the question for wiser thinkers to discuss, " Is it right to tax GOD'S HOUSE ? " [1]

[1] It is with pleasure that the writer adds further coincident thoughts from the noble letter of Gen. Dix, not sorry to draw attention to these constellations of thoughts, worthier, though here sunk below the horizon-line : —

" The scheme should be repudiated and denounced in all its parts. One can hardly debate it without a feeling of debasement. It is not a subject for human logic; it is not a problem of profit and loss, to be argued by religious obligation on one side, and cupidity on the other. It is a matter of instinct, of inborn reverence, of the consciousness which every mind not perverted by the sophistications of worldly science has of its own immeasurable inferiority to the Sovereign Ruler of the universe, and of the homage it owes him as its Creator and Redeemer. There is something revolting to the moral sense in its normal state in the idea of making a mercenary profit out of an edifice consecrated to his service. When this inner sense is wanting, argument is useless.

" The most attractive objects which meet us in our travels in Europe are the cathedrals. Amid all the wars, the bloodshed, the barbarities, the desolation, which nations have visited upon each other under the misguidance of their evil passions, these monuments of their faith and their devotion come out from the dark background of the picture in bright relief as sacred tributes to the Creator of the universe. No man can stand beneath their domes and vaulted roofs without feeling that they atone for much of the wrong committed by their authors, who lavished on them without stint the wealth they would otherwise have wasted on ostentatious gratifications or unholy indulgences. Heaven forbid that the lesson of these comparatively uncivilized ages should be lost on us, and that, in this day of intellectual light and social refinement, the tax-gatherer should be sent to fill his bag of lucre by levying contributions on the sanctuaries of the living God!

" I do not believe that any community which seeks to throw its burden of secular expenses on the worship of God, by levying contributions on the edifices consecrated to his services, can long escape the chastisement it provokes. It is not necessary to look for special visitations of ill as manifestations of his displeasure. Cupidity, selfishness, rapacity, the profanation of things which should be held sacred, carry with them, by the force of immutable laws, the retribution denounced by the codes they violate.

" All religious denominations have the same interest in preventing their houses of worship from becoming desecrated and secularized by taxation. As was beautifully expressed by Madame de Staël, 'Their ceremonies are strongly contrasted ; but the same sigh of distrust, the same petition for support, ascends to heaven from all.' It seems to me that this whole movement is calculated to create in the breasts of reflecting persons a feeling of profound sorrow and unmitigated disgust. The proper mode of treating it is to scout it out of the committee-rooms, legislative halls, and social circles which it has defiled by its presence. To give it any countenance would be to furnish new ground for the national reproach too often cast upon us, that the almighty dollar is the chief object of our adoration." — JOHN A. DIX: *New-York Herald.*

THE STATE AND THE CHURCH.

THE STATE AND THE CHURCH.

DRIVEN by the necessities of close thinking, and by eagerness to penetrate to the heart of the important subject named above, — for the maxim is evermore true, " He who would pile high must dig deep," — we found ourselves pushing beyond the Ultima Thule of all we could find written on this subject, and indeed beyond all methods of analysis of the subject, and reading Heard's "Tripartite Nature of Man," and Delitzsch's "Biblical Psychology," and sections of Julius Müller on "Sin," and pondering especially the distinction between the *spirit* and the *soul*. This distinction, we believe, is at the root of the separation of Church and State.

We need not dwell tediously upon the "spirit" and the "soul." To have drawn attention to the discrimination of the two is, perhaps, sufficient: at least, abstruse, extended discussion of the nature of man is not needful or in place here. Yet, on second thought, perhaps it is best — considering the exceeding practical value of this discrimination, and yet that very little is made of it in popular works — to enter a little more deeply than the ordinary reader will enjoy into the distinction between

THE SOUL AND THE SPIRIT.

We warn the popular reader that we are about to enter upon several pages of metaphysical dulness, which we invite him to skip to commence at once upon the argument. But the thorough student will wish to understand this distinction sufficiently to appreciate its reality and importance, and how it underlies the subject we are handling. Hence this dull metaphysical section, which we would willingly have thrown into an appendix, were it not that it is properly prefatory to the subject, and therefore in place just here. Allowing the popular reader to pass on to the argument, with the student we dwell a moment on the soul and the spirit.

The profound thinkers, before noted, all arrive at that important discrimination of the spirit from the soul. The *spirit* seems to be man's inner personality and individuality, *detached* from nature and creation, from his body and from the universe: *soul* seems to be the spirit as *attached* and connected, and resident in nature and in the body, and as modified by nature.

Plain men understand the "spirit" best by observing how, apart from philosophical study, they naturally and unconsciously discriminate it from "soul." Though the qualities of the spirit derive very easily to the soul, so that we can say "a generous *spirit*," "a generous *soul*," yet that the words are not synonymous is seen from the fact that they are not interchangeable in such expressions as "a holy spirit," "a keen spirit," "a discerning spirit," "a wise spirit," where the word "soul" could not properly be used; from the fact, also, that this reference to the inner, detached personality passes over into the word "spirit," used to express the *mood* of the "spirit" itself; as, "He acted in a devout spirit," "He criticised in an appreciative spirit."

Other simple ways of studying these two words in discrimination is to observe that we speak of "disembodied *spirits*," rather than disembodied souls; that the demons are called "evil *spirits*," not souls.

The Scriptures move with the ease of perfect understanding, and of unconsciousness of difficulty in this discrimination. They speak, indeed, of "*dividing asunder* soul and spirit." Thus man *became* a living soul; that is, a spirit put into and *living in nature.* "Try the spirits;" that is, the *personal* qualities of those in contact with us. "The first man was made a living soul: the last man is a quickening spirit." "God is a

Spirit ;" that is, a being above nature. When we conceive of God as *immanent in nature*, we call him the "Soul of all things," or, as Emerson does, "the Over-Soul." In *soul* there is always reference to the personality as dwelling in nature, and as adapted to that nature-life.

The "Holy Spirit," not the Holy Soul.

From such ways of discriminating, we come to the clear sense that *spirit* is the pure personality by and in which one is what he is ; by which he discerns, and is in contact with or repulsion from, other personalities, whether they be equal, inferior, superior, or the Supreme. The spirit is man in his power to know his own personality ; to comprehend the quality of other beings, and hold converse with them ; above all, with God. Delitzsch says the *spirit* is "that whereby he becomes evident to himself, recognizes his own distinct individuality, is conscious of himself, the divine image in man, the principle of his personality." As to the *soul*, Müller defines it "the personal life of the individual, *Ichleben*, arising from the entrance of the spirit into the earthly organ of the body."

Now, from the preceding considerations, there is no doubt that the *spirit*, as everywhere represented in Scripture, is the *fountain* of divine life to the whole being ; because by the Holy Spirit, or God in his quickening personality, man's perverted personality is rectified, restored to its original, namely, a miniature "likeness" of the Divine Personality, so in accord with the Divine Personality, and therefore, for the first time, receiving an inflow or "communion" of the Divine Personality.

It is in the *spirit* that man cries, "Abba, Father." "The *Spirit* beareth witness with our *spirit*." The two personalities, divine and human, meet in harmony, and therefore in mutual recognition of their harmony.

The soul is properly reached, controlled, moulded, by the spirit. There is philosophy in the consecution, "I pray God your whole *spirit* and *soul* and *body* be preserved blameless." The spirit ripples out the qualities of its personality into soul and body. On the other hand, body and soul, containing somewhat of God not in the spirit, may have something of good to ripple back into the spirit. But, at the last, man's spirit from within is to form all which he is, or is to be,—even the body in its transient acts ; as we speak of "the spiritual look" on the face.

Christ was once asked, Clement tells us, when the end would come. Part of his threefold answer was, "When that which is *without* is as that which is *within*."

But now observe carefully, as needful to discussion of the topic, State and Church, that it by no means follows, because one's own spirit is the formative power of *his own soul* and *his own body*, that therefore *another's spirit*, in the divine order, is to be allowed to control and form the soul and body of the first.

Further is it to be considered, that there is so much of God in nature, in the body and the soul, which is not in the spirit, — nature being divine, since from God, — that it is not a certain thing that a man's spirit at any particular time is superior in character to his soul and body. The reverse may be true, — that his body and soul, his human *nature*, may be nobler than his spirit. This is often seen. One may be a disobedient spirit, but a noble soul. We sometimes appeal from the man's evil spirit to his nobler soul, his more generous nature. Therefore, before absolutely subjugating one's soul to one's spirit, wise were it, needful indeed is it, to be sure that the formative spirit invoked is superior to the soul. To form society, one must be sure the *spirit* he invokes is equal to nature, is plenitudinous and multitudinous as nature ; in other words, is the Holy Spirit, who "knows the mind of God," in nature. Nature may be stronger, nobler, because God is infallibly in it, than any other spirit, or even than that Spirit if hindered so that he have not "free course." It might not be safe to invoke the spirit of Napoleon to form all society and government ; but it might give a glow of satisfaction to see a colossal representation of Thorwaldsen's "Christ in Benediction" on our national capitol, invoked as the spirit which should mould nation and government. "Try the spirit," be sure it has a right to subordinate all nature to it, before you undertake to subordinate all nature to it.

One must also note, as necessary to this discussion, that the soul has so much of spirit in it, and so much of nature — in which God is — in it, that it has a certain moral life and moral conduct. It has not direct sense of God's personality, except as an observed fact: that belongs to spirit alone. But the soul is competent to perceive *God's work,* and thence have inference of his existence and character, and

"Look through nature up to nature's God."

The soul can perceive God's laws and moral order, and observe them. Luther says, "The natural man is one who, though he stands *apart from grace,* is still endowed to the fullest degree with understanding, sense, capacity, and art." So Aristotle, " Soul is that by which we live, feel or perceive, will, move, and understand." "Thus," says Heard, " the *psyche*" [soul] "is the sum total of man's natural powers, the life as born into the world, and all that it contains, or can attain unto." "The *psyche* is the life of man in its widest and most inclusive sense, embracing not only the animal, but also the intellectual and moral faculties, in so far as their exercise has not been depraved by the fall." "It is exactly where Aristotle leaves off that the Scripture begins to treat of human nature, and tells us of a faculty — let us call it God-consciousness" [we should say more widely *personality*-consciousness] — "which is dead or dormant in a great degree" [we should say *dormant* only, and that *mainly* as towards God], "and which" [as towards God and spirits renewed in his image] "it is the office and work of the Holy Spirit, first to quicken, and then to direct, sanctify, and govern."

The thought to be dwelt upon is this: the *natural* man may know *about* God, and may recognize his *moral order* in the world, and observe it, and regard him as the Author and Governor of that moral order : the *spiritual* man knows *God himself,* his spirit being in accord with the Divine Spirit.

This distinction of spirit and soul, natural and spiritual, has great uses in one's personal spiritual life ; valuable homiletic uses also. We are now observing that it underlies the separation of Church and State.

We may seem to have dwelt too long on this distinction between spirit and soul, the spiritual and natural man, — here we believe for the first time clearly drawn as the thought at the root of the separation of Church and State, — but no longer time than many a bulkier volume spends upon preliminaries not one tithe as important.   This distinction would have aided Vinet to answer more summarily and satisfactorily the objection over which he wearily labors, made to his theory of the separation of Church and State, — the objection that "the State ought to reproduce the entire man, which it cannot do in the separation of Church and State."   Holding, as that great thinker did with singular clearness, that religion, personal religion, is of the *indi-vidual*, and therefore not to be attributed to an organization, he said clearly to this objection, " The State *cannot* have personal religion, which is the predicate of individuality ; " but with this distinction prominent to his mind,[1] of the natural man and the spiritual man, he might have gained greater clearness as to the true and full connection of God and religion with the State, and summarily have answered the objector, — The State *is* a *natural* man *entire*, — " one great stature of an honest man," as Milton says, — and can therefore have *natural religion*, that recognition of God, righteousness, morality, which is identical and common in all natural, psychical men.

Dry and uninteresting, abstract and abstruse, then, as this discussion may thus far have seemed, we believe our time has not been wasted.   The French Directory were impatient at the slow and tedious work by which the youthful Napoleon got his artillery into position before Toulon ; but, when that work was done, Little Gibraltar was untenable, and Toulon was evacuated. So these distinctions between spirit and soul may have been tedious ; but by them is found untenable the domination of the State by the Church, or of the Church by the State.

We foreshadow our argument in two paragraphs.

In the superiority of the spiritual to its natural, and its legitimate control over its own natural as its formative, guid-

---

[1] Vinet, it is just to say, comes nearest to glimpses of this distinction. — e. g., pp. 242, 258; but he does not state it, least of all insist on it.

ing, and corrective power, arises the plausible demand for the domination of the State by the Church.

On the other hand, in the fact that the natural is in its sphere, no less than the spiritual, a true life, — represented in governments and institutions, — which recognizes God and a divine order, and a divine law; and in the fact that no one spirit has so recovered itself and elevated itself as to be worthy to subject and form the natural life in nations, and generally in the earth; that no spiritual organization is so recovered and elevated as worthily to subject and form all nations; that the one Spirit who was perfect, and endued with dominant power, permitted and respected the natural as divine in its sphere, and never sought to impose his spiritual dominion, perfect and powerful as it was, upon nations and governments as such, — arises the counter-claim and valid consideration, that the State should be free from the Church.   The above is the general view before our minds as we proceed.

STATE AND CHURCH.

Let us commence here : *The State is not to be dominated by the Church.*   This Pius IX. emphatically denies.[1]

Here we pause to asseverate, in the amplest and most decided manner, that we draw a distinction between *Romanism* and *Catholicism.*   We have no conflict with Catholics in religion, nor with Catholicism, nor with Pius IX. as the " Holy Father," so called, of a large class.   Our conflict, in which we have the company of many of the noblest Catholics, the living and the dead, — our conflict is with Romanism, which, in its *very first principles*, is an enemy to the independence of nations.   In Bismarck's words, " I have to deal here with politics, and not with dogmas."

But we return to repeat, Pius IX. emphatically denies that the State ought to be independent of the domination of the Church.

Here we are obliged to make another pause to draw attention to the remarkable fact, the *delusive fact* to many, that not only newspaper editors, but some of the highest dignitaries, bishops,

---

[1] Syllabus, §§ 55, 77, 78.

archbishops, and even cardinals, in the Romish Church, deny in the most positive manner that the Papacy assumes to control governments. But, be it observed, *no pope* was ever known to make such a denial. History, Jesuits, strict Romanists, all agree with the Papacy ; and the Papacy understands itself ; and, meanwhile, the denials of cardinals and all " *minora sidera*" go for absolutely nothing.

Very emphatic and weighty, too, are these denials of Romanists : strong as Doric pillars they seem ; but mere stubble are they before the Papal purpose. How weighty and emphatic is this, for example ! — In 1825 Bishop Doyle appeared before Parliament, and, as we believe, with the utmost candor and truthfulness gave the following opinion, which is *Catholic*, indeed, but not at all *Romanist :* " Our obedience to the law," he says, " and the allegiance which we owe to the sovereign, are complete and full and perfect and undivided, inasmuch as they extend to all political, legal, and civil rights of the king and his subjects. I think the allegiance due to the king and the allegiance due to the pope are as distinct and as divided in their nature as any two things can possibly be." He was not alone, but was backed by the " Declaration," in 1826, we believe, of the Vicars Apostolical. Who, after that, could be so ungenerous as to attribute to Rome sinister designs against governments ?

Bishop Kenrick, quoted with approval by Döllinger, says, " The obedience which we owe to the Pope has regard only to matters in which the salvation of souls is concerned : it has nothing to do with the loyalty and allegiance which belong to the civil government."

In his book on the " Primacy " he says, " Primacy is essentially a spiritual office, which has not, of divine right, any temporal appendage." " In making Peter the ruler of his kingdom, he " [Christ] " did not give him dominion or wealth, or any of the appendages of royalty." [1]

Cardinal Antonelli, the man nearest the Papal throne, whose opinions might appear coincident with, if not the echo of, the

[1] R. W. Thompson: Papacy and the State.

Pope's, said that it was never taught "that it was allowable for a pope to interfere with their temporal rights and blessings;" and Döllinger, who quotes this, adds, "I do not know what could be said more clearly or distinctly."

The superficial therefore think, and they will keep on thinking, — and they include some of the noblest Catholics, like Döllinger and some of our American fellow-citizens, — that the Papacy means no danger to nations.

But all these utterances go for nothing, betoken nothing hopeful, except to show — what is almost the only hopeful thing in the connection of Catholicism with free governments — that *Catholics are not all Romanists.* Probably two-thirds of Catholics are not Romanists : but *Rome* is *Romanist;* and Antonelli's word does not count against the word of the *Infallible,* explaining the true Papal idea. It is but the promise of a *child* of what *his father* will do. For Pius IX., in the Syllabus (§§ 55, 77), anathematizes as *errors,* "That the Church ought to be separated from the State, and the State from the Church;" "That in our times it is no longer expedient that the Catholic should be the religion of the State, to the exclusion of all other religions." And, enveloping the same thought (§ 78), "Whence it has been wisely" (this, observe, is stigmatized as an error) "provided by law, in some countries called Catholic, that persons coming to reside therein shall enjoy the public exercise of their own worship." "And, in Article 24 of this document, the denial to the Church of authority to avail herself of any force, or of any direct or indirect temporal power to extend her faith, is similarly denounced."[1] "Pope Gregory XVI., in his Encyclical Letter of 1832, denounces as 'a most pestilent error, as the ravings of delirium, the opinion that for every one whatever is to be claimed and defended the liberty of conscience.'" "In 1864 Pius IX. issued his Encyclical Letter, in which he says 'that liberty of conscience and of worship is the right of every man' is an erroneous opinion, 'most pernicious to the Catholic Church and to the salvation of souls.'"

This is fidelity to the history and traditions of the Papacy,

---

[1] Lorimer.

from Hildebrand down ; to the Papacy's idea of itself, that it is the only legitimate spiritual power, already in a perfect and absolute and infallible form, and the world its own proper natural, to be ruled by it; to the Romanists, who, like the Jesuits, understand the "true inwardness" of the Papacy. These either deny to government any distinct organic life, or they assert a clerocracy, that the State should be subject to the Church, like horse to rider. Père Hyacinthe quotes with highest approval an idea of government, which, he says, moulded his own: "The Abbé Serbati, a genuine Italian to the very marrow of his bones, has helped me to the best conception of civil society. According to him, civil society has for its object, not — like the family in the natural order, nor like the Church in the supernatural order — the *substance* of rights, but simply the *modality* of rights. It does not create rights." "The mission of the State consists, then, in fixing the *modality* of rights ; that is, in regulating the best way in which the reciprocal duties of individuals and families should be exercised in order to help rather than hinder each other in their common development," "and to extend over them what in England is so beautifully called the 'Queen's Peace.'" "Such are the natural frontiers of civil society and domestic society."[1] He means, if we understand him, that nationality and loyalty are a mistake ; that government is merely a police to protect the family and the church.

Yet, only thirty pages farther on, Father Hyacinthe, with strange inconsistency, but in noble words of truth, says, "What makes a nation is its soul. There is a soul in nations as in individuals, and this soul is their life." "This people has a common conscience in the present, a common stock of beliefs, affections, interests, morals ; and it is in the profound consciousness of this collective life that it declares its unity to itself before declaring it to its rivals. Now, in this national soul, I do not hesitate to say the largest and best place belongs to religion."[2] "If I saw in my country nothing but an institution of human contrivance, a sort of social clock-work, whose number-

---

[1] Discourses: Civil Society and Christianity, 27.
[2] Discourses: Religion in the Life of Nations, 58.

less little wheels are ticketed off in the bulletin of laws, and set in motion by the myriad hands of the bureaucracy; if I saw in it nothing but a patch of common earth occupied by people foreign and sometimes hostile to each other, — how could such a France as that waken in my heart one throb of enthusiasm?"
"When I was yet a boy, I used to read those noble lines of one of our greatest poets:—

> 'Ye nations, pompous name for savage hate!
> Can love be halted at your boundary-lines?
> Tear down those envious flags, and hear the voice —
> That other voice — that speaks this stern reproach:
> Self-love and hate alone possess a country;
> But brotherly love has none.'

> 'Nations, mot pompeux pour dire barbarie!
> L'amour s'arrête-t-il où s'arrêtent vos pas?
> Déchirez ces drapeaux; une autre voix vous crie:
> L'égoïsme et la haine ont seuls une patrie,
> La fraternité n'en a pas.'
>
> DE LAMARTINE: *La Marseillaise de la Paix.*

"These are fine lines; but they are false." This was spoken in December, 1867. But notwithstanding these noble, spontaneous words of patriotism, yet in a volume of his published later, but in a discourse spoken a year earlier, he says, "The *Nation.* The second form of society — not natural, but artificial, since it is man's own creation — is civil society." "The object of this government is, not to suppress or to create individual or family rights, but to regulate the *manner* of exercising all rights; to extend over them the protection of justice, and, if necessary, the protection of the sword, against all attack, whether from without or from within."[1] It is this same unpatriotic view which he promulgates Dec. 1, 1867, only two weeks before the noble words of patriotism already quoted on "Religion in the Life of Nations." Either this view of Père Hyacinthe, or the subjugation of temporal to Papal Church dominion, as horse to its rider, is the relation of Church and State in the idea of the Pope. "When I say the Pope," as Coleridge says, "I understand the Papal hierarchy, which is, in truth, the *dilated Pope.*"

---

[1] The Family and the Church, 63.

Geffcken[1] traces this claim of supremacy of Church over State farther than to Hildebrand. "'The emperor,' says Chrysostom, 'governs the body; the priest governs the mind: therefore the emperor must bow his head under the hand cf the priest.' The theory is established in detail in Augustine's work on the 'City of God,' wherein he contrasts the Church as the *Civitas Dei* with the State as a purely human society (*hominum multitudo aliquo societatis vinculo colligata*). The State does not receive its true mission and consecration until it has submitted its allegiance to the Church. Although, therefore, it continues to receive the obedience of the Church in all matters of purely temporal concern, on the other hand, whenever it refuses to obey her in spiritual matters, it accomplishes its own destruction; and as to what are spiritual matters the Church can alone decide."

Guizot, as a faithful historian, speaking of the fifth century,[2] says that "the Church endeavored with all her might to establish the principle of theocracy, to usurp temporal authority, to obtain universal dominion." "She said, 'What! have I right, have I an authority, over that which is most elevated, most independent in man, — over his thoughts, over his interior will, over his conscience, — and have I not a right over his exterior, his temporal and moral interests?'" "The spiritual order had a natural tendency to encroach on the State." "When she failed in this, when she found she could not obtain absolute power for herself, she did what was almost as bad: to obtain a share of it, she leagued herself with temporal rulers, and enforced with all her might their claim to absolute power at the expense of the liberty of the subject."

Now, it is not a little singular that no one, not even Mulford, has presented the counter idea of the State with more clearness and cogency than some Catholics who were not Romanists; notably Mr. O. A. Brownson, in his work, "The American Republic." "Nations," he says, "are only individuals on a larger scale. They have a life, an individuality, a reason, a conscience, and instincts cf their own, and have the same general laws of development and growth, and perhaps of decay, as

---

[1] Church and State, i. 124.   [2] Guizot, i. 55.

the individual man." "A nation has a spiritual as well as a material, a moral as well as a physical, existence, and is subjected to internal as well as external conditions of health and virtue, greatness and grandeur, which it must in some measure understand and observe, or become weak and infirm, and stunted in its growth, and end in premature decay and death." [1] "Every living nation has an idea given it to realize, and whose realization is its special work, mission, or destiny. Every nation is, in some sense, a chosen people of God." "The Church not only distinguishes between the two powers, but recognizes as legitimate governments that manifestly do not derive from God through her." [2]

This, the Transalpine Catholic idea, is in direct antithesis to the Cisalpine and to the Syllabus.

Now, having taken a view of the two theories, the hierarchical and the national, we can pass to considerations showing where the truth lies, that

THE STATE IS NOT TO BE DOMINATED BY THE CHURCH.

I. The most obvious consideration, probably, that which comes most promptly and irrepressibly to the mind, as to the independence of States, is, that STATES EXISTED BEFORE THE CHURCH, AND ALSO QUITE APART FROM IT.

This chronological argument can hardly be gainsaid. What is a *nation* but a people, or complexity of peoples, in the providence and vocation of God, united by similarity of race, language, by one geographical theatre in which to act, and by one government, into one spirit and general oneness of destiny and aim? Now, if this is the true idea of the nation, consider that two great nations, to speak of no others, preceded any church or any priesthood which would be considered legitimate, — Egypt and China. These nations still exist; the latter certainly possessing in high degree what we call the spirit of nationality. These nations existed before the Church. It seems to have pleased God that they should exist as nations. Therefore the State can exist, we do not say without God, without righteousness, but without the Church.

[1] Am. Repub., I, 2.   [2] Ibid., 112.

Israel, too, was a nation before it was a church.

Other nations, later in time, and contemporary with the Church in some form, have existed quite *apart* from the Church; Greece and Rome, for example. They did not receive their task from any ecclesiastical organization; yet historians have always regarded them as *nationalities*, existing, in the providence of God, to carry out certain well-defined purposes. The Greek mind gave force in the world to the ideas of freedom in the state, and perfection in art. Rome impressed the universality and majesty of law, also the beneficence of imperial law, as seen in its great roads, great schools, and even in its distant provinces, its great walls built against barbarian enemies of those it had undertaken to protect. These nationalities, as well defined as ever existed, were *apart* from any church.

In modern times, many of the nationalities on the same historic theatre as the Church formed themselves *without* her, if, one might not say, in some cases, in *spite* of her. Russia did not come to its nationality through the fostering of the Church, nor England, nor France, nor, in our own day, free Italy.

We conclude, then, the independence of the State of the Church, because, from historical survey, we find the State existing in complete nationality before and apart from the Church. Some cogent reason will be needed to subject to the Church the State, which exists independent of it, and owns no tie to it of origin in any respect. Passing, now, to philosophical reasons,

II. STATE AND CHURCH SHOULD BE DISTINCT, BECAUSE STATE AND CHURCH HAVE A DIFFERENT BASIS, — the one being an organization of natural men, and viewed as an organism, one grand natural man, existing for natural life and natural ends; the other being an organization of spiritual men, and, as it were, one grand spiritual man for spiritual life and ends.

This embraces several propositions: —

First, Church and State have a different basis. The State is built on man as a soul; the Church, on man as a spirit, — the one as attached to nature, the other as detached from it.

Second, The State is composed of natural men; the Church, of spiritual. The State is made up of men as natural, since it can take no account of the unseen relations of spirits, which are beyond its ken: the Church, the true Church invisible, is made up of spiritual men who are in filial accord with the Father of spirits, and fraternal accord with renewed spirits.

Third, They are both organisms as well as organizations. This is denied by Serbati, but is the popular idea, — the idea of Mulford, Brownson, Tocqueville, and scholars generally. So plain is it, that some have even sought the origin of government in the *family* relation extended. The two, nationality and family, happened to coincide in Israel. Hence Cicero and Washington are named *Patres Patriæ*, and Henry IV. called Frenchmen his children. These facts are adduced only to show that the nation is as naturally thought to be an organism as the family, which, all allow, possesses an organic life. This is the view of Aristotle and Hegel. Milton says, " A nation ought to be like some huge [Christian] personage, — one mighty growth or stature of an honest man, as big and compact in virtue as in body."

Of the two, indeed, the State is more compact as an organism than the Church : so erroneous is the idea that the Church alone has an organic life, and that the State is a mere organized guard to keep it. For while we may start from citizen or state, church-member or church, as unit, the reasons are weightiest to call the *State* on the one side, and the *church-member* on the other, the *primary* unit to which all is most naturally referred. One spirit is worth more than the church visible ; but for the State thousands of citizens sacrifice themselves, all they have in the State. In this one particular the nation is like a federal government, where the interests of the secondary unit, the State, are not forgotten, but subordinated to the whole : the Church is like a confederation, where each *part* of the whole holds itself supremely important. In each man's spirit, as in an interior world, a " kingdom within," religion is enacted.

Alexandre Vinet, in his work, in most respects superlative,[1] points out with sharp distinctness the fact that personal religion appertains only to the person, and can only be loosely and

---

[1] Separation de l'Église et de l'État, 1858.

generally represented in an organization. He distinguishes
between conscience (meaning the general moral sense) and the
particular conscience, " the conscience in the metaphysical sense."
In this sense "consciences are not identical." Then he proceeds : " Christ consecrated the principle of religious *individuality*." " A religion which at its departure or its termination
is not personal is not a religion." " Individuality, religion, —
these two terms are never separated. *A collective religion is not
a religion.*" And again this clear and profound thinker says,
" If Christianity is the religion of the individual, the element of
identity, which is that of civil society, has forever disappeared
from the domain of religion, and every kind of contact is
henceforth impossible between Church and State." From which
the implied claim — that because the Church is an organism,
and, as Serbati says, the State is not, therefore the State must
become corporal's guard to the Church — falls to the ground ;
since, of the two, the State is not only an organism, but the *more
compact organism* of the two.

*Fourth, The State exists for natural ends ; the Church, for spirit-
ual.* The State cares for natural welfare, " life, liberty, and the
pursuit of happiness," with conformity to moral law as the
condition of its health and growth : the Church accomplishes its
high end in ministering means whereby each spirit may come
into closer union with the Divine Spirit. The State, in accomplishing its career worthily, has its good for each man in giving
him freedom, and help in becoming a perfect natural man, in
education, physical development, and the rest, and in setting
before him, in her spirit, history, laws, institutions, great names,
the spectacle of the highest qualities — honor, justice, and the
like — which can exist in the *natural* man : the Church accomplishes its end to each man when she becomes to him the
minister of more perfect life with his God, and exhibits in her
corporate life the manifold perfections of the *spiritual* man.

*The State and the Church, then, are two separate organizations
in different spheres. Nor is there reason why either should dominate the other.* The State cannot dominate the Church, because
the State knows nothing of the unseen life of each person with

God, and has no right to attempt to control it, any more than to give laws to the taste for music, or a society of music. When such an invisible society takes visible form, and intrudes objectionable and lawless acts upon society, the State may take cognizance of them.

The Church should not dominate the State, because the Church is intent on the spiritual good of each of its members, " righteousness, peace, and. joy in the Holy Spirit; " while the State is not aiming at that, but so to maintain the national life that each citizen may fulfil all the conditions of a natural man. The State is a natural man. The natural man is not bound to submit to the spiritual man, unless made to feel that the demand is legitimate. A person's soul feels, when quickened, the authority of his own spirit, if in righteousness. The State has found no other spirit, single or organized, which is its master, except God and its own spirit, *l'esprit de l'état.* Unless the Church can prove to the State that it dominates it by right divine, as the proper spirit of the State, the State must hold itself free from the Church to fulfil its own ends in becoming *a perfect natural man.* The burden of proof is on the Church to convince the State, so as to insure its complete suffrage, that it ought to submit to the Church's guidance.

Of course the State, without subjecting herself to the Church, can perceive that the Church may aid in ennobling the national life, just as Germany might recognize the benefit of her musical societies on national character. This is Coleridge's view of the connection of Church and State : " The Christian Church is not a *kingdom, realm (royaume),* or *state (sensu latiori)* of the *world;* " " nor is it an estate of any such realm, kingdom, or state." " Her paramount aim and object, indeed, is *another* world, — not a *world to come* exclusively, but likewise *another world that now is.*" " It is the appointed opposite to all " kingdoms " *collectively;* the *sustaining, correcting, befriending* opposite of the world ; the compensating counterforce to the inherent and inevitable evils and defects of the *State* as a state, and without reference to its better or worse construction as a particular state." In the same way we may recognize the benefit received from friends, and their moulding influence upon us, without subjecting ourselves, soul and body, to their spirits as a subjugating and controlling force. *State and Church are not Husband and Wife, but Brother and Sister.* It was a most natural utterance of a man who had had forced upon his mind all through life, in stormy days, the purpose and true place of these two organizations, as they stood out to his mind in his final hours, the last words of Cavour, "*Libera Chiesa in libero Stato,*" — " A free Church in a free State."

III. THE STATE HAS AN ENTIRELY LEGITIMATE LIFE APART FROM THE CHURCH, WHICH HAS NO NEED OF SUBJECTION TO THE CHURCH TO SECURE ITS PERFECTION. Undoubtedly Coleridge is right, that the Church is a "befriending" power to the State. But the State has as real and divine a life within her sphere as the Church within her sphere. It does by no means follow that what comes naturally is of necessity to be superseded by what comes spiritually. This is a capital misapprehension of some. The word "spiritual" seems to throw a spell over some as soon as uttered. Is not the planetary system perfect, though its motions are not governed by spiritual laws? The most spiritual power could not interfere with its natural operations. They are directly from God as the creating Spirit. "The earth does not move," said the Church: "*E pur si muove.*" "But it moves for all that," said Galileo ; and it moves as symmetrically as if the Church moved it. God does not do all right things that are done on earth through the Church. Your circulatory system is perfect, divinely perfect in its own sphere, with its never-ceasing systole and diastole. The respiratory system is as normal and right as it can be. The spirit can sanctify, but cannot dominate it. For the Church to rule a free State is like the spirit attempting to give laws to the circulation of the blood, which is as divine as the spirit, as normal as the spirit, though inferior to it. The State is as normal as the Church.

IV. THE CHURCH SHOULD NOT CONTROL THE STATE, BECAUSE THE NOBLY DEVELOPED NATURAL MAN MAY BE SUPERIOR TO THE DISTORTEDLY DEVELOPED SPIRITUAL MAN. Examples are abundant of a greater nobility of soul in *some* unspiritual than in *some* spiritual men. It cannot, therefore, be asserted roundly, that *spiritual* must control *natural.* Satan is a spirit: demoniacal possession of human bodies is not therefore desirable. The natural of a man, left free, may be nobler than dominated by his misguided spiritual. Gerhard, in "Cloister and Hearth," made the pernicious attempt to subject a noble natural to a mistaught spiritual. In Christ, the spiritual duly controlled the natural, and "he went about doing good." In Simon Stylites, a false spiritual subjugated, doubtless, a worthier natural, and he became, against nature, the Column Hermit. His natural would have led him, in naturals, to act better than did his perverted spiritual.

So has it happened in the nation a hundred times, that the State, as the natural man, has been far in advance of the ecclesiastical body in judging its own true aim and destiny. Döllinger says that "Hennersey, in the British Parliament, was called on to name a single man of any intellectual importance in Italy, who, on the question of the Papal States, was on the side of the Papal Government ; and he could name only one, and that one the Jesuit Secchi." Undoubtedly, Italy, in her freed national spirit, understood Italy's national future better than the Vatican. Even Passaglia and Tosti said, "The Papal States must cease altogether, or be completely altered."

America must be allowed to doubt, whether the Pope, in recognizing the Southern Confederacy as a legitimate break-off from the nation, understood American unity and nationality as well as America.

These are not the only times in history when the instincts of a free nation were nobler than the cramped spirit of ecclesiasticism. It is doubtful if the Episcopalianism of the Revolution, nourished as it was by its connection with the Church of England, would have allowed free America to be born. The free instincts of a nation may be wiser than a narrow ecclesiasticism which seeks to control it.

V. Thus far we have spoken as if there were but one claimant to be the proper spiritual to that natural, — the State.

BUT THERE ARE SEVERAL CLAIMANTS TO BE THE CHURCH. Individuals may see but one church, their own; but the State sees at its bar several organizations, founded on supposed receptions of divine revelation, — Mormon, Mahometan, Papal, Protestant. It is somewhat difficult, not to say impossible, for the *State*, being a natural man, to decide as to spiritual claimants. If it could decide; if there were but *one church* in the world; if the State felt, as completely as the soul of a man feels the authority of his spirit when quickened by the Holy Spirit, its right and its sole right to rule it, — then might we think an *ecclesiocracy* possible. But there are contending claimants. Either one of them, the Papal, for example, would say, "Better let the State live its natural life, befriended by all the so-called churches, than have it subject to any other church, — the Mormon or Mahometan."

VI. IF THERE BE ONE TRUE SPIRITUAL BODY, THE TRUE SPIRITUAL MAN, YET IT IS STILL MILITANT, NOT TRIUMPHANT, nor, indeed, predominant, not having vindicated, so far as to command any thing like universal consent, its claim to be the *one sole spiritual*. The persons in the Church are not, therefore, inclusive of all within the *State;* nor will they probably be till the end of time. The *two organizations. are not co-extensive:* therefore they will proceed better each in its own sphere.

Any religious colony, indeed, has a right to build a state upon a church. This our Puritan fathers essayed to do. They had a *right* to do it. "'To construct a commonwealth out of a church,' as Winthrop frankly avowed it, that was the intent of the founders of the colony."[1] "No one," says that distinguished legal gentleman, Prof. Joel Parker, "had a right to come and set up an opposition, and plead conscience. That plea was open to a general demurrer. What of that? You have no right to bring such a conscience here. I submit, the argument is unanswerable."[2] "All I claim is a vindication of the legal and moral right of the Puritan fathers to govern their own commonwealth" "without being accused of persecution."

[1] Rev. George E. Ellis: Lowell Lectures: Massachusetts and its Early History.
[2] Lowell Lectures, 419.

Such a State must, therefore, to maintain its integrity on its original basis, banish summarily and at once all not submissive to the Church.

This might be done; and a Romish, a Mormon colony have right to take possession of unoccupied territory, and establish a church-state, exclude and banish dissenters. With due regard to the growth and ties of family and society, however, this is exceedingly difficult to do; so that, *legally right* and politically necessary as such banishment might be, in a state having such an origin the *expediency* of continuing a *church-state* would be doubtful in the extreme. The same lectures therefore say, " They could not create a state out of a church; for a state grew up which would not come into the church, and which they would not have allowed to come into it."

From all which we observe, that it is almost impossible that the Church, or any one church, should completely overlap the State, so as, justly to the rights of the dissenters, to control it. Beyond all question, a *new church* entering an *old state* not of its forming has no right to control that state in the presence of dissent.

VII. THE CHURCH SHOULD NOT CONTROL THE STATE, BECAUSE WE FIND NO DIVINE WARRANT, NOR ANY THING WHICH MAY FAIRLY BE CONSIDERED A DIVINE WARRANT, FOR IT. " Render to Cæsar the things which are Cæsar's, and to God the things which are God's." Let us examine particularly.

1. *God does not, in nature,* impress on the conscience that the nation is to be subject to a hierarchy. Cavour cannot be regarded by the natural conscience as committing a mortal sin because he made a free nation of Italy. The considerations thus far presented may give us the reasons why, to the Infinite Mind, it does not appear to have seemed wise to subject, every where and in all time, the temporal to the spiritual power. He has put no such law on the tablets of the heart. Since nationality was to be a fact everywhere outside of his revelation, previous to his revelation, in countries where his revelation was — as where is it not? — imperfectly understood and represented, it appears to have seemed best to him that the

morality of the State, since there must be a morality of the State, should *repose directly upon himself by and in nature.*

2. In that book from which the claim of the Papal Church is supposed to come, *God is represented as recognizing, as legitimate, governments which do not derive from any spiritual power* (nor obey any), but only directly, in nature, from himself. To Ishmael it was promised that he should become a nation. The image with golden head shows God's thought of nationalities. God honored and used Cyrus. "Honor the king." "Be subject to principalities." "The powers that be are ordained of God." One quotation is sufficient to show that each nation, though Israel is the "first-born," is yet as his son. Jer. xviii. 7, 8: "At what instant I shall speak against a nation, and concerning a kingdom, to pluck up, and to pull down, and to destroy it; if that nation against whom I have pronounced turn from their evil, I will repent of the evil that I thought to do unto them."

3. *God in the theocracy* is not represented as *assuming* or *demanding* particular control over Israel, but as asking and receiving it at the hands of the nation, as something which it was theirs to give. E. C. Wines ("Hebrew Commonwealth") has made this very plain: "It ought never to be forgotten, that although God, by what he wrought for the Israelites, had acquired all the right to be their sovereign that any man could possibly possess, he still has neither claimed nor exercised that right in an arbitrary and despotic way. Moses, by his direction, permitted the people freely to choose whether they would accept Jehovah as their King, and obey the laws which he might give them. When they had formally assented to this, God was considered their King, but not before. The whole world, indeed, was under his moral rule. His dominion as Creator embraced all the tribes of the earth; but Israel was his peculiar people, who had chosen him for their King. The passages of Scripture to this effect are surprisingly pointed and striking (Deut. vi. 20–24)."

Furthermore, accepted as the nation's King by the plebiscite at Sinai, whom made he his vicegerents? Moses, not Aaron; Joshua, not Eleazar. He did not govern the nation through the

sacerdotal order: that class he kept in their sphere to minister in spiritual things. "*Judges*," not priests, he made his
vicegerents. Theocracy — we need to recall the word's meaning — signifies government of a nation by God as King. Theocracy is not clerocracy: it never was clerocracy or ecclesiocracy in Israel. As a general fact, it may be said, that, in
Israel, *the priestly order never for a day had legitimate control over
the nation.*

Aaron, indeed, while Moses was on Sinai, was irregularly
made for the hour a leader "to return to Egypt;" and Jehoiada
(2 Kings xi.), alarmed at Athaliah's conspiracy, became leader
of the loyal host; but the next chapter shows that he made
himself duly subject to the king. The Maccabees were priest-
heroes; leaders because heroes, not because priests.

4. *There is one figure in this book*, which, to most churches on
American soil, is the fountain of authority, who is said to stand
on earth as in some sense or other "God with us." Observe
his conduct and principles in the matter.

First, Christ, in his lifetime, absolutely refused to dominate
over one kingdom which he was importuned to take, which he
might have taken and controlled; and in the Temptation he
also refused the temporal and political external control of all
the nations of the earth.

Second, Christ nowhere assumes temporal control over kings
and governments as such, or gives us to understand that he ever
will. "My kingdom is not of this world;" that is, in its *nature*
is not, and therefore never will be, of this world. Kings are
nowhere sketched or prophesied as temporal vassals of Jesus.

Third, *A fortiori*, Christ never put into the hands of a spiritual inferior to himself the desire or the prerogative to control
temporal kingdoms, nor into the hands of any organization.

VIII. The State and the Church should be kept asunder because each of them comes to its highest life when
unimpeded by binding connection with the other.

That they may be helpful to each other is not denied.

The State may keep churches from outward encroachments
on each other. The Church, encouraging all virtue, strengthens

good government. What is now asserted is, that Church and State are each in highest perfection when not fettered by a connection which outwardly binds them together. State and Church, we repeat, are BROTHER AND SISTER, *not* HUSBAND AND WIFE.

In the first place, the *State* reaches its highest perfection with-out the domination of the Church. (This is quite different from saying that the State reaches its highest perfection *without God.*)

We could discuss this proposition in the *a priori* method. We prefer simply to point to Greece, to the Athenian republic, to Rome, to the kingdom of Alfred, to the republic of America. Put these in comparison with Italy, Spain, Austria, in a word, any State impeded by connection with the Church, and we be-come aware that a State free to develop its own life according to the national vocation, and aided only by the good influence of the Church, is in the way to most perfect flowering and fruit-age. Every ecclesiastic would acknowledge this in regard to any other church but his own, that the State would fulfil its own career most worthily unimpeded by ecclesiastical domination.

On the other hand, the Church reaches its highest perfection without the domination or compulsive help in her affairs of the State. Some will even think that the Church has reached its highest, purest life when the State has persecuted it, as the primitive Christians and the Pilgrims. But, at most, all.which the Church needs from the State is protection, " the queen's peace ;" then whatever vitality it has will appear, not by favor of the king, but, *Dei Gratiâ*, by the life of God in the Church.

We might argue this also from the nature of religion and the methods of its true growth ; but we prefer to bring two witnesses as sufficient evidence on a point which should not be a difficult one to any reflecting man.

We remember, however, as we write, that some of England's best brains cannot understand how the English Church could flourish without the State. But they are like boys who have always swum with the help of bladders, who cannot conceive how Byron could possibly swim the Hellespont without them.

We adduce two witnesses.

Gibbon, speaking of the effect of Constantine's accession, points out that it was the occasion of bringing into the Church those who could add nothing but worldliness to weaken its spirituality. " The hopes of wealth and honors," he says (chap. xx.), "the example of an emperor, his exhortations, his irresistible smiles, diffused conviction among the venal and obsequious crowds which usually fill the apartments of a palace." " The salvation of the common people was purchased at an easy rate, if it be true, that, in one year, twelve thousand men were baptized at Rome, besides a proportionable number of women and children, and that a white garment with twenty pieces of gold had been promised by the emperor to every convert."

Gibbon, who *cannot* sneer at the Church of the Catacombs, finds it natural to think that the Church of Constantine might be a less spiritual body, and so less impressive, less true to its vocation.

The other witness is *Lyman Beecher*. He was one of hundreds of the greatest and best men who looked with dismay, almost as if in thought of the final dissolution of society, at the threatening separation of Church and State. Viewing his alarm, we confess we have more sympathy for the alarm of our English friends at thought of the rupture of the Establishment.

Beecher struggled with all his might against withdrawing from the Church the support of the State. During that struggle, his daughter Caroline says, " I remember seeing father, the day after the election, sitting on one of the old-fashioned, rush-bottomed kitchen-chairs, his head drooping on his breast, and his arms hanging down. ' Father,' said I, ' what are you thinking of?' He answered solemnly, ' THE CHURCH OF GOD.'"

Beecher replied to her, " It was a time of great depression and suffering." " I worked as hard as mortal man could." " My health and spirits began to fail. It was as dark a day as I ever saw." " The injury done to the cause of Christ, as we then supposed, was irreparable. For several days I suffered what no tongue can tell for *the best thing that ever happened to the State of Connecticut*. It cut the churches from dependence on State support; it threw them wholly on their own resources and on God. They say ministers have lost their influence : the fact is, they have gained."[1]

IX. FINALLY, THE STATE AND THE CHURCH SHOULD BE KEPT SEPARATE, BECAUSE, IN PRACTICE, THEY DO NOT WORK WELL TOGETHER. A few facts oniy from the many pages of history.

The State should not rule the Church. *The State ruling the Church* drove the Christians into the Roman catacombs for three centuries ; threw Polycarp and a thousand others to the lions in the arena; and persecuted so severely, that Diocletian inscribed on a pillar, *"Nomine Christianorum deleto,"* — " The very name of Christian effaced from the earth."[2]

The Church should not rule the State. *The Church ruling the State* lost the skilled brain and hand of the Huguenots to France ; erected the Inquisition, which, in the eighteen years of Torquemada, burnt alive 10,220, besides severely punishing 104,-181; and according to the report of Llorente, secretary of the Inquisition, "immolated on its scaffolds in the space of three centuries upwards of 300,000 persons."

Church and State do not work well together.

Several remarks are needed to complete the discussion.

(1.) "The State and the Church." This is as legitimate a collocation of words as the more frequent " Church and State." We are not speaking of the value of the two organizations, but of their legitimacy. In that view, it is as proper to start with the State as with the Church. Men sometimes say Church and State as they say church and parish ; the parish second, because secondary, the secular of the church. This is the view of men like Serbati and Hyacinthe, who live only in the Church, and see the Church as the only reality. They ask this question, "What is this thing, the State? what is it for?" They are puzzled. They can only answer, "It must be subordinate to the Church, or else a mere protection to Church and family." This view ignores nationality as a prime fact.

But a statesman is just as philosophical in saying the State is

---

[1] Lyman Beecher, Autobiography, i. 344.   [2] Neander, Ch. Hist. i. 154.

the starting-point. This is the view of Mulford in the volume, "The Nation;" and of Milton, "The nation is one huge honest man." Then come the questions, "What relation has the Church, if any, to the *State?*" "What relation has religion, apart from the Church, to the *State?*" It is as legitimate to say State and Church, as well as Church and State, as to speak of music and poetry, as well as of poetry and music.

(II.) This discussion sheds great light on what is meant by *religion* as properly belonging to the State. Much blind thought there is, which strives to utter, in a confused way, that some sort of *religion* appertains to the State. This is constantly said by some of the great Anglicans. The confusion is in the use of religion in two senses,—one narrow, the other wide; the one natural, the other spiritual religion. In the argument, "religion" is an *equivoque,* and the mind unwittingly plays backwards and forwards between its two meanings: hence confusion. The State is a natural man, and ought to have *natural religion,* "what is everywhere and always religion." The State cannot have spiritual religion; nor can it meddle with it in individuals. Much of the confusion of thought in defenders of the Established Church would be cleared up, if they should see that *natural religion,* the recognition of God in government, education, society, morality, is competent to, obligatory upon, the State, as one huge natural man, but that spiritual and revealed religion is entirely a matter between each soul and God, and therefore in no way to be intruded upon by the State. That personal revelation of God to the soul the State has no right to pry into, or seek to understand, much less to formulate, establish, promulgate, and constrain and compel the unwilling to profess to experience. A creed is, in reality, not an intellectual dogma, but a description of God as he deals with a soul. In old New-England times, each candidate for the church wrote out his own creed. Not even a church can constrain a man to a creed: it can only declare how far his religious experience entitles him to fellowship. The more one studies spiritual religion as a revelation of God in the soul, the more will he feel that the State has no right to *touch* personal religion, much less to *teach* it, much less to attempt to *compel* it.

(III.) *The separation of Church and State does not mean the exclusion of God, righteousness, morality, from the State.* This misapprehension seems so common as to be almost universal. Brownson's words deserve careful study : " *They have not only separated the State from the Church as an external corporation, but from God as its internal lawgiver, and by so doing have deprived the State of her sacredness, inviolability, and hold on the conscience.*" This mistake should not be made by thoughtful men.

(IV.) The principles of this discussion not only permit, they really exact, that the State, though not intermeddling with Church, or with the private interviews of the King of kings with individuals, should entertain the highest ideas of God and righteousness, and the highest ideal of humanity, as the ideal of its own life. This is competent to the State within its proper sphere. It is not contrary, but according, to these principles, that all orders of citizens, from the chief magistrate to the humblest voter, should fulfil their duties to the State under the profoundest sense of their responsibility to God to accomplish the divine order in all things — magistracy, franchise, education — which pertain to the State. On the other hand, it is competent to the State to set before it as the model of its own life the highest human life of man. If, for example, the ideas of the Jews should change, there is nothing in these principles to prevent the State entire from accepting the character of Jesus Christ, in the fulness of his reverence, the clearness of his sense of true living, and the amplitude of his beneficence, as the ideal of the State. We are, of course, speaking of Christ entirely apart from his spiritual doctrines and the work he is averred by theologians to do between the soul and God. Were there no objection on the part of a few who will, in a day not far distant, give him fairer study than to-day, there would be nothing incongruous for the entire State, as a natural man, to set Thorwaldsen's *Christus Segnend* on our national capitol as the ideal of our national life. Until that time, it is entirely competent, without departing from these principles, to a statesman like Sumner, to have the deepest sense of God and righteousness in the State, and a constant endeavor — as in his ideas on peace — to form the nation according to the model of the human character of Christ as the Divine Man.[1]

This is the idea which shines dimly, as through a mist, before *some*, when they assert that the nation is a *Christian* nation. That expression, so confusing as to make its use objectionable or impossible, might be true in the sense above indicated, — that the nation, in the general and prevailing thought, recognizes the benevolence and philanthropy, the love of peace, the severe righteousness, the mercy to poor, sick, afflicted, which are, or are popularly believed to be, in Jesus, as the highest ideal of humanity, and so the ideal which the State, consciously or unconsciously, is striving to realize in itself, rather than the manhood of Achilles, or Alexander, or Louis XIV., or Napoleon. In *this* sense, we might call ourselves a Christian nation; but the expression is so equivocal, that its use is hazardous, and, for the present, undesirable.

(v.) State and Church should resist any attempt at a binding alliance : they should either of them resist it as brother and sister would resist the idea of marriage. There are many who are ready with arguments to show the use and beauty of State and Church. Specious arguments might be found even for the marriage of brother and sister. That is primitive, since Cain and Seth must have married sisters ; brother and sister have had longest acquaintance; they would keep the property together ; they might hand down family qualities intensified ; and, perhaps it might be added by way of pleasantry, they would have no mother-in-law. Still we would not seriously advise marriage of brother and sister. Arguments for union of State and Church are, like the above, *surface* arguments, not *bottom* arguments, from the nature of things.

Binding alliance is such a union that either interferes in the concerns of the other. Brother and sister have wide privilege of advice and help, but no compulsion. Husband and wife have certain moral and legal compulsions. State and Church should not be so united, for example, that the Church shall allow the State to choose and locate her pastors, while the State agrees to maintain them.

[1] Charles Sumner: True Grandeur of Nations.

This is an establishment, or established religion, which, as Parkinson defines it in his admirable book, " is an ecclesiastical organization whose teachings are authorized, and whose support is provided by the State." " Any church whose ministers are maintained from the appropriation of a certain portion of the land of the country which would neither have been possible in origin nor in permanence, except by the force of public law, is an established church. Any church whose articles and services have received the legal sanction, and could not be changed without the further sanction of acts of Parliament, is an established church. In the Church of England these two conditions meet, and constitute her the more distinctly an establishment."[1]

The English reader will, perhaps, desire to see the principles of this paper applied to the living problem of his country, — establishment, or disestablishment.

So much that is excellent and venerable, and fruitful of good, — the cathedrals, the English Bible, — has sprung from united State and Church in England, that one must use resolution in penetrating the subject, willing to accept what insight shows, — that, with all the apparent advantages from the marriage, State and Church have been detained by it from higher good.

Israel and England show the two most auspicious experiments of the connection of State and Church. They are worthy of special study.

First, State and Church in Israel.

Passages might be collected from the records in Kings and Chronicles which would make an argument of fair show for the use of the secular arm in promoting worship. Such passages are the frequent use of power by pious kings in cutting down Baal's groves, and the temple-building by Solomon. But, on the other side, observe : —

(1.) Israel is an exceptional case : Israel was called to a particular destiny. God gave to Greece, to Rome, ideas to develop. Through the nationality of Israel during long centuries, God proposed as in solid type to set forth the monotheistic idea, the ritual and Messiah, the written oracles, and the history of Israel,

---

[1] Parkinson, Rev. H. W : State Churches.

itself a tapestry inwoven with God's dealings with his people. At Sinai God called the nation to his work and worship. They accepted it by acclamation. Israel became a theocracy, in which idolatry was treason. Israel was to exist to receive the religious ideas.

The provisions were complete. *God* himself ordained the Church, the ritual, and the worship, even to the minutest arrangements. To the *State* was left nothing to do in the organizing of the Church or the worship. All was done by Jehovah. To the State was left only the *preservation* of the Church, and the holding of citizens to external duties. For that purpose God made arrangements for a succession of divinely chosen men, with heart and wisdom to keep Israel to its mission. Church and State were organized divinely, separately, and established by God himself in relations to each other, as are earth and moon. The State never interfered with the Church in her internal affairs ; nor does the record impress us that the State, except in the destruction of idolatry and the keeping of the Sabbath, used compulsion at all liberally.

Moreover, their politics and their religion had the same proof, obvious and irresistible. The pillar of cloud that led Israel rested over the tabernacle of his worship. He who established the ritual, and gave their Messiah in prospect, was he who revealed himself unmistakably in their history. There could be no doubt of that. The same God who chose Moses chose Aaron. We can hardly imagine a Jew denying that.

Now, this is altogether peculiar.

No other nation will probably ever have a distinctively religious destiny. " To *them* were given the oracles of God." No nation will ever have God distinctly and unmistakably ordain, co-ordinately and " complanted," its State and Church. No nation will again have a church with ritual and worship divinely arranged in its most trifling particulars, even to the " jots and tittles " of the law. No nation will ever again have a divinely chosen and guided chief magistracy. Therefore no State without these important conditions can claim Israel as a proper model in State and Church.

By those conditions, the same divinity unmistakably ordaining Church and State and their connection, State and Church might have been a success.

But now we have to observe a disturbing element.

(2.) Israel rejected the succession of *divinely* called magistrates. They sought a king. God, under protest, yielded to their folly. One great means of the success of the State Church was knocked away. The succession of hereditary kings, with such various characters as Saul and David, Josiah and Ahab, was not calculated to fulfil Israel's mission.

This new governmental arrangement was not, however, wholly fatal. It could not change the idea of Israel's mission, which God did not relinquish, but kept alive in the faithful "remnant." It could not destroy the record and memory of the divinely established worship, nor divert the people entirely from it. It could not prevent the powerful prophetic office and work. But, for all this, the failure of *one link* in the divine chain, the substitution of hereditary monarchy, with fluctuations of religious purpose, in place of a series of divinely chosen judges, — Moses, Joshua, Gideon, Deborah, Samuel, — so vitiated the plan of State sustaining Church, that,

(3.) Taking the whole history of Israel together, no one would probably say that religion prospered in that nation through the force of the government behind it. The building of the Temple seems the most signal advantage to Israel of the secular power ; yet it may be questioned whether David more readily accumulated the wealth for the Temple than Moses for the Tabernacle. There the free-will offerings were so great, that Moses was obliged to stay them.

To speak of no other injuries received from the State, the work of one single king, Jeroboam, is sufficient to condemn the experiment of binding Church to State. By making the two calves at Dan and Beersheba, "he made Israel to sin ; " he cut off ten tribes permanently from the Temple worship ; he propagated his wicked example ; he sundered them, through the retributions of God, from their native land, among heathen idolaters ; he left the nation in a broken condition politically.

and religiously, more ready to misunderstand the Messiah, and receive the condemnation of his rejection.

All this occurred from the failure of *one* only of the peculiar conditions by which God would have made a State Church successful.

In modern days, *all* these conditions fail; and we are not surprised that the clear insight of Benedict Spinoza — a Jew, and not ignorant of the philosophy of his nation's institutions — led him to advocate the theory of the separation of Church and State.[1] Paradoxical as it would seem, he was an Israelite indeed in so doing.

The State Church of England deserves study. We advance to examine it, if not with veneration, at least with respect, and with consideration of the feelings attached to a time-honored State-Church, yet with fearlessness, as those who see it as an incongruous and mischievous union.

" Numerous associations connect themselves with the idea of the Established Church. It has interwoven itself with many national habits and customs. Some of its endowments have come down from an immemorial age. Its fabrics are multiplied in every town, and lift their spires in every village. Its prayers have been the language of devotion to multitudes for ten generations. Twenty thousand clergy derive from it comfortable and sometimes splendid maintenance, and superior social position. No wonder the Established Church has its defenders."[2]

George Herbert's feelings express themselves fervently: —

> " I joy, dear mother, when I view
> Thy perfect lineaments, and hue
> Both sweet and bright."
>
> POEMS : *The British Church.*

But ivies of fond associations grow over rough sheds, and ruins, and unmatched architecture, as well as over symmetrically united adjacent palaces. The English Church has for generations been the object of fond regard. Yet perhaps the Eng-

---

[1] Geffcken: Church and State, i. 458.   [2] Parkinson, 284.

lishman is not discriminating as to how much of his affection clings to the Church as a *Church*, and how little, perchance, to the Church as an *Establishment.* When we think of all which might be meant by the *English Church,* — the Christian activity and living of more than a millennium of years; the Christian men before and since Alfred ; such men as Wycliffe and Tyndale and Baxter and Bunyan and Robertson ; such women as Hannah More, Elizabeth Fry, and Florence Nightingale ; such missionaries as Carey, Marshman, Ward, Martyn, and Duff, pushing the gospel to remotest lands; such evangelists as Wesley and Whitefield ; such writers as Bunyan and others, who have created the finest Christian literature in the world, forever to be read with delight and profit ; when we think of her English Bible ; her hymnology, rich with the spiritual songs of Watts, Charles Wesley, and Cowper ; when we reflect, even in this most cursory way, upon the vast aggregate of England's Christian life and history and achievements, without as well as within the Establishment, — we own that we think the ENGLISH CHURCH, in its broadest sense, is deserving of many fold more veneration than the Establishment alone, however venerable that may seem to be. The English Church, in this broader sense, is large enough to receive all the ivies of affectionate veneration which have been lavished upon that part of the Church called the National Church. Keble and Herbert and Vaughan need not rewrite their fond tributes of verse to the British Church ; but these poems can receive a wider meaning. Were we Englishmen, we would not wish to hear of an English Church which did not include Bunyan, and Robert Hall, and Spurgeon, and Baxter, and Wesley, and Cowper, and a firmament of other sainted names. Indeed, we change our thought ; and should we, as we advance, through compliance with custom, chance to use the title " English Church " of the Establishment alone, we crave pardon of the broadest-minded Englishmen, who want *an English Church which means all England's Christianity.*

One is struck, in reading the arguments for an Establishment by great men like Arnold, Stanley, and the authors of the " Essays," [1]

---

[1] Hole, Dixon, Lloyd: see Parkinson's Preface.

by observing that they seem perfunctory, as if made up by advocates to defend an established institution without regard to the deep principles involved. In no other way can we account for the feeble arguments, and for the strong objections which they state, but do not remove. We suspect that our English churchmen are more governed in their clinging to the Establishment by their feelings, and by a sense of the convenience of having force of law and wealth and respectability behind the Church, than by any well-grounded theory that State and Church *ought* to be united. Born in Boston, Thomas Arnold would never have written his "Fragment on the Church."

Arnold's argument is thus stated by Stanley: "His belief that the object of the State and the Church was alike the highest welfare of man; and that — as the State could not accomplish this, unless it acted with the wisdom and goodness of the Church, nor the Church, unless it was invested with the sovereign power of the State — the State and the Church in their ideal form were not two societies, but one; and that it is only in proportion as this identity is realized in each particular country that man's perfection and God's glory can be established on earth."

This is noble and plausible, but, with due reverence to the great teacher of Rugby, fallacious. True is it, that a country is blessed by a State and a Church: so God gives both, *but not one through the other*.

Arnold seems to confuse natural religion, which may be the national religion, with spiritual religion, with which the State has no more to do than to teach Handel how to write "The Messiah."

Moreover, God does not set before us on earth in all things the highest conceivable ideal. It is the highest possible ideal of human beings to be *Isangeloi*, "angel-like;" but on earth the secondary and temporary ideal is, that they are perfect in marriage. Poetry and music are perfect, perhaps, only as complemented by the other; every poem with its music, all music mated with words. But a secondary ideal, under the imperfections of human nature, probably forever in this stage of existence, makes us call Homer's "Iliad" perfect, and the "Anvil Chorus," or Weber's "Storm." So, though in a celestial commonwealth, — where all beings have angelic cognizance, discrimination, justice, — the State might rule the Church; but the secondary ideal, the only one compatible with earthly limitations, is, that State and Church shall each, like poetry and music, perfect itself, and ennoble man, without interference from the other.

Arnold, Chalmers, and Stanley advance the argument, that a State's power and patronage enable it to set pastors and churches in the extremest hamlets.

We need reply only three words, — *Methodism, American Home Missionary Society, Jesuit Missions.* It is rather the organization and energy of a church which makes it secure places of worship in poorest and remotest villages.

These are the best reasons we have been able to find in such English works as we have seen. Some of the arguments adduced are almost frivolous.

Against the Establishment, the two finest arguments (and to our mind they are both superb and unanswerable) are the volume by Rev. Henry William Parkinson, "State Churches," and the paper by the Hon. J. L. Curry, LL.D., of Richmond, Va., read in 1873 before the Evangelical Alliance in New York, on the "Alliance of Church and State."

Another fine book is Baldwin Brown's "First Principles of Ecclesiastical Truth."

The argument we are about to construct, different in method, will freely use their materials.

(1.) An Establishment is instituted on a wrong principle, and confusion of ideas. The State can, indeed, establish natural religion, the invocation of God in government and school; but for the State to establish a Church is for the State to interfere with the private visits and arrangements of the King of kings. Curry well says, "When Church and State are united, the State practically assumes infallibility, arrogates the capability and the right to sit in judgment upon creeds, and to determine what is a church, what is the Church; what is true and what is false religion."

"Religion, man's relation to his God, is personal and individual, and cannot be vicarious nor compulsory. In the economy of God's grace, a national religion, strictly speaking, is a solecism and absurdity. The Holy Spirit regenerates by units." "State policy may establish a creed, and enforce its outward observance by penalties; but the mind, the heart, and the conscience cannot be fettered. Christ's kingdom is not of this world; and he is the supreme, absolute, single Head. No temporal prince can be." "His kingdom is independent of civil authority. Over his subjects no earthly potentate has spiritual jurisdiction. For a State, by executive or legislative power, to give law to Christian churches, to prescribe creed or ministry, to determine the guests, and the manner of their gathering at the Lord's Table, is a more flagrant usurpation of sovereignty than for one of the Azores to assume to govern the world."[1]

Parkinson keenly says, "The teaching of Christ and his apostles must surely be of supreme significance in the decision as to what ought to be the relation of the Church to the world."[2] "It only remains to refer for a moment to the saying of Christ before Pilate, — 'My kingdom is not of this world: if my kingdom were of this world, then would my servants fight, that I should not be delivered to the Jews: but now is my kingdom not from hence,' — a saying which puts the advocates of Establishments more on their defence than any other. It has been generally acknowledged by expositors who had no purpose to serve, that Christ's meaning is, that now, from henceforth, his kingdom was not to be national, united with the civil power, and employing the secular arm, as it had been among the Jews, but spiritual, employing only such instrumentalities as affect principle and motive; in proof of which his servants did not fight."

"And those who read their New Testaments," says Baldwin Brown, "see a picture of the Church there, to which the worldly, wealthy, creed-bound, disjointed system of the Establishment presents a sorrowful contrast. This apparatus of worldly pomp and dignity seems to them a terrible incubus on the spiritual

[1] Curry.   [2] P. 24.

energy of the Church itself, and a scandal and a shame before the unbelieving world. Men are shrewd enough to see in these days that the Established Church hinders much and mars much free, voluntary effort which would else be put forth for the service of the community; and the life, energy, and rapid increase of the free churches set men thinking about the right and the worth of this costly and clumsy method of attempting — we can hardly say accomplishing — spiritual work." [1]

That a State should establish a Church is, from the State's standpoint, like a fire-company instituting music as one of their regular exercises, and that, too, when one-third have no ear for music.

(2.) An Establishment is unjust.

It is unjust to make half a country pay for worship which they do not attend nor approve.

"From among several denominations government selects one to receive its discriminating favor. It takes this denomination into partnership, patronizes it, supports it by special laws, public property, exclusive privileges." "The government thus places nearer the sovereign power the man or the woman who professes a particular creed. Such a one becomes a member of a privileged fraternity, and, by a sovereign *digito monstrari*, is held up as a more proper person than his less-favored fellow." "Government elects a portion of its citizens, sometimes the majority, and subjects them to inferiority; dishonors them and their religion; puts a penalty on their form of worship; degrades them at the bar, in the college, in the pulpit, in parliament, and in all places of honor and trust. Dissenter is a term of reproach; and such a person is under a stigma, and in a state of uniform degradation. This vexatious, prolonged, corroding insult is not relieved by acts of toleration." "It makes a diploma of a college, a commission in the army or navy, a foreign mission, a crown, dependent on being loyal to the sect which happens, for the nonce, to be in favor with the government. It compels support of a denomination which has not the approval of the tax-payers. It robs of property; for, when a government takes

[1] 324.

more than is necessary for a just and economical administration of its legitimate affairs, it commits robbery." [1]

"The State Church is an offender against the equal rights of all men by the law; and these theories are accomplices after the fact." [2]

(3.) A nation which has a State Church is always the scene of tyrannies and of struggles against tyranny.

The English Church is no exception to this statement.

The course of this Church has been like an asymptote, commencing far away, always approaching, but never to reach, the line of justice. No Englishmen, we suppose, would glory in the State Church under the Tudors or the Stuarts. Even Edward VI. has his reign stained by the burning of Jane Bocher: one such act is sufficient to disgrace a reign.

"There are three degrees of injustice," says Parkinson, "committed by an Established Church upon a community. The first and greatest is when it proceeds to penal infliction; the second, when it imposes civil disabilities; the third, when it bestows invidious privilege."

All these have marked the English Church.

The first of these "is to invade the prerogative of the Almighty; to kill the body for what, in a fallible judgment, are supposed to be the faults of the soul."

The State Church, under one name or other, burnt Cranmer, Latimer, Ridley, Hooper, Ferrar, and Rogers; beheaded Fisher and Sir Thomas More; drove nearly nine thousand Catholics from their benefices on the accession of Elizabeth; imprisoned Bunyan in Bedford jail; set on the statute-book the Persecuting Acts, Conventicle Acts, Five-mile Acts, Test Acts. These are specimens of State-church tyranny.

"The revolution of 1688 turned over that page of English history." This revolution gave the Toleration Act.

"From the time of the Toleration Act the work of removing the disabilities under which the Nonconformists labored has been steadily pursued." "Perhaps its most striking events were Catholic emancipation, the admission of Jews into Parlia-

---

[1] Curry.   Parkinson, 163.

ment, the abolition of church-rates, and the opening of the universities. Other demands, as the right of burial in the parish churchyards, have yet to be decided."

Worcester says, "'In Ireland,' as it is observed by Sir Henry Hardinge, 'five-sixths of the property are Protestant, while five-sixths of the population are Catholics;' yet the established religion is that of the Church of England, with a richly endowed clergy; while the Catholic clergy derive their support from voluntary contributions, and from fees from their people, who are, for the most part, extremely poor.

"In Scotland, a strenuous effort was made to establish the right of congregations to choose their own ministers: but the advocates of this measure, after a long contest, failed of their object; and, in 1843, about four hundred and sixty out of somewhat more than twelve hundred ministers of the Established Church 'seceded, in order to free themselves from the interference of the civil courts in ecclesiastical matters.' The seceders, consisting of the ministry, and such of the laity as followed them, — a large and respectable body, — now form the 'Free Church of Scotland.'"

If, as our own Sumner said, "Nothing is settled which is not right," these tyrannies will, in our generation or a succeeding, cease by the cutting down of the *trunk* itself, — the tyranny of the attempt to establish a religion by the State.

(4.) "The Establishment is an injury to the State. When governments undertake impossibilities, they frequently inflict intolerable grievances, or bring themselves into contempt. Governments have no jurisdiction over the conscience: this is extra-territorial. Governments cannot afford to lose the sympathy, or encounter the just prejudice, of the governed, or do palpable injustice. An Establishment fosters notions of arbitrary government, cultivates opposition to liberal principles." "A reference to the troubled condition of political affairs in Brazil, Mexico, France, Germany, Austria, Spain, and Italy, shows that the union is perplexing governments, obstructing reform, fomenting strife and war." "The State offers a premium to insincerity and hypocrisy. To get honors and emoluments, men become members of the Established Church. Moral principle is eradicated when men affect conversion to be sheriffs, magistrates, and judges, and when a petty constable is forbidden to execute process until he shall have received the sacrament of the Lord's Supper from the hands of a regularly ordained clergyman as a part of the prescribed induction into office."[1]

(5.) The State control over the Church is an injury to the / Church and to religion.

"Public profession of a State religion is sometimes conjoined with private incredulity. Infidelity has taken refuge under cover of an Establishment; abounds where religion is enforced by law. Germany and France, with their scepticism, are not persuasive of an Establishment. All the sovereigns of England, from Henry VIII. to James II., during a period of one hundred and forty years, — the boy Edward VI. excepted, — employed their supremacy to extinguish vital religion.[2] Froude states that at one time ordinations were bestowed on men of lewd and corrupt behavior." "Patronage is invariably a source of corruption." "An endowment secularizes a denomination, and attracts the worldly, the selfish, the ambitious. The system of presentation to benefices is an afflictive malady. Advowsons are regular articles of merchandise, advertised in the newspapers, and sold at public outcry or private sale. From this legal right of presentment, regardless of the consent of the inhabitants of the parish, have come non-residence, huge salaries, starving incomes, sporting and dissolute clergymen. Men of frivolous characters, of infidel principles, hold livings as property, and bestow them for other considerations than a desire to save souls, or promote the Redeemer's kingdom."[3]

In his latest story, Charles Reade — who, we presume, does not libel — sketches, as present with others at a gaming-table at Homburg, "an Anglican rector, betting fivers, and *nonchalant* in the absence of his flock and the Baptist minister."

It is another Englishman, — who, we believe, did not have to leave England to find examples for his well-known *noble portraiture of the ministry*, — who, nevertheless, paints other ex-

---

[1] Curry.   [2] Noel's Union of Church and State, 59.   [3] Curry.

amples under the corrupting influence of a State Church, thus : —

> "But loose in morals, and in manners vain ;
> In conversation frivolous ; in dress
> Extreme ; at once rapacious and profuse ;
> Frequent in park, with lady at his side,
> Ambling, and prattling scandal as he goes,
> But rare at home, and never at his books
> Or with his pen save when he scrawls a card ;
> Constant at routs ; familiar with a round
> Of ladyships ; a stranger to the poor;
> Ambitious of preferment for its gold ;
> And well prepared by ignorance and sloth,
> By infidelity, and love of the world,
> To make God's work a sinecure ; a slave
> To his own pleasures and his patron's pride."
>
> COWPER : *Task*, Bk. 2, 378–391.

"Legal uniformity was the curse of the Church. The state of religion at the accession of William III. was, according to Archbishop Leighton, 'the most corrupt he had ever seen ; and the clergy were equally destitute of strictness in life, and zeal and laboriousness in work :' while Bishop Burnet observes, that they were most remiss in labors among the people ; adding, 'The main body of our clergy have always appeared dead and lifeless to me ; and, instead of animating, they rather seem to lay one another to sleep.' "[1]

Strange, indeed, would it be, if the whole management of the Church, choice of bishops and pastors, by a worldly power, could foster spirituality, or gladden the spiritually-minded.

> "It is not, nor it cannot come to, good."

(6.) Finally, the State Church cannot accomplish so much for religion as a free Church.

Parkinson says, "What the Nonconformists have proved is the might of the principle, — voluntaryism as a means of existence, its sufficiency not only for the maintenance of the ordinances of religion and the support of the ministry, but for the diffusion of the blessings of Christianity both at home and abroad."

[1] Parkinson, 306.

"We hear much," says Baldwin Brown, "of the toleration of the Church of England. I confess to a feeling of strong impatience when I hear and read about it. Three times in the three great crises of her history, — in the sixteenth, seventeenth, and eighteenth centuries, — the Church of England has deliberately purged herself of her noblest, wisest, and most Christian members. She expelled the Puritans; she expelled the Nonconformists; she expelled, practically, the Methodists. Thrice has she purged out her most vital elements; thrice has she destroyed her fertility, and left herself dying in wealth, dignity, and ceremony, while the pure, noble, glowing life which would have quickened her passed outside her pale forever, and organized churches on the apostolic model, which have been the salt and the light of religion in this English land, in her room. And I believe, that, in the very nature of things, it was simply inevitable that it should be so. The Scotch National Church has repeated the same suicidal policy, and has expelled the very men whom it should have been most proud to retain, — the men who proved by their self-sacrifice that the flame of the divine life burnt pure and bright on the altar of their hearts.

"That organization of Christianity which is possible in a National Church leaves little room for burning zeal and intense vitality. Its religious activity must, under the very best conditions, be largely a thing of rule and order and law. The independent movement of a man like Penry or Cartwright, obeying the inspiration of a higher will, can find but little free play within its pale. As matter of necessity, it must look suspiciously on the movement of a. vigorous and independent life. It is the natural and apparently the necessary policy of all highly organized and established churches to expel their most vital elements; and it is their Nemesis. These repeated ejections leave them .exhausted of their divine energy: they waste and perish, while the life which they have cast out grows strong and fruitful, passes into new and independent forms, and creates churches more harmonious with the divine idea, — churches which aim at the national establishment of religion by Christianizing the very heart of the community."[1]

[1] Eccles. Essays, 317.

This is not wonderful when we consider the force of divine
and spiritual motives.   Parkinson says of the idea that the
Church needs the State's patronage, "On such a theory it is
wonderful how the gospel ever came to prevail at all.   It won
its victories, through the energy of preachers who were neither
established nor endowed, over religions that possessed both
these supposed benefits."

"The Nonconformists have multiplied their religious agencies
in still greater proportion.   By them, far more than by the members of the Established Church, has the work of Sunday-school
instruction been carried on.   They have never abated their
advocacy or stinted their aid in behalf of the great catholic and
evangelical religious societies, as the British and Foreign Bible
Society, the Tract Society, and the various modes of town and
city missions; and have often assumed the whole burden of the
local support of such societies, because the clergy have held
aloof from any action that was not of a distinctly 'Church' or
sectarian kind.   They were the first to originate, and, according
to their numbers and wealth, have been far the most liberal in
sustaining, the great missionary societies which have carried
Christianity to India, China, and the islands of the sea, and in
three-quarters of a century have materially changed the aspect
of humanity.   They set the example of using the press for the
spread of religious knowledge, especially among the poor, by
cheap magazines and other publications; and still maintain the
lead in the number of such productions.   They also have gone
far towards solving that problem which is the despair of Church
congresses, — the interesting of what is popularly called the laity
in religious work, and employing them as teachers, preachers,
visitors, class-leaders, managers of church temporals, honorary
secretaries of local religious and benevolent societies, according
to the fitness they may discover amongst the members of their
churches.   And they have done all this in addition to the entire
support of their own religious worship, — from the laying of the
first stone of the building to the payment of the last penny of
the minister's stipend."   "In the doing of Christian work, it
would be the right arm, and not the left, that would be para-

lyzed if Nonconformity in England should cease from its labors." [1]

The accommodation provided by evangelical Nonconformists is already 4,894,548 sittings as against 5,317,915 sittings in the Established Church. Such is the vitality of a church without establishment.

"These two movements," says Baldwin Brown, "have been very plainly concurrent, — the multiplication of voluntary teachers and churches, and the weakening of the Establishment principle, which has at length grown so weak, that, in the judgment of the Primate of all England, it has but a few years' lease of life." [2]

In the English Colonies, voluntaryism or willinghood has, in a short time, borne noble fruit. The Bishop of Ontario in 1854 protested against it with indignation and grief: in 1869 he said, "I candidly confess that I would not exchange the present condition of the Canadian Church for her condition as an endowed Establishment." Just as gladdening fruit has the voluntary system borne in Australia, Jamaica, New Zealand, and the Bahamas. Let one speak for all, — Rev. J. W. Coxe of Adelaide: "We have here no State Church, and none but those who are thus free can tell the blessing of the deliverance."

No American, we hardly need say, wants or feels the lack of a State Church.

Baldwin Brown says, "I am no eulogist of the United States. There is something in their Christian life which contrasts, and to my mind unfavorably, with the tone and temper of ours." Yet he says, "The nation which most constantly recognizes God in connection with all its national experiences, the chastisements, humiliations, and triumphs of its life ; the nation in which the Christian ministry receives its most abundant honor; in which a Christian sanctuary is recognized as the first and most essential structure in every settlement in the wilderness ; the nation in which Christian communities are most numerous and influential, and Christian activities most strenuous and successful, — is the nation in which there is not, and never has

---

[1] Parkinson, 259, 260.   [2] Brown, 320.

been, an Established Church. The comparison between the United States and England in all that concerns the visible marks and badges of a Christian people would be, on the whole, to our disadvantage. Freedom has secured there results which privilege and endowment have failed to secure here ;. and simple preachers of the word — Independents too — there exercise an influence on public affairs which is not approached in England, even by the most distinguished bishops of the Established Church."[1]

Parkinson remarks, "Voluntaryism in America, measured by its results, furnishes abundant evidence of efficiency. It may be safely averred that religion has gained a stronger hold upon the people of that country than it maintains in England to-day, where the enactments and endowments of a thousand years have cursed it with control, and made it to limp by supplying it with crutches."

Williams shows this in the tangible form of figures. "By the census for 1872, there were in America 72,459 religious organizations, 63,082 church-buildings, 21,665,062 sittings, and, in the possession of the religious bodies, not less than £70,896,716 worth of property. It has also been computed that there is religious accommodation for fifty-six out of the fifty-eight per cent of the population for whom it is required; so that there is quite sufficient room in the churches for those who wish to attend them."[2]

"It is supposed that the Protestant churches of America raise annually for religious purposes at least fifty million dollars."

"If any one," says Pres. Woolsey, "were to ask the religious men of all Protestant denominations whether they would accept of State support to religion, given in the least objectionable form, — that of a general tax, — to be devoted according to the ratio of the members of all denominations, or even to all Protestant denominations, they would, I think, with one voice say 'No!'"[3]

[1] Brown, 329, 330.

[2] J. Carvell Williams: Voluntaryism in the United States and Canada.

[3] Rev. Theodore Woolsey, D.D.: Paper before Evangelical Alliance, 1873.

"The more the Church threw herself on willinghood, the richer would be the fruits she would gather."

The words of the Bishop of Ontario are worthy to be the concluding sentence here : "*The Church possesses a salient spring of life when she falls back on first principles ; and surely she has some grounds for thinking that principles, which, in the first three centuries, conquered the conquerors of the world, can do so again, if necessity required.*" [1]

(vi.) On the other side, we recur to the attempt of the Church to control the State.

The nation has a conflict for its sovereign life and liberty — with all which that involves — with any church which seeks to rule it.

Mr. Mulford shall stand as foreman to speak, better than we can, what we have to say on this theme.

"The irreconcilable hostility of Rome to the being of nations has never had more open avowal than in this century." " This antagonism of Roman ecclesiasticism is involved in its necessary postulate," "since it denies to the individual and to the nation a real and integral moral being, the realization of a divine vocation in the moral order of the world, which is not formulated through it." " The Church will concede to the nations, therefore, no spiritual life or powers, no real freedom, no fulfilment of a divine vocation in conscious obedience to a Divine Will. It assumes the working of the divine energy, and the fulfilment of the divine purpose in itself alone, and in the individual and nation only as formulated through it."

"The nations have been involved in a conflict with Rome for their integral unity and being. The struggle has been for their existence, their order, their freedom. There is none, as it has sought to realize its freedom, that has been exempt from the secret or open assault of Rome. Its attack has taken on every form ; and there is no weapon, however cruel, and no device, however false, which it has not used, and no ally, however evil, which it has not engaged. It has appeared on every field as the foe of the life and liberties of nations."

[1] Speech, 1869.

"The Papacy has been the eternal, implacable foe of Italian independence and Italian unity. It never would permit a powerful national kingdom to unite Italy."

"Whether the United States will be involved in an immediate conflict with Rome lies in her future. While there are noble but still few exceptions, her unity and education and freedom will meet, in Roman Catholicism, it may be a guarded and often concealed, but an unceasing antagonist. Those who see in the course of the Christian centuries only the development of a dogma, and regard Protestantism as an intellectual conflict, can find no cause for apprehension. M. Guizot turns from speculations on the essence of Christianity to advocate a confederacy in Italy, and the maintenance of the temporal power of the Pope; but, to those for whom the conflict of so many centuries has a deeper reality, the ecclesiasticism of Rome bears another character. Milton was the statesman of a greater age, and was a wider scholar, and of fairer sympathies; but for him it was 'the old red dragon.' It was to be met by the nation in a struggle of life and death; and the nation will not maintain its unity or its being if she meet it only as a material force. The Church will not give place to an atheistic State, nor to a materialized civilization. The end of history is not attained, and the destination of humanity is not realized, in that. The nation can meet the forces with which it has to contend, only as it realizes its own moral being, and recognizes its origin and end in God."

NO MAN OUGHT TO HAVE OFFICE OR CITIZENSHIP IN AMERICA WHO DOES NOT RECOGNIZE THE STATE AS, UNDER GOD, SUPREME IN HER SPHERE, TO WHICH ALONE HIS CIVIL LOYALTY IS DUE, TO WHICH HE IS WILLING TO SWEAR AND MAINTAIN ALLEGIANCE.

THE STATE SCHOOLS AND RELIGION.

THE RECOGNITION OF GOD IN PUBLIC EDUCATION BY READING THE BIBLE.

A NORTH-EAST wind has been blowing steadily over the land, with intermittent gusts more or less furious, during the last score or more of years, on the Bible in the Public Schools. Hope is that this storm will, on fair discussion, pass its fury, and the air grow calm and sunny again.

A YEAR ago the writer attempted to reach bottom on one of the vexed questions of the day in a paper on " Taxing God's House." Dissatisfied with any of the ways of meeting the kindred question of the Bible in the Public Schools, as not coming to the root of the matter, he ventures this essay on the topic of the heading. These thoughts were first presented a week or two after Bishop McQuaid's address, in Horticultural Hall, on " The Public School Question as viewed by a Romanist." His main principle bearing on this topic is specious, but unsound, — that the parental responsibility for the child's salvation limits his public education by the State to what the father chooses he shall learn. Carried out, this principle would ignore the right of government to punish such a child for crime, or control him in any way. The State, in its sphere, is as responsible that he should be a good citizen, as the father, in his sphere, that he should be a " wise son."

Three procedures in regard to the matter may be thought of, which are, we think, sound in the respective circumstances: —

I. There seems to be no reason why a body of men, like the

Pilgrims or the Hernhutters, might not acquire title to a territory within natural limits, and then, by compact (as in "The Mayflower's" cabin) or by constitution, decree that the country founded should exist to carry out God's purposes. It is a question, whether that will not be the millennial experience. In the schools of such a nation, the Bible would not only be read, it would be studied. Now, it is susceptible of a powerful argument, that the founders, although they may not by law have made these States *Christian*, nevertheless showed their *intention* that they should be built up on the religion and morality of the Scriptures, — an intention shown in the early history of schools, and the motto of Harvard College, "*Christo et Ecclesiae.*" Though this action of the fathers was not positive law, it showed no less what is worthy of perpetual respect, — *a respect shown by sons of the fathers, whatever may be the spirit of foreign-born,— a clear intention to shape the institutions of this land by the Bible.*

And yet, though the intention of the fathers is worthy of full respect, it cannot be considered regnant and binding in the legal or complete moral sense ; since, on this side the Atlantic, law and constitution are not merely the collected opinions of great names in the past, or even the national policy of the past, but only that which is the present will of the people, declared in the present constitutions, in the laws, and in popular vote.

II. Another legitimate procedure would be the appointment of some score of our best statesmen as a high commission to consider this question in a broad, statesmanlike way: Is it true that this book, the Bible, is intimately connected with the welfare of nations? Is it true that New England and Scotland owe much of their intellectual discipline to the Bible? Is it true that you can note the difference between the Protestant and Catholic cantons of Switzerland; that, in sailing up the Danube, you can tell when you pass from the dominion of the Koran to the dominion of the Bible by the neatness and thrift of the villages? Was Victor Cousin right when he said of Luther's Bible, "It has greatly aided in the moral and religious education of the people"? "Every wise man will rejoice in this ; for, with three-fourths of the population, morality can be instilled only through the medium of religion." Was Victoria right, when, in response to the African prince, she sent her ambassador with a costly Bible, with this message from her lips, "Tell the prince that this is the secret of England's greatness"?

Let the opinion and recommendation of such a commission find embodiment in some law, made on the ground that they found that the prosperity of the State is intimately connected with this book. This commission would be greatly facilitated in the acceptance of their work by the simultaneous discussion of the same question by the people in their lyceums and debating clubs.

But now a strong argument might be made, that, in effect, such a high commission has sat in this country; that John Adams, John Quincy Adams, Lewis Cass, Everett, Greenleaf, Jefferson, Kent, McLean, Rush, Seward, Story, Washington, and Webster, in their noble statements,[1] have represented American statesmanship in the affirmation of the connection of the reading of this book with the welfare of the State, as when Greenleaf says, "Without these sanctions, the laws are no longer observed; oaths lose their hold on the conscience; promises are violated; frauds are multiplied; and moral obligation is dissolved. These securities are found in the Bible alone;" and John Quincy Adams says, "The first and almost the only book deserving universal attention is the Bible;" and as Jefferson writes, "I have always said, and I always will say, that the studious perusal of the sacred volume will make better citizens, better fathers, and better husbands;" and as Washington says, "Of all the dispositions and habits which lead to political prosperity, *religion* and *morality* are indispensable supports. In vain would that man claim the tribute of patriotism who should labor to subvert these pillars of human happiness, these firmest props of the duties of men and citizens."

These are the voice of a high commission of American statesmen, not the less powerful that it represents the sense of

---

[1] Homage to the Book. Samuel W. Bailey, New York, 1869.

our public men in all periods of our history. Yet although, in moral impressiveness, these testimonies of America's great statesmen, collected, would be equivalent to the voice of a high commission, still it must be admitted, that unless this commission were legally appointed, or accepted by the suffrage of the people, their report, however valuable and impressive, could not be considered law or constitution.

III. But now a third procedure — that which we proposed to ourselves — is to consider the subject *de novo*, and from a point of view farther back than the book.

We are seeking valid ground, rock foundation, for the Scripture in schools, *under our present free Constitution;* "and the dry land appears."

This view is in accordance with our popular idea, — the severance of Church and State. *This idea being regnant,* what shall we hold in regard to the action of the State in connection with the Scriptures in our schools? We shall present, as we have presented, only such considerations as we believe are irrefragable.

Two guiding thoughts, which "shine aloft like stars," illuminate us in considering the subject of education. *First,* The principle of the Swiss Pestalozzi, who, "for the last hundred years, has exerted a greater influence than any other man on education in England, America, and the north of Europe." Pestalozzi's first principle is, that *"Education relates to the whole man,* and consists in the drawing forth, strengthening, and perfecting . all the faculties with which an all-wise Creator has endowed him, — physical, intellectual, and moral ; or, to use Pestalozzi's own words, ' Education has to do with the hand, the head, and the heart.' " *Second,* The guiding thought, that — to apply somewhat loosely, perhaps, a phrase of Ruskin — *education should be "foundational and progressive."* The heart of a subject, its foundation, its keystone, that by which it "con-sists," should not be neglected or ignored. A man is not educated on any topic so long as he observes not its central fact or facts.

These guiding stars will not quit our firmament while we discuss the grave subject of education in the State.

Two propositions, then, we lay down : —

GOD SHOULD BE RECOGNIZED IN THE PLACE OF PUBLIC EDU-
CATION.

All natural science conducts to the One, to God. Zoölogy,
botany, the "star-eyed science," geology, physiology, all lead to
a great Being. "Each scientist," says Prof. Park, "claims that
his science most illustrates the wisdom of the Creator." Bacon's
well-known "Essay on Atheism" is a philosopher's opinion.
"The mind of man," "beholding the chain " "of second causes,"
"confederate and linked together, must needs fly to Deity and
Providence."

All who heard Agassiz' magnificent oration on Humboldt
well remember the pains which he took to free that man of
science from the imputation of atheism. "To these I venture
to say," says Agassiz, "Humboldt did not belong. He had too
logical a mind to assume that a harmoniously-combined whole
could be the result of accidental occurrences. In the few instances where, in his work, he uses the name of God, it appears
plainly that he believes in a Creator as the Lawgiver, and
primary Originator of all things." And so eager is he to free
Humboldt from what he seems to feel is the unscholarly stain
of atheism, that he quotes two passages from Humboldt's works,
"Gottes erhabenes Reich " ("God's Majestic Realm "); and
the other at the close of his description of the earthquake at
Caraccas, "Es war Gottes nicht menschenhand die hier zum
grabgelaute zwang " ("It was the hand of God, and not the
hand of man, which rang that funeral dirge ").

Since writing the above, the noble incident in the life of
Agassiz himself, from newspaper sources, and also as told in
golden rhyme by the admiring Whittier, has come to my eye.
It is the naturalist and the poet together confessing God.

"On Tuesday, July 8, 1873, Prof. Agassiz opened his Anderson School of Natural History on Penikese Island, in Buzzard's
Bay. He made no parade about it. Every thing was managed
with quiet good sense." "On the eve of his great enterprise
he could afford time to acknowledge God. Standing before his
little company, met for the first time on the scene of new studies

and toil, Prof. Agassiz said that they were in a strange position, and were strangers to each other. He felt more than he could express. He regretted that the gentleman to whom they owed the place was not present. As he knew of no one present whom he could call upon to invoke the divine blessing, he asked all present silently to give thanks to the Creator. After a moment of silence, he proceeded with the services.

"Science," continues the narrator, "is God's handmaid, and the truly scientific man cannot be undevout. The Creator is pleased when the votaries and scholars of science own its divine kindred, and ask him for its gifts. He blessed Solomon above all other kings, and gave the reason thus: 'Because thou hast not asked riches, wealth, or honor, but hast asked wisdom and knowledge for thyself.'

"We know of but few finer pictures than that one on the Island of Penikese, where our acknowledged modern king of science, with bared head and reverent mien, amid the scattered stones and the rude gatherings of his projected work, stood with his forty pupils, waiting on the Almighty Creator."

"Poetry is beautiful truth," said a college classmate. Therefore Whittier saw this noble incident as invested with a halo.

THE PRAYER OF AGASSIZ.

"On the Isle of Penikese,
　Ringed about by sapphire seas,
　Fanned by breezes soft and cool,
　Stood the *master* with his school.
　Said the master to the youth,
　'We have come in search of truth,
　Trying with uncertain key
　Door by door of mystery;
　We are reaching through His laws
　To the garment-hem of Cause, —
　Him the endless, unbegun,
　The Unnamable, the One,
　Light of all our light the Source,
　Life of life, and Force of force, —
　As with fingers of the blind,
　We are groping here to find

What the hieroglyphics mean
Of the Unseen in the seen ;
What the thought which underlies
Nature's masking and disguise ;
What it is that hides beneath
Blight and bloom, and birth and death.
By past efforts unavailing,
Doubt and error, loss and failing,
Of our weakness made aware,
On the threshold of our task
Let us light and guidance ask ;
Let us pause in silent prayer.'
Then the master in his place
Bowed his head a little space ;
And the leaves by soft airs stirred,
Lapse of wave, and cry of bird,
Left the solemn hush unbroken
Of that wordless prayer unspoken,
While its wish, on earth unsaid,
Rose to heaven interpreted."

The recognition of God is part of a scientific education.

History requires the hand of God. The definition by Dr. Edward A. Lawrence, which he has kindly allowed me to use, is philosophical : "History is God's agency in the origin, development, and government of the human race by means of natural law, supernatural forces, and the moral freedom of the subjects ; or, more concisely, it is the actual course of events in the evolution of the divine plan in creating and governing the world."

Gervinus says, " My work is only what all historical narratives ought to be, — a vindication of the decrees of Providence." Says D'Aubigné, " History should be made to live with its own proper life. God is this life : God must be acknowledged — God proclaimed — in history. The history of the world should purport to be the annals of the government of the Supreme King."

No one is educated who fails to see God in history. The American discerns him at Plymouth Rock ; the Israelite, in the Exodus ; the Frenchman, in Joan of Arc ; the Englishman, in the destruction of the Armada. "Afflavit Jehovah, dissipati sunt."[1]

---

[1] Motto of the Armada Medal.

Ethics as the science of duty runs as on a sunbeam up to God. Great legal minds have felt how the second table of the law rests on the first. Duties, the performance of which is a part of good citizenship, and which are needful to make a State virtuous and happy, are felt in some way to derive from God; as witness the taking of an oath to be truthful.

The *science of government* traces back to God. The "social compact" theory would not now be held by an educated man. "The powers that be are ordained of God." It is a part of education needful to a citizen to know that divine right goes with the constituted government, and good citizenship requires a recognition of the "divinity that doth hedge" a magistrate. Cicero (quoted by Lord Bacon) makes a part of true Roman statesmanship "haec una sapientia," &c., "the sole true wisdom, the having perceived that all things are regulated and governed by the providence of the immortal gods, through which wisdom we have subdued all races and nations."

In the schoolroom of the State, therefore, — where a true education, and not merely a congeries of facts, is given, — the place of public instruction, God — the God of science, the God of history, the God of duty, the God of nations — ought to be openly recognized. This recognition should be made distinct and regnant *by reading high and impressive thoughts concerning him, and by reverent address to him.*

Primarily it matters not how this recognition should be made. The Chinese schoolboy always makes his act of reverence to the statue, or the name on a tablet, of Confucius. The question is not concerning one particular book, or the divine claim of any book, or the authoritative teaching of the particular doctrines of any book. The main point is that already insisted upon, — the *recognition of God*. A book of eclectic thoughts on God, from the sages of the world, would be appropriate for a public school. Max Müller says, while speaking of the Vedas, "The late good Bishop Cotton, in his address to the students of a missionary institution at Calcutta, advised them to use a certain hymn of the Rig-Veda in their daily prayers."

The reading from some devotional volume is one of the most

natural devices for expressing and inspiring worship. Religious reading accompanies prayer. The standard thoughts, the highest the race has known, not only most worthily recognize the Being they describe, but are the best prompter to new thoughts. · Alexander, Plutarch tells us, carried his "casket-copy" of the Iliad with him, and laid it with his sword under his pillow at night.

An interesting illustration of the naturalness of recourse to standard devotional works as conveying and prompting worship is found in the works of Benjamin Franklin. In November, 1728, when Franklin was twenty-two years old, he commenced a writing which he called "Articles of Belief, and Acts of Religion." He begins with a quotation from Addison's "Cato," then states his belief in God, and concludes with an "Adoration." Then he proceeds: "After this, it will not be improper to read part of some such book as Ray's 'Wisdom of God in the Creation,' or Blackmore on 'The Creation,' and the Archbishop of Cambray's 'Demonstration of the Being of a God,' &c.; or else spend some minutes in a serious silence, contemplating on these subjects. Then sing Milton's 'Hymn to the Creator,' —

'These are thy glorious works, Parent of good.'"

After which, "Here follows the reading of some book, or part of a book, discoursing on and exciting to moral virtue." This is followed by a "Petition."[1]

But now *there are certain good reasons why the* BIBLE SHOULD BE THE BOOK CONCERNING GOD, WHICH SHOULD BE USED IN RECOGNIZING HIM IN THE AMERICAN SCHOOL.

NOT *because the Bible is inspired.* Our argument does not claim that; nor does it, in any of these articles, proceed on that assumption.

But on these unquestioned grounds : —

1. All the nations of Europe, the languages of Western civilization, hold this book, the Bible, as containing the sublimest, most righteous, most gracious views of this Divine Being. This

---

[1] Franklin's Works, Sparks's Edition, ii. pp. 1 and following.

needs no illustration.   One need only refer to the little volume, "Homage to the Book," and to what is said there by Goethe, Burke, Hale, Locke, Carlyle, Scott, Milton, Everett, Webster, Washington, Seward, Oxenstiern, Jefferson, Guizot, Coleridge, Bacon, Napoleon, and the eminent Oriental scholars, Selden and Sir William Jones.[1]

2. The Bible, early translated into all the languages of Europe, is that book whose language and diction in regard to God permeate all our literatures.   It is not the Scandinavian or the Hindoo phraseology about God, but that of the Scriptures, which is most familiar to all readers of the European literatures.   It might be added, that all these literatures, as has often been proved, owe much of their riches to the germs of Scripture thought ; and the modern literatures cannot be understood without the Bible.

3. The Bible is the book of the founders of our nation's institutions.   They freely used the Bible in moulding their early institutions.   The church-meeting suggested the town-meeting ; and thence, in Jefferson's mind, the democracy of the republic was born.   This book, which shaped our institutions, rather than any other, should have the preference in a public recognition of God.   Rufus Choate once said, "Banish the Bible from our public schools? ·Never ! so long as there is left a piece of Plymouth Rock big enough for a gun-flint."   This is not a mere extravaganza of eloquence.   There is a reason why, in the quick mind of Choate, the Bible and Plymouth Rock flashed together.   At Plymouth our institutions were born of the Bible, as by the Bible they grew in vigor.

It may be added, that the nation is satisfied with the powerful and salutary influence of the Bible upon her institutions and upon public morality.   Ninety-nine hundredths of Americans whose ancestors thirty years back were on our soil coincide with Jefferson's words, already quoted, that " the studious perusal of the sacred volume will make better citizens, better fathers, and better husbands."

4. This book, of all religious volumes in all climes, gives the

---

[1] Homage to the Book, Samuel W. Bailey.

truest cosmogony, the only one which is not open to ridicule, and a view of God throughout which is sublime, and in no way below the teachings of advanced civilization.

5. This book contains, wrapped up in it, and developed in it, the truest political science. The system of circuit judges is biblical; also the idea of associate judges. Democracy in Church and State is set forth as the divine idea. Kingship is not commended as the best type of government; yet obedience to constituted government is commanded. See Wines's "Hebrew Commonwealth."

6. This book deserves the preference, because it is regarded as the best attempt ever made to describe the divine and the human. God is the Supreme Being: man is a being made in his likeness. Any serious attempt to describe these two — God, man — must result in a treatise which will contain vital and educating forces. We do not assert here that this book is inspired, but that, by the almost unanimous suffrage of educated men, this volume is the most successful endeavor to describe man and his Maker. We quote a few eloquent words: "It is the book of God, and the book of man. It is the book of the divine nature. It is the book of man as well as of God. Human nature is as fully revealed as the divine. They are revealed in comparison; they are revealed in contrast; in things similar, and in things dissimilar. The fountains of the great deep of human thought, of human action, are broken up; and man, inward and outward, is contemplated, not in the dim taper-light of time, but the broad light of eternity." [1]

7. This book deserves the preference in the recognition of God in the school, because it contains the one unique, perfect man, Jesus Christ. There can be no doubt his character enters widely and deeply into all modern philanthropy and ethics. Hospitals came from the hem of Christ's garment. "It is Christian, or it is not Christlike," is the modern criterion. Sceptics do homage to Christ's character, and all high art. "In Memoriam," "Paradise Regained," Ary Scheffer's "Christus Consolator," Thorwaldsen's "Christus Benedicens," attest how

---

[1] Dr. Allen Morron: Lecture on the Bible.

this man dominates modern ideas of life and duty and benevolence.

These appearing to us irrefutable reasons *why this book should be used* in the recognition of God in the school, practically one of two ways may be taken *in its use.*

1. The Eclectic Way.   This may seem chimerical, but may be stated thus : The State may call a convocation of venerated doctors in the Bible from different sects, Protestant, Papal, Jewish, who should be empowered to prepare a manual of extracts from the Bible, having for its aim the recognition of God, the same for use in the schools.   As to a prayer, it would seem that there could be no serious objection to the Lord's Prayer, since Rabbi Kalisch of Milwaukee (see " Guide for Inquirers ") claims that every phrase of this prayer, excepting that about temptation, has its germ, or at least corresponding passage, in the old Jewish writings.   But it is doubtful whether such a convocation would be harmonious, or whether such an *eclectic method* would find favor with them.   Our recourse, therefore, is to

2. The Way of the Majority.   That is practically the method of to-day, — *the use of the Bible in the form chosen by the majority in any State*, with such concessions as are due to the conscientious scruples of others.

We do not see how the present law could be made more acceptable to the candid of all religious opinions and orders. We recite it, because we believe many are unaware how far it is from wounding the consciences of any : —

" The school committee shall require the daily reading of some portion of the Bible, without written note or oral comment, in the public schools : but they shall require no scholar to read from any particular version whose parent or guardian shall declare that he has conscientious scruples against allowing him to read therefrom ; nor shall they ever direct any school-books calculated to favor the tenets of any particular sect of Christians to be purchased or used in any of the public schools." — 1862, chap. 57, sect. 1.

In a Jewish commonwealth, if there were one, the Old Testament would be the basis of the devotional reading ; in a

Papal State should there be one, the Douai version; in our States, — as they are, and as we trust they will forever be, free from the domination of any church, — that noble version of the Bible should be used in recognizing God in the school which was contemporary with "The Mayflower," and was used by the fathers of the nation.

GOD IN THE NATION; THEREFORE IN PUBLIC EDUCATION.

As "flying buttresses" to the argument on "The Recognition of God by the Bible in Public Education," for strengthening and symmetrically extending the propositions there built up, these additional essays appear.

The syllogism is this: —

God and Righteousness are essential in the State;

The Public School is the only Preparation controlled by the State for securing good Citizenship and Statesmanship:

Therefore God and Righteousness should have place in the Public School.

The *second premise* needs little remark: its truth will be generally acknowledged. Mr. Beecher, indeed, says, "In our day of general intelligence, we divide the functions of society, letting the Church teach dogma, letting the family teach personal religion, and letting the common school perform the task of teaching intelligence." Now, sufficient righteousness to make a good citizen may perhaps, in general, be taught by the family; but, in case that the State is not satisfied with such righteousness as the family teaches, — such as the Jesuit taught Charles IX. in preparation for St. Bartholomew; such as the Mormon, the Spartan, the Free Lover, the gentleman of light fingers, may please to teach his family, — what then? Has the State no protection to itself against the teaching of cellars, and of the cells of Jesuits? Evident it is, that, however the State may "farm out" to any

128

party the instruction in righteousness which is necessary to her well-being, she is responsible for the result, — her character as a State. Mr. Beecher, we suppose, would not deny this. His words, "we" and "letting," imply that it is a concession to allow the school to teach only "intelligence." The wisdom of "farming out" her necessary instruction in God and morality, in these days of Jesuitism and Mormonism, and home luxury bought by public corruption, is questionable. At all events, the State has a right — nay, on it is laid the imperative duty — to teach righteousness, as Dr. Johnson might say, "sufficient to preserve from putrefaction." And the public school is the only place which she can control to educate her future citizens to this end. It was objected to this statement, in a company of gentlemen before whom this paper was read, that the State could train her citizens in justice and morality by her legislation and her court proceedings. We may gratefully allow the great influence upon a people of righteous law-making and righteous judgment, without retracting the statement made. It rests with the people, however, how far they will give attention to the study of the laws and the judgments of courts. The State, even if it should issue brief reports to the people of these two departments, could not compel their reading. In the school only, the State has a control over her citizens, so far as *to dictate what they shall read, and what moral lessons they shall receive.*

The *first premise* is worthy of more extended remark, that God and righteousness are essential in the State.

Scientifically and philosophically, and then historically, we will view this matter.

THE PHILOSOPHICAL VIEW.

Since the first paper, and, indeed, since meditating most of this, a friend brought to my notice a volume by Mr. E. Mulford, "The Nation." This book, we are told, is the product of years of thought ; and it seems, on partial examination, not unworthy to rank with the famous work of De Tocqueville. In several lines of thought gathered here and there in the book, it "marshals me the way that I was going."

The argument which I make from principles culled from this book may thus be stated as a first proposition on the subject:—

I. THE TRUE THEORY OF THE STATE REQUIRES GOD AND HIS RIGHTEOUSNESS IN IT.

One is glad to set forth the views of so profound a thinker as Mr. Mulford, as coincident with his own. Space forbids little more than the mere statement of such propositions of his book as bear on the matter in hand.

1. "The nation is a moral personality." This he sets in opposition to the false theories of the nation ; as "a necessary evil," "a historical accident," "a jural society," "an economic society." This is the view of Aristotle and Hegel. Milton says, "A nation ought to be like some huge Christian person-age, one mighty growth or stature of an honest man, as big and compact in virtue as in body; for, look, what the ground and causes are of single happiness to one man, the same ye shall find them to a whole State."

2. "The origin of the nation is in the Divine Will." This he sets against the false theories, that the origin of the nation is in "the development of the family," in "mere force or might," in "some instinct or emotion of man," in "the social compact," in "popular sovereignty."

3. "A nation is sovereign."

4. The sovereignty of a nation involves the right of its own independent existence. "In Rome it was asserted in the words, '*Videant consules ne quid detrimenti capiat respublica,*'"—"Let the consuls watch, that the republic receive no injury."

5. The nation has its vocation from God, and its responsi-bility to him, and its preservation and guidance by him. "The realization of its being through its vocation in a moral order is in righteousness : not only the law of its being, but the condition of the realization of its being, is in righteousness. In its neces-sary being, it moves towards this end. Thus, in anarchy and oppression and violence and crime, there is a negation of its being. Thus also, in so far as it fails of its end, it passes from history. As history is the realization of a moral order, in the unity of a divine purpose, when the nation ceases to work in its

own vocation in it, and to act as a constructive power in the harmony of its design, then it no longer has its place in it. It is this constant possibility of evil in the nation that involves the most real obligation, and is the incitement to the utmost energy and vigilance ; and it is this which gives solemnity to history."

He quotes Brownson with approval concerning a recent political school : " It has rejected the divine origin and ground of government, and excluded God from the State. They have not only separated the State from the Church as an external corporation, but from God as its internal Lawgiver, and by so doing have deprived the State of her sacredness, inviolability, and hold upon the conscience."

These five propositions are foundational. Each is a principle. They deserve great study at this period of our history. Men of great ability, borne on surface thought and popular notions, are drifting from fundamentals. These propositions deserve reperusal and study. If they are true, then God and his righteousness are essential in the State.

II. We pass now to another consideration which has been brought to our notice — not in this particular connection, however — by an eminent and admiring spectator of our institutions, who, while rejoicing in the separation, properly speaking, of Church and State, gave it as his opinion, that A REPUBLIC, OF ALL FORMS OF NATIONALITY, SHOULD ESPECIALLY BE RELIGIOUS.

De Tocqueville is discoursing on " The causes which tend to maintain democracy in America," and, while speaking of the opinions of Americans, makes us aware that his sentiments are similar. I transcribe a long but interesting paragraph : " Religion in America takes no direct part in the government of society : but it must be regarded as the first of their political institutions ; for, if it does not impart a taste for freedom, it facilitates the use of it." "I am certain that they hold it to be indispensable to the maintenance of republican institutions." " I have known of societies formed by the Americans to send out missionaries of the gospel into the North-western States to found schools and churches there, lest religion should be suffered to die away in those remote settlements, and the rising States be less fitted to enjoy free institutions than the people from whom they came." " Thus religious zeal is perpetually warmed in the United States by the fires of patriotism. These men do not act exclusively from a consideration of a future life: eternity is only one motive of their devotion to the cause." " They will tell you that ' all the American republics are collectively involved with each other: if the republics of the West were to fall into anarchy, or to be mastered by a despot, the republican institutions which now flourish upon the shores of the Atlantic Ocean would be in great peril. It is, therefore, our interest that the new States should be religious in order that they may permit us to remain free.'" " There are men in France who look forward to a republican form of government as a tranquil and lasting state, toward which modern society is daily impelled by the ideas and manners of the time, and who sincerely desire to prepare men to be free. When these men attack religious opinions, they obey the dictates of their passions, and not of their interests. Despotism may govern without faith; but liberty cannot. Religion is much more necessary in the republic which they set forth in such glowing colors than in the monarchy which they attack: it is more needed in democratic republics than any other. How is it possible that society should escape destruction, if the moral tie be not strengthened in proportion as the political tie is relaxed? and what can be done with a people who are their own masters, if they be not submissive to the Deity?"

III. One more consideration in the same direction, that God and his righteousness are essential in the State, is, that THE BIBLE MAY PERHAPS BE TRUE ; AND, IF IT IS, THEN THE CREATOR OF NATIONS HAS ASSERTED AND SHOWN THAT HE HOLDS THEM STEADILY TO THEIR SPHERE AND DUTY TO HIM. This consideration is different from the first proposition. That concerns a theory, the true ideal of the State: this consideration implies, that, if the Scripture is true, there are positive assertions by One, who is King of kings, that he holds them, as he does individuals, responsible.

This book is remarkable, in that, unlike the Koran, Vedas, Confucian Analects, and, indeed, all other books representing a grand religion, it contains the spectacle of a great nation, from germ and cradle onward, professedly guided by the Almighty, and held to a peculiar work, which it was chastised when not doing. This theory as here sketched seems true even to perverse minds; for even Lord Rochester, in his infidelity, averred that the existing state of the Jews, scattered in the world, but not mingling, was an unanswerable argument for the so-called inspired book.

If this book is true, the nations are, not in a theological, but moral order, his sons or wards. If the nations do not observe this responsibility to God, the failure may be their destruction.

God and his righteousness are set as foundation to the nations. " Righteousness exalteth a nation." " The powers that be are ordained of God." " The nation that will not serve Thee shall perish." One passage explicitly draws out the statement of God, that he holds nations responsible to him for their character, and that he will deal with them according to their character: " At what instant I shall speak concerning a nation and concerning a kingdom, to pluck up and to pull down, and to destroy it, if that nation against whom I have pronounced turn from their evil, I will repent of the evil that I thought to do unto them. And at what instant I shall speak concerning a nation and concerning a kingdom, to build and to plant it; if it do evil in my sight, that it obey not my voice, then I will repent of the good wherewith I said I would benefit them."

If, then, the Bible should be true, by inspiration, — or even if it should have stumbled on the truth, — then even a nation begun as auspiciously as ours by the Pilgrims may well take heed that it set before itself to remember God and his righteousness.

These three considerations, it would seem, should be sufficient to make this truth evident and clear as a theory.

THE HISTORICAL VIEW.

Historically, now, the indications are quite as clear that THE BEST MINDS, THOSE WHICH HAVE BEEN THE LIVING LEADERS

OF NATIONS, HAVE SPONTANEOUSLY AFFIRMED GOD AND HIS RIGHTEOUSNESS IN THE STATE. A few illustrations will be sufficient.

Romulus, as soon as Rome was built, reared an altar to Consus, the god of counsel. Numa not only "called in the assistance of religion," as Plutarch tells us, but gave out that some goddess gave him wisdom in secret interviews. The Delphic oracle consulted by Lycurgus told him that "Apollo had heard his request, and promised that the constitution he should establish would be the most excellent in the world." Solon put his laws into verse, at least began to do it, in these lines : —

> "Supreme of gods, whose power we first address,
> This plan to honor, and these laws to bless."

Draco had already decreed, "It is an everlasting law in Attica that the gods are to be worshipped." Demosthenes not only opens and closes the immortal Oration on the Crown with invocation of the Deity, but in it he acknowledges many times the guiding hand of God in the affairs of Athens. From the height of the Acropolis, Minerva the Protector, a statue in ivory nearly fifty feet high, rose above roofs of homes and temples. Cicero, in his First Oration against Catiline, exclaims, " Magna Diis immortalibus habenda est gratia, atque huic ipsi Jovi Statori, antiquissimo custodi hujus urbis," — "Great gratitude is due to the immortal gods, and most of all to Jupiter Stator, the most ancient guardian of this city." And in his last paragraph he addresses him, "Tu, Jupiter, qui iisdem, quibus haec urbs, auspiciis a Romulo es constitutus, quem Statorem hujus urbis atque imperii nominamus," — "Thou, Jupiter, who wast, in the very auspices of the origin of the city, *declared* by Romulus, and whom we since *name* Stator, guardian of this city and this realm."

Plato reports to us a dialogue in which Socrates was one of the speakers.

Socrates. — If, then, you wish public measures to be right and noble, *virtue* must be given by you to the citizens.

Alcibiades. — How could any one deny that?

Socrates. — *Virtue*, therefore, is that which is to be first possessed, both by you and by every other person who would have direction and care, not only for himself, and things dear to himself, but for the State, and things dear to the State.

Alcibiades. — You speak truly.

Socrates. — To act justly and wisely, both you and the State, YOU MUST ACT ACCORDING TO THE WILL OF GOD.

Alcibiades. — It is so.[1]

When the nation is saved in battle, the " Te Deum " is sung. Even Philistia triumphing over Israel sets the ark before her "fishy god" Dagon. Joan of Arc had on her standard the figure of God in the clouds, with the world in his hand, an angel on each side presenting him with a fleur-de-lis which he was blessing, — beautiful thought of this young girl's mind. The reverse had the crown of France held by two angels.

Collections of coins show that nearly all modern nations send from their mints their creed in God in the gold and silver stamped, " Dei gratia." Religious 'national numismatology, indeed, discloses a wealth of significant inscriptions. England, — sovereign : "Victoria, Dei gratia ;" also "Dirigit Deus gressus meos." France, — Louis d'òr, "Imperator Christianissimus ;" crown, " Sit nomen Domini benedictum." Spain, — doubloon, " Carol. IV., Dei gratia ;" dollar, " Fernando VII., por la gratia de Dios y la constitution." Portugal, — " Dei gratia ;" "In hoc signo vinces ;" " Nata stab. subq. sig." Switzerland, — " Domine, conserva nos in pace ;" " Dominus providebit ;" " Cuncta per Deum ;" " Benedictus sit Jehovah Deus, Dux." Austria, — " Dei gratia." Germany, — " Dominus Protector meus ;" " Gott und das Vaterland ;" " Dominus Mihi Adictor ;" " Dei gratia ;" " Gott segne Unterhalte unsere Bergwerke ;" "In Deo consilium." Tuscany, — " Dirige, Domine, gressus meos ;" " Dominus spes mea a juventute mea." Belgium and Holland, — "Gentium et Ipse dominabitur ;" " Nomen Domini turris fortissima ;" " Domini est Regnum ;" " Forti et spes nost. Deus." Jerusalem, — " Justus Jehovah Judex."

Even in time of trouble we stamped one coin, " In God we trust." Medals for victories often have an ascription to the

---

[1] Prefixed by Daniel Webster to his Argument on the Girard Will, Works, vi. 135.

Almighty.   Fasts and thanksgivings are State recognitions of
God, chaplaincies also in legislature, army and navy, and in
criminal and benevolent institutions.   L'Enfant's Plan of
Washington City (1792) included " (D.) A *church* intended for
national purposes, such as public prayers, thanksgivings, funeral
orations," &c.

The fathers of the republic looked to the outstretched arm
of the Almighty.   We may well in these days, in which we heed
especially the commandment " not to be righteous overmuch,"
study the outspoken recognition of God by the founders.
"When intelligence was received that the British army had
capitulated at Yorktown, it was immediately

"*Resolved,* That Congress will, at two o'clock this day, go in procession to the Dutch Lutheran Church, and return thanks to Almighty
God for crowning the allied arms of the United States and France
with success, by the surrender of the whole British army under the
command of the Earl Cornwallis."

The day after that surrender, Gen. Washington issued an
order, that " Divine service shall be performed to-morrow in the
different brigades and divisions.   The commander-in-chief
recommends that all the troops that are not on duty do assist
at it with serious deportment, and that sensibility of heart which
the recollection of the surprising and particular interposition òf
Providence in our favor claims."

" The auspicious event was commended to the whole nation
as a subject of thankfulness in a proclamation which begins,
' Whereas it has pleased Almighty God, the Father of mercies,
remarkably to assist the United States of America,'" and contains this sentence : " Through the whole of the contest, from
its first rise to this time, the influence of the Divine Providence
may be clearly perceived in many signal instances, of which we
mention but a few."

An error it would be, we believe, to attribute the omission
from the Constitution of the United States of the name of
God to atheistic feeling, or intention to exclude mention of the
Father of nations.   It would, indeed, have been grateful and

graceful to have commenced the National Constitution, as did so many of the States, by some such expression as "With gratitude to the Supreme Governor of nations," or the like. But the omission of this was not necessarily exclusive of God. We have sought in vain in the Federalist and in the Constitutional Debates for any evidence that the Divine Name was *ruled* out.

The fathers of the republic had before them the arduous task, — a task so arduous and perplexing, that they well-nigh failed, — to set forth the political framework of the State in such a way as to represent fully the American idea, and, at the same time, to satisfy thirteen separate Colonies. That problem seems, if you will glance at the debates, so to have absorbed all their powers, that it appears not to have occurred to them to define or express the relation of the State to God. So some astronomer might have his mind so taxed with some question of the stars, that he might forget to say, "The heavens are telling God's glory." For all that, relieved from the problem, he may prove a devout man.

It has been remarked as singular, that there is one book in the Bible which does not contain the name of God, — the Book of Esther. The interesting thought has been suggested in connection, that thus, by a suppression of his name, yet by the constant sense of him throughout, this book resembles nature. The writer of Esther was not an atheist. Had the divine name been in that book, we should not have grieved ; but neither shall we petition to have it inserted.

Neither were our ancestors atheists. The Pilgrims commenced their compact, "In the name of God, Amen." "The charters of all the Colonies acknowledged God. The articles of the old Confederation acknowledged him. All the earliest constitutions of the States acknowledged him." The Declaration of Independence speaks of the "Creator," "the God of nature," and "appeals to the Supreme Judge of the world for the rectitude of their intentions," "with a firm reliance on the protection of Divine Providence." Even the Constitution speaks of the Sabbath, requires the taking of an oath, and recognizes the rights of personal religion. Surely, in any true sense of the word, our Constitution is not atheistic. Undoubtedly the framers were absorbed by the mighty task of adequately embodying their new political ideas, and adjusting the unaccustomed relations of the branches of the government. Were the Constitution revised, we would insert some distinct recognition of God ; but we would not do it as a rebuke to the fathers, but rather to make their recognition of God *distinct* in the Constitution as they made it elsewhere. " Sicut patribus, sit Deus nobis." Yet, in reality, there is no more atheistic intent in the omission of God's name from the Constitution than in its omission from the Book of Esther.

" The recognition of the origin and continuity of the nation in God is repeated in the inaugurals of the first Presidents."

President Jefferson, at the close of his inaugural, said, " I shall need, too, the favor of that Being in whose hands we all are ; who led our fathers, as Israel of old, from their native land, and planted them in a country flowing in all the comforts and necessaries of life ; who has covered our infancy with his providence, and our riper years with his wisdom and power ; and to whose goodness I ask you to join in supplications with me." President Lincoln was equally recognizant of God in his state papers.

President Grant's excellent proclamation for a Centennial Fourth-of-July service is worthy of citation here : " The founders of the government, at its birth and in its feebleness, invoked the blessings and protection of a Divine Providence ; and the thirteen Colonies and three millions of people have expanded into a nation of strength and numbers commanding the position which then was demanded, and for which fervent prayers were then offered. It seems fitting, that, on the one hundredth anniversary of our existence as a nation, a grateful acknowledgment should be made to Almighty God for the protection and the bounties which he has vouchsafed to our beloved country. I therefore invite the good people of the United States, on the approaching fourth day of July, in addition to the usual observances with which they are accustomed to greet the return of the day, further, in such manner and at such times as in their respective localities and religious associations may be most convenient, to mark its recurrence by some public religious and devout thanksgiving to Almighty God for the blessings which have been bestowed upon us as a nation during the centenary of our existence, and humbly to invoke a continuation of his favor and of his protection."

Daniel Webster, in his last address not political, delivered before the New-York Historical Society, concluded in these words: "And let me say, gentlemen, that if we and our posterity shall be true to the Christian religion; if we and they shall live always in the fear of God, and shall respect his commandments; if we and they shall maintain just moral sentiments, and such conscientious convictions of duty as shall control the heart and life, — we may have the highest hopes of the future fortunes of our country: and if we maintain those institutions of government, and that political union exceeding all praise as much as it exceeds all former examples of political associations, we may be sure of one thing, — that, while our country furnishes materials for a thousand masters of the historic art, it will be no topic for a Gibbon; it will have no decline and fall. It will go on prospering and to prosper. But if we and our posterity reject religious instruction and authority, violate the rules of eternal justice, trifle with the injunctions of morality, and recklessly destroy the political Constitution which holds us together, no man can tell how sudden a catastrophe may overwhelm us, that shall bury all our glory in profound obscurity."

Such was the feeling of the relation of God and righteousness to the nation in the mind of the great "Defender of the Constitution."

We cannot forbear transcribing the grand supplication of Bishop Simpson at the opening of the Centennial Exhibition: "We beseech thee, Almighty Father, that our beloved republic may be strengthened in every element of true greatness, until her mission is accomplished by presenting to the world an illustration of the happiness of a free people, with a free church, in a free State, under laws of their own enactment, and under rulers of their own selection, acknowledging supreme allegiance only to the King of kings, and Lord of lords; and as thou didst give to one of its illustrious sons first to draw experimentally the electric spark from heaven, which has since girdled the globe in the celestial whispers of 'Glory to God in the highest, peace on earth, and good-will to men,' so to latest time may the mission of America, under divine inspiration, be one of affection, brotherhood, and love for all the race; and may the coming centuries be filled with the glory of our Christian civilization!"

But perhaps the most illustrious and striking example is that now to be recounted. It was the recognition of the Supreme Guidance, not by some sacerdotal orator, but by a calm philosopher, at a time, too, when even the birth of our nation was a matter of grave doubt and earnest solicitude.

It was in the Constitutional Convention in 1787 that a difficult question was presented as to the composition of the future Senàte of the United States. The Constitution seemed about to be wrecked on this point. "There was much warm and some acrimonious feeling exhibited by a number of speakers: a rupture appeared almost inevitable; and the bosom of Washington seemed to labor with the most anxious solicitude for its issue." In this juncture Dr. Franklin arose, "the Mentor of our body." He moved an adjournment for three days to give time for calm reflection, and then proceeded in a speech which ought to be set in fair letters in our schoolrooms, which was one of the declamations of our younger years, and may well continue to be given to the youthful speakers, the future statesmen of America: —

"In this situation of the Assembly, groping, as it were, in the dark to find political truth, and scarce able to distinguish it when presented to us, how has it happened, sir, that we have not hitherto once thought of humbly applying to the Father of lights to illuminate our understanding? In the beginning of the contest with Great Britain, when we were sensible of danger, we had daily prayer in this room for the Divine Protection. Our prayers, sir, were heard, and they were graciously answered. All of us who were engaged in the struggle must have observed frequent instances of a superintending Providence in our favor. To that kind Providence we owe this happy opportunity of consulting in peace on the means of establishing our future national felicity. And have we forgotten that powerful Friend? or do we imagine we no longer need his assistance? I have lived, sir, a long time; and, the longer I live, the more convincing proofs I see of this truth, that God governs in the affairs of men. And, if a sparrow cannot fall to the ground without his notice, is it probable that an empire can rise without his aid? We have been assured, sir, in the Sacred Writings, that, 'except the Lord build the house, they labor in vain that build it.' I firmly believe this; and I also believe, that, without his concurring aid, we shall succeed in this political building no better than the builders of Babel. I therefore beg leave to move, that henceforth prayers imploring the assistance of Heaven, and its blessings on our deliberations, be held in this Assembly every morning before we proceed to business."

This motion was seconded by Roger Sherman.

It matters not whether, as some say, the motion was not put, for several reasons. This address stands, as recorded by Madison, as the profound impression of Franklin, the philosopher-statesman, of the dependence of our nation upon God. It also remains on record in the words of another eye-witness: "Never did I behold a countenance at once so dignified and delighted as was that of Washington at the close of his address."

And, now, were these founders and these wise men wrong? Were Washington and Franklin and Jefferson and Lincoln wrong, that a nation must confess God? Were Solon and Lycurgus, and Numa and Romulus and Demosthenes, and Cicero, Milton, and De Tocqueville, clear-sighted as to where lies the strength and safety of nations? As Ruskin says on another theme, "I will only ask you to give its legitimate value to the testimony of these great men, consistent as you see it is on this head. Can it be supposed that these men, in the main work of their lives, are amusing themselves with a fictitious and idle view?"

Our syllogism stands completely argued, — God and his righteousness are essential in the State; The public school is the only preparation controlled by the State for citizenship and statesmanship : *Therefore* the public school should recognize God and his righteousness.

Since writing the foregoing, I came upon this coincident sentence of Rev. Charles Brooks : "The maxim among the Prussians seems to be this, *Whatever we would have in the State we must first introduce into the schoolroom.*"

In what way this should be done is a problem which we discuss — not here. That it should be done — done not timidly and questioningly, as now ; done in a more pronounced and understanding manner, more effectually and prominently than now — can hardly be denied by one who sees the lack of " God and his righteousness " in the State. "The First Prayer in Congress " would be a good picture to adorn the schoolroom, "Washington at Prayer at Valley Forge," " The Departure from Delft Haven," and the " Pilgrims' Prayer on Landing." Some scheme for declaiming such addresses as that of Franklin, and of Corwin on Mexico, might be devised. I have been more solicitous to establish the principle than to show its practical working. But, beyond all other means, what can be better than for the youth of the republic, in the school preparatory to the State, to recognize the God of the nation by reverent prayer and selections from that book which makes prominent by precept and example that " righteousness exalteth a nation," and of which Edward Everett said, that " all the distinctive features and superiority of our republican institutions are derived from the teachings of Scripture " ?

MOTHER AND CHILD; BIBLE AND SCHOOL.

INGRATITUDE is not reckoned among the virtues. The viper stinging the befriending farmer is not fabled to us to excite to emulation. The "Ungrateful Guest," so branded by Philip of Macedon, is a stain on the historic page. Towards one whose beneficence is still virent, fruitful, and blossoming for more fruit, ingratitude is especially odious. Basest of all is filial ingratitude. The bestowal of valuable life, the guarding and shaping of the early life, are the great boon, especially where only good was given in giving existence. Æneas bearing "Pater Anchises" from burning Troy, Cleobis and Biton in the harness drawing their mother to the temple, are admirable; but Nero putting Agrippina to death is execrable.

What if it should possibly be susceptible of demonstration, that for the school to eject the Bible is for child to thrust parent out of doors?

. What is the relationship of Scripture and school? Is not Orestes slaying his mother the most tragic of tragedies? Did the Furies spare him, even though called Gracious Goddesses? or Œdipus, though unwittingly he slew his father? Faustulus knew Romulus and Remus not the offspring of the she-wolf, but was not wise enough to trace the twin-brothers to their royal ancestry; but time revealed who gave them birth.

There is reason to suspect, to begin with, kinship between Bible and school. Bunsen says, "A glance at the mental development of humanity during the last eighteen centuries would compel us to assume the existence of some singularly exalted holy Personality as the cause, and not simply the occasion, of that revolution in man's view of the universe, the mightiest of all mental revolutions; being no less than the introduction of a new formation of life." By having the personality of Jesus Christ in it, "the Best," if no otherwise, the Bible is a vital book, influencing religious and mental life.

Religion and intellect have connections. Mental philosophers have taken note of this. Religion — which makes and keeps the will divine in its choice, the conscience clear and unperturbed, makes hope serene, the eye docile and looking to the Highest, imparts lofty purpose, evolves hidden energies, the "faith which energizes by love " — must needs quicken intellect; might even awaken a slumbering intellect.

A common thing is the waking up of mind in and consequent on a religious experience. "To the Bible Spurgeon ascribes the discipline of his mental powers." "Once," he declares, " he put all his knowledge together in glorious confusion; but now he has a shelf in his head for every thing. ' Ever since I have known Christ, I have put Christ as my central sun; and each secular science revolves around it.' He can learn any thing now; and from his own experience he exhorts to build a studio and raise an observatory on Calvary."

John Müller, whom D'Aubigné calls the "prince of modern historians," writes to Charles Bonnet, "Ever since I knew the Saviour, I see all things clearly: with him there is no difficulty which I cannot solve."

Emerson says, "If your eye is on the Eternal, your intellect will grow, and your opinions and actions will have a beauty which no learning or combined advantages of other men can rival." "Genius takes its rise out of the mountains of rectitude." "People of superior moral quality are nearer to the secret of God than others; are bathed by sweeter water: they hear voices, they see visions, where others are vacant. We believe that holiness confers a certain insight, because not by our private but by our public force can we share and know the nature of things." Hamerton says, "The two most powerful mental stimulants — since they overcome even the fear of death — are unquestionably religion and patriotism : ardent states of feeling, both of them ; yet this ardor has great moral strength in all who have come to intellectual greatness."

We are not surprised at " Bene orasse est bene studuisse,"— " To have well prayed is to have well studied ;" nor at the Frenchman's outburst, —

> " Nòus ne voyons rien
> Sur terre on dans les cieux,
> Si nous ne nous mettons pas à genoux,"—
> " We see nought
> On earth or in heaven,
> Unless we put ourselves upon our knees."

But enough to show that this connection is fully recognized between moral and intellectual.

Further, now, the kinship is not a distant one. MODERN EDUCATION IN EUROPE AND AMERICA IS THE CHILD OF THE BIBLE. This is the proposition which this paper is to prove and illustrate. The reader may be as much surprised as was the writer at the unanimity and amplitude of the evidence which shows that the Bible and school are parent and child.

Modern education is in question. The schools of Greece and Rome, and the schools of the Arabians, which shed such splendor of learning, need not engage our attention, because, *first*, they are utterly perished, leaving not a vestige behind ; and, *second*, because they are in no way the germ, or fountain, or even suggestion, of modern education ; and, *third*, because modern education did not copy their forms and methods. They lacked "elements of immortality." Modern education, commencing with Christianity, receiving consistency under Charlemagne, bids fair to last the lifetime of the race. This education is the child of the Bible.

The Chinese schools have been greatly the wonder of our scholars ; yet neither in method nor results can they be compared with ours. Moreover, — and this is the point now, — modern Western education has derived nothing from them ; nor is it likely to ingraft any of the peculiarities of Chinese method. On the contrary, Williams says,[1] " The defects of the tuition here briefly described, extent, means, purposes, and results, are very great. Such, too, must unavoidably be the case until new principles and new information are infused into it. Considering it in its best point of view, this system of education has effected all it can in enlarging the understanding, purifying the heart, and strengthening the minds, of the people ; but in none of these, nor in any of the essential points which a sound education aims at, has it accomplished half that is needed."

This is illustrated, not to quote to a tedious length, by the fact that " no other branches of study are pursued than the classics and histories, and practice in composing. No arithmetic, or any department of mathematics, nothing of the geography of their own or other countries, of natural philosophy, natural history, or scientific arts, nor study of other languages, are attended to." The schools are kept by private tutors. " There are no boarding-schools, nor any thing answering to infant-schools ; nor are public or charity schools established by government or by private benevolence for the education of the poor." There are no public female schools. " It is vain to expect that any change in the standing of females, or extent of their education, will take place, until influences from abroad are brought to bear upon them."

It will be sufficiently evident that not only does modern Western education owe nothing to China, but that China is one day to receive quickening influences from the education born of the Bible.

The assertion that modern education is the child of the Bible is explained thus : It is not meant that unusual activity in the reading of God's word was always the occasion of schools. Rather this is meant : *Education received its impulses from pious men, men founded and grounded on the Bible,* often, though not always, at periods of marked religious interest. Further : lest question should arise to obscure this conclusion, the piety of these men was *scriptural* rather than *ecclesiastical;* since these

---

[1] Middle Kingdom, i. 434, 427, 431.

men were as numerous in Protestant as in Papal churches, in
Dissenting as in Established churches. And, furthermore, periods when the Bible has come into unusual prominence have
been periods of revival of learning. Furthermore, on the other
side, men who have not been under the influence of Scripture
have not been prominent in modern education; nor, with very
few exceptions, have they followed the spirit of modern education in building institutions of learning.

" After the introduction of Christianity, and its accession to
power,[1] the duty of the authorities to educate the young was
speedily recognized by the bishops and clergy. The object of
this education was, of course, their training in the doctrines
of Christianity; but it was the recognition of the duty of giving
instruction to the masses. In 800 a synod at Mentz ordered,
that, in the parochial churches, priests should have schools in
the towns and villages; 'that the little children of the faithful
should learn letters from them. Let them receive no remuneration from the schools.' " The Roman Government organized
institutions of learning. Guizot says, " Roman Gaul was covered
with large schools. The principal were those of Treves, Bor-
deaux, Autun, Toulouse, Poitiers, Lyons, Narbonne, Arles,
Marseilles, Vienne, Besançon, &c. Some were very ancient:
those of Marseilles and Autun, for example, date from the first
century.[2] " All things in the fifth century attest the decay of the
civil schools."[3] " The intellectual aspect of Christian society
was very different."[4] " The foundation of the greater portion
of the large monasteries of the southern provinces belongs to
the first half of the fifth century."[5] Matthew Arnold says,
" Then came the invasion of barbarians, and the break-up of
the old order of things. For some time, schooling ceased to be
a concern of lay society: it went on in the shelter of the
Church, and for the benefit of the ecclesiastical body. The
great schools, from the fourth century to the twelfth, are the
monastery schools. There were four hundred monks studying

---

[1] American Encyclopædia.
[2] Civilization in France, i 349.
[3] Ibid., 52.   [4] Ibid., 353.   [5] Ibid., 354.

at St. Medard in the sixth century." Here is the transition from Roman education and the incoming of Christian education. Roman education had one method, — that of self-appointed teachers, drawing to their place of instruction such as came voluntarily, such as were able to pay. This method is practically obsolete, except in the case of the teachers of elocution, music, painting, gymnastics, penmanship, or some other specialty. The modern educational institutions, all of them under some form of Christian civilization still extant, are the monastic school, the parochial school, the university, the endowed public school, and the free school. *Every one of these* owes its *origin*, and, almost without exception, its *separate establishments*, to men under the influence of the Scriptures. This is evident, of course, in regard to all those vast schools which once held principal sway, — the parochial and monastic schools. The others — the university, the endowed school, the free school — require verification as to their origin.

First, the UNIVERSITY. Gladstone, in his " Inaugural," calls universities among the greater lights and glories of Christendom. "It is a fact," he says, "and, if so, it is a fact highly instructive and suggestive, that the university as such is a Christian institution. The Greeks, indeed, had the very largest ideas upon the training of men, and produced specimens of our kind with gifts that have never been surpassed. But the nature of man, such as they knew it, was scarcely at all developed ; nay, it was maimed in its supreme capacity, in its relation to God." "Such a conception as that of the university was surely the appropriate ally of Christianity." " There is a fit association and a noble and lofty harmony between the greatest gift of the Almighty to our race, on the one hand, and the subordinate but momentous ministries of those chief institutions of learning and education."

" The University of Paris," says Guizot, " was the first establishment of its kind in Europe." An " imperial circular," issued by Charlemagne, " doubtless suggested by the learned Alcuin," did not remain without effect : it resulted in the re-establishment of systematic studies in the episcopal cities and in the great monasteries. From this epoch date the majority of the schools, which soon afterward acquired such celebrity, and from which proceeded the most distinguished men of the following century. Alcuin was "the intellectual prime-minister" of Charlemagne. He had been the Archbishop of York, in England, in whose monastic school he had been instructed. Says Guizot, "Alcuin himself labored at a complete revisal of the sacred writings," and sent his work to Charlemagne as the most noble of gifts. He presided over a private school, the School of the Palace, from 787 to 796. This is believed to be the origin of the Paris University, which has been called "the first school of the Church." In the mediæval times it took on its present form, and assumed great importance. "The great Middle Age University," says Arnold, "was the University of Paris." It received the lofty titles, — "Fountain of Knowledge," "Tree of Life," "Candlestick of the House of the Lord."

Across the Channel, learning was revived by Alfred. Guizot informs us that the monasteries and schools of Ireland and England were flourishing; that of York in England especially, whence came Alcuin. But learning had declined, until, south of the Thames, Alfred could not find a priest who could read his prayers in English, or translate a letter from Latin. Six *Christian* men, bishops and other ecclésiastics, helped the pious king to fan the dying flame, one of whom is particularly described as "most learned in the Holy Scriptures." Uncertain tradition ascribes the first English university to Alfred. Of *Oxford*, John Rous, an antiquary of the fifteenth century, affirms that Alfred "built in this town three halls in the name of the Holy Trinity." This is disputed by one, who, however, adds, "Soon after Alfred, schools of learning appear to have been established in Oxford; but these were either of a private character, or were attached to the religious houses with which the town abounded. It is certain that Oxford was a place of study in the reign of Edward the Confessor."

Rapidly run the eye over the universities, observing their origination by men under the influence of the Bible.

"It is probable that *Cambridge* first became a seat of education in the seventh century, when, according to Bede, Siegbert, King of the East Angles, with the assistance of *Bishop Felix*, instituted in his kingdom a school for learning, in imitation of those which he had seen during his exile in France."

Durham was at first "an academical institution, in connection with the Cathedral Church."

London University's charter was "for the advancement of religion and morality, and the promotion of useful knowledge."

St. Andrew's University originated (1411) with Henry Wardlaw, *Bishop* of St. Andrew's; *Glasgow*, thus: "In the year 1450, Pope *Nicholas V.*, at the solicitation of William Turnbull, *Bishop* of Glasgow, issued a bull establishing a *studium generale*, or university for theology, the canon and civil law, the arts, and every other lawful faculty."

Aberdeen (1494) was established by bull of Pope *Alexander VI.*, on representation of James IV., "for teaching divinity, canon and civil law, medicine, and the liberal arts;" *Marischal*, by Earl Marischal. *Edinburgh* has this history: In 1579 "the magistrates, encouraged by the *ministers* and other public-spirited individuals in the city, commenced buildings. The chief promoter was James Lawson, the successor of Knox as minister of Edinburgh."

Dublin University (1592) was built by *Archbishop* Loftus on the grounds of a dissolved monastery.

Similar is the history of the universities of Germany and of Spain. So far, testimony is uniform that the originators of universities were men under Scripture influence.

We shall see, in further study, how education with the course of empire "westward took its way," and that not only the universities of the New World, but new educational institutions born on our soil, sprang from the brain of men inspired by the Bible.

Coming to this side of the great water, our history is instructive, and strikingly illustrative of the fact that modern education is the child of the Bible. One of the New-England fathers writes, "After God had carried us safe to New England, and we had builded our houses, provided necessaries for our liveli-

hood, reared convenient places for God's worship, and settled
the civil government, one of the next things we longed for and
looked after was to advance learning, and perpetuate it to
posterity, dreading to leave an illiterate ministry to the churches
when the present ministers shall be in the dust." In 1638,
only eighteen years after that one hundred and one landed
in winter snows at Plymouth, — when Boston contained some
twenty-five houses, and Massachusetts twenty-five towns, — Harvard College was founded. *Rev.* John Harvard was its foster-
parent, who bequeathed to it half his property. He was a
dissenting clergyman, "reverend," "godly," a "lover of learning."
Rev. Henry Dunster was "patron and first president;" *Rev.*
Charles Chauncey the second president. President Quincy generously acknowledges the work of our pious ancestry two hundred
and fifty years ago : —

"The Congregational clergy next demand our notice. To
them this institution is perhaps more indebted than to any other
class of men for early support, if not for existence. The power
which they possessed they exerted for the college with zeal and
affection. They promoted its interests by every instrumentality
of authority, and every legitimate form of influence at their
command. It was the constant topic of their sermons, and the
constant object of their prayers. They were active for it in
private, solicitous and urgent in public assemblies. Its founder
was a member of their body. Those of them who had wealth
contributed, according to their means, in money and books.
Everywhere they were its unceasing and unwearied advocates.
They identified its success with all the prospects and all the
hopes of religion in the province.

"Above all, we are probably indebted to the clergy for the
catholic and liberal spirit breathed into the first and into each
successive constitution, in every period its vital principle and
distinguishing characteristic, to which may be chiefly ascribed
its success and prosperity.

"Dec. 27, 1643, a college seal was adopted, having, as at
present, three open books on the field of an heraldic shield,
with the motto *Veritas* inscribed. The books were probably

intended to represent the Bible.   This was soon exchanged,
'though without known authority,' for ' In Christi gloriam,' and
' Christo et Ecclesiæ.' "

Yale College had an equally significant history.   In 1700 ten
of the principal *ministers* of the Colony met at New Haven, and
associated themselves as trustees to erect and govern a college.
They brought from their libraries forty volumes.   Rev. Mr.
Pierson was appointed rector.   Similar to this is the religious
origin of our other American colleges.   *Princeton* was founded
in 1746 by the Synod of New York, " for the purpose of supplying the Church with learned and able preachers of the Word."
Brown University was started by Baptists of Philadelphia
Association, at the instigation of *Rev.* Morgan Edwards, a
distinguished Welsh clergyman of Philadelphia.

Dartmouth " was originated (1769) in the warmest spirit, and
established in the most elevated principles of Christian piety."
It grew out of an Indian charity-school in Lebanon, Conn., instructed by *Rev.* Eleazer Wheelock, D.D.   *Rev.* Samson Occum
(the Indian who wrote the hymn, " Awaked by Sinai's awful
sound ") and *Rev.* N. Whittaker raised for it ten thousand
pounds in England.

Dickinson College (1783) is Methodist, and *Hampden-Sydney*
(1776) Presbyterian.   *North Carolina* had a minister for its first
professor.   *Williams* (1793) had *Rev.* Ebenezer Fitch for first
principal.   *Bowdoin* (1794) was started " at the petition of an
association of ministers and county-court session."   *Union*
(1795) " derived its name from the co-operation of several religious denominations in its organization."   "*Amherst*," says
Prof. W. S. Tyler, "grew out of a charity-school which was
established for the education of indigent young men for the
ministry and missionary work.   It was born of the prayers, and
baptized with the tears, of holy men.   It was one of the earliest
institutions which grew up under the influence of the foreign
missionary enterprise, called ' Missionary Colleges.' "   "*Western
Reserve College* was founded by domestic missionaries to furnish pastors for the infant churches on the Reserve.   *Illinois
College* originated in two independent movements, — Home Mis-

sionary operations in Illinois, and a Missionary Society at Yale. The site of *Wabash College* was dedicated to God in prayer by its founders kneeling upon the snow in the primeval forest. *Marietta* was founded mainly to meet demands for competent teachers, and ministers of the gospel. In fact, nearly all of those institutions which have lived and•prospered, and exerted a decided influence even in our literary and political history, were established by evangelical Christians, and have been taught, for the most part, by evangelical ministers." Prof. Tyler adds, " Institutions established by worldly men for mere worldly objects have not prospered. Infidelity has yet to make its first successful enterprise of this sort." To the same purport Dr. Edward N. Kirk says, " Infidelity can found colleges if it will ; but it rarely does, or in the world's history seldom if ever did. The experiment was tried in Virginia ; but the anti-Christian feature of the university has, on experience both of its inefficiency and the public aversion to it, been removed. An infidel judge remarked to President Pierce," adds Dr. Kirk, "'They made me a trustee of that college ; but I would not serve. I knew I should not attend faithfully to it ; and I do not know anybody but you ministers and Christians that will.' " And he adds further, " I believe it would be easy to bring this audience to tears by reciting what has been endured within ten years by the professors in Western colleges. Nothing has held them there but the love of Christ."

Such is the history of universities, which originated in the Christian mind, and which, almost without exception, were established and sustained by men under the inspiration of the Bible.

The history of GREAT ENDOWED SCHOOLS speaks exactly the same thing. The historian says, " To prevent the growth of Wickliffism, it had been made penal to put children to private teachers ; and the consequent excessive influx to only a few schools rendered, in 1477, grammar-learning so low, that several *clergymen* of London petitioned Parliament for leave to set up schools in their respective churches in order to check seminaries of illiterate men. Thus commenced grammar-schools, properly so called." The history of the great schools of England verifies our proposition. Let us enumerate. *Eton,* "founded by the most pious but most unfortunate of English monarchs," Henry VI. *Winchester,* by William of Wykeham, of whom Froissart writes, "There was a *priest* about the kynge of Eng-londe, called Syr William Wyoam, who was so great with the kynge, that all thynge were done by hym, and withoute hym was nothing done." *Harrow, Merchant Taylors' Charter House,* are due to the general spirit of education fanned by religion; *Rugby,* to Lawrence Sheriff, a "stanch Protestant."

Westminster came from the grammar-school of the Monastery of St. Peter. *St. Paul's* was founded by John Colet, *Dean* of St. Paul's, in the time of Henry VII. "Its creation was solely due to the desire of a great scholar and an enlightened Christian for the diffusion of pure doctrines in religion and learning."

To men and women acting under the same influence were due our American schools of the same character, as is seen in the origin of *Dummer, Phillips,* and *Exeter* Academies, and of *Ipswich, Mt. Holyoke, Wheaton, Wellesley, Abbott,* and *Bradford* Female Seminaries. The Western ladies' seminaries were founded by warm-hearted Christians. The very idea of female seminaries was conceived in the brain of a Christian minister, *Rev.* John Emerson of Byfield, preceptor of Mary Lyon. These seminaries, and others which we need not mention, were founded by men and women under Bible influence ; and the story of their origin is one of the most interesting pages in the history of Christian endeavor.

And is the COMMON SCHOOL, too, due to Christianity? It is one of the plainest facts of history, though it is not so well known, or distinctly remembered among the people, as such a remarkable fact ought to be. Imperfectly and sporadically, the *idea* of education of children at public expense appears a few times in antiquity. "In Sparta, under the system of Lycurgus, the State undertook the education of the children ; but the in-struction imparted was mainly physical, and did not reach the peasant classes." Plato, it is said, in one passage, expresses an idea of public education as we understand it. Nowhere, then, in antiquity, is public literary education found. "After the captivity, the Jews developed an excellent system of paro-chial schools in connection with the synagogues. In Rome, while private schools were numerous, the advantages accrued only to the patricians and such plebeians as possessed property." Germany, France, England, and the rest, had only universities, parochial, monastic, and endowed schools. A great impulse was given to school education by the Reformation. In 1524 Luther wrote his "Address to the Common Council of all the Large Cities of Germany in Behalf of Christian Schools." In 1528, with the aid of Melancthon, he drew up the Saxon School System. In 1560 John Knox urged the necessity of schools for the poor, to be sustained at the charge of the kirk.

Education was in like manner encouraged by Zwingle and Calvin. But this was not yet *common-school education.* It was reserved for that new people, who, drinking directly from Scripture wells, made "a church without a bishop and a state without a king," who had grave sense of the necessity of the intelligent understanding of the Bible and equally grave sense of the duties of the State, to originate the common school.

The American Encyclopædia says, "The free public school, the common school of our time, was of New-England origin ; but whether it was first established in Massachusetts or Con-necticut is a mooted question." Observable is the coinci-dence of the locality of the early common schools in the same States as the two universities, which were founded, as we have seen, by religious men. Indeed, Prof. Tyler says, "The whole history of education in our country shows that colleges and common schools form different and essential parts of one and the same great system." Pres. Kingsley says, "The source of the wide-spread and incalculable benefit of popular education in America may be traced, without danger of error, to a few of the leading Puritans. If the early Pilgrims, more particularly of Massachusetts and Connecticut, had not strug-gled and toiled for this great object, and if they had not been immediately succeeded by men who had imbibed a large portion of their spirit, the school system of New England would not now exist."

Before the year 1650 the Colony of Massachusetts Bay made provision by law for the support of schools at the public expense, for instruction in reading and writing, in every town containing fifty families ; and for the support of a grammar-school, to prepare young men for the university, in every town containing one hundred families.   The preamble of this school law shows how the Bible was the fountain of these schools: "It being one of the objects of Satan to keep men from the knowledge of the Scriptures, as in former times keeping them in unknown tongues ; . . . therefore, to the end that learning may not be buried in the graves of our forefathers in church and commonwealth, the Lord assisting our endeavors, it is ordered by this court that every township," &c.   Almost simultaneously, whether before or after, a similar system sprang up in Connecticut.

That the common-school system may be plainly seen not to be due to Anglo-Saxon ideas, or to the spirit of that age, but only to a free Bible in a free State and in free minds, this interesting fact is adduced.   In 1670, in answer to certain questions from England, the governor of Connecticut wrote, "One-fourth of the annual revenue is laid out in maintaining free schools." To the same question Gov. Berkeley of Virginia replied, "I thank God there are no free schools nor printing, and I hope we shall not have these hundred years."

We quote only one more authority, — Chancellor Kent: "The interests of education had engaged the attention of the New-England colonists from the earliest settlement of the country ; and the system of common and grammar schools, and of academical and collegiate instruction, was interwoven with the primitive views and institutions of the Puritans.   The word of God was at that time almost the sole object of their solicitude and studies.   We meet with the system of common schools in the earliest of the colonial records.   The system of free schools, sustained and enforced by law, has been attended with momentous results ; and it has communicated to the people of this State, and to every other part of New England in which the system has prevailed, the blessings of order and security to an extent never before surpassed in the annals of mankind."

Thus modern education was born of the Bible. Not only the monastic and the parochial schools, but the university, the endowed school, the common school, are the work of men under the influence and inspiration of the Bible. *Quod erat demonstrandum.*

And, now, does it remain for the school of this century, after the Bible has given birth to our education and nourished it, and given it new shapes for a thousand years, and it is potent and ample in its educational benefactions across a continent, and even to the fair isles of the Pacific, still virent, fruitful, and blossoming for more fruit, — does it remain for the school, which so proudly exhibits itself at the Centennial before the nations, to banish this benefactor by an ostracism of ingratitude ? Shall the College cut from its regnant place and from its conspicuous escutcheon the volume *Veritas?* Shall the proud child, the Common School, thrust its parent, the Bible, into the street? Majestic and plaintive as when they first came from the imperial Cæsar under the stab of the foster-son will the words be heard again, while *this Imperial Volume* suffers, but *will not die,* — "*Et tu quoque,* MI FILI?" — "And thou, too, MY SON ?"

FREE AMERICA BORN OF THE BIBLE.

THAT one of the Pilgrims, who on the memorable day of debarkation, in December, 1620, stood with Plymouth Rock beneath his feet, and with the Bible which he had brought up from "The Mayflower's" cabin in his arms, expressed three great things: *First*, the great continent beneath and before them, — the sea and the Old World left behind, — which was strong enough and rich enough to bear them up, and to become the homestead of a great nation; *second*, the English race, thoughtful and sturdy enough to become a wise and vigorous people; and, *third*, the English Bible, which contained the germs and principles of the civil and religious institutions which were to dominate on this continent.

When young Edward VI. of England was crowned, and the three swords were brought to him as token of his being king of three kingdoms, he said there was yet one wanting. The noblemen around him inquired what that was. He answered, "The Bible." "That book," said the young prince, "is the sword of the Spirit, and to be preferred before these swords. That ought in all right to govern us, who use them for the people's safety by God's appointment. Without that word we are nothing, we can do nothing, we have no power: from that alone we obtain all power and virtue, grace and salvation, and whatsoever we have of divine strength." "After some other similar expressions," adds the historian, "Edward commanded the sacred volume to be brought with reverence, and so carried before him."

158

There were fifty issues of the Bible in his short reign.

In Madagascar, in 1868, was seen a sight marvellous to those who reflect, that, within the lifetime of most of those present, her jagged rocks had been sprinkled, almost poured, with the blood of martyrs.   Ranavalona, — not the Cruel, but the Christian, — "preceded by a hundred ladies of rank, who walked before her palanquin, advanced across the plain, and ascended the richly-decorated platform.   There, surrounded by the high officers of her court and kingdom, — for it was her coronation-day, — she took her seat beneath the canopy, on the front of which were inscribed in shining letters the Malagasy words, 'Glory be to God;' on the other sides, 'Good-will among men,' 'On earth peace,' 'God shall be with us.'   On one hand of her Majesty stood a small table with the crown; on the other hand a table, where, at a preceding coronation, had stood an *idol*, but where now was seen the handsome *Bible* sent to her predecessor by the British and Foreign Bible Society."

If, looking at these countries, which had — at least the former — emerged so gradually from barbarism that some might evade allowing the transforming power of this book in their history, we thrill as at the sight of a deed nobly done at the public acknowledgment by these monarchs of the paramount influence of the Scriptures on their nations, how much more should we think the public acknowledgment of this book — inspired or uninspired — right and comely in America, whose corner-stone was a Bible!

If these two island monarchs, sundered by two continents and by more than two centuries, set the Bible in honorable position before them, before their people, *publicly on their coronation-day*, A FORTIORI should the Bible be set in some conspicuous place of honor by the State in the American Republic. For the child, for the youth, that public *place* where the State should honor the book of her life and institutions is a special desk in the *public school*.   Or will you thrill with a sense of the sublime fitness of things when these monarchs publicly own the secret of their greatness, yet look on as at a comely deed while that book — which, uninspired or inspired, is *transcendently* the secret of *our* greatness — is contemptuously swept from the pedestal where it stands in honor before American youth? We believe history, that Plymouth Rock had a Bible on it: we know that American life and liberty has the Bible in it.

The survey of modern education, from Charlemagne down to our time (Mother and Child, Bible and School), was necessarily exhaustive. To our readers conversant with American history, we need give only a brief presentation of a few out of many considerations to make the impression fresh and clear, that. FREE AMERICA OWES HER LIFE AND, HER INSTITUTIONS TO THE BIBLE.

We present first, not those considerations which naturally occur first, but those which have already received mention and illustration in these papers.

I. THE AMERICAN SABBATH, ESSENTIAL TO OUR FREE INSTITUTIONS, WAS DUE, IS DUE, TO THE BIBLE.

However others received the septenary day of rest, we derived it from the Bible. For its continued beneficent observance we are indebted to the invitation and command of the Bible, and the weekly ministrations from that book, which induce men to leave shop and home, and congregate in the place of worship. We are not claiming that the book is inspired: our argument, being throughout *on the ground of natural religion*, neither requires that nor permits that. The undeniable fact alone is averred, that our Sabbath is derived from the Bible, and that that Sabbath is essential to our national life.

We need not at length repeat the proof that there is a vital connection between free institutions and the Sabbath. Still we will recall our witnesses, lest we should have forgotten the weight of their words. Pres. Hopkins, in his discourse on "The Sabbath and Free Institutions," maintains these propositions: *First*, a religious observance of the Sabbath or the *religious* Sabbath would secure the permanence of free institutions ; *second*, without the Sabbath religiously observed, the permanence of free institutions cannot be secured." Says another, "He who has made the Sabbath for *man* has ordained the connection between the sacred day and that *manliness* which can

brook no bonds." One writes a report on the European Sabbath, and calls his report "The Holy Day of Freedom and the
Holiday of Despotism." A French writer says, "Why are the
French people incapable of sustaining free institutions? Because they have no Sabbath." Pierre Duval exclaims, after a
visit to America, and observation of our Sabbath, "I understand
why this people is a great people. I know why for a century it
has been free, — yea, the freest people which has been found.
'Woe to America,' says one, 'if it ever ceases to keep holy the
Lord's Day!' Yes, woe to America! and woe then to liberty!"

Webster said, "The Sabbath school, as an institution, is
priceless. It has done more to preserve our liberties than
grave statesmen and armed soldiers." "There is not," says an
eminent writer, "a single nation, possessed of a popular form of
government, which has not our theory of the Sabbath. Protestant Switzerland, England, Scotland, and America cover the
whole ground of popular freedom; and in all these this idea
of the Sabbath prevails with a distinctness about equal to the
degree of liberty. Nor do I think the result an accidental one."
We adduce now a new witness. Theodore Parker, who was not
given to eulogizing the Bible, pays this tribute to the Sabbath:
"Sunday, though enforced by superstition, has yet been the
education-day of New England, the national school-time for the
culture of man's highest powers: therein have the clergy been
our educators, and done a vast service, which mankind will
not soon forget." "But for that superstition, we might have
had the same anarchy, the same unbridled license, in the seventeenth century which we saw in the eighteenth." "How much
farther English atrocities would have gone than the French
did go, how long it would have taken mankind by their proper
motion to re-ascend from a fall so adverse and so low, I cannot
tell: I see what saved them from the plunge." "But without
that Sunday, and without that preaching, New England would
have been a quite different land, America another nation altogether, the world by no means so far advanced as now. New
England with her descendants have always been the superior
portion of America." "She is superior in intellect, in morals:

that is too plain for proof.   The prime cause of that superiority must be sought in the character of the fathers of New England; but a secondary and most powerful cause is to be found also in those two institutions, — Sunday and Preaching."   " The acorn is not more obviously the parent of the oak than those two institutions of New England the parent of such masculine virtues as distinguish her sons."   " Why is it that all great movements, from the American Revolution down to antislavery, have begun here?   Why is it that education societies, missionary societies, Bible societies, and all the movements for the advancement of mankind, begin here?   Why, 'tis no more an accident than the rising of the tide.   Once in a week they paused from all work; they thought of their God; they listened to the words of able men exhorting them to justice, piety, and a heavenly walk with God; they trembled at fear of hell; they rejoiced at hope of heaven."

To the Sabbath, therefore, to the Bible, free America, enlightened America, is due.   *Clark's Island*, the observance of the first *Pilgrim Sabbath* in America, is one spring which feeds our river of life as a nation.

II. AMERICAN EDUCATION, ESSENTIAL TO OUR FREE INSTITUTIONS, IS DUE TO THE BIBLE.

It is so common a remark as to be trite, — it has been in the mouths of patriotic orators for more than a hundred years, — that education is essential to the maintenance of free institutions. But the education which led our fathers hither, which our fathers set in their polity as living spring of good citizenship and statesmanship, was not only born of the Bible, but contained the Bible.

All modern education — we need not repeat the long and massive array of facts — is the child of the Bible.   The fathers of America were especially indebted to that education sprung from the Bible, in the two forms, the university and the endowed schools, and, we may add, the parochial schools.   " The university," says Gladstone, " as such, is a Christian institution." The endowed schools also owed their suggestion and establishment only to men nourished by the Bible.   These were the schools — with the parochial, also due to the Bible — which taught the Pilgrims to read the English Bible, and to compose the compact in the cabin of " The Mayflower." They established the same education here, born of the Bible, in the same forms, — the university and the endowed school. And here, on American soil, the religious origin of these institutions was, perhaps, even more marked than in the 'mother-country. Harvard was founded and fostered by religious men ; Yale was due to ten ministers ; Dartmouth grew out of an Indian charity-school ; Wabash College was " dedicated to God in prayer by its founders kneeling upon the snow in the primeval forest." Dr. Kirk says, " Infidelity can found colleges if it will ; but it rarely does, or, in the world's history, seldom if ever did." Besides establishing universities and schools on the model handed down to them, education, in the minds of these men, religious and free, took the third form, — that of public free schools. We recall as worthy of repetition what was said in a previous paper. Pres. Kingsley says, " The source of the wide-spread and incalculable benefit of popular education in America may be traced, without danger of error, to a few of the leading Puritans. If the early Pilgrims, more particularly of Massachusetts and Connecticut, had not struggled and toiled for this great object, and if they had not been immediately succeeded by men who had imbibed a large portion of their spirit, the school system of New England would not now exist." Chancellor Kent's words are also memorable : " The institutions of education had engaged the attention of the New-England colonists from the earliest settlement of the country ; and the system of common and grammar schools, and of academic and collegiate instruction, was interwoven with the primitive views and institutions of the Puritans. The word of God was at that time almost the sole object of their solicitude and studies. We meet with the system of common schools in the earliest of the colonial records. The system of free schools, sustained and enforced by law, has been attended with momentous results ; and it has communicated to the people of this State, and to every other part of New England in which the system has prevailed, the blessings of order and security to an extent never before surpassed in the annals of mankind."

But not only did the education established by the fathers, which has enlightened America, come from the Bible : they set the Bible in that system of education. In the Ordinance of 1787 they declared, " Religion, morality, and knowledge being necessary to good government and the happiness of mankind, schools and the means of education shall be forever encouraged." Fifty million acres have been set apart for education.

" In 1709 the town of Boston, on the report of a committee, voted, ' annually to appoint a certain number of gentlemen of liberal education, together with some of the reverend ministers of the town, to be inspectors of the schools ; ' ' and, at their visitation, one of the ministers, by turns, to pray with the schools, and entertain them with some instructions of piety especially adapted to their age and education.' " [1]

The system of education adopted by the *town* of Boston prescribed in the Latin School " The Greek Testament ; " " the Bible to be read once a day by the first and second classes in course, excepting such parts as the masters may deem it best to omit ; " " Beauties of the Bible ; " " that it be the indispensable duty of the several schoolmasters daily to commence the duties of their office by prayer, and reading a portion of the Sacred Scriptures, in the morning, and close the same in the evening with prayer."

Pres. James Walker says, " In this college (Harvard), still purporting to be dedicated to Christ and the Church, the Greek New Testament was for more than a century the only text-book in the language."

In this spirit the fathers set the Bible in the school ; and there, as their legacy, it continues at this day.

To her education, therefore to the Bible, free America is due. Passing now to fresh considerations : —

III. THE PILGRIMS AND PURITANS WERE MEN ENLIGHTENED AND INCITED BY THE BIBLE. We may acknowledge all the noble influences which have flowed from the other colonizations in America, — from New York, Pennsylvania, Maryland, Virginia, and the rest ; but no one can gainsay the fact that Plymouth

[1] Quincy's Boston.

Rock is the corner-stone of America. The institutions and principles, like the Thanksgiving, of New England, have passed beyond the narrow limits of a State, and are recognized as dominant in the whole land. The descendants of the Pilgrims, moving westward and southward, have carried and planted whatever institutions were their life and their pride. Dr. Christopher Cushing says,[1] "Bancroft, in his History, first published in 1837, testified, that, at that recent date, the Puritans of New England were 'the parents of one-third of the whole white population of the United States.'"[2] Now, the Pilgrims and the Puritans were men of the Bible. So much were they men of the Bible, that they even established their commonwealth — unwisely as we now think — upon it. As Dr. Ellis and Joel Parker show, they planted here what these writers call a "*biblical commonwealth.*" They quote Cotton's words to Lord Say and Sele: "When a commonwealth hath liberty to mould its own frame, I conceive the Scripture hath given full direction for the right ordering of the same." And Davenport, in his life of Cotton, writes, "Considering that these plantations had liberty to mould their civil order into that form which they should find to be best for themselves, and that here the churches and commonwealth are complanted together in holy covenant and fellowship with God in Jesus Christ, Mr. Cotton did, at the request of the General Court in the Bay, draw an abstract of the laws of judgment delivered from God by Moses to the commonwealth of Israel, — so far forth as they are moral, that is, of perpetual and universal equity among all nations, — wherein he advised that theocracie, i.e., God's government, might be established as the best form of government, wherein the people that choose rulers are God's people in covenant with him."

We see how completely the Bible and its ideas saturated the whole mind and heart of these men. But we are now considering the *men*, and their characters as men, rather than their institutions. The vital moral forces of the Bible had penetrated them as deeply as we might argue that they would from the hold

---

[1] Past Century of Congregationalism, 7. [2] i. 468.

the Bible ideas had gained upon them. Our greatest orators have spoken excellent words on the religious character of the Pilgrims, and its influence on the national character. Edward Everett, in his Plymouth oration, says, "Religious reformation was the original principle which kindled the zeal of our Pilgrim Fathers, as it has been so often acknowledged to be the main principle of the greatest movements of the modern world;" and he speaks of "the first emigration to New England, from which, under a kind Providence, has flowed, not only the immediate success of the undertaking, but the astonishing train of consequences auspicious to the cause of liberty, humanity, and truth." Webster, in his memorable oration at Plymouth in 1820, tells us, "The morning that beamed on the first night of their repose saw the Pilgrims already established in their country. There were political institutions, and civil liberty, and religious worship." "They were politic, intelligent, and religious men." "Who would wish for other emblazonry of his country's heraldry, or other ornaments of her genealogy, than to be able to say that her first existence was with intelligence, her first breath the aspirations of liberty, her first principle the truth of divine religion?" "Finally, let us not forget," continues he, in the massive sentences of his peroration, "the religious character of our origin. Our fathers were brought hither by their high veneration for the Christian religion. They journeyed by its light, and labored in its hope. They sought to incorporate its principles with the elements of their society, and to diffuse its influence through all their institutions, civil, political, or literary. Let us cherish these sentiments, and extend their influence still more widely, in the full conviction that that is the happiest society which partakes in the highest degree of the mild and peaceable spirit of Christianity."

To the Pilgrims, therefore to the Bible, free America is due. The Pilgrims made a free America: the Bible made the Pilgrims. "Banish the Bible from the public schools of America!" indignantly exclaimed Rufus Choate. "Never, so long as there is a piece of Plymouth Rock big enough to make a gun-flint!"

Monstrous would it be to prohibit in public schools the

story of the Pilgrims, of William Penn and George Calvert, since they are our nation's founders. Monstrous it is to interdict the Bible, since free America was born of the Bible.

The proofs accumulate.

IV. THE SEPARATION OF CHURCH AND STATE, WHICH IS ONE OF THE MARKED ADVANTAGES OF OUR POLITICAL SYSTEM, IS DUE TO THE BIBLE.

The Bible, indeed, contains the spectacle of a theocracy; but that, be it observed, properly understood, is not a state in which the priesthood controls the government, nor even in which the *Church* controls the government, but in which *God* controls it. In Israel, as a *general* truth, God did not raise the "judges," or presidents, from the sacerdotal order. The *mode* of Israel's theocracy implies, indeed, the natural freedom of the State, since the theocracy was always felt to be, not a universal thing, but the peculiarity of Israel. Whoever, therefore, is impressed with the idea *deepest* in Israel's government, must believe in the natural separation of the State, not only from the sacerdotal order, but even from the theocratical government of God. The theocracy was accepted by Israel at Sinai, when, by *plebiscite*, they chose their Deliverer as their King. "It is never to be forgotten," said Wines, "that although God, by what he wrought for the Israelites, had acquired all the right to be their Sovereign that any man could possibly have, he still neither claimed nor exercised the right in an arbitrary and despotic way. Moses, by his direction, permitted the people freely to choose whether they would accept Jehovah as their King, and obey the laws which he might give them. When they had formally assented to this, God was considered as their King, but not before." Wines dwells on this.

Now, in this *chosen* theocracy, there is not "Church and State" in the modern sense, but the contrary, — a recognition of the moral freedom of the State in general. The Bible, then, really implies the separation of Church and State. True, the Puritans did not see this; but, with an open Bible, they *would have come* to see it.

Parkinson says of the Puritans, "Even to have half acquired

the lesson was to be in advance of their times, and prepared them for a further development of their principles." [1]

Mitchell says, "The full history of toleration is yet to be written;" [2] and he refers to Lord Bacon's letter to Cecil, advising the toleration of the Irish Papists, and to a volume appearing before 1606, in which the argument of the "Tares" is used, and these words: "If Christ will have it thus, why do you blame my advice that a Christian king should do the same, rather than use the sword of force and violence upon the like occasions?" But, notwithstanding these and other sporadic utterances, such as William Blackstone's "I did not flee from the lord bishops to obey the lord brethren;" and notwithstanding Cotton's assertion, that others besides the *one* thought Church and State should be separate, — the honor must be conceded to that one, ROGER WILLIAMS, of having distinctly and broadly enunciated the doctrine of separation of Church and State, and of having incorporated that idea into a constitution, that of Rhode Island. That is now the American doctrine everywhere. To it is due much of the success of our political system. Gervinus, Uhden, and Bancroft in his noble tribute, ascribe this revolution to *Roger Williams.* But Roger Williams was a minister; and, further, he built his political doctrine on the Bible. "Christ Jesus," says he, "is the deepest politician that ever was; and yet he commands the toleration of anti-Christians." The parable of the "Tares" is a favorite argument with him. "It pleased not the Lord Jesus, in the first institution of his Church, to furnish himself with any such civil governments as unto whom he might commit the care of worship."

So America owes the separation of Church and State, her safety and her pride, to the Bible.

V. THE IDEAS OF DEMOCRACY AND REPUBLICAN LIBERTY IN AMERICA ARE DUE TO THE BIBLE.

Tocqueville must needs name his volume of thoughts on our country by the central idea of our institutions, "Democracy in America." "America," says he, "is the most democratic coun-

---

[1] State Churches, 245.   [2] Westminster Assembly Minutes.

try in the world." That democracy came from the Bible.
During centuries, the old English spirit, in a select part of her
people, was nourished, from Wycliffe down, by Bible-truths.
"When we speak," says Phelps, "of the sway of European and
American mind, we speak of the conquests of the Scriptures.
The elemental ideas of the Bible lie at the foundation of
the whole of it." "In English form the Bible stands at the
head of the streams of English conquests and of English and
American colonization and commerce." The Puritans, the
most assiduous readers of this book, imbibed to the greatest
degree the principles of liberty. Hume emphatically acknowledges the indebtedness of English liberty to these Bible-readers. "So absolute was the authority of the crown, that the
precious spark of liberty had been kindled by the Puritans
alone ; and it was to this sect that the English owe the freedom of their constitution." Hallam calls them the "deposita-
ries of the sacred fire." It is not difficult to see whence they
derived this principle. The internal management of the theocracy of Israel was essentially that of a commonwealth.
Wines has abundantly displayed this in "Hebrew Commonwealth." Religion always gives man the idea of his personal
value. Christ made his church a theocracy as regards himself,
a democracy as regards each other. "All ye are brethren,"
"Tell it to the Church," is the principle of democracy. King
James saw by intuition the drift of Puritan doctrines. To
Reynolds he said, "No bishop : why, then, no king." *Had
Christ's order in the Church been carried out for five centuries,
Europe would have been republican the other thirteen,* and have
avoided regal tyrannies, and wars due to royal caprice and am-
bition.

The New-England town-meeting was modelled after the New-
England church-meeting. Otis and Warren learned free speech
and the rights of legislative assemblies in the town-meeting and
the church-meeting. Phelps says, " History has learned to
recognize the founders of New England among the civilizing
powers of the world. This power is for the most part latent,
like the forces of Nature. It has been working now for two

centuries and more ; yet to-day it is going on with its creations, giving birth to states, fashioning institutions, breathing life into nations, with the same unconcern of its own majesty which belongs to gravitation." " *'Democracy is Christ's government,'* " he says, "was the theme of a pamphlet by a humble pastor of Massachusetts in 1687, which, nearly one hundred years later, on the eve of our Revolution, was republished as a political document becoming to the times." Jefferson, it is said, learned the democratic idea from observing the manner of proceeding in a little country church in Virginia.

To the democratic idea, therefore to the Bible, is due free America.

VI. THE ARDENT SPIRIT OF THE REVOLUTION, WHICH MADE US AN INDEPENDENT NATION, WAS DUE TO THE BIBLE. This is apparent to the thoughtful reader in perusing such a book as Magoon's " Orators of the Revolution." Otis's " Vindication of Boston " appeared in 1762. " Your opposition preceded ours," writes Jefferson. Otis was born on the shores of Massachusetts Bay, and was descended, on his mother's side, from those who came in " The Mayflower." Samuel Adams is called " the last of the Puritans," " a class of men to whom," says Everett, " the cause of civil and religious liberty on both sides of the Atlantic is mainly indebted for the great progress which it has made for the last two hundred years ; and, when the Declaration of Independence was signed, that dispensation might be considered as brought to a close. At a time when the new order of things was inducing laxity of manners, Samuel Adams clung with greater tenacity to the wholesome discipline of the fathers. His only relaxation from the business and cares of life was in the indulgence of a taste for sacred music, for which he was qualified by the possession of a most angelic voice, and a soul solemnly impressed with religious sentiments. Resistance to oppression was his vocation." " It is significant that he prepared himself for the ministry." " He must be regarded as the great leader of our Revolution." He made " the first public denial of the right of the British Parliament to tax the Colonies without their consent, the first denial of parliamentary supremacy, and the first public suggestion of a union on the part of the Colonies to protect themselves." Whatever credit is due to others, it is to be remembered that Gordon declared — truly, no doubt — that "Mr. Samuel Adams has long since said, in small confidential companies, 'This country shall be independent, and we will be satisfied with nothing short of it.'"

John Adams, too, was of Puritan descent, of whom Jefferson wrote, "The great pillar of support to the Declaration of Independence was John Adams. He was the colossus of that Congress."

"The meeting-house, the school-house, and the training-field," said he, "are the scenes where New-England men were formed."

Besides this, the *patriot preachers* of the Revolution were among the foremost leaders. Says Phillips, "In those days, Adams and Otis, advocates of the newest and extremest liberty, found their sturdiest allies in the pulpit. Our Revolution was so much a crusade, that the Church led the van." The Old South Church, loved by patriots, hated and feared by Great Britain, honored by Edmund Burke, was one of the great nurseries of the Revolution. "Here," says the eloquent Phillips, "the fit successors of Knox and Hugh Peters consecrated the pulpits with the defence of that doctrine of the freedom and sacredness of man which the State borrowed so directly from the Christian Church." "Here Samuel Adams, the ablest and ripest statesman God gave to the epoch, forecast those measures which welded thirteen colonies into one thunderbolt, and launched it at George the Third." "The State House," says Dr Manning, "and this sanctuary, have been called the Moses and Aaron of New-England freemen."

"Perhaps no livelier illustration of this common conviction of the vital connection which was felt at that time to exist between politics and religion could be furnished than is given in an incident which happened just before June 14, 1774. Dr. Byles succeeded in creating a real panic among the British troops by reporting, that, on June 14, forty thousand men would rise up in opposition to them, with the clergy at their head ; the fact being, that that day had been appointed as a day of fasting throughout the province. It was wisdom, as well as wit." "In that day, in this province, it meant in all literalness an army of twoscore thousand men headed by their clergy, and animated by the dangerous resolution to defend their liberties."[1]

"That great word, of independence," says Everett, "which, if first uttered in 1776, was most auspiciously anticipated in 1620, means much more than a mere absence of foreign jurisdiction. I could almost say, that, if it rested there, it would scarcely be worth asserting. In every noble, in every true acceptation, it implies not only an American government, but an American character, an American feeling."

The evidence will warrant us in saying with something of positiveness, that,

VII. THE UNION OF THESE STATES IS DUE TO THE BIBLE. We are not prepared to say how far the early colonists had forecast the future of the continent ; though we do not forget in 1643 *the United Colonies of New England*, of which one says, "That was the sapling, the United States are the tree ;" nor how far they had forecast the future of the continent, and discerned by what vinculum the Colonies would eventually be bound. The necessities of common defence and common weal, probably, rather than any ideal of confederation, led them to their first unions. Yet these Bible-readers had in the Book the very model of our government, as has been beautifully described,[2] in the twelve united — not confederate, but united — tribes of Israel. "The God of our fathers has divided us, according to his own primeval idea of beauty and glory, as manifested in his own Israel, into states." "Pleiades among the nations, land of commonwealths !" That ideal was in the mind of New England, latent, if not produced, waiting only for events to bring it out into distinct consciousness.

"On a Sabbath morning, — the 8th of June, 1766," — says Prof. Phelps, "when the old charter of Massachusetts was in

---

[1] Mather Byles to Thomas Starr King : Rev. George L. Chaney.
[2] N. Adams, D.D. : Our Family of States.

peril, Jonathan Mayhew, pastor of the West Church in Boston, hallowed his last day of health in that city by writing to James Otis, 'You have heard of the communion of churches. While I was thinking of this in my bed, the great use and importance of a communion of colonies appeared to me in a strong light, which led me immediately to set down these hints to transmit to you.' That was the germ," says Phelps, "from which sprang the union of these States."

This idea thus cast by this Boston pastor into patriot minds did not die. In an emergency of the Colony, six years later, Nov. 2, 1772, on motion of Samuel Adams, a committee of correspondence was chosen "to state the rights of the colonists, as men, as Christians, as subjects." This committee was instructed to correspond with all the Colonies on the subject of their rights. " Out of this original committee of correspondence," says Magoon, "grew the union of the Colonies and the Congress of the United States." If it be true, then, as Tocqueville said, that "the maintenance of the existing institutions of the several States depends in part upon the maintenance of the Union itself;" and as Webster said in his reply to Hayne, that " to that Union we owe whatever makes us prosperous at home and respectable abroad;" and if that Union is due to the thought of a Christian pastor meditating the analogy of the communion of churches with the possible union of the colonies, and to the energy of a Christian statesman,—free America, in its present united and prosperous condition, is due to the Bible.

VIII. NOT THE ORIGINAL CORNER-STONE ALONE, — THE EARLY COLONIES, — BUT AS WELL THE LINE OF NEW STATES FROM THE ALLEGHANIES TO THE PACIFIC, THE LONG COLONNADE OF MASSIVE AND BEAUTIFUL PILLARS ON WHICH THE ARCHITRAVE OF THE NATIONAL TEMPLE REPOSES, HAD THEIR ORIGIN AND STRENGTH FROM THE BIBLE.

De Tocqueville's observation shows that this fact struck his open and discerning mind, — that the Atlantic States were making the new States to the westward. " I have known of societies," he observes, "formed by the Americans, to send out missionaries of the gospel into the North-western States to found schools and churches there, lest religion should be suffered to die away in those remote settlements, and the rising States be less fitted to enjoy free institutions than the people from whom they came." " Thus religious zeal is perpetually warmed in the United States by the fires of patriotism." " They will tell you that all the American republics are collectively involved with each other : if the republics of the West were to fall into anarchy, or to be mastered by a despot, the republican institutions which now flourish upon the shores of the Atlantic Ocean would be in great peril. It is, therefore, our interest that the new States should be religious in order to permit us to remain free."

Tocqueville here is only discerning what had early been the policy of the new nation, — to quarry the ever-lengthening line of columns from the same granite quarries from which the corner-stone had been taken.

Such emigrations, indeed, from the East, as were prompted by no special religious purpose, carried with them religious institutions. The first emigration to the North-west Territory was, we believe, that called the Marietta Colony, led by Gen. Putnam, which, in 1788, sailed down the Ohio in a vessel which they had built, and significantly named " The Mayflower," and landed on the Muskingum. River. They were " principally descendants of the Puritan fathers." " They retained a portion of the good old customs and steady habits of their Pilgrim ancestors, and also of their veneration for the institutions of religion, literature, and morality. Hence it was, that, as soon as they had provided for shelter for themselves and their families, they directed their attention to the erection of a church. A school was also organized at the same time. These were the first institutions of the kind got up within the North-west Territory." [1] This was New England transplanted. Rev. Marcus Whitman saved Oregon to the United States. But direct efforts on a large scale were made to plant religion and education in the West and South. What else mean these time-honored names, — " Home Missionary Society," " Society for

---

[1] Burnet: Early Settlement of North-west Territory.

Collegiate Education," "American Missionary Association"?
Great men have not undervalued that great empire growing up
beyond the Mississippi. In 1835 Lyman Beecher made his
"Plea for the West," of which it is said significantly, "It was
delivered in several of the Atlantic cities." "The West," said
he, "is a young empire of mind and power and wealth and free
institutions, rushing up to a giant with a rapidity and a power
never before witnessed below the sun ; and, if she carries with
her the elements of her preservation, the experiment will be
glorious, the joy of the nation, the joy of the whole earth, as
she rises in the majesty of her intelligence and benevolence
and enterprise for the emancipation of the world."

A Christian layman, in 1842, wrote, "I feel a strong persuasion that this country (the West) some time hereafter will be the
main support, reliance, and life of our government, or it will be
its poison, destruction, and death. If knowledge, virtue, justice,
temperance, righteousness, and all sound moral and religious
principles, abound and increase with the increase of the country,
it will, almost beyond the possibility of a doubt, permanently
strengthen, support, enrich, and ennoble our government, promote the prosperity and happiness of the whole people, and diffuse blessings over our whole country and the world ; but, if this
is not the case, . . . then this great country will become a curse
instead of a blessing."

This apprehension, this hope, have excited commensurate
efforts. "There have been three great efforts made to supply
the whole population of the United States with Bibles, which
were inaugurated in 1829, 1856, 1866," in the last of which
nearly five and one-half millions of families were visited. Malt-
by, in 1825, arguing for a National Home Missionary Society,
says, "A system aiming not at itinerant missionaries *alone*, but
at planting in every little community that is rising up men of
learning and influence to impress their own character on those
communities, — a system, in short, which shall gather up the
resources of philanthropy, patriotism, and Christian sympathy,
throughout our country, into one vast reservoir, from which a
stream shall flow to Georgia, to Louisiana, to Mississippi, and to

Maine." This was a mighty plan. In 1873 six million five hundred thousand dollars had been disbursed in the West.

Bushnell said, in remarking the effects of these efforts, even in 1847, "It was religion, dispensed by missionary societies, which finally turned the crises of Vermont, Western New York, and Eastern Ohio." "A society now hovering over Michigan, Indiana, Illinois, Wisconsin, Iowa, and other regions beyond." From that great city of the West, Chicago, twenty-four years later, Bartlett points out the whitening harvest of these efforts: "Why should I cite De Tocqueville to show that her principles 'have involved the whole confederacy,' or 'The Evening Post' to prove that the descendants of those 'forefathers are clearly the dominant power in the United States'? Why tell again the story of those who planted the church, the school, and the college in Ohio, Illinois, Wisconsin, Iowa, Minnesota, and the Pacific slope? How trace the great silent forces carried West by Theron Baldwin and his noble comrades forty years ago? Why repeat the tale of the Andover Band in Iowa? Why tell of the Dartmouth graduates who preached the gospel first in Buffalo, Marietta, and Western Reserve? of the thirty Yale-Seminary ministers in Ohio, and the forty in Illinois? This society has planted more than five-sixths of the Presbyterian and Congregational churches in the great Western States, which sent one-fourth of their male population to the war." "The Home Missionary Society has become an eminent historical power; a plastic organic force in the genesis of new empires; the most effective factors of Christian civilization, order, and life, in new States of imperial vastness and aspirations which have sprung up along the march of our nation from ocean to ocean."

Of course we fail in any brief space to speak fittingly of the great movements which have carried westward and southward civilization, religion, education. The Presbyterian, the Moravian, and the Episcopalian have had their share in the work. No one can fail to observe the immense influence of Methodism in forming the character of the South and West. "Methodism, with its 'lay preaching' and its 'itineracy,' could alone afford the ministrations of religion to the overflowing population : it was to lay the moral foundations of many of the great States of the West." [1] Baird writes, "We recognize in the Methodist economy, as well as in the zeal, the devoted piety, and the efficiency of its ministry, one of the most powerful elements in the religious prosperity of the United States, as well as one of the firmest pillars of their civil and political institutions." [2] "The historian of the republic says that it has 'welcomed the members of Wesley's society as the pioneers of religion ;' that 'the breath of life has wafted their messages to the masses of the people, encouraged them to collect the white and the negro, slave and master, in the greenwood, for counsel on divine love, and the full assurance of grace ; and carried their consolation and songs and prayers to the farthest cabins in the wilderness.'" [3]

In our day, it is still *men of the Bible*, as represented in such societies as the American Missionary Association (incorporated 1849), which have taken upon them the task of moulding three millions and a half of freed slaves into Christian citizens, and to exercise like religious influence upon the thousands of strangers from the land of Confucius and upon the tribes of the red men.   It was Gen. O. O. Howard, "the Christian man, the indefatigable worker, and the impartial friend of white and black," who was chosen chief commissioner of the Freedmen's Bureau (1865).

The West, religious and free, is essential to free America : therefore free America is due to the Bible.

The final consideration which we adduce is, that,

IX. THE GREAT RELIGIOUS AND MORAL MOVEMENTS IN AMERICA, BORN OF THE BIBLE, HAVE BEEN THE CONSERVING FORCE IN THE AMERICAN NATION.   They have been what salt and motion are to the sea, — its preservators.   This is a theme little pondered ; but these great movements, with all their faults, are worthy not only of respectful study by the statesman, but also of his frank acknowledgment.   Who shall estimate the in-

---

[1] Stevens : History American Methodism, 18.
[2] Religion in America.   [3] Bancroft, 7, 261.

fluence upon America of about twenty-five of her clergy? We do not speak of their spiritual, but their moral work, — renovations of individuals and communities, which are matters, not of ecclesiastical computation, but of common observation. Benjamin Franklin was led to dedicate himself " to a perpetual effort to do good in the world " by reading Cotton Mather's " Answering the Great End of Life." Many a New-England man learned his antislavery doctrines at the feet of Dr. Channing, who wrote as early as 1835 against slavery, and in 1837 headed the petition for the use of Faneuil Hall for that stormy meeting where Wendell Phillips commenced his career of agitation. Jonathan Edwards, Dr. Dwight, Emmons, Nettleton, Finney, Edward Payson, Lyman Beecher, Bushnell, Wayland, Channing, many eminent presidents of colleges and seminaries, not to speak of the eminent living, — men like these are essential to America as we have it. They were charged with vital and saving forces. They awakened and formed, at every period of our history, the young men who have been our statesmen and educators. Dr. Dwight was a bulwark against the spirit of the French *illuminati*, which might have given us a French revolution. Lyman Beecher's "Six Sermons on Intemperance" were the unsealing of the fountain of American temperance. To Finney and Oberlin we owe a tidal wave of antislavery influence. Some of these men understood the relation of great religious movements to the future of their country. Finney speaks in 1831 of the conversion of a hundred thousand, and of larger numbers since, and makes us aware how much that number of morally-renewed men can affect a nation. And, when the simplicity of our ancestors had passed away, could any thing have resisted corruption, and kept us from moral decay and destruction, but these great tides of holy influence which have come with the preaching of the Bible? " In 1801 there was one professed Christian for ten inhabitants, in 1834 one for seven, in 1843 one for five and a half, in 1850 one for four and a half, in 1860 one for four and a quarter." " Communicants have increased more than fourteen-fold." " Church-membership has increased two and one-half times

faster than the population."[1] Now, if, for " salt without savor,"
you reckon, even unreasonably, as, for instance, the extreme proportion of one-half, still who can estimate the influence of one
renewed man in every eight ? — five million men, women, and
children, who profess to owe the commencement and sustaining
of their moral life to the Bible.   Is it too much to suppose that
these five million people, — to reckon them so few, — morally
renewed, may have been, must have been, in the various crises
of our history, sails, ballast, rudder, which have kept our nation and the " Ship of State " from wreck ?   *Yet these five million profess that they were morally renewed by the Bible.*

Who shall estimate the vitalizing and conserving influence
upon American life and character of the work of Dwight L.
Moody, who has not only stirred up thousands to a renewed
life, but who has so put before our great cities — Chicago,
Boston, Philadelphia, New York — the thought of honest, manly
living and dealing, that business-men remark, as one said to
me, " In Boston, a pound is sixteen ounces nearly everywhere
to-day."

"There never was an age, and never a city or state," says
Hedge, "in which moral corruption was not too rife.   In such
as survive the ever-threatening destruction and death, it is the
more prevailing virtue of the few which overcomes the abounding vice of the many, and rights at last the sinking world.   In
every age, those 'ten righteous' have been the saviors of their
time.   They have served it with their excellent works and the
more excellent beauty of their lives.   Without ostensibly com-
bining for that end, with no visible conspiracy, without art or
device, or shrewd organization, or policy, or plot, by being
what they are, and living what they are from the heart of faith,
by walking uprightly, doing justice, and loving mercy, in their
several spheres, with the still conservatism and counter-attrac-
tions of miraculous goodness, they have kept the world from
going to pieces with the wear and tear and centrifugal strain of
disintegrating vice.   These 'ten righteous' are the secret and
immortal cabal which unconsciously plots the preservation of

---

[1] Rev. Daniel Dorchester, D.D.

the State, as selfishness, and low chicanery, and political intrigue, are forever plotting its destruction." [1]

These five million men — to call them so few — profess that they were morally renewed by the Bible ; to which we must add the devout and noble Catholics and Jews throughout the land who drink the same living waters.

As the legend is, that in Germany there was an estate on which every rock, being split, and every tree, being cut, showed the heraldic device of the owner, so America, in every township, in all her institutions, bears the imprinted device of the Bible.

More senseless than the French commune, which pulled the bronze Napoleon from the Vendôme column, wreathed with the story and the glory of French victories, is the spirit of to-day, the American commune, which would hurl from its place, where set by the State, "full high advanced" before the eyes of youth, — from the desk in the public school, — the Bible, golden, glorious, on the summit of the column which is wreathed from pediment to capital with the achievements of this book, the story of all that is great and good in American history.

[1] Primeval World, pp. 261, 262.

THE BIBLE IN PUBLIC SCHOOLS, AND THE RELIGIONISTS.

How the sons of the Pilgrims, the descendants of the settlers at Jamestown, and, in general, those of English ancestry in our country, regard the Bible in the public school, is apparent. Exotic faiths have appeared since the days of the fathers. Rare plants or weeds, whichever they be, they have right to equal place in our free soil with the primitive American religion, whose root is the open, the entire Bible. Though these religionists are new-comers, they are not, legally and constitutionally, interlopers.

And, at least when they come to have considerable numbers, their voice is equally potent with that of original Americans in forming the State and its institutions. The State, however tenacious of her original policy, is to change it upon a fair representation of a sufficient number, and especially upon serious and well-grounded objection that the sacred rights of conscience are invaded. But the State would be unwise to depart from an original sound policy on the mere clamor of invasion of conscience, when a more penetrating and comprehensive study of the situation would discern no such invasion of conscience, but would discover, that, by fair explanations, her policy would seem to contravene no man's conscience, but, on various grounds, would appear a policy to be judiciously yet firmly held to. This, to the writer, is the present policy of the State in retaining the Bible in its place in the school.

This paper will consider the *view of the Pantheist, the Hebrew, the Freethinker, and the Romanist, on the Bible and the School.* We shall find ourselves coming to the view that " the recognition of God by the Bible in public schools," rightly understood, infringes no right of conscience, cannot give just offence to any, while it still remains the high and solemn duty of the State to itself.

THE PANTHEIST

has not, I believe, felt moved to declare himself directly upon the subject. From the utterances of these seers, we presume that no objection would be made by them, except, perhaps, an objection to the idea of limiting worship and divine thought to book and time and place. This could not be a serious objection. The sayings of these men make us feel, the rather, that, as God is all and in all, the devout soul would appropriately enter into study by some act of devotion.

Three leading Pantheists have uttered themselves in what may bear on this subject, — one German, a second English, the third American, — Goethe, Carlyle, Emerson.

Goethe, in "Wilhelm Meister's Travels,"[1] has stirred in every reader delightful and suggestive thoughts in describing the "Great Institution" of youthful education. Every one is as much struck as was Wilhelm by the "Three Reverences : " —

" The youngest laid their arms crosswise over their breasts, and looked cheerfully up to the sky; those of middle size held their hands on their backs, and looked smiling on the ground ; the eldest stood with a frank and spirited air, their arms stretched down. They turned their heads to the right, and formed themselves into a line ; whereas the others kept separate, each where he chanced to be."

Wilhelm asked explanation. "One thing there is on which all depends for making man in every point a man," — " Reverence 1 " " We inculcate a threefold reverence, which, when commingled and formed into one whole, attains its highest force and effect. The first is reverence for what is above us.

[1] Chapter x.

That posture, — the arms crossed over the breast, the look turned toward heaven, — that is what we have enjoined on young children, requiring from them thereby a testimony that there is a God above, who images and reveals himself in parents, teachers, superiors." Wilhelm in one field saw some children who did not perform the reverence, but kept at work. He asked what it meant. "It is full of meaning; for it is the highest punishment which we inflict on our pupils: they are declared unworthy to show reverence, and obliged to exhibit themselves as rude and uncultivated natures." It can hardly be doubted that Goethe would not object to an act of reverence in opening the public school. He would be more apt to be of the mind of Charles Lamb: "Why have we no 'grace' for books, those spiritual repasts, — a grace before Milton, a grace before Shakspeare, a devotional exercise proper to be said before reading 'The Fairy Queen'?" What he thinks of the Scriptures, Wilhelm tells us, in traversing the first of the three great departments. "One great advantage" of the Hebrew nation "is its excellent collection of sacred books. These stand so happily combined together, that, even out of the most diverse elements, the feeling of a whole still rises before us. They are complete enough to satisfy, fragmentary enough to excite, barbarous enough to arouse, tender enough to appease; and for how many other contradicting merits might not these books, might not this one book, be praised!"

One cannot believe that Goethe would have any hesitation, if a boy at the school-form, to hear this book read.

Carlyle speaks no otherwise. Discoursing on Jesuitism, he exclaims, "The Hebrew Bible, is it not before all things *true* as no other book ever was or will be?" "Every nation, I suppose, was made by God, and every man too: only there are some nations, like some men, who know it, and some who do not. The great nations are they that know it well: the small and contemptible, both of men and nations, are they that either have never known it, or soon forgotten it, and never laid it to heart. Of these comes nothing. The measure of a nation's greatness, of its worth under this sky to God and to man, is not the quantity of cotton it can spin, the quantity of bullion it has realized, but the quantity of heroisms it has achieved, of noble pieties and valiant wisdoms that were in it, that are still in it. Beyond doubt, the Almighty Maker made the English too, and has been and is miraculously present here. The more is the pity for us if our eyes have grown owlish, and cannot see this fact of facts when it is before us! Once it was known that the Highest did of a surety dwell in this nation, divinely avenging, and divinely saving and rewarding; leading, by steep and flaming paths, by heroisms, pieties, and noble acts and thoughts, this nation heavenward, if it would dare."

"The early nations of the world — all nations, so long as they continued simple and in earnest — knew, without teaching, that their history was an epic and Bible, the clouded, struggling image of a God's presence, the action of heroes and inspired." Carlyle, evidently, would not banish the "*truest book*" from its place of inspiring the future citizens and statesmen of England.

The American Pantheist speaks thus: "The religious sentiment is divine and deifying. It is the beatitude of man. It makes him illimitable." "The expressions of this sentiment affect us more than all other compositions. The sentences of the oldest time, which ejaculate this piety, are still fresh and fragrant. This thought dwelled always deepest in the minds of men in the devout and contemplative East, not alone in Palestine, where it reached its purest expression." "Europe has always owed to Oriental genius its divine impulses. What these holy bards said all sane men found agreeable and true. And the unique impression of Jesus upon mankind, whose name is not so much written as ploughed into the history of this world, is proof of virtue of this infusion." "That Supreme Beauty ravished the souls of those Eastern men, and chiefly of those Hebrews." "The Hebrew and Greek Scriptures contain immortal sentences that have been bread of life to millions."

We cannot imagine, after these unanimous utterances, that the Pantheists would thrust out the Bible from the place of culture and preparation for citizenship.

THE HEBREW

varies in his view of the Bible in the schools, according to the manner in which the Bible is to be read. The writer has lately had an interesting conversation with an intelligent lady, daughter of a rabbi whose name is well known in the United States. While she does not place a high value on the devotional exercise as now conducted — and who can? — she does not object to the reading of the Bible in the schools. She objects to the *teaching* of the doctrines of the New Testament, but not to the reading of it, without note or comment, as a good and moral book. Jesus she esteems as a great and good man; to her mind, in some respects, an enthusiast, but not an impostor : but in his words, and in the Lord's Prayer, she finds nothing original, no advance upon the Hebrew Scriptures. She would, if a teacher, and if left to herself, read entirely from the Old Testament; but, if reading from the New Testament were in the regulations, she would not hesitate to read, as from a good book ; nor would she fail in having the Lord's Prayer recited, if prescribed. From her standpoint, her view is simple and consistent ; and it must, one would think, be the view of every fair-minded Jew.

Still it is well known, that, in the Cincinnati discussion, some, though not all, of the leading Jews advocated the exclusion of the Bible, yet not bitterly like some religionists. This lady believed *they* did so on the ground that the *doctrines* of the New Testament were also *taught.*

In this " The Jewish Times " agrees. " That citizens of the Hebrew faith object to the reading of the New Testament, and prayers and hymns recognizing the divinity of Christ, requires no illustration." " Whether a conscientious Israelite can ever consent to allow his children to listen to the creed and dogmas evolved from the reading of the New Testament, or to specific Christian prayers and hymns, may be safely left to the decision of impartial and unprejudiced hearers."

And of course there can be no doubt what " impartial and unprejudiced men " would say; namely, that the teaching of *personal religion* is not the office of public education; nor does the objection lie against the simple reading, without note or comment, of the Scriptures, Old and New.

The only objection, then, which a Jew would consistently make, would be that of an extreme Jew, if such there now are, who, first, regards Jesus as an impostor, and so saturated with the element of inveracity; and, second, who believes that the New Testament teaches any immorality. We do not know of any Jew who censures the New Testament as immoral; and to "put ourselves in his place" by comparison of our own feeling in the supposed case of the reading in school with the Bible of moral parts of Mohammed's book, the Koran, we see no reason for conscientious scruples on the part of any Jew against hearing the New Testament read. But we are relieved on this point by the Hebrew himself:[1] "It is not the ethics of the New Testament to which we object; for what else are they but the echo or the very copy of our own Bible? Moreover, we hold that a moral precept or maxim is good, whether contained in the New Testament, the Koran, or Zend Avesta, whether uttered by Epictetus or Seneca, provided it does not militate against our own biblical standard."

To a Scripture service from both Old and New Testament, properly conducted, as we shall hereafter describe it, the Jew could therefore have no conscientious or decided objection; while if conducted aright, and, as it ought to be, unsectarianly, his religious nature would approve it.

How should a Jew be ashamed of *the most illustrious Israelite,* — the Rabbi, who with his disciples, also Israelites, has given more truth to the world than Plato; who broke the pericarp, and scattered the seeds of Israel's oracles over the earth; whose followers have translated Moses and the Psalms into a hundred and fifty languages, and taught monotheism to the Greenlander and the Pacific-Islander?

THE FREETHINKER

has bitter objections against the reading of the Bible in the public schools; but, set in sunlight, they evaporate like dew.

---

[1] Jewish Times, Jan. 28, 1870.

The Freethinker entertains one of two notions, — either there is no God, or there is no Word of God. This second Freethinker sometimes says, further, that the so-called Word of God contains not even a worthy conception of God and his righteousness.

First, the Freethinker who is an Atheist, and believing in no God, of course believes not in providence, prayer, scripture, or the nation's responsibility. Such men, happily rare, I say it deliberately, are to be deemed *monstrosities* of human nature ; nor can the State desist from her duty in bringing up her nursling children in recognition of the providence of God because a *monstrosity* does not believe in a God. "Whilst I was in America," says Tocqueville, "a witness who happened to be called at the sessions of the county of Chester, state of New York, declared he did not believe in the existence of God, or in the immortality of the soul. The judge refused to admit his evidence, on the ground that the witness had destroyed beforehand all the confidence of the court in what he was about to say."

The other Freethinker objects to the Bible, because, though he believes in God, he believes in no Word of God. But this need not make any scruple in his mind, if the service is con-ducted aright, and as we shall hereafter describe it ; for the view we are all along taking goes only so far as that the Bible is a word *about* God, and, in the apprehension of American statesmen, the *best*. The Freethinker, then, could have no more scruple in reading the Bible in public school than in read-ing Emerson's essay on the " Over-Soul."

But the Deistic Freethinker sometimes .goes farther, and declares the Bible ungodly and immoral. Now, this is a ques-tion entirely for the State to decide by some Moral Board of Health. A mere *ipse dixit* does not remove a building which is averred to be a nuisance ; nor can the Freethinker's *ipse dixit* stand against the verdict of the State, agreeing with Jefferson, that "the studious perusal of this volume makes better citizens, neighbors, and husbands." But the Freethinker says there are certainly parts of the Bible which are not fit for public reading. Nobody denies this. A gentleman was once riding with Prof.

Greenleaf of Harvard Law School, and making this objection to considering the Bible the word of God, that there are parts of it which he would not read before his family. " Do you sit in your parlor before your family with your naked feet displayed?" — " Certainly not." — " Then God did not make your feet." [1]

No one proposes to read all the Bible in the public school: not that there is any thing inveracious or immoral; but it is not all suitable for the time, occasion, and youthful audience.

There seems no ground for any conscientious Freethinker to object to recognizing God in his child's education by reading before him select passages from *a* book *about* God which has the veneration of the majority of men, and is called the Bible.

It remains to consider the view of

THE ROMANIST.

The Catholic says four things : —

I. *Allow me to teach my religion in the public schools.*

This, it must be admitted, the Catholic Church could insist upon in an ecclesiastical State of her own founding. Thus Massachusetts was for some seventy years, as is shown in the Lowell Lectures by George E. Ellis and Joel Parker, a "biblical Commonwealth." But in a free State the case is different. Here the State recognizes herself as a "moral personality," responsible directly to God. Examine the claim above, when made in a free State.

The Catholic has three elements in his religion : —

1. *Natural religion,* the belief in God and morality. This is not peculiar to him, but is common to all men. The State takes cognizance of this natural religion, lives by it, and should give it a place in education. Brownson well says, "The American State recognizes only the catholic religion. It eschews all sectarianism. The State conforms to what each holds that is catholic, that is always and everywhere religion; and whatever is not catholic it leaves, as outside of its province, to live or die, according to its own inherent vitality, or want of vitality. The State conscience is catholic, not sectarian."

[1] N. Adams, D.D.: Our Bible.

2. *His own peculiar dogmas,* such as the homage to the Virgin, purgatory, worship of the saints, transubstantiation, and the like. These are a part of *personal* religion, and, with all else which concerns a man's personal acceptance with God, is by no means to be taught by the State.

3. *The control of government by the ecclesiastical, the papal power.* This, indeed, Brownson denies, and so takes the true American ground. " Canonists have maintained that the subjects of other States may even engage in war with the Pope as prince, without breach of their fidelity to him as pontiff, or su: preme visible head of the Church." " The Church not only distinguishes between the two powers, but recognizes as legitimate governments that manifestly do not derive from God through her. St. Paul enjoins obedience to the Roman emperors for conscience' sake." So far, so good ; but he adds, " No doubt, as the authority of the Church is derived immediately from God in a supernatural manner, and as she holds that the State derives its authority only mediately from him in a natural mode, she asserts the superiority of her authority, and that, in case of conflict between the two powers, the civil must yield." Edward Beecher, in " Papal Conspiracy Exposed," has shown what is known to every reader of history, — how the Papal power has claimed dominion over States. This doctrine of the Papal creed cannot be taught in the schools of a free State. It is against the ideas that the " State is a moral personality ; " that " it is sovereign ; " that " it has a right to independent exist ence."

The American people may as well learn now as after the extreme disaster to the nation, that this Papal idea is *destructive of the nation.* " Obsta principiis." Bring forth all the rifles at Springfield, let there be Borodinos, before we admit the thinnest blade of this entering wedge, whether called a political or religious idea, that the Papacy rules States.

A late writer, describing Bismarck, says, " I shall never forget the frantic look of surprise and rage which took possession of the group of clericals seated right in front of him as he related the old incident of Henry IV. standing in his shirt at

Canossa until it was the Pope's pleasure to receive him. 'We desire,' said he, without changing a muscle of his face, or raising his voice in the least, — 'we desire to live in peace with the Romish Church, with bishops, and with pope ; but, still,' — pausing and stammering, — '*we are not going to Canossa !*' The effect was indescribable ; and, from that day to this, Germany has repeated Bismarck's 'We are not going to Canossa.'"

The Catholic cannot teach his religion in the public school, or the Jesuit his politics.

Failing in this, the Catholic proceeds, —

II. *Give me, then, my part of the school money, and allow me to have my part of the schools under my control.*

It is impossible to concede this ; for,

1. *The State knows nothing of ecclesiastical bodies*, neither one nor another. The State, as Mulford has said, is herself a "moral personality," responsible directly to God for her character ; and her citizens are responsible to her.

2. *She is solicitous for her public morality*, and is aware that her integrity and existence depend upon it. She cannot allow Jesuits, Mormons, Freelovers, to have separate schools, uninspected and uncontrolled, where, for all she may do, all history may be falsified, and morality may be so mistaught that the State character may be honeycombed, and fall.

With all deference to the holy and good men in this church, this ecclesiastical organization — as in the Jesuits, for example, and in the defence of the violation of the safe conduct of Huss — has promulgated such a doctrine of inveracity as no State, with the remembrance of St. Bartholomew before it, can allow to be taught in schools for which she is responsible.

3. *The State has great ends to gain by public schools* in which all her future citizens shall mingle. Guizot said, forty years ago, " It is in general desirable that children whose families do not profess the same creed should early contract, by frequenting the same schools, those habits of reciprocal friendship and natural tolerance, which may ripen later, when they live as grown-up citizens, into justice and harmony."

Dr. William Taylor, in "Home Missionary," 1875, says, "When we think of the thousands of immigrants, of different nationalities and various faiths, who are continually landing on our shores, and passing on to the far Western settlements, the necessity for keeping up this blessed system becomes imperative.

"The common school is the great assimilating organ of the body politic. Children go into it English, Irish, Scotch, German, Danish, Norwegian, French, Italian: they come out American. In the experiences and companionships of the school they lay up memories which bind them to each other and to the country ever after."

"There is nothing, therefore, so important for the giving of unity and homogeneousness to our population as the maintenance and extension of the public-school system."

4. *She owes it to herself to teach systematically that she is not a vassal, but an independent personality*, responsible directly to God, and her citizens responsible in her sphere only to her. She never can safely allow any body of her citizens to be brought up in seclusion, and as a kind of secret society, to hold that nationality is subject to Papacy. That is *treason*, as Bismarck has dealt with it. She cannot, perhaps, interfere with private teaching of this doctrine ; but she can at least neutralize it, and insist that all her youth shall receive her teaching on this matter.

Failing in this also, he goes on to say, —

III. *Concede to me, then, that, in the public school, there shall be absolutely nothing said about religion;* that education shall be absolutely secular.

This, too, is impossible ; for,

1. *The State is a moral personality, responsible to God*, and therefore, as a State, and in schools preparatory to the State, MUST recognize him.

2. *The State* MUST *teach so much morality as will preserve her.*

These two things the State *must* do. In addition,

3. *The State has a* RIGHT *to have religious exercises* for her youth from a book which her statesmen consider the best book

about God, the parent of public education, and the best fosterer of republics.[1]

4. *The State has a* RIGHT *to introduce the Bible as literature.*

Failing in all his representation to secure the State's approval and concession, the Catholic next says, in the wail of
complaint before the people, —

IV. *My rights of conscience are invaded.* "If it were so, it
were a grievous fault," and should be rectified. The State
undoubtedly should respect the conscience of her citizens. It
was a "grievous fault," and just occasion for mutiny, that the
Sepoys were compelled to use cartridges made with hogs'
grease. But the cry of "Conscience" by the Papist can be
plainly shown not to be just. Here we dwell. We desire to
grind to powder, and fling to the winds, this claim of conscience abused. Here is the strength of the great hierarchical
opposition to the Bible in the schools, that they have been able
to confuse the minds of a people like ours, because sensitive,
and regardful of conscience and personal rights. If I mistake
not, we shall find that their cry of abuse of conscience is altogether an empty one.

Let us address ourselves calmly and philosophically to the
problem. The State should respect individual conscience.
Thus the State is right in adapting the Sabbath laws to the
Jew, who understands that the ETERNAL lays upon his conscience to keep the seventh day.

But the State is not bound to give up great and positive benefits on account of merely *constructive commands*, even if addressed
to the conscience. If, in time of war, the Jew carries the observance of the Sabbath to the fanatic extent of the Jews
against Titus, the State does not, therefore, excuse him from
picket and other military duty on that day ; nor does the State,
on plea of conscience, excuse the Quaker from military service;
or, what is the same thing, obtaining a substitute.

They perform these duties under protest as individuals, and
in deference to the divine State, where they are not sure they
have *positive* command from God, faithfully as *atoms of the State.*

[1] De Tocqueville.

Finding no positive or moral command to make the matter stringent on their conscience, men feel at liberty to subordinate themselves to the State, and disregard these constructive commands, and do these things rather than endure martyrdom, which they would do if commanded to lie, or worship idols. This might be the case in regard to the Romanist in reading King James' version, even had he conscientious scruples. Not to read this, at most, is only a *constructive* command of God, made through another, who arrives at the idea that that is God's will, only after meditation and inference, in both which may lurk error which vitiates the result; and the State may righteously hold the citizen to this act, and he may, without injury of conscience, perform it, even if, as in the cases above, there is in some sort a *conscientious* scruple.

But now, in the case of the Catholic and King James' version, there is no *conscientious* scruple. This I hope to make plain.

Observe a distinction, now, we believe, for the first time drawn, yet, we believe, true and plain, and greatly to be regarded in this discussion. There is a *scruple of conscience*, and there is a *scruple of antagonism.*

Conscience is the moral faculty deciding right and wrong, as in the lie, disobedience to authority, and the like. It has been called "the voice of GOD in the soul of man." The peculiarity of conscience is, that it impresses us *directly*, as the direct voice of *God* to *us*, which we must observe in our direct responsibility to God. *Antagonism* is such a condition of mind and sensibilities as will not allow one to regard with acceptance or peace, or other than aversion, the thing in question. The scruple of the Puritans against the Maypole on Merry Mount was one of antagonism; also their scruple against Christmas. They could not like it, because it was "Popish." Roger Williams and Gov. Endicott, cutting the cross out of the colonial flag, followed a scruple, not of *conscience*, but of *antagonism*. So, whoever, *unbidden*, took sword to slay on St. Bartholomew's Day, acted from antagonism, not conscience.

Now, it is not said that an individual or a state should lightly disregard scruples of antagonism ; but it is obvious that they should not erect those antagonisms to the dignity of clear, grand, moral appeals of conscience.   The two are clearly studied, side by side, in the Jew's righteous demand for permission to observe the seventh day commanded ot God, and the Puritan's prejudice against Christmas.   One is *conscience;* the other, *antagonism.*

Some one tells the story of the " Indian's conscience."   He said his conscience forbade him to do a certain thing.   " Conscience ! what do you mean by conscience ? "— " Something in here," laying his hand on his breast, " which says *I won't.*"

The scruples of the Roman Catholics in the present case are scruples of antagonism.

(I.) *The scruple of the Catholic is one of antagonism against State schools.*   It is simply against all his idea of education that it should be connected with the State, especially a State where Protestants are numerous.   Dr. Peabody says, that, after a time, the Catholics left an evening school which he had established. He expostulated with the priest.   The reply was, " Education is so great a boon, that we are unwilling that our people should be indebted for it to heretics.   We would rather have them utterly ignorant than that their gratitude to Protestant teachers should make them look with favor on the religion of their teachers."   This is plainly a scruple of religious repulsion, not of conscience.

Cincinnati was unwise enough to allow the Catholic children to sequester themselves from the public schools.   A committee of conference with the archbishop, — think of the *degradation,* — to bring about some union, received this reply, that, " during the sitting of the Œcumenical Council at Rome, he would ask the opinion of Pope Pius IX. on the subject, and then communicate to the School Board the result of his mission."   " What ! " said Mr. Mayo of the School Board, " shall we, the free citizens of this gigantic country, wait for the decision of a prince whose political influence is reduced to a minimum, and who was the only prince of Europe who recognized the rebel States as a government?   Never, never ! "   This unwillingness to enter

State schools is a scruple of antagonism. A man does not go four thousand miles to make inquiries before a scruple of conscience leaps upon him. The State does not yield because of this scruple of antagonism, but requires all her youth to attend public school.

(II.) *A scruple of antagonism it is against King James' version of the Bible.* It is not denied that it is a good translation of the Bible. Bishop McQuaid, we believe, admitted it. These two books are translations of the same original. They are as near as any two translations of any book. What Catholic can say that one of these — the poorer translation, not directly of the inspired original — is *sacrosanctus*, and the other sinful? As to King James' version, "Geddes, the most learned biblical scholar among the Romanists," says Dr. Peabody, "speaks of it as of all versions the most excellent for accuracy, fidelity, and the closest attention to the letter of the text. An influential American priest in one of our great cities said, 'I admit that the English Bible is a perfectly fair translation, and I think it far preferable to the Douai Bible; but our foreign ecclesiastics, and especially the authorities in Rome, cannot be induced to look upon it in that light, and could not fail to regard our acquiescence in its use as schismatic.'" It is therefore not a scruple of conscience, but of sectarian repulsion, which leads a Roman Catholic to dislike the English translation of the Bible. Worse than that, it is by their own confession the scruple of repulsion, *not so much of the American ecclesiastics, as of foreign ecclesiastics who dominate the American.*

There is a common misunderstanding about the Douai version which it is worth while to correct. "The Catholic World" says (November, 1870), "We Catholics have actually no standard English Bible; and, as no particular edition is made compulsory on any, we are not likely to force any on our fellow-citizens." "It is an impression with some, that the Douai Bible was approved at Rome: this is an error. Rome does not give any approbation to vernacular versions; the decision as to them, in point of orthodoxy, fidelity, and purity of language, being left to the bishop in whose diocese the volume appears. Hence the

wide latitude for various versions, and the corresponding difficulty of making any one edition a standard."

(III.) *The scruple is also one of antagonism when the two are
united, the Bible and the public school.* Neither is King James'
version Protestant, but only an English version; nor is the
public school a Protestant school, but only a State school; and
any attempt to represent the reading of this book as a Protestant domination over the religion of Catholics is an attempt
to arouse to still higher pitch, not scruples of conscience, but
scruples of antagonism.

(IV.) *Under one condition only can there be considered a real
scruple of conscience in this case;* namely, if the Pope of Rome
shall *command* American citizens not to read King James' version
in our public schools. I weigh well my words, and speak deliberately, when I say, that that is a tyranny worse than the Colonies ever suffered from King George; that the sooner *the Pope
of Rome pleases to ordain by pontifical bull, that, in the public free
schools of America, any class of American citizens shall not read or
hear read any moral and proper book whatever which the State
thinks best to be read for her welfare, which, for two centuries,
she has decreed should be read, the sooner will come the solution of
the question, whether the palace of the Vatican or the American
legislature rules America; the sooner will come the war of direct
antagonism, and perhaps of arms, by some prophesied, between the
Papacy and the free government. And, if "the war is inevitable,
let it come."*

Until that *mandate* shall go forth from the Roman Vatican,
that American Catholics *shall not* read King James' version of
the Bible at the bidding of the State in her public schools, the
scruples of Catholics are scruples of antagonism, and not of
conscience.

Yet the writer admits that the biblical service is to be conducted, under the State, *more firmly and decidedly than now,* yet
so as to give no needless offence to our Romanist citizens. The
plain way is to establish by law and statute that Catholic teachers and scholars are at equal liberty to read from the Douai
Bible, and from that version repeat the Lord's Prayer; and, in

the pericope of the appointed sections of the Scriptures for daily reading, they should have fair hand in the seotions to be made. But the practical carrying out of the views which have been discussed in these essays will be set forth in another paper.

Yet it must be said emphatically, as the final word of America, that however considerate, to the last extreme of what is proper, of the feelings of all men in the *manner* of recognizing God in public education by the Bible, and by reverent address to God, the *thing* itself — American as it is, as it has been for two centuries, and for two centuries beneficial, if not essential, to the State, and becoming in itself — will not be given up *at the beck of a foreign monarch*, whether his throne be on the Seven Hills, or on the Bosphorus, or in Pekin. "WIR GEHEN NICHT NACH CANOSSA," — "WE ARE NOT GOING TO CANOSSA."

STATE SCHOOLS AND CHURCH SCHOOLS.

SHOULD we allow Rome to pass the *Danube*, the BALKANS will be the STATE SCHOOLS.

For this is the order of the conflicts before us: —

First, If not the Papal, then no religion in public education.

Second, Papal-church schools, instead of State schools, for Catholics.

Third (the Constantinople), Papal-church schools for the nation, and compulsory on all.

This, we know very well, will provoke a smile; but the time may not be far off when it shall cause a groan. Fifty years hence, this volume may be burnt under the Great Elm. "You do not feel in America," said an English lady to me, "as we do in England. There we see the places where Rome burnt the martyrs. When I was a little girl, my father took me to the place, and said, 'Here, on this spot, Cranmer was burnt.'"

We forget Mexico, though she touches elbows with us on the continent; we forget that a Catholic emperor sent over ocean and gulf a Catholic prince; we forget the Ahualulco mob of 1874, excited by the priest, in which Stephens was assassinated; and the San Miguel massacre of two summers ago, in which the mob had "passports to heaven," signed by the bishop.[1]

We say America is strong. Samson lacked not strength. The strong slept: he arose weak, "like any other man,"

---

[1] Harper's Weekly.

shorn by "the liers in wait" of his locks of strength, which God had bidden him preserve. Not ignorance, but presumption, was his fatal fault: it is ours. Rome *tells us distinctly* — not, perhaps, through American mouths, but from her Italian throne — what she means to do.[1] America settles herself to slumber, *knowing* that Philistia wakes and waits.

But, says one, America has an unconquerable free spirit. France, too, once had her Henry of Navarre, and her Gallican church and bishops.

Rome is audacious and plausible in her demands. Rome knows when to rest her claims, and when to press them. But let it be remembered, that while all other religions confess that they have been marred by imperfections, and with shame repudiate some things in their past, and have always believed with Pastor Robinson that "new light will break out of the Word," Rome boasts that she is "*Semper eadem.*" We can therefore always reason from her past to her future. Says one Romanist writer (Brownson), "The answers which the Church gives to all great practical questions have become historical. These answers are, in many instances, no doubt, very offensive to the spirit of the present age, and such as the prevailing public opinion denounces ; but there they stand on the page of history, and can neither be honestly nor successfully denied, or explained away. What the Church has done, what she has expressed or tacitly approved in the past, that is exactly what she will do, expressly or tacitly approve, in the future, if the same circumstances occur."

There is plausibility and quiet persistence in the cry of the sectarianism of public schools in which the English Bible is used, — plausibility and quiet persistence in the demand for church schools in lieu of public schools. When this demand grows loud, our superficial men, — for there has not yet arisen a STATESMAN on this subject, — such men as Bismarck, as Vinet, Guizot, Cousin, or as our own Horace Mann, are needed to apply their broad minds profoundly and patiently to this theme, and then give the Achillean shout which will rouse the Greeks, —

---

[1] Syllabus, §§ 55, 78, &c.

our superficial men, flustered, perturbed, as the matter presses for instant action, will yield to clamor, because they have not thought down to the foundations.

Try we, then, while we may, to think this subject clear, — forge anchor strong in these sunny days, — State schools and Church schools. Let us not yield to the plausibility of Church schools, but understand the rationality and validity of State schools.

The mind, at the mention of this theme, naturally turns to the discussion, "The State and the Church." That subject fitly precedes this. It is necessary, indeed, to the round understanding of the theme before us. We do not mind telling the reader that a portion of that was originally studied as a preparation and preface for this; but, on after-thought, it seemed co-ordinate with the other problems, and worthy of a separate place. The reader will not do amiss to recall that idea of State and Church, as a stiff stalk to hold the fruited branch, the theme we now pass to consider.

That State schools should not give way to Church schools, to one Church's schools, or to separate Church schools, should, it would seem, be obvious from that preceding argument. But some considerations need to be dwelt upon.

I. THE GENERAL OBJECTS OF STATE SCHOOLS AND OF CHURCH SCHOOLS ARE NOT THE SAME. The State school aims to make a citizen and a man: the Church school aims to make a disciple and a redeemed spirit. The Church brings up the child in things relating to the realm of man's intercourse with God, and personal growth in the divine nature. The Church school may then add enough of natural learning to make him a Newton; or, if so disposed, can leave him unable to write his own name.

The State, on the other hand, sets, as its object, to make the child a perfect natural man in himself, and, towards her, a good citizen. She pours into him a complete education of mind, heart, body (not spirit), and loyalty to the State.

II. ONE OBJECT OF STATE SCHOOLS, A UNITED CITIZENSHIP, IS MARRED BY SEPARATE CHURCH SCHOOLS. Even so far as they must be allowed to go, sects separate and weaken the body politic. Were every State in the Union a sect, a Mormon State, an Episcopalian State, a Catholic State, a Presbyterian State, the bond of national union would be essentially weaker. It is doubtful whether, even to advanced scholars, it is beneficial to sequester them from each other in denominational colleges. It cannot be for the advantage of a State, like Massachusetts, that, within its borders, the children should be segregated, — these into a Catholic school, these into an Episcopalian, a Presbyterian, a Methodist, a Mormon, a Mohammedan, a Chinese school. This cannot be conducive to union or loyalty. Guizot said forty years ago, "It is, in general, desirable that children whose families do not profess the same creed should early contract, by frequenting the same schools, those habits of reciprocal friendship and natural tolerance, which may ripen later, when they live as grown-up citizens, into justice and harmony." Dr. William Taylor, in "Home Missionary" (1875), says, "When we think of the thousands of immigrants of different nationalities and various faiths who are continually landing on our shores, and passing on to the far Western settlements, the necessity for keeping up this blessed system becomes imperative.

"The common school is the great assimilating organ of the body politic. Children go into it English, Irish, Scotch, German, Danish, Norwegian, French, Italian : they come out American. In the experiences and companionship of the school they lay up memories which bind them to each other and to the country ever after."

"There is, therefore, nothing so important for the giving of unity and homogeneousness to our population as the maintenance and extension of the public-school system."

III. State schools are more apt than Church schools TO GIVE A COMPLETE DEVELOPMENT TO THE NATURAL MAN.

The Church school may *deliberately* curtail all education not spiritual. The answer of Omar to his general, as to what he should do with the captured Alexandrian Library, comes to mind "If these writings agree with the Koran, they are use-

less, and need not be preserved ; if they disagree, they are pernicious, and ought to be destroyed." The Church is apt to
think natural learning injurious. "The more knowledge of the
world, the more worldly-minded." A Church school will naturally place more value on reciting a list of her officers than on
the whole curriculum of learning.

Further : the Church may fail to give wide development, *because she does not appreciate the glory of the natural man.* Greece
had men magnificently endowed and disciplined, though they
were not spiritually-minded. But the State, an enlarged natural
man, is more likely to give a wide scope to all that is great in
human nature to be and to know, — from gymnastic training to
microscopic studies, from geology and astronomy to logic, and,
on another side, from the gallantry of Sir Philip Sidney to the
patriotism of a Sumner. No Church which assumes to control
States will be apt to reckon the development of the natural man
of so high worth.

There are other less creditable reasons why a Church school
might limit education, since it is asserted that some hierarchies
foster ignorance ; but those above are sufficient, and we need
not stain our page with unkind words. But the result of
Church schools will generally be less fully developed men.

IV. Church schools may limit education in all secular knowledge to the minimum. This is natural. Sometimes this occurs without evil intentions ; sometimes from discreditable reasons. We find no fault now and here with Catholicism as a religion, except to say, that, being merely a church,
it cannot be expected to care much for merely secular knowledge. It is, therefore, no more than what we might say as
Catholic critics, were we of that church, when we adduce the
following facts to show that Church schools, with creditable or
discreditable intentions, limit secular knowledge to a minimum.

First, there is the obvious yet striking fact, that children,
restrained from public schools by ecclesiastics, are sent afterwards by their parents, who cannot forego the superior secular
education. Joseph Cook, in one of his Monday Talks, names
an American city where the Roman-Catholic children were

taken out of the public schools. "After being drawn into ecclesiastical Roman schools for a fortnight or a month, those children were found to be making very unsatisfactory progress; and the parents came to the School Board in many cases, and said, 'Take our children back: they will behave themselves now.' 'We know that objections are made in ecclesiastical quarters; but your schools are better than ours, and our children must have the best schools.'" An eminent professional man writes me, "I have been acquainted for years with instances in various communities where the direct and explicit prohibition of the Romish Church has availed only to keep Catholic children out of our public schools for a season; the parents having worldly wisdom enough to see, that, if their sons and daughters are to get places in life, those places will be procured by actual acquaintance with *secular learning*, not by certificates from some priest's school. In a word, the *bread-and-butter argument* is obviously and heavily on the public-school side."

Napoleon Bonaparte, desiring an efficient national-school system, removed every priest from national schools. "Very little was taught, except the creed and the elements of the Papal faith."

Victor Hugo, in one of his speeches, shows, we will not say how intentionally destructive, but how *regardless*, ecclesiasticism may become of good learning. He is speaking, we believe, of the Jesuits.

"Thanks to you, Italy, mother of genius and nations, which has spread over the universe all the most brilliant marvels of poetry and the arts, — Italy, which has taught mankind to read, now knows not how to read. Yes, Italy is, of all the States of Europe, that where the smallest number of natives knows how to read.

"Spain, magnificently endowed; Spain, which received from the Romans her first civilization, from the Arabs her second civilization, from Providence, and in spite of you, a world, — America; Spain, thanks to you, to your yoke of stupor, which is a yoke of degradation and decay, — Spain has lost that secret power which it had from the Romans, that genius which it had from the Arabians, this world which it had from God ; and, in exchange for all which you made it lose, it has received from you — the Inquisition."

Coleridge, at Cologne, July 2, 1825, writes, "During the summer of last year I made the tour of Holland, Flanders, and up the Rhine as far as Bergen ; and among the few notes then taken I find the following : Every fresh opportunity of examining the Roman-Catholic religion, on the spot, every new fact that presents itself to my notice, increases my conviction, that its immediate basis, and the true grounds for its continuance, are to be found in the wickedness, ignorance, and wretchedness of the many ; and that the producing and continuing cause of this deplorable state is, that it is the interest of the Roman priesthood that so it should remain, as the surest, and in fact only, support of the Papal sovereignty and influence against the civil powers, and the reforms wished for by the most enlightened governments, as well as by all the better informed and wealthier class of Catholics generally.   And as parts of the same policy, and equally indispensable to the interests of the triple crown, are the ignorance, grossness, excessive number and poverty, of the lower ecclesiastics themselves, including the religious orders."

We will not insult the intelligent Catholic by calling this the result of his *religious faith,* nor by supposing that such result is less displeasing to him than to us ; but we ask him to observe, rather, as we observe ourselves, that this minimum of good learning in all natural things is sooner or later the result of ecclesiasticism and hierarchical organizations, intruding where they do not belong, and hacking the trees of good learning, even where they may be honestly trying to prune them.   The hierarchy would fetter Galileo because the astronomy of Nature is not taught directly in the Bible.

We call upon all enlightened Catholics to observe this injurious tendency of ecclesiastical schools to diminish good learning, and, if you will, follow the sentiment of Brownson : "Keep your Catholicism; but *leave Europe behind you.*"   "We need,"

he says, "the Catholicity, but not the *foreignism.*" "The spread
of Catholicity," he adds, "associated with the foreign civilization throughout the country, would destroy the American order
of civilization, and reproduce in our New World that of the Old
World, on which ours is, in our judgment, a decided advance."

To all this it will be said by the shallow, that an adequate
provision against this possible reduction of general education
to the minimum in Church schools will be found in supervision
of all schools, church and public, by one educational board, and
by public compulsory examinations.

To which the reply is immediate and obvious: If the State
allows the Church to have separate schools, it must do so on
one of two grounds: either, *first,* on the Church's own claim,
that the Church is the only proper teacher of youth; or, *second,*
on the State's ground, as her assistant or deputy, giving this
instruction to future citizens in behalf of the State.

If, now, education is relegated to the Church *on the first
ground,* on which she claims it, then, by the same reason, if she
has the sole right to educate, as she claims, she must also have
the sole right to set the standard of education, order examinations, and do all other things which are a part of her alleged
right to educate.

On the second ground, if education is yielded to the Church, as
to a deputy assistant, in behalf of the State, there will be this
twofold struggling force always operating, and successfully, to
prevent any further control by the State over Church schools:
first, that the Church will always contend and protest, year by
year, against examinations, on the allegement that her view is
the right one, that she is not deputy of the State, but, in her
own right, educator, and, being thus persistently aggressive,
will in twenty years establish her view; and, *second,* that the
same overshadowing influence, religico-political, by which she
gained the greater, separate schools, will grant her, within a
decade, absolute control of her separate schools. 'Tis the letting out the genie from the kettle, — easier to prevent than to
remedy. When the genie has emerged in full size, think not he
will be obsequious to you.

Public supervision could not, for five years, control an established Church-school system. After conceding into *their* hands the system, do we imagine *we* could *administer* the system? What, then, would prevent the Church school from limiting attendance to two hours a day, or general studies to the most rudimentary? Do we have such an exalted idea of the Papal schools for the whole people, that we believe Rome would be strenuous to make her schools promotive of general education? Macaulay, impartial judge, who speaks generously of Rome before the Reformation, says of Rome since the Reformation, "To stunt the growth of the human mind has been her chief object. Throughout Christendom, whatever advance has been made in knowledge, in freedom, in wealth, and in the arts of life, has been made in spite of her." "Whoever, knowing what Italy and Scotland naturally are, and what, four hundred years ago, they actually were, shall now compare the country around Rome with the country around Edinburgh, will be able to form some judgment as to the tendency of Papal domination." "Whoever passes in Germany from a Roman-Catholic to a Protestant principality, in Switzerland from a Roman-Catholic to a Protestant canton, finds that he has passed from a lower to a higher order of civilization."

Catholic brother, we can believe you desire the "*higher order of civilization*" as well as we: therefore give your weight against ecclesiastical schools, whose inferior education and development is a patent fact, clear to observation, clear on the page of history.

V. Church schools may teach pernicious morals.

We do not say they *will;* but they *may.* That is sufficient to bar them out, that they *may* teach pernicious morals. *They cannot be prevented.*

But since Rome boasts herself *semper eadem*, and Jesuits are unchanged, it would not be asserting too much, that, sooner or later, Church schools *will* teach pernicious morals.

The Mormon in his Church school will, of course, teach polygamy, which in the State is crime. The Papist will teach reverence to the Jesuits as the saintliest of men, of whom Pascal says, " The Jesuits and the Inquisition are the two scourges of the truth." The Mohammedan Church teaches proselyting by the sword, — " the faith, tribute, or the sword." The State morality, as the natural morality, is more likely to be a unit, and more likely to be true to nature, than these diversities of studied morals.

" ' There is some one,' says Talleyrand, speaking of worldly politics, ' more clever than Voltaire, more sagacious than Napoleon, more shrewd than each minister, past, present, and to come ; and that some one is *everybody*.' There is some one, we may say, in ecclesiastical politics, more learned, more able, and more versatile, than any individual bishop, more likely to be right than the Pope of Rome, or the Wesleyan Conference, or the Geneva Assembly ; and that is the *whole community*."

Papal-church schools will teach that huge immorality, —*persecution for religion*.

Rome sowed that teaching so deeply into Europe, that the revered Calvin could not unlearn it.

Rome will teach persecution thus : —

Pope Pius IX. denounces as errors, that " The Church ought to be separated from the State, and the State from the Church ; " " In the present day it is no longer expedient that the Catholic religion shall be held as the only religion of the State, to the exclusion of all other modes of worship ; " " Whence it has been wisely provided by law, in some countries called Catholic, that persons coming to reside therein shall enjoy the public exercise of their own worship." It is an error that " The Church has not the power of availing herself of force or indirect temporal power."[1]

Liberatore : " Amongst the rights appertaining to a perfect society is that of coercing enemies, internal and external. Where, between the State and the Church, there is reciprocal alliance, there the right is exercised by the latter through the agency of the former ; but, where this alliance happens to be broken, manifestly this right of the Church cannot perish," &c.

American Editors : " There is, ere long, to be a State religion

[1] Syllabus, §§ 55, 77, 78, 24.

in this country; and that State religion is to be Roman Catholic." [1] "Religious liberty is merely endured until the opposite can be carried into effect without peril to the Catholic world." [2] "Protestantism of every form has not, and never can have, any rights where Catholicity is triumphant." [3]

Historically she will teach it in one word, THE INQUISITION.[4]

By defences of the Inquisition: "A sense of duty obliges me to say that an heresiarch, an obstinate heretic, and a propagator of heresy, *should indisputably be ranked among the greatest criminals.*" [5] "That institution you may value as you choose; you are at liberty to condemn the abuses and the cruelties of which it has been guilty through the violence of political passions and the character of the Spaniard: yet one cannot but acknowledge, *in the terrible part taken by the clergy in its trials,* THE MOST LEGITIMATE AND MOST NATURAL EXERCISE OF ECCLESIASTICAL AUTHORITY." [6]

Rome will teach "*ecclesiastical utility,*" — that that is right which is useful to the Church. In the canon law, "An oath taken contrary to ecclesiastical utility is not binding." Again: "Oaths taken contrary to ecclesiastical utility are not oaths, but perjuries." [7]

Papal schools — which are Jesuit schools — will teach *Jesuit morals.*

We renew our demurrer, that we do not attack the Catholic faith, but only Roman ecclesiasticism, in what we are about to adduce. Nine-tenths of plain, honest Catholic people and Catholic priests will be as much horrified as are we to see what immorality ecclesiasticism, distorted by long centuries of casuistry, can bring itself to teach. Should Church schools be allowed, there is no reason why, as fast as American ecclesias-

---

[1] Father Isaac Hecker.   [2] Bishop O'Connor, Pittsburg.

[3] Catholic Review, January, 1852.

[4] Eugene Lawrence, Hist. Studies, 1876; Dominic and the Inquisition, 358.

[5] Le Maistre's Letters on the Spanish Inquisition, published by Donahoe, Boston, 1843.

[6] Mgr. Ségur: Plain Talk about Protestantism, also published by Donahoe, Boston. R. W. Thompson, 81.

[7] "This maxim gave the most unlimited privilege to the popes of breaking all faith of treaties which thwarted their interest or passion, — a privilege which they constantly exercised." — HALLAM.

tics can be brought down to it, they may not teach these morals from approved standard works.

Some one may interrupt with the inquiry, Cannot the Romish Church *now* teach what she chooses? To which we answer: —

First, The State is not responsible for what the Church teaches in her private sphere; but the State is responsible for making her *assistant teachers* of the boys and girls of the republic churches which may teach immorality and crime.

Second, The State is able, in the State, to neutralize the private teachings of churches by her own teaching of natural morals.

We again beg pardon of all noble-minded Catholics at supposing that they could sit patiently under such teaching as that which follows: yet *as fair-minded men as any of us have been brought down to it;* and there can be little doubt, that, in due time, if Church schools were rooted in American soil, just these doctrines would be taught in them.

For we are about to transcribe from *standard works.*

Father Joanne Petro Gury, born in 1801, was for thirty-five years professor of moral theology at Vals, and afterwards in the Collegio Romano. He died in 1866. "No modern treatise," says Cartwright,[1] "can show a more formidable array of guarantees than Father Gury's 'Compendium of Moral Theology.' It has been appointed in Roman-Catholic seminaries in all lands as the standard manual of moral theology. It has been printed in every country, and translated into every tongue. In the new issue of De Backer's 'Dictionary of Jesuit Writers' there are enumerated no fewer than twenty-four editions. The one we quote from was issued in 1872 from the presses of the Propaganda at Rome, — the highest possible voucher for the entire approval of every line and every word in the book by the supreme representatives of the Roman-Catholic Church. The volume on 'Cases of Conscience,' by the same author, is a commentary in practical elucidation of the larger work."

Cartwright undertakes to examine the morals taught in these standard Jesuit works. He glances at the whole field in this sentence: "Advocate and antagonist alike will admit that the

---

[1] W. C. Cartwright, M.P.: The Jesuits, their Constitution and Teaching.

system of lax opinions popularly charged against Jesuit divines rests on three cardinal propositions, — of *Probabilism*, of *Mental Reservation*, and of *Justification of Means by the End*." For a full understanding of these subjects, we refer the reader to Cartwright's work, "The Jesuits," and Pascal's famous "Provincial Letters." We shall get merely a few glimpses of these teachings.

Probabilism is this : "*Opinio probabilis* is any judgment resting on some really grave motive; though with fear of the opposite." "That means," says Cartwright, "that notwithstanding an irrepressible inward impression that truth is really in opposition to a given *opinio probabilis*, yet any opinion in behalf whereof there can be adduced what is technically termed a 'grave motive' may be safely accepted as full warrant for action." "In case of a person unversed in letters, it is enough that he can point to a particular opinion as having fallen from any one whom 'he himself deems to be possessed of learning and insight,' for his confident acceptance of such opinion as a rule of action."

Mental reservation is of two kinds, — "*strictly* and *broadly* mental." The latter only, Gury considers justifiable.

The doctrine of *Means by End*, "notwithstanding their denial, has been taught by an unbroken chain of Jesuit divines, of first-rank standing, from Busenbaum down to Gury and Liberatore."

Now we run together in miscellaneous way a few of the cases of conscience under these three Jesuit moralities.

"Can servants who are of opinion that their wages are inferior to the work done by them make use of clandestine compensation, *occulta compensatio* ?" asks Gury. "Not generally ; but there are exceptions." "Servants who have contracted for inadequate wages, under physical constraint, or moral fear, or strain of necessity ; such being declared entitled to help themselves to what they deem their rightful due." [1]

What do Americans think, — all, of whatever religion ? Shall we have Church schools, where it should be even *possible* for the boy in preparation for future citizenship to be thus taught? Yet this is from a standard Jesuit book of morals.

---

[1] See. in connection. Pascal's story of Jean d'Albe.

Gury asks, "Can a missionary, for purposes of concealment, assume the dress of ministers of a false religion, so that he may seem one of them?" Which is answered in the affirmative: "For dresses primarily serve for covering the body, and are not merely declaratory signs of some religion."

A similar instance is given in Pascal's "Letters:" "In the Indies and in China they permitted Christians to practise idolatry itself, with the aid of the following ingenious contrivance: they made their converts conceal under their clothes an image of Jesus Christ, to which they taught them to transfer mentally those adorations which they rendered ostensibly to the idols Cachinchoam and Keum-fucum."[1]

"It is startling," says Cartwright, "to find it enumerated as a principle in the standard handbook for the instruction of Roman-Catholic youths in moral obligations, that an oath may be repudiated with perfect impunity, if only the person who has sworn will plead to having been at the time influenced in his mind by some apprehensions of possibly injurious consequences to himself, unless he had so sworn."

Gury says, "An individual sets poison or a snare in a locality where his enemy, though very rarely, passes, with the express intention that he might perish if he should chance to come by. A physician applies the degree of attention he is bound strictly by his calling to exercise, but, out of hatred, is resolved to apply none beyond, in order that the patient's death might ensue." "Gury asks whether these men should be held guilty of having wrongfully caused death, if this actually came about from circumstances prepared with so much deliberation. His answer is, that, according to the more *accredited opinion*, they should be held exempt from guilt, 'because, on the one hand, the external act is not unjust, inasmuch as, in human dealings, the mere possibility of another man's injury has not to be taken into account: and, on the other hand, an internal act is not rendered unjust in virtue of intention; for intention has influence neither for the efficacy of a cause, nor for peril of injury. Consequently, the result must be said to

---

[1] Pascal, who gives authorities, Letter 5.

have happened by mere accident; and of this an evil intention does not change the nature.'"[1]   "No one," remarks Cartwright, "need ever be disturbed in his conscience as to any moral liabilities being consequent on intentions, however wicked, if these have only been artfully connected with agencies of which, by some ingenuity, it could be plausibly pleaded, that, in some conceivable contingencies, they might prove harmless."

Gury asks, "Whether you are bound to make any reparation for the harm that has befallen another in consequence of your unjust deed; as, for instance, if the theft were imputed to him of that which you yourself had stolen?" And he answers in the negative, "Even though you should have expressly striven to get your own action imputed to him." The example he gives of *Quirinus* fully illustrates the answer. To these strange. chapters of *moral instructions*, so called, we might add similar teachings in regard to "hush-money and its extortion," "evasion of taxes," "smuggling," and underrating the value of property in deeds.[2]

Church schools for the citizen boy ?   Never !

Blaise Pascal's earnest and witty "Provincial Letters" ought to be read by all.   There all which Gury teaches is abundantly illustrated from the Jesuit fathers by citations, of which Pascal says, "I have twice read 'Escobar' throughout; and, for the others, I got several of my friends to read them : but *I have never used a single passage without having read it myself in the book quoted*, without having examined the case in which it is brought forward, and without having read the preceding and subsequent context, that I might not run the risk of citing that for an answer which was in fact an objection ; which would have been very unjust and blamable."

Take a few bits from Pascal, fair *specimens*, since we cannot cite amply.

Of probabilism he makes his priest say, who converses with him, "Why, sir, it is the foundation, the very A B C, of our moral philosophy."

From *Emmanuel Spa*, Jesuit doctor : "A person may do what

---

[1] Gury, vol. i. 366, 367.   [2] See Gury; Cartwright on Jesuits.

he considers allowable according to a probable opinion, though the contrary be the safer one. The opinion of a single grave doctor is all that is requisite."

Vasquez : "On what occasions may a monk lay aside his religious habit without incurring excommunication?"—"If he has laid it aside for an infamous purpose, such as to pick pockets, or to go *incognito* into haunts of profligacy, meaning shortly after to resume it."

John d'Alba was servant to the fathers in Clermont College. Dissatisfied with his wages, he purloined, and was arrested by the fathers. The case came to court April 16, 1647. He confessed to taking the pewter plates, but maintained he had not stolen them : according to the doctrine of his masters, he had taken them as *occulta compensatio*, clandestine compensation. His plea was not allowed : on which Pascal wittily says to his interlocutor, that his doctrine satisfies the *priests*, but not the *judges*. "In following your probabilities, they are in danger of coming into contact with the whip and the gallows. This is a sad oversight."

The doctrine of the *Direction of the Intention* he counts almost equal to probabilism.

Sanchez : "A man may swear that he never did such a thing, — though he actually did it, — meaning within himself that he did not do so on a certain day, or before he was born." "And this is very convenient," &c. Or he may do this : "After saying aloud, *I swear that I have not done that,* to add in a low voice, *to-day;* or, after saying aloud I *swear,* to interpose in a whisper, *that I say,* and then continue, *that I have done that.*" There is a remarkable illustration, in Cartwright, of a woman who has deceived her husband.

Escobar (from whom the word *escobarderie,* meaning *duplicity*): "Promises are not binding, when the person in making them had no intention to bind himself." *Escobar,* further : "We call it killing in treachery when the person who is slain had no reason to suspect such a fate. He, therefore, that slays his *enemy,* cannot be said to kill him in treachery, even though the blow should be given insidiously, and behind his back."

"He that kills an enemy with whom he was reconciled under a promise of never again attempting his life cannot be *absolutely* said to kill in treachery, unless there was between them all the stricter friendship." *Escobar:* "It is lawful to kill an accuser whose testimony may jeopard your life and honor."

Father L'Amy (François Amicus) uses these words: "An ecclesiastic or a monk may warrantably kill a defamer who threatens to publish the scandalous crimes of his community or his own crimes, when there is no other way of stopping him."[1]

Father L'Amy's doctrine was censured in 1649 by the University of Louvain. "And yet," says Pascal, "two months have not elapsed since your Father des Bois maintained this very censured doctrine, and taught that 'it was allowable for a monk to defend the honor which he had acquired by his virtue, EVEN BY KILLING the person who assails his reputation, — *etiam cum morte invaseris.*'"[2]

"The doctrines advanced by L'Amy are too gross for repetition: suffice it to say, that they sanctioned the murder, not only of the slanderer, but of the person who might tell tales against a religious order; of one who might stand in the way of another enjoying a legacy or a benefice; and even of one whom a priest might have robbed of her honor, if she threatened to rob him of his character. These horrid maxims were condemned by civil tribunals and *theological faculties*" [observe this, to the honor of the nobler Catholics]; "yet the Jesuits persisted in justifying them."[3]

In following out this doctrine, "a Bavarian parish-priest, by name Riembauer, in 1808 murdered his mistress with revolting cold-bloodedness, because he feared she would make their intimacy public, to the ruin of his position. Being brought to trial, Riembauer, who displayed much morbid ingenuity, defended himself, on the plea that the deed was in strict accord with the maxims he had been taught in the seminary, — that it was quite lawful to put out of the way any one from whom

---

[1] Cours Théologique.   [2] Letter 13.
[3] Nicole, Latin translator of Pascal's Letters: Notes, IV. 41.

there was reason to dread a ruinous denunciation ; and this he sustained by extracts from Statler's 'Ethica Christiana,' at that time a standard manual.   No doubt, this was an extreme case : still that miscreant could appeal with perfect plausibility to maxims in divines of authority, which, without any strained construction, did seem to justify his deed."[1]

Sanchez, quoting, says, "Navarre justly observes, that, in certain mentioned cases, it is lawful either to accept or to send a challenge, — *licet acceptare et offerre duellum.*   The same author adds, that there is nothing to prevent one from despatching one's adversary in a private way."   "By this means we escape at once from exposing our life in the combat, and from participating in the sin which our opponent would have committed by fighting the duel."[2]

On another matter, the killing for a buffet, "Lessius lays it down as a point which no casuist has contested.   He quotes a great many that uphold, and none that deny it, and particularly Peter Navarre, who, speaking of affronts in general (and there is none more provoking than a box on the ear), declares, that, 'by the universal consent of the casuists, it is lawful to kill the calumniator, if there be no other way of averting the affront, — *ex sententia omnium, licet contumeliosum occidere, si alter ea injuria arceri nequit.*'"[3]

"According to Father Baldelle, quoted by Escobar, 'you may lawfully take the life of another for saying you have lied, if there is no other way of stopping his mouth.'   Lessius and Hereau agree in the following sentiments : 'If you attempt to ruin my character by telling stories against me in the presence of men of honor, and I have no other way of preventing this than by putting you to death, I may, and that even though I have been really guilty of the crime which you divulge, provided it is a secret one, which you could not establish by legal evidence. And I prove it thus: If you mean to rob me of my honor by giving me a box on the ear, I may prevent it by force of arms; and the same mode of defence is lawful when you would do me

---

[1] Cartwright, 224.
[2] Sanchez, Moral Theology; Pascal, Letter 7.   [3] Letter 7.

the same injury with the tongue. In fine, honor is dearer than life ; and, as it is lawful to kill in defence of life, it must be so to kill in defence of honor.' " [1]

On the other hand, observe the Jesuit teachings on uttering calumny. In their public theses at Louvain, in 1645, they taught, " What is it but a venial sin to calumniate, and forge false accusations to ruin the credit of those who speak evil of us ? " " Quidni non nisi veniale sit detrahentes auctoritatem magnam, tibi noxiam, falso crimine elidere ? " Dicastillus defends this audaciously. " ' There can be no doubt,' says Caramuel, ' that it is a probable opinion that we contract no mortal sin by calumniating another in order to preserve our own reputation, for it is maintained by more than twenty grave doctors, by Gaspard Hurtado and Dicastille, Jesuits, &c. ; so that, were this doctrine not probable, it would be difficult to find any one such in the whole compass of theology.' "

Pascal shows the working of this maxim in the daughters of the empress, and in a dispute of the Jesuits with M. Puys, curate at Lyons, in 1650, whom they calumniated as " scandalous from his gallantries." The curate explained that his book was not directed against their society. Whereupon Father Alby immediately addressed him a letter : " Sir, it was in consequence of my believing that you meant to attack the society to which I have the honor to belong, that I was induced to take up the pen in its defence ; and I considered that the mode of reply which I adopted was *such as I was permitted to employ.* But, on a better understanding of your intention, I am now free to declare that there is *nothing in your work* to prevent me from regarding you as a man of genius, profound and *orthodox* in doctrine, and *irreproachable* in manners ; in one word, as a pastor worthy of your church." [2]

But why transcribe more ?   Is it not enough ?

Being of mild disposition, we are not accustomed to use severe words ; but Carlyle has a rich vocabulary of just such words as we feel like using : " Ignatius' black militia, armed with this precious message of salvation, has now been campaigning over

---

[1] Letter 7.   [2] Letter 15.

all the world for about three hundred years, and openly or secretly has done a mighty work over all the world. Who can count what a work? Where you meet a man believing in the salutary nature of falsehoods, or the divine authority of things doubtful, and fancying, that, to serve the good cause, he must call the Devil to his aid, there is a follower of Unsaint Ignatius." " They have given a new substantive to modern languages. The word *Jesuitism* now, in all countries, expresses an idea for which there was in nature no prototype before." " They have done such deadly execution on the general soul of man, and have wrought such havoc on the terrestrial and supernal interests of this world, as insure to Jesuitism a long memory in human annals." " There had been liars in the world before ; " " but there was in this of Jesuit Ignatius an *apotheosis* of falsity, a kind of subtle quintessence and deadly virus of lying, the like of which had never been seen before." " It is to be hoped one is not blind withal to the celebrated virtues that are in Jesuitism, — to its missionary zeal, its contempt of danger, its scientific, heroic, and other prowesses, of which there is such celebrating," — " small residue of pearls from such a continent of putrid shell-fish." [1]

But we doubt not attempt will be promptly made by Papists to break the force of these overwhelming revelations of Jesuit morality. The nail, though deep driven, will be withdrawn, unless clinched. They will say two things : —

1. These doctrines will never be taught in America.

To which we reply: *First,* It is sufficient to our argument against Church schools, that these morals *may* be taught in them. *Second,* They are taught abroad. Gury is a standard. " The same maxims which it may have been deemed the shafts of Pascal's wit must have banished forever are being inculcated at the present day in every Roman-Catholic school, college, and seminary where Jesuit doctrine prevails ; and this comprises the vast majority." [2] *Third,* In the United States there are, says " St. Peter," a Catholic paper in New York (1871), *twelve colleges under Jesuit charge,* and *three hundred Jesuit priests.*

---

[1] Carlyle: Jesuitism, Latter-day Pamphlets.   [2] Cartwright, 147.

The Papist will further strive to break the force of these damaging revelations by saying, —

2. These representations are slanderous and false, exaggerated and overstrained; and they were answered long ago by Father Daniel and others.

To which we make reply: *First*, We do not need to rebut this for our argument's sake, since if they *may* be genuine and authoritative, and *may* be taught to children of the republic, that *possibility* is sufficient to induce the State to anchor fast to State schools, and not allow Church schools. But, *Second*, The pages of Gury are open to all; they are standard; they contain these Jesuit morals, if not always to such outrageous extent as those of two centuries ago, yet such as we have just read them. *Third*, As to Pascal, we have read his avowal that he had carefully read his authorities; and, indeed, he foot-notes them. Moreover, we know that one pope at least abolished the Jesuits, and died with blackened body shortly after.[1] The European States, in their days of clearest vision, have jealously watched, restrained, or ejected them. "If Pascal's solemn deposition, emitted by one whose heart was a stranger to deceit, and whose shrewdness placed him beyond the risk of delusion, is not accepted as sufficient, we might refer to the mass of evidence collected at the time in the *Factums* of the curés of Paris and Rouen, to the voluminous notes of Nicole, and to the Apology of Petitdidier, in which the citations made by Pascal are authenticated with a carefulness which not only sets all suspicion at rest, but leaves a large balance of credit in the author's favor, by showing, that so far from having reported the worst maxims of the Jesuitical school, or placed them in the most odious light of which they were susceptible, he has been extremely tender towards them. But, indeed, the truth was placed beyond all dispute, through the efforts of the celebrated Bossuet, in 1700, when, by the sentence of an assembly of the clergy of France, the morals of the Jesuits, as exhibited in these 'monstrous maxims which had been so long the scandal of the Church and of Europe,' were formally condemned, and when it

---

[1] Clement XIV. Cartwright: Steinmetz, Hist. of Jesuits, iii. 615.

may be said that the 'Provincial Letters' met at once their full vindication and their final triumph." [1]

Remember, Catholic fellow-citizen, *Church schools* will be *Jesuit schools;* for this is not an extinct and antiquated society, but still "the sword whose hilt is on the Tiber," the "janizaries of the Papacy."

Remember, the Propaganda issued an edition of Gury in 1872. Only about *thirty years* ago, it was "discovered that the theology of Dens was still taught by the Jesuits in Ireland, — a collection of the most wicked and obscene maxims of casuistical morality." "Dr. Gilly mentions a publication at Lyons, in 1825, which is so bad, that the reviewer says, 'We cannot, we dare not, copy it: it is a book to which the cases of conscience of Sanchez were purity itself.'" [2]

But these are mere casuistic speculations, one imagines. Yet "according as a man *thinketh,* so *is* he."

These and similar teachings have not only borne abundant fruit, as could be shown, between citizen and citizen, but on a large scale, on the page of history, instances *gloom* forth like black columns of smoke. Edward Beecher gives examples: "Ladislaus, King of Hungary, formed a treaty with the Sultan Amurath, and the king and sultan confirmed it by mutual oaths on the Gospels and the Koran. Eugenius IV., the Pope, by his legate Julian, declared it in the highest degree criminal to observe an oath so much opposed to '*ecclesiastical utility.*' 'I absolve you,' said the legate, 'from perjury, and sanctify your arms.' 'The Sultan,' writes Edgar, 'it is said, displayed a copy of the violated treaty in the front of battle, imploring the protection of the God of truth, and called aloud on the prophet Jesus to avenge the mockery of his religion and authority.'" Ladislaus was defeated and slain. "An enumeration," says Edward Beecher, "of popes and councils, would present at least twenty cases of teaching perjury on the great scale, by professing to dissolve national oaths." [3]

---

[1] Thomas M'Crie, D.D., Introduction to Pascal; Vie de Bossuet, iv. 19; Tabaraud, Dissertation sur la Foi, &c.

[2] M'Crie, Introduction, Pascal, lxxv.

[3] Edward Beecher, D.D., Papal Conspiracy Exposed.

Are the moral teachings which produced St. Bartholomew's Day to be inoculated into the State by her own permission?

John Huss, summoned to appear before the council, received from the Emperor Sigismund a safe conduct, in the amplest words, " to go, to stop, to remain, and to return safely." This safe conduct he gave honorably, intending to maintain it.

" Notwithstanding this safe conduct," says Dackery, an eyewitness, in his German history of the council, " the deputation, in a long speech, persuaded the emperor, that, by *decretal authority*, he should not keep faith with a man accused of heresy." Huss was burnt. The Council of Constance then decreed, " Nor ought any faith or promise to be observed to him, to the injury of the Catholic faith, by any law, natural, divine, or human."

—— " I'd rather be
A Pagan, suckled in a creed outworn,
So might I "

learn to speak and act the truth.

Brought up in a far different school was he who said, that, " if truth were to be banished from all the world, it ought to have a place in the heart of kings ; " or that great Roman, who informed the hostile general of his physician's offer to poison him, and the Epirote Pyrrhus in admiration exclaimed, " It is easier to turn the sun from the heavens than Fabricius from the path of honor ; " or the Gothic Alaric, when he had taken Rome, " Kill only the armed, spare those who have taken refuge in churches ; " or Saladin, who at his death bequeathed a large sum of money to the poor, whether Mussulman or Christian or Jew, to show that all men are brothers ; or the Chevalier Bayard, " sans peur et sans reproche," who, dying, looked on the false Constable of Bourbon, and said, " It is not *I* who am an object of commiseration : it is *you*, who are fighting against your king, your country, and your oaths."

THE STATE SCHOOL, by plain instruction of virtue, teaching Sigismund to keep his word! — rather than CHURCH SCHOOLS, sophisticated, and sophisticating Sigismund into breaking faith with his subjects!

VI. CHURCH SCHOOLS, FINALLY, MAY BRING UP SCHOLARS TO
DIVERSE, AND EVEN HOSTILE AND NATIONALLY DESTRUCTIVE,
POLITICAL IDEAS.

In the American Revolution the Episcopal schools probably
taught, "God save the King." What might not have been the
effect, during our "war of restoration," had the Catholics had
separate schools, and had the teachers, under instructions from
the Tiber, chosen to impress on scholars, and through them on
their parents, that "the Pope has acknowledged the Southern
Confederacy"? Would our citizens from across the seas have
shown such steadfast loyalty and such heroic gallantry for the
Union? This is only saying that in a less open, but no less
potent manner, *Jesuitism in politics* may be imparted in youthful instruction; which both France and Germany having tried,
spewed it out of their mouth as treason to the State.

In these Church schools, in the first decade possibly, the ideas
of Catholics who are not Romanists — Brownson, Doyle, Döllinger — *might* be imparted.

But — and here is the argument — these Church schools
might, as *soon as secluded* (and nothing could then prevent
them), teach all the American youth called Catholic the political ideas of Serbati and Liberatore, and Brownson in his earlier
years.

Brownson once said, when more of a *Romanist* than at the
ripening of his life, "*Either the popes usurped the authority they
exercised over sovereigns in the middle ages, or they possessed it
by virtue of their title as vicars of Jesus Christ on earth.*" "Say
what we will, we can gain little credit with those we would
conciliate. Always, to their minds, will the temporal power of
the Pope by divine right loom up in the distance; and always will they believe — however individual Catholics here
and there may deny it, or nominally Catholic governments
oppose it — that it is the real Roman-Catholic doctrine, to be
re-asserted and acted the moment that circumstances render it
prudent or expedient. We gain nothing with them but doubts
of our sincerity." This doctrine "is the most logical, the most
consonant to Catholic instincts, the most honorable to the dig-

nity and majesty of the Papacy; and it has undeniably the weight of authority on its side.   The principal Catholic authorities are certainly in favor of the divine right ; and the principal authorities which he " (Charles Butler) ." is able to oppose to them are of parliaments, sovereigns, jurisconsults, courtiers, and prelates and doctors who sustained the temporal powers in their wars against the popes.   The Gallican doctrine was, from the first, the doctrine of the courts, in opposition to that of the vicars of Jesus Christ, and should, therefore, be regarded by every Catholic with suspicion."   There spoke Brownson, the true *Roman* Catholic, before he became an *American* Catholic, — *American in politics, while Catholic in faith.*

Is it for the interest of the State that it should allow one-third or one-half its youth to be brought up, denying that the State is "sovereign," "independent"?   But so Serbati would teach, as he taught Hyacinthe, that "civil society has for its object, not — like the family in the natural order, the Church in supernatural order — the *substance* of rights, but simply the *modality* of rights ;" that is, that government is merely a useful police system to guard the family and church, — an iron fence, of no value or honor in itself, but only to protect the enclosed trees.

Can the State, safely or honorably to herself, send one-third of her youth to have the grand ideas of *nationality* and *citizenship* and *loyalty* stamped and crushed out of them in a Church school ?

The State, by a system of *compulsory education* reaching all her children, is to insist that all her youth, for a term of years, — if not for the whole ten years of their school life, from five to fifteen, at least for seven years, from five to twelve, or from eight to fifteen, — shall be under her immediate eye and instruction, to receive those moral and political ideas that will fit them for their place as citizens in the State, and fellow-citizens to each other.

Suppose Father Liberatore were the State Superintendent of Church Schools in Massachusetts : he would order that these his words should be taught to the future — shall we say *citizens* of *America,* or to the future *subjects* of *Rome in the province of America?* "The State," declares Father Liberatore, "must understand itself to be a subordinate sovereignty, exercising ministerial functions under a separate sovereignty, and governing the people conformably to the will of that lord to whom it is subject."

"*Church schools*" means that one-third of American citizens are to be brought up to hold as politics and faith that AMERICA IS A PROVINCE OF ROME.

THE "ENGLISH" AND THE "DOUAI."[1]

By what marvellous lack of sifting and straining must it have happened, that a volume in the English language, extant for a period of more than quarter of a thousand years, — two centuries and a half, or, to give the full time, two hundred and sixty-seven years; a volume which, during that long course of years, had received recension and revision many times (near a dozen times in England, and two at least in this country);[2] a volume professedly a book, — pre-eminently the Book of all books, — at any hour, of many millions, and these present millions to be multiplied by eight generations, — that this volume, in so late a recension as that of 1852 (its latest, we believe), should, at this day of schools and universities, retain such remarkable pieces of composition as these? —

"The Lord ruleth me, and I shall not want. He hath set me in a place of pasture. He hath brought me up on the water of refreshment. He hath converted my soul. He has led me on the paths of justice for his own name's sake.

[1] Since scholars disagree practically in writing this name, it may not be thought petty to vindicate our spelling by showing the weight of authority. *Douai*, Encyclopédie Moderne, Firmin Didot Frères, Printers of the French Institute, Paris, 1853; Murray, Handbook of France; Encyclopædias Brittanica and American (latter also, Douay); Webster's Dictionary (also Douay); English Encyclopædia of Geography; McCulloch's Geographical Dictionary; Lippincott's Pronouncing Gazetteer (or Douay). On the other hand, *Douay*, Chambers' Encyclopædia; Worcester's Dictionary; Colton's, Johnson's, and Collins' Atlases. The weight of authority is thus for *Douai ;* and it is easier to see how Douai fell into Douay than the reverse. The pronunciation is that of Worcester, accented on the first syllable, rather than that of Webster, on the last. *Doway* is a corrupted form, in print or pronunciation, and has no good authority.

[2] John G. Shea: Bibliography of Catholic Bibles printed in U.S. 1859.

224

"For though I should walk in the midst of the shadow of death, I will fear no evils ; for thou art with me. Thy rod and thy staff, they have comforted me. Thou hast prepared a table before me, against them that afflict me. Thou hast anointed my head with oil; and my chalice which inebriateth me, how goodly it is! And thy mercy will follow me all the days of my life. And that I may dwell in the house of the Lord unto length of days."

And this, in the midst of much that is excellent : —

"Him, therefore, when Peter had seen, he saith to Jesus, Lord, and what shall this man do? Jesus saith to him, So I will have him to remain till I come, what is that to thee? Follow thou me. This saying, therefore, went abroad among the disciples, that that disciple dieth not: but Jesus did not say to him, He dieth not; but, So I will have him remain till I come, what is that to thee?"

This volume is entitled the Douai version of the Latin Vulgate, so called. The English reader need not have his attention called to the barbarisms and infelicities of diction in his vernacular, and the classical reader need not have one point out the obvious departures from the sense of the Hebrew Psalm and Greek paragraph.

Astonishing as this English is, which is published and set before English readers to-day in the great cities of polite speech and writing of our language, unchanged, uncensured, unchallenged, the explanation is near at hand. This book *never was* sifted, as one would suppose, from its conspicuous position and its immense nominal constituency, it must have been. This book has, indeed, been placed *on* the sieve ; but it never was *sifted*. The translation, it is true, was duly made ; the recensions were put forth by ecclesiastics ; they were laid *upon* the sieve : but the sifting never took place, — the necessary mental agitation, the constant, critical, thoughtful reading by millions of eager minds, which shakes a translation to sift it like wheat,. throws aside its crudities, and makes the final product smooth and refined, as well as essentially correct.

To say that this sifting never took place is to say no disputable, and, from the Catholic side, no invidious thing. In the commentaries and footnotes, indeed, studied by the learned, some of these inaccuracies are remarked ; but they are not set in any fresh translation, in the plain text, for the common readers, even were those readers numerous. If that beautiful Psalm were read and repeated from the Douai a hundred thousand times a year, — as it probably is from the authorized version, — and if there were among us the same freedom in private translating as among the Romanists, how long would the words be tolerated in print, " My chalice which inebriateth me, how goodly it is " ?

We repeat, it is no disputable or invidious thing to say that this Douai version never was thus sifted by universal and earnest reading. This is no libel. · No general statistics are before us from which we can predicate, or even estimate, the generalness of Catholic reading of this version ; but one fact which has come to our knowledge may, we believe, not unfairly be considered as a specimen of the extent to which this book is possessed by the common people. Mr. Willey visited nearly 3,000 Catholic families in Lowell, Mass., of which 1,200 had the Douai Bible ; in Lawrence he visited 1,950 Catholic families, in only 515 of which, " a little more than one-fourth of the families," did he find the Douai Bible.[1] In New England are few Protestant families — persons, we might almost say — who do not own a Bible. May it fairly be supposed, also, that presumably the *same proportion of interest* is taken in the reading of the Douai version by those who own a copy, the same proportion as between the large *number* of those who own an English and the small *number* of those who own a Douai ? Be this as it may, we need not pry into houses, nor demand a census at the doors, to find how many, even in American homes, possess the Douai Bible, and read it constantly and eagerly. For the fact is acknowledged, — nay, it is claimed as a Catholic peculiarity and excellence, — that the Bible is not so much to be read by the people, but that the religious teachers should study and digest it, and present to the people what, in their judgment, it is

[1] Report of Massachusetts Bible Society, for 1876.

best for them to learn. This is the common Catholic theory, and has been for centuries. Mr. John Shea opens his catalogue of Catholic Bibles (1859) by saying, " In the Catholic Church the Holy Scriptures do not occupy the same position as in the various denominations formed among those who left her bosom in the great schism of the sixteenth century. To the Catholic the Bible is neither a school-book, a ritual, nor a popular treatise on theology : consequently, Bibles are not profusely scattered. For reverential perusal and devout meditation a comparatively small number of them suffices."

This is no " private interpretation." of the Catholic idea. So early as 1199, the Waldenses were prohibited from reading their vernacular version. The Council of Toulouse, in 1229, decreed, " Prohibemus ne libros Veteris Testamenti aut Novi laici permittantur habere : ne praemissos libros habeant in vulgari translatos, arctissime inhibemus," — " We prohibit the laity from reading the books of the Old or the New Testament ; and we most strictly forbid their possession of them translated into the vernacular." In 1234 the Council of Tarragona anathematized as " heretic any one who within eight days should not give up a Bible owned by him." The Council of Trent decreed that " no man may read the Scriptures in the vulgar tongue unless he have obtained permission from the bishops and inquisitors."

Leo XII., in his bull as late as 1824 against Bible societies, prohibited Bible-reading. Bellarmine, in one of his six arguments against vernacular translations, says that " it is dangerous for the people to read the Scriptures. All heresies have sprung from misunderstanding of the Scriptures." Molanus, royal and Papal censor of books, says, " We deny that the study of the Scriptures is required of laymen; yea, we affirm that they are safely debarred the reading of the Scriptures, and that it is sufficient for them to govern the tenor of their life by the directions of the pastors and doctors of the church."[1]

Cardinal Ximenes says, " The word of God should be wrapped in discreet mystery from the common people, who have little

---

[1] Practical Theology.

reverence for what is plain and obvious." "The Scriptures should be confined to the three sacred languages symbolically written on the cross." And the Douai translators, in their preface, wrote, "They do not publish it upon an erroneous opinion of its being necessary that the Holy Scriptures should always be in our mother-tongue, or that they ought to be read indifferently of all, or could be easily understood of every one that reads or hears them in a known language. . . . But they translated the sacred book upon special considerations of the present time, state, and condition of their country," &c. In a Catholic bookstore, you will observe the small number of Bibles as compared with the costly and elegant "manuals" and "prayer-books." Bibles were printed by individual publishers, at the limited numbers possible to them, until so late as 1869 ; since which time they are also issued by a Catholic publication society.

The Romanists did indeed, in the early years, co-operate in the printing and circulating of Bibles in Germany and Hungary ; but this happy work, foreign to the Papal genius, — though, we are willing to believe, germane to many Catholic hearts, — was of short duration ; for it was nipped in the bud as by cruel frost, the society at Presburg and that at Ratisbon being summarily abolished about 1817 by Papal bull. The Russian autocrat stamped out the Russian Bible Society in 1826.

To us it sounds melancholy as the booming of the bittern, the complaint which Cardinal Wiseman makes, somewhat too facilely, of the lack of biblical studies among Papists : "The appearance of any work upon biblical literature is, unfortunately, a phenomenon amongst us." "We are utterly unprovided with even elementary and introductory works upon the Scriptures," "whether intended for the education of our clergy, or the instruction of our people : we possess not a commentary suited to the wants of the times or the advances made in biblical science ; and are obliged to seek information either in voluminous, rare, and old writers, or in the productions of men whose religion differs essentially from ours."[1] Geddes, nearly

---

[1] Essays, 1836, i. 74.

a hundred years ago, complained that Catholic England had no Bible.

D'Aubigné well represents the two extremes of the Papal Church in setting before us two facts. "Catholic Christians, those of Port Royal, during the age of Louis XIV., wrote these beautiful and touching words: 'To forbid Christians the reading of the Scriptures, and especially the gospel, is to deprive children of light and life, and place them in a sort of excommunication.' The Pope hurled against them the bull 'Unigenitus.'"

On the other hand, "I was in Rome in 1843. Gregory XVI., predecessor of Pius IX., who occupied the Papal throne, had upon his accession pronounced against the modern times. He had even interdicted railroads. But he had done still more, and thousands of people had been thrown into prison. A little after, he published a brief against the Bible societies and the reading of the Bible. This was not very needful at Rome. If one had ransacked all the bookstores, he would not have discovered in them a single copy of the Holy Scriptures in Italian. The Epistle of St. Paul to the Romans was not to be found in Rome itself. Verily, the time is far away when Bossuet could say that Rome was more proud of one letter of St. Paul than of all her triumphs. The Romans read not in the mother-tongue the epistle which St. Paul addressed to their ancestors. It is read by thousands, by millions, in the valleys of Switzerland, upon the banks of the Elbe and the Rhine, beside the Thames, in the highlands and the plains of Scotland, along the shores of the Atlantic and the Ohio. It is not read — strange fact l — on the banks of the Tiber, whither yet it was sent by Paul."

How significant is the striking contrast, that for seventy-three years (since 1804) the British Bible Society, and since 1816 the American Bible Society (and in 1870 it was reckoned that there were somewhere near *thirteen thousand* societies, auxiliaries and branches, in both hemispheres), have been pouring forth Bibles for the multitudes of the earth; in 1846 and 1847 alone, sending out nearly 3,000,000 copies of the Scriptures, and in all these years more than 100,000,000 copies of God's word! But the Douai Bible has never had the sifting of such a multitude of eager and intelligent readers.

In the inevitable connection of these two versions — rival versions as (considering their constituency only) they may be called — with the school-question for the next quarter of a century or less, — if happily by God's favor to us as a nation that question may be settled so soon in a safe and satisfactory and statesmanlike way, — we find the occasion to set forth a comparison of these two famous translations.

The thought which we would meet — an indistinct thought, working mischief from its very indistinctness — is this: You speak of reading the Bible in the schools. *But which translation? Each sect claims to have the best: therefore, to avoid the strife and irritation of discussion, let us have neither.*

But we say, Have *either*, or *both:* both are good translations of the revered book, as like as any two translations of any classic; yet one is superior to the other on scholarly grounds, and vindicates its claim to be considered the "English version."

There is, therefore, no reason to put the Bible out of the schools from mere impatience of thought at deciding what to do about rival versions.

Our attempt will be to present such a view of the versions as shall approve itself to scholarly minds as a clear though brief account of the two volumes, and may remain in hand, easily referred to, during the time of this agitation, as a satisfactory history and criticism of the "English" and the "Douai;" while, on the other hand, we will endeavor to make the discussion as little abstruse as careful scholarship will permit, and set the two versions in a plain and candid light before the intelligent general reader who desires information.

Nearly a hundred years ago, Alexander Geddes, the most learned scholar among the Catholics, speaks of the Douai as a "barbarous translation made at Rheims and Douai from an uncorrected copy of the Vulgate." [1]

This remark of Geddes suggests the two lines of study which will present us with a clear and sufficiently full idea of the

[1] Address to the Public, 3.

DOUAI VERSION.

First, "an uncorrected copy of the Latin Vulgate;" second, "a barbarous translation made at Rheims."

(1.) *First, the history of the Latin Vulgate.* This we cannot better give than by a condensation of the learned, critical, elaborate, and voluminous article in Smith's "Bible Dictionary" on the Latin Vulgate, from Westcott's pen.[1] We assume a sufficient interest in the subject, or desire for information on our reader's part, to follow some details of the narrative of this version.

"The history of the earliest Latin version of the Bible," he says, "is lost in complete obscurity. All that can be affirmed with certainty is that it was made in Africa. During the first two centuries, the Church of Rome, to which we naturally look for the source of the version now identified with it, was essentially Greek. The Roman bishops bear Greek names; the earliest Roman liturgy was Greek; the few remnants of the Christian literature of Rome are Greek." Tertullian "distinctly recognizes the general currency in Africa of a Latin version of the New Testament in the last quarter of the second century." "But, while the earliest Latin version was preserved unchanged in North Africa," — in the churches, that is, of which Carthage was the centre, — "it fared differently in Italy. There the provincial rudeness of the version was necessarily more offensive." "Thus in the fourth century a definite ecclesiastical recension (of the Gospels at least) appears to have been made in North Italy by reference to the Greek." Augustine makes this plain.

"The *Itala* appears to have been made with some degree of authority: other revisions were made for private use." "The next stage in the deterioration of the text was the intermixture of these various revisions; so that, at the close of the fourth century, the Gospels were in such a state as to call for that final recension which was made by Jerome." It is to be borne in mind — what even the scholar familiar with it is apt to let slip from his field of vision — that every new copy of the Scriptures

---

[1] Vulgate, 3451–3482.

was separately done by hand of man.   There was no stereotype
to throw off a hundred thousand copies, nor even common type
to print an edition of Bibles, each, by necessity of common origin, word for word, and letter for letter, exactly like the other;
but each new copy was substantially a new and various edition.
This, of course, was a constantly growing evil.

"In the crisis of danger, the great scholar was raised up,"
continues Westcott, "who probably alone for fifteen hundred
years possessed the qualifications necessary for producing an
original version of the Scriptures for the use of the Latin
churches. *Jerome* (Eusebius Hieronymus) was born in 329
A.D. at Stridon in Dalmatia, and died in Bethlehem in 420
A.D.   From his early youth he was a vigorous student, and age
removed nothing from his zeal.   Jerome went to Rome A.D.
382, probably at the request of Damasus the Pope.   His active
biblical labors date from this epoch.   These were threefold.
They are worthy of a somewhat detailed account, — the revision
of the Old Latin Version of the New Testament, the revision
of the Old Latin Version (from the Greek) of the Old Testament, the new version of the Old Testament from the Hebrew."

Coming to these labors, Jerome found no easy task before
him.   "There were almost as many forms of text as copies,"
says Jerome, "tot sunt exemplaria pene quot codices."   " Mistakes had been introduced 'by false transcription, by clumsy
corrections, and by careless interpolations ;' and, in the confusion which had ensued, the one remedy was to go back to the
original source.   (Graeca veritas, Graeca origo.)   The Gospels
had naturally suffered most.   Jerome therefore applied himself
to these first."   "But his aim was to revise the old Latin, not to
make a new version."

"His second work was the revision of the Old Testament
from the Septuagint Greek.   He revised the Psalter by the
Greek ; but the work was not very complete or careful."   This
revision was called "The Roman Psalter," and was used in the
Roman Church till 1566.   In a short time he produced a new
revision, which has been called "The Gallican Psalter."   The
same has been used in the Romish churches since 1566.   " From

the second (Gallican) revision of the Psalms, Jerome appears to have proceeded to the revision of the other books of the Old Testament; restoring all, by the help of the Greek, to a general conformity to the Hebrew."

But, the longer one proceeds with labors of revision, the more conscious does he generally become that he must begin *de novo;* must translate, instead of revise. This became so apparent to Jerome, that, in the growing sense of what should be done, he counted his revisions as entirely inadequate. With the love of thoroughness which is part of a true scholar, he made preparations for radical work. Jerome commenced the study of Hebrew when he was already in middle life — at the age of forty-five, in the year A.D. 374 — with "excessive zeal." It was an age when there were no Hebraists, when every thing Jewish was hateful, when Jerome exposed himself to censure for his unexampled resort to Hebrew teachers. But, with the sagacity and insensibility of a great scholar, he sequestered himself to the very heart of Judaism to learn Hebrew. At Bethlehem, the very birthplace of his Lord, as he must often have reflected, whither the wise men had brought their offerings of homage, he commenced his version, which was issued book by book, beginning 391 A.D. "The Books of Samuel and Kings were issued first." "The work was executed with the greatest care." Jerome speaks of the translation as the result of constant revision, — "crebrius vertendo et emendando sollicitius." "The whole translation was spread over a period of about fourteen years, from the sixtieth to the seventy-sixth year of Jerome's life. But still parts of it were finished in great haste." "The three Books of Solomon were translated in 398 in three days, when he had just recovered from a severe illness."

His version, after the clamor of ignorance passed away, was received in succeeding centuries with great and increasing favor, and it has continued in the Roman Church the object of the most profound veneration.

A word of critical estimate is in place here. "Jerome himself admits from time to time that he had fallen into error. In many places he gives renderings which he prefers to those which he had adopted." "Yet," continues Westcott, "such defects are trifling when compared with what he accomplished successfully. The work remained for eight centuries the bulwark of Western Christianity; and, as a monument of ancient linguistic power, the translation of the Old Testament stands unrivalled and unique. It was at least a direct rendering of the original, and not the version of a version." " Generally it may be said that the scriptural idioms of our common language have come to us mainly through the Latin." "The vast power which they have had in determining the theological terms of Western Christendom can hardly be overrated. By far the greater part of the current doctrinal terminology is based on the Vulgate, and, as far as can be ascertained, was originated in the Latin version. Predestination, justification, sanctification, salvation, mediator, regeneration, revelation, propitiation, first appear in the old Vulgate. Grace, redemption, election, reconciliation, satisfaction, inspiration, scripture, were devoted there to a new and holy use. Sacrament and communion are from the same source; and, though baptism is Greek, it comes to us from the Latin." "The Latin versions have left their mark upon both our language and our thoughts." "The study of the Vulgate, however much neglected, can never be neglected with impunity. It was the version which alone they knew who handed down to the reformers the rich stores of mediæval wisdom; the version with which the greatest of the reformers were most familiar, and from which they had drawn their earliest knowledge of divine truth."

"But the Latin Bible which thus passed gradually into use under the name of Jerome was a strangely composite work." "Thus the present Vulgate, including the Apocrypha, contains elements which belong to every period and form of the Latin version, — (1) unrevised Old Latin; (2) Old Latin revised from the Septuagint (the Psalter); (3) Jerome's free translation from the original (Judith, Tobit); (4) Jerome's translation from the original Old Testament (except the Psalter); (5) Old Latin revised from Greek MSS. (Gospels); (6) Old Latin cursorily revised (the remainder of the New Testament)."

The condition of the Vulgate, therefore, in its best estate, was this, — that *all the Old Testament*, with the important exception of the Psalms, is *the noblest work of the master-hand of Jerome, his direct translation in free and noble Latin from the Hebrew original;* albeit he afterwards "in many places gives renderings which he prefers to those which he adopted, and admits from time to time that he had fallen into error." The Gospels, too, are from the hand of the master, — a secondary though valuable work, — his *revision* of the old Latin by reference to the best Greek manuscripts. The rest of the New Testament did not receive his best labor, only a cursory revision. *His direct work of making a version is limited to the Old Testament,* — the Psalms, unfortunately, excepted. Geddes, whose opinions as the great and candid Catholic scholar we have frequent occasion to transcribe, says, — referring, I suppose, not to Jerome's portion of the work, which he elsewhere extols, but to the whole composite, party-colored volume, — "The great defect of Jerome's version is its want of uniformity: it being sometimes strict, and sometimes loose; now barbarously literal, and now widely paraphrastic. Every translation made from it, then, must partake of this variety."

But the Vulgate, as it was soon called, did not remain stationary, even the noble work of Jerome. "Meanwhile the text of the different parts of the Latin Bible was rapidly deteriorating. The simultaneous use of the old and new versions necessarily led to great corruptions of both texts." Then followed revisions, among them those of Alcuin, 802 ; the Complutensian by Cardinal Ximenes, 1517 ; that of Stephens, 1528 ; and others. Later, after the Council of Trent had been apprised that the text was "so corrupt that only a pope could settle it," came the Sixtine by Pope Sixtus V., in 1590, which he solemnly declared perpetual. But hardly was he in his grave when his anathemas were disregarded, and his edition, so full of errors, was set aside, and the Clementine revision was substituted. Such was the imperfect state of the Vulgate, itself originally a work not all Jerome's, very far from being of equal merit. How much more imperfect — before the thorough revision by

Sixtus and Clement, at the time of the report to the Tridentine Council, that "the corrupted text could only be restored by a pope" — must the unemended Vulgate have been! Yet, as we shall see, it was at this period of a corrupted text that the Douaists took the Vulgate in their hands still further to deteriorate and degrade it by rendering it into barbarous English.

(2.) *The Douai Translation.* This Latin Vulgate, with all the faults of its origin, with all the errors of transcription of eleven centuries, — for this was only the dawn of printing, — gathered into it, and with the text as yet substantially unemended, —

> "Even in the blossoms of its sin,
> With all its imperfections on its head,
>   .   .   .   .   unaneled," —

was in the hands of Gregory Martin and his two compeers about 1575, twelve years *before* Pope Sixtus undertook the revision of a "text so corrupt that only a pope could correct it ; " and in this deteriorated condition it was made the basis of the present Romish version.[1] Dr. Alexander Geddes, the learned Catholic scholar, gives the following account of this translation : " From the days of Wycliffe there was no version made from the Vulgate until the year 1582, when the English Catholics, who had, in the beginning of Queen Elizabeth's reign, taken refuge in Flanders, and were now removed to Rheims on account of the war, published a translation of the New Testament only. The publication of the Old Testament did not take place till after the return to Douai, in 1609. Hence the whole version is known by the name of the Douai Bible. It is a literal and barbarous translation from the Vulgate before its last revision. Their residence in a foreign country, and what they deemed a cruel exile from their own, had corrupted the translators' language, and soured their tempers." [2]

Westcott says, " The Rhemish Bible, like Wycliffe's, lies properly outside the line of English Bibles, because it is a second-

---

[1] Gregory Martin, "an excellent linguist," the principal translator, his death hastened by his excessive toil ; William Allen (Cardinal) ; Richard Bristow ; "men of no small erudition," says Dr. Eadie, "but thorough devotees of Rome." Thomas Worthington is said to have assisted. John Reynolds also assisted.

[2] *Prospectus,* 109.

ary translation, based upon the Vulgate." "Such translations as these have no claim to be cónsidered vernacular renderings of the text: except through the Latin, they are unintelligible."[1]
- Nothing can be more certain than that it is not the noblest work of scholarship to make a *translation* of a *translation*.

But this the Douaists did, and not, as appears, from lack of knowledge of the original, but *upon principle*, for reasons stated in the preface. They alleged especially that the originals had been more corrupted by Jew and Byzantine than the Vulgate had been ; so that the Vulgate was even better than the originals.

Lest we should seem to imply that we think the Rhemish translators utterly absurd, and wanting in extenuation for their course, we transcribe what Westcott calls their "very interesting and ingenious defence of their method:"—

"We translate the old Vulgate Latin text, not the common Greek text, for these causes: (1) It is so ancient, that it was used in the Church above thirteen hundred years ago (1609) ; (2) It is that, by all probability, which St. Jerome afterward corrected, according to the Greek, by the appointment of Damasus the Pope; (3) Consequently it is the same which St. Augustine so commendeth ; (4) It is that which, for the most part ever since, hath been used in the Church's service ; (5) The Holy Council of Trent, for these and many other important considerations, hath declared and defined this only of all other Latin translations to be authentical; (6) It is the gravest, sincerest, of greatest majesty, least partiality, as being without all respect of controversies, specially those of our time ; (7) It is so exact and precise according to the Greek, that delicate heretics therefore reprehend it of rudeness ; (8) The adversaries themselves, namely Beza, prefer it before all the rest ; (9) In the rest there is such diversity and discussion, and no end of reprehending one another, and translating every man according to his fancy, that Luther said, 'If the world should stand any long time, we must receive again' (which he thought absurd) 'the decrees of councils for preserving the unity of faith, because of so diverse interpretations of the Scripture ;' (10) It is not only better

[1] **English Bible, 334.**

than all other Latin translations, but than the Greek text itself
in those places where they disagree."

Now, it so happens that all scholarship is against them, both
as to facts and as to the true theory of translation, — all scholarship, that is, which is not overborne by ecclesiastical authority,
or the profound veneration which the nobler parts of the Vulgate have excited in those brought up from childhood to this
grand version, or those whose sensibilities (as were those of
one whom I once knew) are so peculiarly alive to the sono-
rousness and majesty of the old Roman language, that nothing
on earth is comparable to it ; nay, as this man used to declare,
that to his mind the Latin must be the language of the celes-
tials.   Universal scholarship — and the biblical scholars of this
day, in addition to the rich inheritance of wisdom which they
hold from the past centuries, are themselves men of great critical discernment and clear good sense — is decided that *any first-
rate translation is to be primary, not secondary; that is, is to base
itself upon the original corrected to date*, and is to avail itself to
the fullest extent of all versions as auxiliary.   " The very idea,"
says Geddes, " of translating from a translation is a strange
idea.   We have an excellent French version of Plutarch, by
Amyot ; but would any Englishman sit down to translate Plutarch through the medium of Amyot's translation ? "   " In the
very first transfusion from one idiom to another, some part of
the author must necessarily evaporate : how much more must
he lose on a second or third operation ! " [1] 'Tis an Italian pun,
Traduttori, traditori, "Translators, traitors," " who do not render, but surrender, their author's meaning."   Thrupp [2] speaks of
the means and aids to translation in this order, — "manuscripts,
versions, and citations."   " The first are peculiarly liable to
errors from transcription.   The last two are liable to this cause
of corruption, and also to others."   " Some uses of the article
and of prepositions cannot be expressed or distinguished with
certainty in translations.   Glosses or marginal additions are
more likely to pass into the text in the process of translation

[1] Prospectus, 105.
[2] Art. Old Testament in Smith's Dictionary.

than in that of transcription." "The mutually corrective power of the three kinds of testimony is of the highest value."

These are fair specimens of the opinions of scholars, which entirely agree with what the general reader at first thought would suppose, — that *the prime resource of a translator should be directly to the volume in its original form.* "Graeca veritas, Graeca origo," is evermore the true starting-point of the translator. No fault would be found with the Douai, if it modestly acknowledged its inferiority ; if, like Wycliffe's Bible, it went to the Vulgate because the scholarship of the day did not permit it to go farther, or from veneration, or from the novelty of launching — as even Wycliffe had not done — into the broad sea of original translation. But such translation cannot be defended on theory as giving promise of the superlative translation. "The only plausible reason," says the Catholic writer already quoted, "that can be offered for translating from the Latin, rather from the originals, is, that, the Vulgate having been once adopted as the public Latin version, uniformity seemed to require that all vernacular versions should be consonant thereto." [1] But that a Catholic, in the opinion of her intelligent men, does not become a heretic in retaining his scholarship, and his scholarly opinion that versions should be based on the originals, and not on the Vulgate, Geddes shows, both in his own version, so far as completed, made from the Hebrew, and in the examples he adduces: for he did not conceive himself to be less a Catholic because he founded his translation on the original rather than on the Vulgate ; and he says, "But although the Catholics in general have made their vernacular versions of the Bible from the Vulgate, yet they have not done so without exception. Two Italian translations are professedly made from the originals. In France there are two complete manuscript versions of the whole Bible." [2]

As to facts, the plea of the Douaists is no more conclusive. "The conclusions were by no means fairly deducible," says Geddes, "that, because the Hebrew was in many places corrupted where the Vulgate was not, therefore the Vulgate was

---

[1] Prospectus, 104.   [2] Prospectus, 111.

everywhere preferable to the Hebrew text. This absurd opinion," &c., " St. Jerome and St. Augustine denied, that the Jews
corrupted the Hebrew."   He uses the expression, " The wonderful uniformity of all the Hebrew manuscripts, and the perfect
agreement with the printed copy."   " There is every reason,"
says Thrupp, " to believe that in Palestine the text was both
carefully preserved and scrupulously respected.   The boast of
Josephus,[1] that, through the ages that had passed, none had
ventured to add to, or take away from, or to transpose aught of,
the sacred writings, may well represent the spirit in which, in
his day, his own countrymen acted."   " In the translations of
Aquila and the other Greek interpreters, the fragments of whose
works remain to us in the Hexapla, we have evidence of the
existence of a text differing but little from our own ; so, also, in
the Targums of Onkelos and Jonathan ; so, also, in Origen's
transcription of the Hebrew text."   " And yet more important
are the proofs of the establishment of the text, and of substantial indemnity with our own, supplied by the translation of
Jerome."

If it may not be affirmed that the Vulgate unrevised, which the
men of Douai had in their hands, was as much corrupted from
its original as the Greek text was corrupted from its original, —
and we are by no means prepared even to withdraw this hypoth-
esis, — of this, at least, we think no one could make question,
that, if we may put it in this algebraic way, the corruption of
the Vulgate from its original, *plus* the departure and variation
of the original Vulgate from the evangelistic, and especially the
apostolic Greek, placed the Vulgate of the Douai period at a
very much farther distance from the primal Greek of the evangelists than the mere errors of transcription had placed the
Greek manuscripts.   With all the exceeding merits of the Vulgate, it must never be forgotten that its Psalms and Testament
— precisely what we prize ·most, and bind together as the
" finest wheat " of the Scriptures — are not the best work of
Jerome.

Then, again, — for we think it useful to dwell a moment further,

[1] Contra Apion, i. 8.

that this claim of the Douaists in regard to the Vulgate as the proper starting-point and basis of translation may now and here receive final disposition, — it cannot now be doubted that the various *Greek manuscripts*, gathered from all climes, East and West, whither Christianity was scattered, would in their collation afford a better basis for a perfect text than the Vulgate, even after recension. The discovery of that ancient Greek manuscript by Tischendorf, in Mt. Sinai's convent, sent a greater thrill of delight into scholars' hearts everywhere than if he had found three manuscripts of the Latin Vulgate.

Once more: the *numerous versions combined plus* the *Greek manuscripts* are immeasurably more trustworthy than the Vulgate, even though we had it fresh from Jerome's hand and final touch. We have the Greek manuscripts — themselves vastly transcending the Vulgate in power to represent the primitive Greek — plus three Syriac, the Coptic, Ethiopic, Gothic, and other independent versions. The Vulgate ranks as one of these versions, — one of the best; some would say absolutely the best of these versions, — but only one. From these, using the manuscripts as basis, and the versions as auxiliary, scholars are wont to reform the text. This is the method of Lachmann, Griesbach, Tischendorf. Never would an unbiassed scholar make the Vulgate the foundation text to be corrected by Greek manuscripts and versions. If the illustration be not too abstruse: Given, on the one hand, a pitcher of a liquid which appears to have been red and blue exposed to the air; on the other hand, Given a pitcher of some liquid which appears to have been red, yet which has been changed by exposure to the atmosphere; given several pitchers of the same liquid mixed mechanically with yellow, indigo, and the other rainbow colors; and from all these, by observing the red scarcely changed, and by thorough knowledge of the laws of mixture and reduction of colors, a nearer approximation would be made to the original color than by a study and reduction of the one pitcher of red mingled more or less — we know not how much — with a blue color. The stream of the Vulgate, flowing in one language, and that the ecclesiastical language of all Western Europe, it might he

thought that its departures from purity might be readily traced;
and yet, on the other hand, it is far more advantageous to trace
a considerable number of streams, not quite so observable in
their course, in search for the elements which they derived in
common from the fountain of their origin.   Better study all the
independent versions for the original sentences than any one
version, even were it of great excellence.

To this it must be added, — a consideration not to be forgotten,
— that one of these versions, at least, claims an equality, if not
a superiority, to the Vulgate.   The Gothic version made by
their bishop Ulphilas, whose history is so remarkable, is of
value.   "The Memphitic and Thebaic are among the first of the
aids to sacred criticism;"[1] but the earliest *Syriac* version is of
exceeding importance.   One need only read the remarks in
Murdock's translation of this version, called the "Peshito,"
to see this.   "The great value of this translation," says Murdock,[2] "depends on its high antiquity, — it is ascribed to the
first century, some say to apostolic times, — on the competence and
fidelity of the translators, and on the near affinity of its language to that spoken by our Lord and his apostles.   In these
respects it stands prominent among the numerous versions of
the New Testament.   To give the substance of what is written,
and in the plainest, simplest manner possible, seems to be its
sole aim.   In these respects it stands alone among all the
ancient versions of the Bible."   "The true import of the New
Testament," says Ludovicus de Dieu, "can scarcely be learned,
except from the Syriac."   The Vulgate, then, even at its best, —
even supposing that modern scholarship would detract somewhat from Murdock's estimate of the Syriac (Scrivener[3] and
Westcott[4] abate little or nothing from Murdock's valuation of
the Syriac), — has a rival, and perhaps a superior, in this translation, made, as some suppose, in Antioch.

One conspicuous defect, finally, the Latin language has, known
to all scholars, which alone of itself must needs put any Latin

---

[1] Scrivener, Six Lectures, 96.   [2] Appendix, 497.
[3] Six Lectures on New Testament, 1875, 92.
[4] Canon of New Testament, 213.

version of any Greek book far below the Greek original as a basis for translations into other languages, — the conspicuous defect of the absence of the article in the Roman tongue. Every one must feel what a mutilation of the book, — in itself, and as a basis for translations, — as to the exactness and niceties of expression, must take place by expunging every article in the New Testament and the Old. Stuart says, "The eloquence of Cicero and all his power over language could not enable him to translate adequately and fully into his own mother-tongue the simple words OI AETOI."

"In many cases the relative meaning of words is entirely changed by the presence or absence of the article." Middleton speaks of the article as a "part of speech on which the meaning as well as the elegance of so large a portion of Greek composition must evidently depend."

Middleton's work on the Article,[1] now too rare, is deserving attention. He commences his preface, "The student in theology cannot have failed to remark that the exposition of various passages of the New Testament is, by commentators, made to depend on the presence or the absence of the article in the Greek original."[2] "Michaelis has well observed that 'the difference even of an article must not be neglected in collating a MS.'" "Hints tending to prove the importance of the subject may be traced even in the writings of the fathers. In Justin, in Irenæus, in Clement of Alexandria, in Origen, in Athanasius, in Epiphanius, in Chrysostom, and in Theophylact, we find that stress is sometimes laid on the article as prefixed to particular words; and a Latin father, Jerome, remarking on Gal. v. 18, that 'spirit' is there anarthrous" (without the article), "adds, 'Quae quidem minutiae magis in Graeca quam in nostra lingua observatae (qui ἄρθρα penitus non habemus) videntur aliquid habere momenti,'" — "These minutiæ, indeed, observed more in Greek than in our language, — for we have no articles at all, — seem to be of considerable importance."[3]

Several interesting cases Middleton mentions of the impor-

---

[1] Thomas Fanshaw Middleton, Bishop of Calcutta: Doctrine of the Greek Article. 1808.
[2] P. xxxix.   [3] Preface, xl.

tant use of the article : as, "The word πνεῦμα is employed, by eminence, to denote the Great and Pre-eminent Spirit ; and in this acceptation it is worthy of remark, that πνεῦμα, or πνεῦμα ἅγιον, is never anarthrous, except, indeed, in cases where other terms, confessedly the most definite, lose the article." "In the passages which, from their ascribing personal acts to the πνεῦμα ἅγιον, are usually adduced to prove the personality of the Blessed Spirit, the words πνεῦμα and ἅγιον invariably have the article." [1] On the contrary, Luke xi. 13, "How much more shall your Father give holy spirit to them that ask him ;" [2] for which, accordingly, the Greek scholiast has χάριν πνευματιχήν, "spiritual grace." Another interesting case is Luke xviii. 13, τῷ ἁμαρτωλῷ, "*the* sinner," whether you say with Wetstein, "τῷ habet emphasin," "the chief of sinners," or with Middleton, "The article here marks the assumption of its predicate :" and the strict meaning of the publican's prayer is, "Have mercy on me, who am *confessedly* a sinner;" or, "*Seeing that* I am a sinner, have mercy on me." [3] Still another valuable use of the article, which even carries an argument with it of the writing of the Gospels before the Epistles, is quoted from Gersdorf, that "the four evangelists always write ὁ Χριστός, but Peter and Paul usually Χριστός, as this appellative had in their time become a 'proper name." These are a few among the many valuable uses of this little part of speech, carefully used in Greek, but absolutely unknown to the Latin. Winer (Greek Grammar, Andover ed., 1870) says, "In the language of living intercourse, it is utterly impossible that the article should be omitted where it is decidedly necessary. Ὄρος can never denote *the* mountain, nor τὸ ὄρος *a* mountain." (Matt. v. 1, τὸ ὄρος.)

Now, the Latin takes a stylus, or pen, and goes through the Bible, from Genesis to Revelation, sixty-six books, and *expunges every article.*

A writer in "The Edinburgh Review" eulogizes the Greek thus : "We cannot refuse our admiration to that most wonderful and perfect machine of human thought, to the flexibility, the harmony, the gigantic power, the exquisite delicacy, the infinite

[1] 125.   [2] 227.   [3] 231, 232.

wealth of words, the incomparable felicity of expression, in which are united the energy of the English, the neatness of the French, the sweet and infantile simplicity of the Tuscan. Of all dialects, it is best fitted for the purposes of science and of elegant literature. The philosophical vocabularies of ancient Rome and of modern Europe have been derived from that of Athens. Yet none of these imitations have even approached the richness and precision of the original. It traces with ease distinctions so subtle as to be lost in every other language. It draws lines where all other instruments of the reason make blots."[1] This is the language from which the New Testament was taken. To what was it translated? This author says, perhaps too strongly, "The want of a definite article and of a distinction between the preterite and the aorist tenses are two defects which are alone sufficient to place it below any other language with which we are acquainted. In its most flourishing era it was reproached with poverty of expression. Cicero, indeed, was induced by his patriotic feelings to deny the change ; but the perpetual recurrence of Greek words in his most hurried and familiar letters, and the frequent use which he is compelled to make of them in spite of all his exertions to avoid them in his philosophical works, fully prove that even this great master of the Latin tongue felt the evil which he labored to conceal from others."[2] In a word, *the Greek Testament was plunged into the Latin language*, and *came up with the loss of all its definite articles and aorist tenses*.

We have spent so much time — not too much, may we think — on this point, that we might here and now forever dispel that baseless illusion, which is seen from so many considerations to be utterly groundless, that the Vulgate is the one proper and correct basis for a translation. This, we repeat, is as baseless an illusion as if a man should imagine that the apple-tree is loftier than the elm. With Jerome we say, "*Graeca veritas, Graeca origo.*"

. If this discussion be abstruse, this fact is not, that the great scholar, beginning with translation of the Vulgate, outgrows that, and feels that he must go farther back, and translate from

---

[1] Edinburgh Review, 43, 331 : art. London University.   [2] Ibid., 329.

the original. Wycliffe began with the Vulgate : Tyndale ended with the Hebrew and Greek. Jerome's first work was revisions : by the unerring good sense of perfected scholarship, his final labors were direct translations. It is worth while, perhaps, in this connection, to trace the growth of the mind of the enthusiastic Geddes. He was, though a Catholic, brought up to read the " English " version. "When I had acquired," he tells us, "a sufficient knowledge of Latin, the Vulgate was put into my hands. . . . And now I perceived a considerable difference between it and the English translation. The latter appeared to me rugged, constrained, and often obscure, where the former was smooth, easy, and intelligible. The one seemed to read like a translation, the other like the original. When, in 1762, I began to read the originals, I had both versions constantly before me ; and now I discovered the cause of the great difference between them. The chief study of the English translators I found had been to give a strictly literal version at the expense of almost every other consideration ; while the author of the Vulgate had endeavored to render his originals equivalently into such Latin as was current in his age. ' If ever I translate the Bible,' said I then, ' it must be after this manner.' " [1]

Such was his predilection for the noble Latin, especially, no doubt, in Jerome's portions ; for he says, "His style is plain, easy, and unaffected ; and, although his Latinity is not that of the Augustan age, it is neither barbarous nor inelegant. In his diction and phraseology there is a peculiar grace and noble simplicity which it is not easy to imitate, and which no other Latin version, except that of Houbigant, in any degree possesses." [2] And yet he is obliged later to come to a source other than the Vulgate as a translator ; for he says, " It is well known that there are many places in the Vulgate badly rendered. It is also allowed that other faults have crept into it since the days of its author." [3] " A considerable part of the Vulgate, including the whole Psalter, is not Jerome's, but a translation from a translation none the best, and, moreover,

---

[1] General Answer to Criticisms, 3.
[2] Prospectus, 47.	[3] Prospectus, 105.

contaminated by corruptions that are not in the Greek : hence
it is often unintelligible." " The great defect of Jerome's version is its want of uniformity ; it being sometimes strict, and
sometimes loose ; now barbarously literal, and now widely paraphrastic: every translation made from it, then, must partake
of this variety." "It was my first intention to translate from
the Vulgate, and even to make the Douai version with Challoner's emendations, in some respects, the basis of mine. But I
soon found that this was an absurd idea, and that, by patching
and piecing what had been pieced and patched, I should make
a strange composition indeed. An entirely *new* translation
from the Vulgate, but with such corrections as were manifestly
warranted, was next in my contemplation, and partly executed.
But a very short trial convinced me that neither would this
method ever produce a tolerable version. Had I pursued this
method, I must have been perpetually confronting the Vulgate
with the originals, and very often correcting it by them, or presented my readers with a very unfair and imperfect representation of the sacred text." [1]

This is the conclusion to our numerous, and to some, perhaps,
tedious testimonies, that, in translation, *perfected scholarship
starts from the original ;* that whoso starts from a version starts
from a lower plane ; and that the Douaists, in starting from
principle on the Vulgate to make a translation for Englishmen,
committed a capital error, and one which would forever pre-
clude their work from being thought of as a superlative English
translation of the Scriptures.

Yet, notwithstanding their Latinized English, these men must
be considered deserving of great credit, when we reflect, that
notwithstanding the Catholic aversion to vernacular translations,
and notwithstanding that the apathy of the Papal world fur
nished little incitement or inducement to enter so huge a work,
they entered upon it, and prosecuted the work with such euthusi-
asm. They are to be honored for having given their Catholic
countrymen the best version which they have, and the only
complete version of the Scriptures. It is one of the highest

---

[1] Address to Public, 4.

honors and services a man can attain to be the author of any translation of the Scriptures into the people's language, which remains a standard among any part of them for a hundred years.

Let it be understood, then, we are grateful for their work; and we pause from our disparagement of it, in *comparison*, to refresh the reader by the perusal of Pope Pius VI.'s letter to them, whose sentiments are indeed worthy. He writes, "You judge exceedingly well that the faithful should be exhorted to the reading of the Holy Scriptures. For these are the most abundant sources which ought to be left open to every one, to draw from them purity of morals and of doctrine, to eradicate the errors which are so widely disseminated in these corrupt times. This you have seasonably effected, as you declare, by publishing the Sacred Writings in the language of your country, suitable to every one's capacity." O si sic semper Papae!

But to return. Commencing on this low plane of an un-emended Vulgate, it must now be added, that, as an *English* version, their translation descended to a still lower plane; and this by reason of two separate defects. In the first place, of principle and design and avowal they rendered the Vulgate verbally as nearly as possible, intelligible or unintelligible, elegant or inelegant. The result, as might have been expected, was not a noble, nor even always an intelligible English. Then, in the second place, the translators were not men of such superior genius as (even had they aimed at it) could have produced, in point of English style, a masterly translation. There sometimes arise men (they are as infrequent as great poets), who have such complete scholarship, such universality of spiritual and emotional apprehension and comprehension, and who wield such a weighty, graceful, pliant, adaptative style, that alone they are competent to render the composite Scriptures into their vernacular, running the Bible at once and forever into such a mould of strong and beautiful and appropriate diction, that it takes its abiding-place till the end of time in the hearts of a nation. Such men were Jerome and Luther. But these men were neither Luthers nor Jeromes; nor did they compensate for their mediocrity by their numbers and by remarkable special gifts ; so that, even if a worthy English had been their ambition, they might have divided and revised their labors in such a way as conjointly to have produced an English translation worthy to endure.

The result is such an English style as we find in the Douai, which, in many portions, is a good translation, but in many passages is written in the foreign and un-English language seen in the specimens given : hence we cannot wonder at the opinions of scholars concerning the Douai. Geddes has already been quoted. Though a Catholic, he felt no scruple in saying, " It is a literal and barbarous translation from the Vulgate before its last revision. Their residence in a foreign country had corrupted the translators' language."[1] " It is a translation that hath need to be translated," said old Fuller. Westcott says, " As it stands, the Douai Bible is simply the ordinary, and not the pure Latin text of Jerome in an English dress. Its merits, and they are considerable " (be it far from us to forget that), " lie in its vocabulary. The style, so far as it has a style, is unnatural ; the phrasing is most unrhythmical ; but the language is enriched by the bold reduction of innumerable words to English service."[2] " The translators did not scruple to leave the version unintelligible or ambiguous where the Latin text was so."[3] " The correspondence with the Latin text is thus absolutely verbal ; and it is only through the Latin that the English, in some places, becomes intelligible. But, on the other hand, Jerome's own greatness as a translator is generally seen through the second version." " The Psalter is the most unsatisfactory part of the whole book. Even where the sense is sufficiently clear to remain distinct through three translations, —from Hebrew to Greek, from Greek to Latin, from Latin to English, — the stiff foreign style sounds strangely unsuited to words of devotion ; and, where the Latin itself has already lost the sense, the English baffles understanding."[4]

(3.) Incredible now as it may seem, there is *a yet further deg-*

---

[1] Prospectus, 110.
[2] History English Bible, 328.
[3] Ibid., 327.
[4] Ibid., 3.0, 331.

radation in the Douai since it left their pen.   Mr. Shea says, "Few comparatively, either among Catholics or non-Catholics, are aware, that, among the many Catholic Bibles and Testaments, very few are exact reprints of any previous edition, but that, in fact, there are nearly as many versions, or at least recensions, as there are editions, and that the names Rheims and Douai have become actual misnomers."

"The Catholic World" (November, 1870) says, "In 1752 an edition of Challoner's New Testament appeared, varying in more than two thousand places from Challoner's edition of 1750."   "But these changes are not all. 'The mass of typographical errors to be found in some editions,' says Cardinal Wiseman, 'is quite frightful.'   In point of fact, then, we have neither the Douai Bible, nor Challoner's Bible, in the current edition; and no one knows whose we have.   The evil is a great one.   Archbishop Kenrick endeavored to meet the want by a new translation ; but, with all his biblical and theological learning, his edition has not met such favor as to insure its adoption, even in this country.   It was put forward as an essay, in a limited edition, and is not in a shape for general use."

Cardinal Wiseman says, "To call it any longer the Douai or Rhemish version is an abuse of terms.   It has been altered and modified till scarcely any verse remains as it was originally published ; and, so far as simplicity and energy of style are concerned, the changes are, in general, for the worse. . . . New and important modifications have been made in every edition, till at length many may appear new versions, rather than revisions of the old."   "The mass of typographical errors to be found in some editions is quite frightful, from many of them falling upon important words, and not so much disfiguring them as transforming them into others that give a correct grammatical, but unsound theological sense." [1]

This volume, then, must stand by its name, and read with historical discernment of the words — such as this inquiry has gained for us, its name describes it — the "*Douai*" version of the "*Vulgate;*" nor can it ever aspire to the high position of

---

[1] Wiseman's Essays, Catholic Versions, i. 75, 77, 78.

being regarded by the more than a hundred millions who read the language of Shakspeare and Milton as superlatively the "*English*" translation of the "*Scriptures.*"

Recent Romish Claims.

Before passing from our account of the Douai, we entertain the suggestion of an eminent scholar, that no monogram on these two versions ought to omit to consider the claim made by recent Catholics, of the superiority of the Vulgate over the Greek text in the hands of the King James' translators, on the ground that the Vulgate, made in 391, represented earlier and more correct manuscripts.

We make no pretensions to original or critical diplomatical scholarship. We confess, therefore, that, in addition to our previous reading, we have given three days or more to the perusal and consideration of the best authorities, — Westcott, Davidson, Scrivener, Tregelles, Bentley, — some of which we had read before; not omitting the Douaists' Preface nor the English translators' Preface. After due reflection, we see no reason to change the statements already made; and we believe the view of Cardinal Wiseman and others can, without great difficulty, be shown to be *not the full and final landscape of the case* as it stands out clear and distinct to the glass truly adjusted.

We will first allow them fully and fairly to state their view.

Cardinal Wiseman, speaking of Kenrick's revision of the Douai, says, "First, it is intended to vindicate the Catholic Vulgate, and show its superiority to the Anglican version. The work acquires, in our minds, an additional importance from another consideration. It is the first attempt to bring before the notice of ordinary Catholic readers the critical study of the text. It is an undoubted fact, that all modern judicious critics will give great weight, and even preference, to the Vulgate, or Latin version, beyond the ordinary Greek text, where the two differ. The reason is simple. On these occasions, the oldest and best manuscripts and the most ancient versions almost invariably agree with the Vulgate; and their concurrent testimony establishes the fact, that the Vulgate represents manuscripts more accurate than have been used to form the received Greek text. When we consider the scorn cast by the reformers upon the Vulgate, and their recurrence, in consequence, to the Greek as the only accurate standard, we cannot but rejoice at the silent triumph which truth has at length gained over clamorous error. For, in fact, the principal writers who have avenged the Vulgate, and obtained for it its critical pre-eminence, are Protestants. But though such a judgment has long been passed by the learned, the great bulk of readers, including men of education, no doubt fancy as yet that the Greek must always have the pre-eminence ; and even Catholics may not be free from this opinion. Now, Bishop Kenrick has taken the simplest mode of removing it. He shows, in few words, that where the Anglican version agrees with the Greek, but differs from the Latin, the best modern Protestant critics give the preference to the latter."[1]

This is *all* which we find in Wiseman's writings on this subject.

Bishop Kenrick, in his Preface, says, "The Vulgate version of the New Testament is almost as ancient as the text, having been made in the age of the apostles" (he refers to the Old Latin, of which the Vulgate is a revision), "or not long afterwards, and retouched by St. Jerome at the close of the fourth century: consequently it represents a Greek manuscript of the highest antiquity." "At the Reformation, the Greek text, as it then stood, was taken as a standard." "The text was full of interpolations and corruptions of various kinds ; whilst the Vulgate faithfully represented the text as it stood in the fourth century, or even in the first century."[2]

"Since the famous manuscripts of Rome, Alexandria, Cambridge, Paris, and Dublin, were examined, a verdict has been obtained in favor of the Vulgate. In the vast majority of instances in which it differs from the common Greek, Protestant judges, with astonishing unanimity, have declared its correctness." "I deemed it all-important to prove in detail, by the testimony of unsuspected witnesses, that the Vulgate version of the Gos-

---

[1] Wiseman's Essays, i. 103, 104: Parables.

[2] Amazingly unscholarly is this statement, particularly in one supposed to be a special student of the Vulgate, oblivious to all modern criticism of the Vulgate as it was three centuries ago, and of the Roman criticism of that period upon it.

pels is a faithful representation of the original text; whilst the Protestant translation, taken from the common Greek, abounds in inaccuracies."[1]

With much more learning, the Douaists state this view in their Preface: "It is not only better than all other Latin translations, but than the Greek text itself in those places where they disagree." "And this the adversary himself, their greatest and latest translator of the Greek, doth avouch against Erasmus in behalf of the old Vulgate Latin translation, in these notorious words: 'How unworthily and without cause (saith he) does Erasmus blame the old interpreter,[2] as dissenting from the Greek! He dissented, I grant, from those Greek copies which he had gotten; but we have found, in more places than· one, that the same interpretation which he blameth is grounded upon the authority of other Greek copies, and those most ancient. Yea, in some number of places we have observed that the reading of the Latin text of the old interpreter, though it agree not sometimes with our Greek copies, yet it is much more convenient, for that he seemeth to follow some better and truer copy.' Thus far Beza. In which words he unwittingly, but most truly, justifieth and defendeth the old vulgar translation against himself and all other cavillers that accuse the same because it is not always agreeable to the Greek text; whereas it was translated out of other Greek copies, — partly extant, partly not exant at this day, either as good and as ancient, or better and more ancient, such as Augustine speaketh of, calling them *doctiores* et *diligentiores*, the more learned and diligent Greek copies, to which the Latin translations that fail in any place must needs yield." "If it disagree here and there from the Greek text, it agreeth with another Greek copy set in the margin." "If all Erasmus' Greek copies have not that which is in the Vulgate Latin, Beza had copies which have it, and those most ancient (as he saith) and better."

We believe our readers have before them the objection in the amplest and strongest statements. We presume that they appear to the common reader to establish the Latin Vulgate

[1] Bp. F. P. Kenrick: Pref. to Gospels, 1849.   [2] Jerome.

as the only document worthy to be considered a basis for an English translation.   Nevertheless, our reply need not linger, nor need it gather any thing from uncandor to display the strength of the real truth.

We acknowledge with gratitude that our Roman-Catholic fellow-citizens have so good a version of the Holy Scriptures in the vernacular, which contains the full light of "the glorious gospel of the blessed God," which is "able to make wise unto salvation." "By far the greatest part of the Sacred Text (thank God)," says the great Bengel,[1] "labors under no important variety of reading."[2]

We recognize its merits and its helpfulness, especially — since the Vulgate strove to retain even the Greek *order* — in what Wiseman so finely calls "inversion, where congenial at once to the genius of our language and to the construction of the original."[3]

We recognize gladly the great work which Jerome, a "supremely great man" as Westcott calls him, was raised up to do, in giving to the world the Latin Vulgate, one of the noblest of versions.   Through that, Western Europe received the Scriptures for more than a thousand years, and permanently an extensive and exceedingly valuable addition to its religious diction.   That version, so early made from the best manuscripts of fifteen hundred years ago, is of great critical value.   As an aid to the understanding of many passages, we prize it, espe-

---

[1] Preface to Gnomon.

[2] Lest any youthful reader of this book should stumble at our much talk of corrupt text, variations, &c., we take pains to say that these variations, while they are important in considering one document as an exact and critical copy of another, may have little importance in causing substantial change of meaning. "Prof. Moses Stuart gave this testimony to the general correctness of the present text of the Bible in the original languages: 'Out of some eight hundred thousand various readings of the Bible that have been collated, about seven hundred and ninety-five thousand are of just about as much importance to the sense of the Greek and Hebrew Scriptures as the question in English orthography is, whether the word *honour* shall be spelled with a *u* or without it. Of the remainder, some change the sense of particular passages or expressions, or omit particular words or phrases; but no one doctrine of religion is changed, not one precept is taken away, not one important fact is altered, by the whole of the various readings collectively taken.' "

[3] "Ipse verborum ordo mysterium est" (Jerome). "The very order of the words is a mystery." Bentley first drew the attention of critics to this, as indicating what might be expected of the Vulgate as a copy of the Greek in the structure of sentences. — ELLIS: Critica Sacra, xvii.

cially in Jerome's Old Testament. We believe every biblical scholar ought to own the Vulgate. We confess that we are glad that we have the Vulgate Latin on our shelves, and the Rhemish New Testament. The variation in translation ,stimulates thought, and examination of the original.

But with our appreciation of the Douai, and with our *high* appreciation of the Vulgate, we must express our clear sense of the *two versions in comparison* by a few plain propositions, which, we believe, cover the whole subject.

1. No scholar — not even these Papal scholars — would think of saying that the DOUAI VERSION is to be compared with the ENGLISH VERSION as a representative of the original Scriptures.

The reader has probably received, from the Papal authors quoted, the impression that it is the *Douai* which they are exalting at the expense of the English version. We take it for granted that these worthy men did not *intend* to convey that meaning; for certainly they do not *say* that, nor would they risk their reputation for scholarship by saying that. The Douaists themselves were, of course, speaking of the Latin, not of their version. Wiseman is comparing, if you observe, the Vulgate — not the Douai — with the "English." "To show the superiority of the Vulgate over the Anglican." Kenrick, though inclined to be more rash in statement, if you regard his words, will be seen not to assert that the Douai, but only the Vulgate, excels the "Protestant version."

No scholar — not even of Catholics — denies that the *Douai* is inferior to the *English*. It matters not whether that inferiority come from a *faulty original* or from an *obscure translation:* the inferiority of the product is undeniable.

We may, then, dismiss the court, since there is really no case. The *Douai* is not *claimed* to be the equal of the *English*. It is not *Henry* Paine who is asserted to be a better man than Arthur Stanley, but his *father, William* Paine. Not the Douai, but the Latin Vulgate, is asserted to be better than King James' version.

But perhaps it may be imagined these authors *meant* to speak of the Douai, or *might* have spoken thus of the Douai. That they *did not* is conclusive that they *could not.*

Extended proof is unnecessary. Geddes, the Catholic scholar, calls it "a barbarous translation made at Rheims." "It is a translation that hath need to be translated," said old Fuller. Westcott says, "The translators did not hesitate to leave the version unintelligible or ambiguous where the Latin text was so." "It is only through the Latin that the English in some places becomes intelligible. The Psalter is the most unsatisfactory part of the whole book. Even where the sense is sufficiently clear to remain distinct through three translations, — from Hebrew to Greek, from Greek to Latin, from Latin to English, — the stiff foreign style sounds strangely unsuited to words of devotion ; and, where the Latin itself has lost the sense, the English baffles understanding."[1] He gives examples, of which we quote two as specimens : (Ps. lvii. 10) " Before your thorns did understand the old brier ; as living so in wrath he swalloweth them." (Heb. xiii. 16) "Beneficence and communication do not forget ; for with such hosts God is pre-merited." "Such translations," he adds, "have no claim to be considered vernacular translations of the text : except through the Latin, they are unintelligible."

Romanists themselves show their low appreciation of the Douai by their "faint praise," or no praise ; by the many revisions, beginning with Challoner's revision in 1750, *by King James*;[2] and a second, which corrected two thousand errors, in 1752 ; by dissatisfaction with these revisions ;[3] and by certain remarkable things in connection with these revisions. For example : Wiseman shows these amazing errors corrected in the Dublin revision, 1810: (Matt. xvi. 23) "Thou favorest not," instead of "savorest;" (Rom. vii. 18) "To accomplish that which is good, I find *out*," instead of "find not ;" (Gal. iv. 9) "How turn ye again to the *work* (for *weak*) and poor elements?" (v. 23) "charity" for "chastity ;" also "Sin, which was asleep before, was *weakened* by the prohibition," instead of "awakened." He adds, as if in despair, "It is far from our

---

[1] Westcott: History English Bible, 327, 328, 331, 334.
[2] "Dr. Challoner corrected the style, chiefly from King James' translation."— GEDDES, 110.
[3] See Wiseman.

purpose to undertake a complete exposure of the many passages which want emendation : such a task would require a
treatise."

Kenrick had the smoothest part of the Bible and the simplest, — the four Gospels ; and he ostentatiously marks all the
trifling readings where the Vulgate excels, amounting, as we
counted in Matthew, to a few over one hundred and twenty,
nine-tenths of them variations like the omission of "and,"
"also," &c. But, on the other hand, he fails to show in how
many places the English is superior ; and his corrections of the
Douai by the English he very *quietly* places as footnotes.
These, for the most part, do more towards altering the text.
Still he leaves such confusing or erroneous phrases (in Matthew alone) as, " Touched the tuft of his garment ; " " My yoke
is sweet ; " " Out of the mouth," &c., " thou hast drawn praise ; "
" They put over his head his cause in writing ; " " They wagged
their heads, and said, Vah : " and these sentences, " Nobody
putteth a piece of raw cloth to an old garment ; " " If the mira-
cles," &c., " had been done in Sodom, perhaps it would have
remained ; " " Peter said, Lord, mercy upon thee ; this shall
never befall thee ; and he, turning, said to Peter, Go behind
me, Satan ; thou art a scandal to me ; " " Whosoever will be the
greater among you, let him be your waiter."

It is *not* of this book, but of another, — and who wonders ? —
that Westcott says, who represents scholarship on this point,
" From the middle of the seventeenth century, the King's Bible
has been the acknowledged Bible of the English-speaking nations throughout the world, simply because it is the best."[1]

Our argument might stop here, and *should, logically*, stop here,
since no one denies that the English is better than the Douai.
But, since the subject is before us, we add several propositions
in regard to the originals. There are times when objections
should not only be answered, but driven to their inner works,
and annihilated.

2. No scholar would say that the LATIN VULGATE text, which
was before the Douaists, was a better basis for a translation of

---

[1] **History English Bible,** 160.

the Old Testament than the HEBREW text, which was before the English translators.

What was before the Douaists was (1) a Latin Psalter translated from the Greek, which was translated from the Hebrew; and (2) the rest of the Old Testament, in noble Latin, translated by Jerome, yet still a *translation*, and therefore not equal to the original, though admirable, we gladly admit, as Davidson describes the Vulgate: "Even in its present state, with all its corruptions, it generally coincides with the Masoretic text." .

What was before the Anglicans was the *Hebrew text itself.* It is indeed true, that there is said to be something yet to be desired in the critical emendation of the Hebrew text;[1] yet Davidson's words represent scholarship as to the general purity of the text of the Hebrew Scriptures: "The result of all the collations of the Hebrew manuscripts which have been instituted is the confirmation of the text lying at the basis of the Masorah. All known codices exhibit substantially that text. The oldest versions, which adhere most to the original, had nearly the same text. Little alteration has been made in it since settled by the Masoretes; and the earliest Targums show, that, about the time of Christ, it was essentially what it afterwards appeared in the Masoretic period. When we try to go up farther — to the time when the canon was completed, and onward to the return of the Jews from exile — in search of what the primitive text then was, we cannot conceive of it as differing much from its present condition. The Jews after the exile were very careful in preserving it. They guarded it against corruption with watchful jealousy. Every thing conspires to show that we have the original now in a correct state. The genuine text has been handed down with purity."[2] Josephus is a witness to this extreme care of the Hebrew text: "Now, it appears from the facts how far we have believed in our own Scriptures; for, although already so many ages have passed, no one has ever dared either to *remove* or *add* or *transpose* any

---

[1] Schaff says that there are only 1,314 various readings of importance in the Hebrew Bible, of which only 147 affect the sense.

[2] Davidson: Introduction to Old Testament, 44. See also Westcott: English Bible, 170. Geddes: Prospectus, 17.

thing. And it is for all the Jews, as a thought born with them from the first generation, to call them the teaching of God, to abide in them, and, if necessary, to die with joy to maintain them."[1]

There were five printed editions of the Hebrew Bible before King James' time.

The Hebrew Bible, then, which was before the English translators, is better than the Vulgate, which was before the Douaists, noble as that is.

Concerning the New Testament alone, therefore, as to the superiority of the Greek text or the Latin Vulgate, can question arise.

3. No scholar would assert that the Latin Vulgate, in the *most ancient and valuable copies we* NOW *have,* could compare as a basis for translation with the Greek text, as also represented in the *oldest Greek manuscripts* NOW *accessible.*

We hardly need argue this before scholars. Briefly we may show what copies of each are now accessible. Most of the best codices of each have come to light since the two translations.

Of the *Old Latin* we have several valuable codices: *Vercellis,* of fourth century, found in 1726; *Veronensis,* "hardly less ancient or valuable;" another, of sixth century from Brescia; *Sarzannensis,* also of fifth century.

Of the *Latin Vulgate* we now have, Codex *Amiatinus,* a noble copy of the whole Bible, written by the hand of the Abbot Servandus, A.D. 541. Only five years younger is the Codex *Fuldensis.* There are other codices also of great value.

Of the Greek we have the following, all greatly valuable : —

A. Codex *Alexandrinus,* presented to Charles I. of England by the Patriarch of Constantinople. This manuscript was written at Alexandria, and belongs to the fifth century.

B. Vaticanus, in the Vatican since 1209, not properly published till 1857. This belongs to the fourth century, as early probably as Jerome.

א (Aleph.) *Sinaiticus,* found by Tischendorf — his story of

---

[1] *Against Apion,* i. 8.

the finding is graphic — in the Convent of St. Catharine, on Mt. Sinai.

It is as interesting as a romance, how Tischendorf, in travels in search for Greek manuscripts, in May, 1844, came to the Convent of St. Catharine, at the foot of Mt. Sinai; how he saw a large basket full of old manuscripts, and the librarian told him that two heaps of such mouldered papers had already been committed to the flames. In this heap Tischendorf found part of a very ancient Old Testament in Greek. The authorities allowed him forty-five sheets, which were going to the flames. Rendered suspicious by his enthusiasm, they allowed him no more. He enjoined their preservation, returned to Saxony, made a second visit to the convent in 1853, came away unsuccessful; obtained, after great opposition, the favor of the Russian emperor; arrived the third time at the convent in 1859; when about to depart, was casually shown by the convent-steward the manuscripts he came in search of; affected indifference, asked to take them to his chamber, and there *gave way to his transport of joy!* "I cannot now, I confess," he says, "recall all the emotions which I felt in that exciting moment, with such a diamond in my possession. Though my lamp was dim, and the night cold, I sat down at once to transcribe the Epistle of Barnabas." This manuscript was eventually by the convent presented to the czar, who had splendid copies taken, and deposited in the great libraries of the world.[1]

Tischendorf ascribes this manuscript to the fourth century. It may, he thinks, be one of the fifty copies made at Constantine's order in 351. "The value of this acquisition," says Kitto, "can hardly be over-estimated."

C. Codex *Ephraemi*, written in Egypt in the fifth century.

All these have been made accessible *since* 1600, as also the ancient and valuable Old Latin and the Vulgate Latin manuscripts mentioned.

Now, exceedingly valuable as are the new-found manuscripts of the Vulgate, two of them only one hundred and fifty years

---

[1] Tischendorf: When were our Gospels written? With a narrative of the discovery of the Sinaitic manuscript. Am. Tract Soc., 1866, pp. 132.

after the great translator himself, yet no scholar would for a moment hesitate which to sacrifice, — the Greek manuscripts we *now* have, or the Latin Vulgate manuscripts we *now* have, or even the Old Latin manuscripts we now have.

Or even the Old Latin. These manuscripts, *Vercellis* and *Veronensis*, of the fourth century, are extremely valuable ; for they represent Greek manuscripts, it may be as old as 170 A.D., about which time the Old Latin was made. Some might think for a moment that they might be superior to our ancient Greek manuscripts. But, —

1. The Douai is derived from the Vulgate, not from the Old Latin ; and the Vulgate follows the Old Latin mostly in the Epistles, and somewhat in the Gospels, the Old Testament scarcely at all.

2. The *Vercellis* and *Veronensis* are Latin copies, of a Latin certainly not before 170 A.D., from a Greek before that.

The Vatican and Sinaitic are Greek, *possibly*, — certainly direct and without the loss in translation, — *possibly*, we say, from the very manuscripts of John and Paul, Matthew and Peter. It cannot be shown that they *are not*.

Thus far our propositions have been made with the utmost confidence, as in asserting the indisputable. That which we now make is made with less *positiveness*, yet as our *confident belief*, as suggested by our reading on the subject, that, —

4. No scholar would maintain that the *Latin Vulgate* TEXT, which the Douaists had before them, represented the original New Testament better than the *Greek* TEXT which the English translators had before them.

It is true that the Greek text at that period was not critical ; but, on the other hand, the Vulgate was confessedly corrupt. We find no scholars asserting, in comparison, which was most wide from its original ; but we certainly find no assertions, except that of Kenrick, absolutely without attempt at proof, that the Latin was any nearer to its original.

Scrivener says of the New Testament,[1] " None of the most ancient Greek manuscripts had then been collated ; and, though

---

[1] Cambridge Paragraph Bible, 1873: Introduction, xxxii.

Codex Bezae (D) had been for many years deposited in England, little use had been made of it." "It would be unjust to assert that the translators failed to take advantage of the materials which were readily accessible; nor did they lack care or discernment in the application of them. Doubtless they rested mainly on the later editions of Beza's New Testament, whereof his fourth (1589) was more highly esteemed than his fifth (1598), the product of his extreme old age. But, besides these, the Complutensian Polyglot, together with several editions of Erasmus and Stephanus of 1550, were constantly resorted to."

Such manuscripts of the New Testament would not rank high by the side of those since collated.

Ellicott says, "In the fourth edition of Erasmus, we really have the mother-text of our own authorized version." "Such it is; and yet, by the providence of God the Holy Spirit, and through the loyalty and reverence with which the word of God had been transmitted, and that faithfulness which stirred in the hand and heart even of the writer of the meanest cursive manuscripts, *it is what it is*, so far substantially in accord with what now we may rightly deem the true text as justly to call forth our enduring thankfulness for this mercy and providence of Almighty God." [1]

But, on the other hand, the Latin Vulgate was in no better state. *Codex Amiatinus*, Scrivener says, was seen, we are *told*, by the translators; but he adds, their work does not show it. None of these noble copies of the Old Latin or of the Vulgate were at their hand. Geddes calls the Douai "a barbarous translation from an *uncorrected copy of the Vulgate*." The Council of Trent was told that the text was "so corrupt, that only a pope could settle it." Sixtus tried to amend it, but, though a scholar, ridiculously failed; and Clement, as all scholars confess, has presented to us something which is far from Jerome's Vulgate. "It is only right to state," says Scrivener,[2] "that neither the Sixtine Bible nor the Clementine" "can be relied upon in the least for critical purposes. They are constructed in a loose and unintelligent fashion on manuscripts too recent

---

[1] Ellicott : On Revision, 38.   [2] Six Lectures, 104.

to be trustworthy." "The true readings must still be sought for in the older copies."

Tregelles says,[1] " In the twelfth and thirteenth centuries, *Correctoria*, prepared by the University of Paris and others, afford, at times, good evidence against the modern Vulgate, showing that it exhibits a Latin text, which has suffered even since the thirteenth century." "When about the middle of the fifteenth century the art of printing came in, of course it was out of the question to suppose that any critical skill or care was brought to bear upon the *text* thus multiplied." " The labor of Erasmus was not directed to the restoration of the Vulgate, but to the formation of a version which should, he hoped, take its place. Indeed, that scholar was so impressed with the corruption of the Vulgate, and with its contrariety to classical Latin, that he thought it could not be the actual version of Jerome." Yet " the modern Vulgate is *substantially* the version of Jerome, though the variations from it are frequent, and the changes are always for the worse."

Bentley says, in a letter to the Archbishop of Canterbury, April, 1716, " Popes Sixtus and Clement, at a vast expense, had an assembly of learned divines to recense and adjust the Latin Vulgate, and then enacted their edition authentic ; but I find, though I have not yet discovered any thing done *dolo malo*, they were quite unequal to the affair. They were mere theologi ; had no experience in manuscripts, nor made use of good Greek copies ; and followed books of five hundred years before those of double that age : nay, I believe they took these newest ones for the older of the two ; for it is not everybody that knows the age of a manuscript." "So that, to conclude in a word, I find that by taking two thousand errors out of the Pope's Vulgate, and as many out of the Protestant Pope Stephens', I can set out an edition of each, in columns, without using any book under nine hundred years old, that shall so exactly agree, word for word, and, what at first amazed me, order for order, that no two tallies nor two indentures can agree better."

The emended Vulgate, then, to Bentley, seemed no better text than Stephens' New Testament.

[1] Introduction to New Testament, 248.

But the Douaists had before them an *unemended* Vulgate.

It was, moreover, a *translation*, and, though originally good, was — the New Testament, that is — not the best part of Jerome's work.

5. One final proposition concludes, we believe, what is necessary to a full and fair comparison of these translations, — the English and the Douai, — that the English had *gathered into itself*, not all that it might with benefit, but *a not inconsiderable part of the excellences of the Vulgate.*

The Douaists had made some attempt to avail themselves of other scholarship than the version before them. Westcott tells us that the "earlier English translations formed the groundwork of their version." Challoner, we have seen, corrected the Douai by King James'.

But, on the other hand, the English version receives *constant accessions from the Vulgate* at every fresh revision. Wycliffe's version was from the Vulgate; and this Latin (and his English) was inwrought into the minds of all intelligent and especially scholarly people, above all, of those who came forward to translate the Bible afresh. Besides this, the Vulgate was prized as a help during all the century of translation. We run together a few sentences from Westcott.

"It is impossible to read through a single chapter without gaining the assurance that Tyndale rendered the Greek text directly, while still he consulted the Vulgate, the Latin translation of Erasmus, and the German of Luther." Coverdale's "Pentateuch may be fairly described as the Zurich translation rendered into English by the help of Tyndale, with constant reference to Luther, Pagninus, and the Vulgate." "As far as I have observed, Taverner used no help but the Vulgate in the Old Testament;" and, passing over the others, the authorized version made great use of the Vulgate. "A single epistle furnishes the following list of Latin words which King James' translators have taken from the Rhemish Testament: *separated* (Rom. i. 1), *consent* (i. 32), *impenitent* (ii. 5), *approvest* (ii. 18), *propitiation* (iii. 25), *remission* (id.), *grace* (iv. 4), *glory* in tribulations (v. 3), *commendeth* (v. 8), *concupiscence* (vii. 7), *revealed*

(viii. 18), *expectation* (viii. 19), *conformable* (viii. 29), *confession* is made unto salvation (x. 10), *emulation* (xi. 14), *concluded* (xi. 32), *conformed* (xii. 12), *instant* (xii. 12), *contribution* (xv. 26)." [1] Besides this, nearly all the modern versions — French, Italian, Spanish, &c. — had been made from the Vulgate, which versions were used as helps by the King James' men ; and thus from all these upland washings from the Latin, and its derivative versions, this fair meadow, the "English," received much of the worth and wealth of the Vulgate.

THE ENGLISH VERSION.

The English version needs not so long a description as we have given to the Douai Vulgate : not, however, of course, because its genesis, and progress to final completion, are any less interesting ; for what can be more interesting than that translation which had its origin from Wycliffe, whose bones, dug up, were burnt to ashes, and scattered on the Avon ; from Tyndale, master of seven languages, but strangled and burnt at Vilvorde ; and with which are connected the names of Rogers the martyr, Cranmer the archbishop, Reynolds the Puritan scholar, Queen Anne Boleyn, and James the King ; and which was wrought out in Geneva and Cologne and Worms and Brussels, as well as in London and the university towns of England? The story of the English version, therefore, is amply worthy of full narration ; but for these reasons it needs it not. Its story has been more than once told in popular form ; and then, again, — which reason in the present case is prevailing, — its progress is neither obscure nor indirect. Commencing with Wycliffe, or rather with Tyndale, it marches steadily forward to its completion under King James ; and as this history is so recent, all of it having occurred, we might almost say, under our eye, since the darkness of the mediæval period ; and as the successive versions have recorded themselves in immortal and accessible type ; and as, moreover, the methods and spirit of their translation are for the most part clear and undisputed, — there is little obscurity to remove, and little which is questionable to rebut.

[1] Westcott : Eng. Bib. 334.

A plain, brief account of the English version, not entering, as we would like, if the length of our paper permitted or its needs required, into the interesting scenes connected with it, will satisfy our present purpose, — the comparison of the two versions.

Wycliffe has been called the "morning-star of the Reformation." And certainly his Bible, and the living soul, which, first in imagination, and soon in reality, saw its pages in to his eyes more glorious than illuminated text, — namely, in the vernacular words which carried the enlightenment and cheer of God's word to all who tilled the soil and plied the loom in England, — did much to usher in this latter-day glory, when, since the century began, a hundred millions of English Bibles have been sent out over earth and seas as widely as the sun scatters its all-penetrating beams. Wycliffe was born in 1324: he died in 1384. While regarding his work as in the very van of English translations, we must not forget to name with honor the fragmentary versions of the venerable Bede and royal Alfred and others, which, though read only within extremely narrow limits in their day, and too crude and imperfect to exercise any formative influence upon the present version, nevertheless showed the longing of Englishmen, as early almost as England had a history, and before she had a well-formed language, to have the Scriptures in their vernacular Anglo-Saxon, rude though it was.[1]

"It was a great day for England when John Wycliffe first conceived the idea of giving to his countrymen the whole Bible in the common language. The execution of that idea is the leading event of the fourteenth century. It would not be too much, perhaps, to call it the leading event in Anglo-Saxon history."[2] In a sermon at Lutterworth, Wycliffe exclaimed, "O Christ! thy law is hidden in the sepulchre: when wilt thou send thine angel to remove it?" He himself was sent as that angel.

Wycliffe, "being ignorant of the Hebrew and Greek languages,

---

[1] Anglo-Saxon translations: Bishop Adhelm, Psalms, 705; Bishop Egbert, Four Gospels, a little later; Bede, portions of the Scriptures (he died dictating part of John's Gospel), a few years later; Alfred, about 900, Psalter; Elfric, several books of the Old Testament, 995.

[2] Mrs. H. C. Conant: English Bible, Popular History.

which he had no opportunity of learning, was under the necessity of translating from the Vulgate." "Wycliffe may indeed be regarded as the father of English prose." "Scarcely an attempt had been made to use it in composition till Wycliffe, with his great heart of love for the people, laid hold of it as the vehicle of religious instruction. He took the rude elements directly from the lips of the despised ploughmen, mechanics, and tradesmen. He gave it back to them in all its unadorned, picturesque simplicity, but fused by the action of his powerful mind into a fitting instrument of thought, and enriched with the noblest literature which the world has produced, — the utterances of inspired poets, prophets, and apostles, the inimitable histories, narratives, and portraitures, through which Divine Wisdom has told the sublime story of providence and redemption." [1]

His translation was completed about 1384, a hundred and eight years before the discovery of America, and a hundred and thirty years before Luther. It was the first English Bible, and for a hundred and forty-one years it was the only one. A vast number of transcriptions were made by priests : there are even now extant a hundred and seventy copies. They were read to, and read by, the common people.

> "The Sacred Book,
> In dusty sequestration held too long,
> Assumes the accents of our native tongue ;
> And he who guides the plough, or wields the crook,
> With understanding spirit now may look
> Upon her records, listen to her song,
> And sift her laws."

"In the century and a half during which it was the well-spring of the religious life of England, that long dark day when persecution kept the flock of Christ fast by the source of strength and consolation, its homely, childlike, expressive phraseology had become too deeply hallowed in the English mind as the medium of inspiration ever again to be dissevered from it. A comparison with the subsequent versions which have found favor with the common people will show them to be, in this respect,

[1] Conant, 98.

all offsprings of·this parent stock. Improved in many important particulars so as to reflect with greater exactness the sense
of the inspired originals, they are yet substantially in form and
manner but reproductions of that in which our unlettered forefathers first read the revelation of God."[1] Prof. Marsh says,
"The difference between the version of Wycliffe and that of
Tyndale was occasioned partly by the change of the language
in the course of two centuries, and partly by the difference of
the texts from which they translated,; and, from these two
causes, the discrepancies between the two versions are much
greater than those between Tyndale's, which was completed in
1526, and the standard version which appeared only eighty-five
years later. But, nevertheless, the influence of Wycliffe upon
Tyndale is too palpable to be mistaken ; and it cannot be dis-
guised by the grammatical differences, which are the more important points of discrepancy between them. If we reduce the
orthography of both to the same standard, conform the inflec-
tions of the fourteenth to those of the sixteenth century, and
make the other changes which would suggest themselves to an
Englishman translating from the Greek instead of the Vulgate,
we shall find a much greater resemblance between the two
versions than a similar process would produce between secular
authors of the periods to which they belong. Tyndale is merely
a full-grown Wycliffe ; and his recension of the New Testament
is just what his great predecessor would have made it, had he
awaked again to see the dawn of that glorious day of which his
own light and labors kindled the morning twilight. Not only
does Tyndale retain the grammatical structure of the older
version, but most of its felicitous verbal combinations ; and,
what is more remarkable, he preserves even the rhythmic flow
of the periods, which is again repeated in the recension of 1611.
Wycliffe, then, must be considered as having originated the
diction and phraseology which for five centuries has constituted
the consecrated dialect of the English speech ; and Tyndale as
having given to it that finish and perfection which has so admirably adapted it to the expression of religious doctrine and

[1] Conant, 104.

sentiment, and to the narration of the remarkable series of historical facts which are recorded in the Christian Scriptures."[1] "Of the influence of Wycliffe's labor, no person seems to have obtained a clearer view than Dr. Lingard. 'He made,' says this historian, 'a new translation, multiplied the copies with the aid of transcribers, and by his poor priests recommended it to the perusal of their hearers. In their hands it became an engine of wonderful power. Men were flattered with the appeal to their private judgment; the new doctrines insensibly acquired partisans and protectors in the higher classes, who alone were acquainted with the use of letters; a spirit of inquiry was generated; and the seeds were sown of that religious revólution which in little more than a century astonished and convulsed the nations of Europe.'"[2]

Even dead, he yet spoke to England; and his enemies — the enemies of God's truth — dug him up after he had been thirty-one years in his grave, burnt his bones, and cast the ashes into the Speed, a little English brook which flows into the Avon. In this they did but give an emblem of his work, destroyed as they hoped, but rather scattered over the world.

> "The Avon to the Severn runs,
>   The Severn to the sea;
> And Wycliffe's dust shall spread abroad
>   Wide as the waters be."

Wycliffe's translation, as we have seen, was promulgated only by transcription and faithful preachers. "Whatever power it exercised in preparing the way for the Reformation of the sixteenth century, it had no perceptible influence on later translations. By the reign of Henry VIII., its English was already obsolescent; and the revival of classical scholarship led men to feel dissatisfied with a version which had been avowedly made at second hand, not from the original. With Tyndale, on the other hand, we enter on a continuous succession. He is the patriarch, in no remote ancestry, of the authorized version."[3]

---

[1] George P. Marsh: Lectures on English Language, 627.
[2] Encyclopædia Britannica, art. Wycliffe, 951.
[3] Smith's Dictionary: Version, Authorized (Edward H. Plumptre), iv. 3424-3445. The

"I perceived with experience," says William Tyndale, "how that it was impossible to establish the lay people in any truth except the Scriptures were plainly laid before their eyes in their mother-tongue." It was, then, by far-reaching design, and as means to an end, that Tyndale set about his work. At thirty-six years of age (1520), to a certain divine, who had affirmed, "We were better to be without God's laws than the pope's," he said, "If God spare my life, ere many years I will cause a boy that driveth the plough to know more of the Scriptures than he."[1]   Tyndale's version appeared in 1526.   Since Wycliffe's day, Faust and Gutenburg had invented printing; and, by a happy coincidence, the first volume issued in type had been a Bible.[2] Every heart responds to Coverdale's reflection: "Methinks we have great occasion to give thanks unto God that he hath opened unto his church the gift of *interpretation* and of *printing.*"   Yet Tyndale had not dared to print the Bible in England: so he commenced his work at Cologne, but was forced to snatch his sheets, and fly to Worms, where he completed the version. His was a master-mind.   He was "a scholar, skilled in seven languages, and one of these is Hebrew.   He prepared himself for the work by years of labor in Greek and Hebrew."   "All external evidence goes to prove Tyndale's originality as a trans-lator."   "The translation of the New Testament itself is proof of its own independence."   "It is impossible," says Westcott, "to read through a single chapter without gaining the assur-ance that Tyndale rendered the Greek text directly, while still he consulted the Vulgate, the Latin translation of Erasmus, and the German of Luther."[3]   A worthy eulogy is given by Geddes: "In point of perspicuity and noble simplicity, propriety of

apparent disagreement between Plumptre's estimate of the influence of Wycliffe's version and that of Marsh and Conant is, perhaps, due in part to a real difference of opinion; but more, probably, to their different point of view. The latter have in mind the effect of his English on the later versions. This must have been considerable. Tyndale was doubtless familiar with Wycliffe's Bible, and its phrases must have run in his mind; but Tyndale translated directly and with originality from the originals, and it is doubtful if he directly and actually consulted Wycliffe's version. Plumptre is right in his assertion that "Tyndale is the patriarch," &c.

[1] Foxe: Acts and Monuments, 542, Carter's edition.
[2] Mazarin Vulgate, from press of Mainz, Gutenberg and Faust, 1455.
[3] History English Bible, 174.

idiom, and purity of style, no English version has yet surpassed it." [1] He has impressed his genius forever upon the English Bible. " To Tyndale," says Plumptre, "belongs the honor of having given the first example of a translation based on true principles ; and the excellence of later versions has been almost in exact proportion as they have followed his." " To him it is owing that the versions of the English Church have throughout been popular, and not scholastic. All the exquisite grace and simplicity which has endeared the authorized version to men of the most opposite tempers and contrasted opinions — to J. H. Newman and J. A. Froude — is due mainly to his clear-sighted truthfulness." [2] " Throughout there is the pervading stamp, so often wanting in other like works, of the most thorough truthfulness." Tyndale's noble simplicity is seen in translating, " not ' grace,' but 'favor ;' not 'charity,' but 'love ;' not 'confessing,' but 'acknowledging ;' not 'penance,' but 'repentance ;' not 'priests,' but 'seniors' and 'elders ;' not 'salvation,' but 'health.'" " Some of these we are now familiar with. In others, the later versions bear traces of a re-action in favor of the older phraseology." " When we study our Testaments, we are in most cases perusing the identical words penned by the martyr Tyndale nearly three hundred and fifty years ago." [3]

Tyndale's version was ordered to be bought up and burned in England ; and Sir Thomas More ordered possessors of this translation to be set on horseback, with their faces towards the horses' tails, and thus to carry their copies to the place to be burned. Tyndale's noble life was crowned by martyrdom. He was strangled and burned at Vilvorde, near Brussels.

The Beatitudes, as given by Wycliffe and by Tyndale, will serve to show their similarity and dissimilarity to each other and to our version, and also the growth of the language and the improvement in diction during these periods. They were both in Old English, — the first written, the latter printed.

WYCLIFFE, 1380 : " And Jhesus seynge the peple, went up into an hil ; and whan he was sett, his disciplis camen to him.

---

[1] Prospectus, 89.   [2] Dublin Review, June, 1853.

[3] Marsh : Lectures English Language, 625.

And he openyde his mouthe, and taughte hem; and seide,
Blessid be pore men in spirit; for the kyngdom of hevenes is
herun.   Blessid ben mylde men; for thei schulen weelde the
erthe.   Blessid ben thei that mournen; for thei schal be coum-
fortid.   Blessed be thei that hungren and thirsten rightwisnesse; for thei shal be fulfilled.   Blessed ben merciful men;
for thei schul gete mercy.   Blessed ben thei that ben of clene
herte; for thei schulen se god.   Blessed be pesible men; for thei
schulen be clepid goddis children.   Blessed ben thei that suffren
persecucioun for rightwisnesse; for the kyngdom of hevenes
is hern.   Ye schul be blessid whanne men schul curse you,
and schul pursue you; and schul seye al yvel agens you liynge
for me.   Joie ye and be ye glade: for your meede is plenteous
in hevenes: for so thei han pursued also prophetis that weren
bifore you."

TYNDALE, 1526: "When he sawe the people, he went vp into
a mountayne, and when he was sett, hys disciples cam vnto
hym, and he opened his mouth, and taught them sayinge:
Blessid are the povre in sprete: for thers is the kyngdom of
heven.   Blessed are they that mourne: for they shalbe comforted.   Blessed are the meke: for they shall inheret the erthe.
Blessed are they which hunger ánd thurst for rightewesnes; for
they shalbe fylled.   Blessed are the mercyfull: for they shall
obteyne mercy.   Blessed are the pure in hert; for they shall se
god.   Blessed are the maynteyners of peace; for they shalbe
called the chyldren of god.   Blessed are they which suffre per-
secucion for rightewesnes sake; for theirs is the kingdom of
hevene.   Blessed are ye when men shall revyle you, and perse-
cute you, and shall falsly say all manner of evle saynges agaynst
you for my sake.   Rejoice and be gladde, for greate is youre re-
warde in heven.   For so persecuted they the prophetts which
were before youre dayes."

Next follows rapidly — now that Tyndale and printing have
awakened England — a succession of versions, in which we
observe as a prime characteristic the oscillation backwards and
forwards from extreme vernacular simplicity to ecclesiastical
loftiness, until both found their just, golden mean, and in

which we observe, also, a somewhat richer scholarship in the original, and a growing perfection of our language until the Elizabethan age, — the acknowledged golden age of English literature, — and withal a diction as applied to the Scriptures perfected and enriched and ennobled by the work of each succeeding mind, which, during the course of almost an entire century, in rendering the noble originals, strove to surpass all former versions in representing them felicitously in our mother-tongue.

Coverdale issued his version, probably at Zurich, in 1535. King Henry VIII. did not like Tyndale. "There was no hope of obtaining the king's sanction for any thing of Tyndale. Cromwell pushed Coverdale to the work. He translates at second-hand 'out of the Douche' (Luther's German version)." "In practice he oscillates between penance and repentance, love and charity, priests and elders." "He acknowledges, though he dares not name it, the excellence of Tyndale's translation."

Matthew's version followed in 1537. The singular history of this book was probably this: "Coverdale's translation had not given satisfaction: least of all were the most zealous and scholarlike reformers contented with it. As the only complete Bible, it was, however, in possession of the field. Tyndale and John Rogers (the martyr), in the year preceding Tyndale's imprisonment, determined on another, to include Old Testament, New Testament, and Apocrypha, but based throughout on the original." Left to himself, "after Tyndale's betrayal and burning, Rogers carried on the work, probably at the expense of the same Antwerp merchant (Poynz) who had assisted Tyndale." "Rogers' name, known as Tyndale's friend, is concealed under the name Thomas Matthew. Cranmer and Cromwell approve ; and a 'copy was ordered by royal proclamation to be set up in every church.'" "It reproduces Tyndale's work in the New Testament entirely, in the Old Testament as far as Second Chronicles, the rest being taken, with occasional modifications, from Coverdale." "What has been said of Tyndale's version applies, of course, to this. There are, however, signs of a more advanced knowledge of Hebrew."

Taverner's edition, 1539, is next in the line of succession. "The boldness of the translators had, as has been said, frightened the ecclesiastical world from its propriety. Coverdàle's version was, however, too inaccurate to keep its ground." Taverner's edition professes "to be newly recognized, with great diligence, after the most faithful exemplars." "The edition acknowledges the labors of others (i.e. Tyndale, Coverdale, and Matthew), though he does not name them, 'who have neither undiligently nor unlearnedly travelled;' owns that the work is not one which can be done 'absolutely' (i.e., completely) by one or two persons, but requires 'a deeper conferring of many learned wittes together, and also a juster time and longer leisure.' But the thing had to be done: he had been asked to do it. In other respects, this may be designated as an expurgated edition of Matthew's."

Cranmer's Bible, also called the Great Bible, came out the same year, 1539. The preface declares the book to be "truly translated after the verity of the Hebrew and Greek texts" by "divers excellent, learned men expert in the foresaid tongues." "The oscillating character of the book is shown in the use of 'love' instead of 'charity,' in Cor. xiii., and 'congregation' instead of 'church,' generally, after Tyndale ; while in 1 Tim. iv. 14 we have the singular rendering, — as if to gain the favor of his opponents, — 'with authority of priesthood.' "

The famous *Geneva* version followed. Cranmer had followed Coverdale too closely to please the Geneva exiles. Whittingham, Goodman, Pullain, Sampson, and Coverdale himself labored "for two years or more, day and night." The New Testament was "diligently revised by the most approved Greek examples." "The Geneva Bible was unquestionably for sixty years the most popular of all versions. Eighty editions came from the press between 1588 and 1611. It was, after 1576, printed by Barker, in whose family the monopoly of printing Bibles remained for a hundred and thirty-two years. This was the first Bible in Roman type. It was the first which, following the Hebrew example, recognized the division into verses. It was in a cheaper and more portable form, a small quarto. The notes were spiritual and evangelical. *It was the Bible of the great Puritan party."*

Then at length came the *Bishops' Bible*, originated by Archbishop Parker, made by eight bishops, with deans and professors. It was hoped that it would establish its claim against the Genevan version. "In some respects it followed previous translations, and was avowedly based on Cranmer's." "Of all, it had the least success. Though some of the translators were good Hebraists, it did not command the respect of scholars. Though sanctioned by authority, it could not displace the Genevan.

We come then, by gradual ascent, to the present version. *King James' version* was due to a singular providence, — a suggestion by Dr. Reynolds the Puritan, during a conference of three days at Hampton Court, between the king, bishops, Puritan ministry, and others. The idea came as an inspiration to the mind of James, who discerned in it what would be an honor to his reign. Aided by counsellors, he was five months in selecting the translators, fifty-four in number. There were clergy of the Puritan party as well as of the Church party, laymen also, "that so our intended translation may have the help and furtherance of all our principal learned men." John Broughton, who could talk Hebrew as well as English, was not invited, on account of his unmanageable disposition. Reynolds and Lively, the best Hebraists, soon died. Yet the forty-seven who accomplished the work were men of no mean scholarship and critical judgment. Thirteen were heads of colleges. Six were bishops. Dr. Layfield was chosen for his skill in architecture. Bishop Andrewes was familiar with fifteen languages, besides Hebrew, Chaldee, Syriac, Greek, and Latin. Bedwell was the best Arabic scholar of his time. Lively was Regius professor of Hebrew. Five others also, then or afterwards, held the chair of Hebrew at Oxford and Cambridge. Saville was Greek tutor of Elizabeth.[1] A volume would be required to tell the story of this version. Briefly must it here be related. The whole body of translators, divided into six

---

[1] Their biographies are given in Townley's Illustrations, iii. 200, seq.

companies, and working at Oxford, Westminster, and Cambridge, observing certain rules given to make their labor more uniform and thorough, in three years completed the work, which was then revised by a select company, and given to the world in 1611. Every part received *fourteen revisions.* Dr. Sanderson, one of the youngest of the translators, in a sermon, afterwards censured a part of the translation, giving three reasons why a certain word should have been differently translated. In the evening Dr. Kilbie said to him, "We had considered those reasons, and found *thirteen more considerable reasons* why it was translated as now printed."[1] The marginal readings are *an integral part of their work,* and often superior to the text. Selden, in his "Table-Talk," says, "The translation in King James' time took an excellent way. That part of the Bible was given to him who was most excellent in such a tongue; and then they met together, and one read the translation, the rest holding in their hands some Bible, either of the learned tongues, or French, Spanish, Italian, &c. If they found any fault, they spoke; if not, he read on" (p. 6). In their preface they tell us they "brought back to the anvil that which they had hammered;" so that some of their work was revised fourteen to seventeen times. Geddes says, "The means and the method employed to produce this translation promised something extremely satisfactory, and great expectations were formed from the united abilities of so many learned men."[2]

The work was to be based on the Bishops' version, though other versions were fully read. And if no *Romanist* scholar was among the translators, yet *the labors of Martin, Allen, and Bristow are inwrought into the volume;* for the Rhemish and Genevan "contributed most largely of all to the changes which the revisers introduced." The translation, of course, is neither uniform nor perfect; yet this eulogy on Isaiah fifty-third will apply with nearly equal force to all their work: "Throughout, the most delicate care is given to the choice of words; and there is scarcely a verse which does not bear witness to the wisdom and instinctive sense of fitness by which it is guided."

---

[1] J. Comper Gray: Bible Lore, 95.   [2] Prospectus, 92.

" No kind of emendation appears to have been neglected ; and almost every change which they introduced was an improvement."[1] "It contained," says one, "the wealth of seven antecedent versions, and of as many contemporaneous versions in other tongues."

With all the imperfections of this translation, — and they are such, no doubt, as *necessitate a revision*, principally as a version, but also as a fabric of English, — this version has come to be considered as, on the whole, unrivalled. It is the admiration, if not the marvel, of scholars. Our argument, as well as inclination, requires that we mass here the wealth of scholarly homage, in marked contrast to the scholarly estimate of the Douai version, to the " unrivalled English version."

"Two hundred and fifty-seven years ago the English Bible was given to the world, when Shakspeare and Bacon and Raleigh and Ben Jonson and Drayton and Beaumont and Fletcher were living, to read and admire the richest formation of that great and plastic era of our language, the bright consummate flower of saintly labor and scholarly genius, the wonder of literature coming down with the words of Shakspeare, and, like them, preserving to us the wealth and force of the Saxon tongue, — our mother English, in its simplicity and perfect beauty, — the picturesque structure of an age long gone by, already gray with antiquity, in whose familiar forms of speech the voices of our forefathers and kindred linger, and the inspiration of the Almighty seems to speak as with the majesty of an original utterance, — the English Bible, which has impressed itself upon the Christian heart of to-day, and is looked upon in many cases as if it were the actual product of the ancient scribe, and its pages are read and pondered over as if they contained the ultimate and unalterable expression of divine truth."

This may seem undue eulogy; but a scholar whose mental culture is satisfied in this book can hardly help soaring in its praise. Geddes, the Catholic scholar, though in one place he asserts his preference for Tyndale's work, and indeed for all

---

[1] Westcott: Hist. Eng. Bib., 364.

the English translations,[1] is hardly less eulogistic: "The highest eulogisms have been made on it, both by our own writers and by foreigners; and indeed, if accuracy, fidelity, and the strictest attention to the letter of the text, be supposed to constitute the qualities of an excellent version, this, of all versions, must, in general, be accounted the most excellent. Every sentence, every word, every syllable, every letter, and every point, seems to be weighed with the nicest exactitude, and expressed in the text or in the margin with the greatest precision. Pagninus himself is hardly more literal; and it was well remarked by Robertson, above a hundred years ago, that it may serve for a lexicon of the Hebrew language as well as for a translation."[2]

Prof. Marsh remarks, "The English Bible has been more universally read, more familiarly known and understood, by those who use its speech, than any other version, old or new." "It has now, for more than two centuries, maintained its position as an oracular expression of religious truth, and at the same time as the first classic of our literature, — the highest exemplar of purity and beauty of language existing in our speech."[3]

"An analysis of the style of our present version has been made by Prof. Marsh,[4] in connection with that of fourteen eminent writers from Spenser to Johnson; and it has been found the best representative of true English among the whole nation: one thirty-third part only of its words, or three out of a hundred, have a foreign origin; while one-third of Gibbon's, and one-fourth of Johnson's, originally came from abroad." Prof. Marsh says of our translation, "It was an assemblage of the best forms of expression applicable to the communication of religious truth that then existed, or had existed in all the successive stages through which the English had passed in its entire history."[5] "To attempt a new translation of the Bible, in the hope of finding within the compass of the English language a

---

[1] Different scholars distribute variously, among the long line of revisers, the merit of the final product, the English version.

[2] Prospectus, 92.

[3] George P. Marsh: Lectures on English Language, 617, 619.

[4] Ibid., 120.   [5] Ibid., 622.

clearer, a more appropriate, or a more forcible diction than that of the standard version, is to betray an ignorance of the capabilities of our native speech with which it would be in vain to reason." [1]

 , *Walton* says, "*Eminet inter omnes.*" *Selden*, at the time of the completion of that version, said, " The English translation of the Bible is the best translation in the world, and renders the sense of the original best." [2] *Davidson* writes, " Our English version of the Bible deserves much of the praise which it has received. Its merits are conspicuous. Fitted to be a national possession, it has moulded our tongue to an extent scarcely realized. Its pure and homely idioms are a part of the language which cannot die. It has enriched the mother-tongue with Hebrew and German turns of expression." [3] *Westcott* has this meed of praise : " A German writer somewhat contemptuously remarks that it took nearly a century to accomplish in English the work which Luther achieved in the fraction of a single lifetime. The reproach is exactly our glory. Our version is the work of a church, and not of a man ; or, rather, it is a growth, and not a work. Countless external influences, independent of the actual translators, contributed to mould it ; and, when it was fashioned, the Christian instinct of the nation, touched as we believe by the Spirit of God, decided on its authority." [4] And elsewhere he says, " When every deduction is made for the inconsistency of practice, and inadequacy of method, the conclusion yet remains absolutely indisputable, that the work of these revisers issued in a version of the Bible, better, because more faithful to the original, than any which had been given in English before." [5] *Tischendorf* says, " Their translation of the New Testament has not only become an object of great reverence, but has deserved to be such. The English Church possesses in it a national treasure." It was " executed with scholarship, conscientiousness, and love." *Trench* also says, " The dictionary of our English version is nearly as perfect as

[1] George P. Marsh: Lectures on English Language, 632.
[2] Table-Talk, 5.   [3] Revision of Old Testament, 1.
[4] History English Bible, 370.
         [5] Ibid., 364.

possible." "The words used are of the noblest stamp, alike removed from vulgarity and pedantry. We do not find in our version, as in the Rheims, whose authors seem to have put off their loyalty to the English language with their loyalty to the English crown, 'odible,' nor 'impudicity,' nor 'longanimity,' nor 'coinquinations,' nor 'comessations,' nor 'contristate,' nor 'zealatours,' nor 'agnition,' nor 'suasible,' nor 'domesticals,' nor 'repropitiate.'"[1] "Our version, besides having its own felicities, is the inheritor of the felicities in language of all the translations which went before. Tyndale's was singularly rich in these;" "and, though much of his work has been removed in the successive revisions which our Bible has undergone, very much of it still remains." "To him we owe such phrases as 'turned to flight the armies of the aliens,' which may be thought to be obvious; but the Rheims does not get nearer to it than 'turned away the camp of foreigners.'"[2] "We hardly know the immeasurable worth of its religious diction till we set this side by side with what oftentimes is preferred in its room."[3] "Each time," says *Lightfoot*, "I read the marvellous episode on Charity in the thirteenth chapter of Corinthians, I feel with increased force the inimitable delicacy and beauty and sublimity of the rendering, till I begin to doubt whether the English language is not a better vehicle than even the Greek for so lofty a theme."[4] *Dr. Schaff* says, "The popular English Bible is the greatest blessing which the Reformation of the sixteenth century bestowed upon the Anglo-Saxon race." "It has formed the style and taste of the English classics. It has a hold upon the popular heart which it can never lose. Its vocabulary and phrases, its happy blending of Saxon force and Latin dignity, its uniform chasteness, earnestness, and solemnity, its thoroughly idiomatic tone, its rhythmic flow, its more than poetic beauty and harmony, have secured the admiration of scholars, and the affection of whole churches and nations in which it is used."[5]

Blunt (J. H. Blunt, "The English Bible," 96) says, "The translation thus completed has kept its hold on Englishmen for

---

[1] On Authorized Version, 9, 10.   [2] Page 12.   [3] Page 25.
[4] On Revision, 32.   [5] On Revision, xx.

two centuries and a half. Its excellence is admitted far and wide by the learned; the dignified yet sweet rhythm of its sentences is dear to the unlearned; and the spiritual *satisfaction* which myriads of good and holy minds have found in it is no small proof that a divine blessing has rested upon it."

Eadie says, "It is still abroad in its might; not, as of old, in heavy folios, but in handy volumes, — closet and pocket companions. It costs only a trifle, so that it is within the reach of every one. It has found a home under the Southern Cross, in Australia and New Zealand; and in the United States it has multiplied itself with inconceivable rapidity. The sun never sets upon it. It has spread, and will spread, with the English name and influence, round the globe. All people speaking our tongue are united by their common Bibles, common temples, and the blessing of a common salvation. Our forefathers gave it welcome, and their descendants can never bid it farewell; for the oracle is always fulfilling itself, 'Tell ye your children of it, and let your children tell their children, and their children another generation.' Englishmen shall never weary of reading the Blessed Life told in these Gospels, and in that charming style, which, rising above all provincial peculiarities, forms one fraternal speech to 'all that in every place call upon the name of Jesus Christ our Lord, both theirs and ours.' Centuries have passed over it; but its youth abides. Many volumes far younger than it have perished in the wreck of years. The majority of books published among us are connected with it, either against it, or for it, or on it. Though revised, it will ever preserve its identity; as the statue is the same, though its features be brightened when the dust is blown off it. It can be superseded only when the higher relations and developments of its truths are revealed to us in another sphere."[1]

Plumptre praises in these words: "The language of the authorized version has intertwined itself with the controversies, the devotions, the literature, of the English people. It has gone wherever they have gone, over the face of the whole earth. The most solemn and tender of individual memories are for the

[1] John Eadie, D.D.: The English Bible, ii. 333.

most part associated with it.   Men leaving the Church of
England for the Church of Rome turn regretfully, with a yearn-
ing look at that noble 'well of English undefiled' which they
are about to exchange for the uncouth monstrosities of Rheims
and Douai."

Thus *Faber*, a "pervert to Rome," writes: "Who will not
say that the uncommon beauty and marvellous English of the
Protestant Bible " — why can he not have the grace to call it,
with all scholarship, solely and simply the *English* Bible? — " is
one of the great strongholds of heresy in this country?   It lives
on the ear like a music that can never be forgotten; like the
sound of church-bells, which the convert hardly knows how he
can forego.   Its felicities often seem to be almost things, rather
than mere words.   It is a part of the national mind, and the
anchor of national seriousness.   Nay, it is worshipped with a
positive idolatry, in extenuation of whose grotesque fanaticism its
intrinsic beauty pleads availingly with the man of letters and the
scholar.   The memory of the dead passes into it.   The potent
traditions of childhood are stereotyped in its verses.   The
power of all the griefs and trials of a man is hidden beneath
its words.   It is the representative of his best moments; and
all that there has been about him of soft and gentle and pure
and penitent and good speaks to him forever out of his English Bible " (here his mental sense spontaneously names the
volume aright).   "It is his sacred thing, which doubt has
never dimmed, and controversy never soiled.   It has been to
him all along as the silent, but, oh! how intelligible, voice
of his guardian angel; and, in the length and breadth of
the land, there is not a Protestant, with one spark of religious-
ness about him, whose spiritual biography is not in his Saxon
Bible." [1]

Froude, the historian, is stirred beyond his wonted calmness
by the contemplation of this volume: " The peculiar genius, if
such a word may be permitted, which breathes through it,
the mingled tenderness and majesty, the Saxon simplicity, the

[1] Dr. F. William Faber: Lives of the Saints, xxv. 116. In Dublin Review, June, 1853.
Also Eadie: English Bible, ii. 158.

preternatural grandeur, unequalled, unapproached, in the attempted improvements of modern scholars, — all are here, and bear the impress of the mind of one man, and that man William Tyndale." [1]

Is any thing further needed to glorify the English version but to remember that this volume is no more sectional than sectarian; to recall the remark of Plumptre, "It has gone wherever Englishmen have gone, over the face of the whole earth;" to reflect with Anderson, that "the English Bible is at the present moment in the act of being perused from the rising to the setting of the sun"? *"This Bible is the only one on which the sun never sets."* [2] And all this has warrant and verification in the issue, in little more than half a century, of a hundred million "English Bibles" to the intelligent readers of the language of "Paradise Lost" and of the "Declaration of Independence," scattered in all climes, and under all constellations.

When we consider the sober statements of linguists, both Catholic and Protestant, eulogistic of its exceeding accuracy and fidelity to the originals from which it was directly translated; the encomiums of scholars, both Catholic and Protestant, to its language and diction as "marvellous English;" the way in which, both as a translation and as a fabric of English, it was built up, not as the autocratic work, however excellent, of one sole man, but, in the long course of nearly a hundred years, by the concomitant and successive labors of nearly a hundred learned and enthusiastic scholars of all spiritual temperaments, and church predilections, and preferences of style and diction, and bringing their work, after multifarious revisions, to completion in the very Augustan period, the golden age of English literature; and, finally, the universality of the reception of their work among all those who speak the English tongue, unless — and hardly then — they are debarred by ecclesiastical authority or religious scruple, — when we review all these considerations, is any thing further needed to vindicate the claim of this volume to be regarded everywhere, in the legislative

---

[1] History of England, iii. 84.   [2] Anderson: Annals of Bib. Pref., x. 11.

hall and in the public school, among all English-speaking nations, as superlatively *the English translation of the Scriptures,* the ENGLISH BIBLE?

One final excellence this English Bible has, a grand excellence, — some might consider it the supreme excellence, — its illimitable capability of revision. Every one was struck with admiration when Agassiz described his immense plan of a Zoölogical Museum, one-fourth of a mile in the circuit of the lines of its walls, yet, as he said, to be developed afterwards, only two-fifths of one wing to be constructed at first; and, in the plans in the reports, the future additions are hinted at by the dotted lines, showing the completion of the ample extension. So the English Bible has this crowning excellence, that it is capable, and will be to the end of time, of bearing revision; that its acknowledged perfection and its cherished position will not suffer it to be set aside like all previous versions, but that it can gather into itself, at the ripe times, century by century if need be, the accumulated results of linguistic and archæological scholarship and of perfected English. This is its eternal privilege and prerogative, and stamps it as forever, in the true lineal and royal succession, the English Bible.

Lightfoot says, " Our English Bible owes it unrivalled merits to the principle of revision; and that principle it is proposed once more to invoke. ' To whom ever,' say the authors of our received version, ' was it imputed for a failing, by such as were wise, to go over that which he had done, and to amend it where he saw cause ? ' "[1]

Ellicott says, "If it is to be a popular version, it can only become so by exhibiting in every change that may be introduced a sensitive regard for the diction and tone of the present version, and also by evincing, in the nature and extent of the changes, a due recognition of the whole internal history of the English New Testament. In other words, the new work must be on the old lines."[2]

Davidson says, "No man who intends to supersede King James' will do so otherwise than by working upon it. He will

---

[1] On Revision, 32.   [2] Revision of Authorized Version, 52.

make a new translation by subjecting that of 1611 to thorough revision."[1]

A Catholic writer says, "The Catholic Church never has made, and most probably never will make, a vernacular translation." To Westcott's words all scholars respond: "Our Bible, in virtue of its past, is capable of admitting revision, if need be, without violating its history. As it has gathered into itself, during the hundred years in which it was forming, the treasures of manifold labors, so it still has the same assimilative power of life."[2]

[1] Revision of Old Testament, 145.　　[2] History English Bible, 370.

THE IMPERIAL EXILE.

DANIEL WEBSTER, in that speech of which Winthrop said, "Beyond all doubt it was the speech of our constitutional age," — "*Nil simile aut secundum;*" which Choate refrained from setting in rivalry to Demosthenes' great oration, simply because the Gothic languages, as he said, had not the words to make a "crown speech" of, — in an outburst in the magnificent peroration of that address in which he showed his love and reverence for the American Union, then threatened, exclaims, "I have not allowed myself to look beyond the Union to see what might be hidden in the dark recesses behind." [1]

So does one feel in contemplating the possibility that the Bible — the luminary which has created and constantly vivified all modern education and the American republic — should be blotted from our firmament. The mind repels the thought.

"*Horresco referens.*"

Reluctantly, therefore, the writer accedes to a suggestion that he should set forth *what would be the result were the Bible exiled from the school,* — reluctantly, yet *eagerly;* for even while these papers were first appearing, within the half-year of our Centennial triumph, Law has put her finger on the lip of Public Education, — and that, too, in Boston, — and forbidden her to say that word, which, more than any other, taught us that "all men are created equal," — the word "Our Father." The apathy, nay, more, the sophisticated and crude ideas, on this sub-

[1] Webster's Reply to Hayne.

ject, of really great men, are marvellous. Men whose views are wide and comprehensive on other subjects miss the point, are politicians and not statesmen here. Pursued by public clamor, they, in their haste and perturbation, are ready, like Medea, to fling even their brother to the pursuer. They write as if they were trying to adapt themselves to popular notions, and save our public-school system by yielding all that any one pleases to call "sectarian," rather than attempting to discern and stand upon, "first, midst, and last," *the just and eternal connection between State schools and God and righteousness.* Not thus will these men preserve either their power to serve their country, or the respect of those who clamor, or the public-school system. These opponents care little for our concessions; for what they are pressing towards is the destruction, first, as far as they are concerned, and then utterly, of the public-school system itself. The only wise and philosophical way is to study how far religion — catholic, unsectarian religion — *belongs, in the nature of things*, to the education of youth in the public school as a preparation for the State, take our stand there, and make the struggle — which, strangely enough, many are oblivious to — for free institutions in America.

> "Swiftly the politic goes : is it dark ? he borrows a lantern :
> Slowly the statesman and sure, guiding his feet by the stars."

Our hesitancy, therefore, gives way to eagerness, — "*Facit indignatio versum.*"

It will not be the writer's object to prophesy the visible and palpable evils which will come from banishing God and moral instruction from schools. Rather, this paper will set forth the *departures from wisdom* in the exile of the Bible, leaving to the reader, if he choose, to fancy the outward evils which will result.

I. TO EXILE THE BIBLE FROM THE PUBLIC SCHOOL WILL BE TO DISPENSE WITH SALUTARY, WITH AMERICAN INFLUENCES, JUST WHEN THEY ARE MOST NEEDED. If the Bible has not' been misconceived, it imparts a salutary influence. If we have not been entirely misreading American history, the influence which has moulded our past, and which ought to mould our future, is from this book. Now, in that period when we are throwing our doors — Atlantic and Pacific — wide open to an un-American, and, in a large proportion, ignorant and unelevated throng of emigrants, we come, in our unspeakable sagacity, to the height and pitch of wisdom of *diminishing* salutary and American influences. Consider these statistics, given by Mr. Charles Wyllis Elliott, in a lecture, and afterwards furnished me in correspondence. "Population of Massachusetts in 1870, United-States census, — native born, 478,821; foreign born, 353,319; of foreign parents, 626,211; total of foreign nationality, 979,530; total population, 1,458,351. Over two-thirds of the population of Massachusetts are foreign born and of foreign parentage." And yet, in face of this, we propose to *diminish* the vitalizing American influences. Wisdom says, In periods of rapid immigration, to preserve the original institutions, increase their efficiency, not diminish it. As you increase the meal, increase the leaven. But Americans have learned a new wisdom, and say, As you increase the meal, *decrease* the leaven.

II. To exile the Bible from the public school is to yield the outmost and strongest fortress which protects American institutions, when we have distinct warning that they are to be attacked and destroyed.

This proposition is not identical with the preceding. The foreign throngs come to our shores foreign in spirit, indeed, needing the leaven of our institutions; yet we acquit them, speaking generally, of any intention to subvert our institutions: on the contrary, we believe they come, not only with the design, but with the wish, to submit to the beneficent influences in this Western Republic. Moreover, let it be understood that we acquit *Catholics*, as such, of any intention to do violence to the land of their adoption. But we do not acquit *Romanists* of such designs. We distinguish by a clearly-marked line between Catholicism and Romanism. *Catholicism* is a church with dogmas: *Romanism* is a hierarchy, whose seat is on the Seven Hills, which aims to subjugate all nations as its provinces. The Catholics have no evil designs; but the Romanists dominate the Catholics, and the Jesuits are the heart of the

Romanists. Romanism does have and avow the intention to destroy American institutions. Bungener says, "The true and only Catholics are the Jesuits."[1] "At the Council of Trent, when Lainez, the general of the Jesuits, undertook to set forth his theory of the infallibility of the Pope, he forced every one to admit that he and his brethren alone were, if not in the right, at least the only honest and complete applicants of the principle of authority." Although, then, the larger part of Catholics are attached to American institutions, it behooves us to ask, What says the Jesuit, the core of Romanism, which finally subjugates Catholicism to its inner force and purpose? This is the Jesuit oath : "I do renounce and disown any allegiance as due. to any heretical king, prince, or state named Protestant, or obedience to any of their inferior magistrates or officers ;" "and I will do my utmost to extirpate the heretical Protestant doctrine, and to destroy all their pretended powers, regal or otherwise." The Papal Syllabus of 1864, as is well known, condemns the public-school system, or any other, "withdrawn from all authority of the Church."

The attack upon American institutions comes, then, not from Catholics, but from Romanists.

This proposition contains two points : *first, an assertion that we have distinct warning* that American institutions are to be attacked and destroyed. Bishop O'Connor of Pittsburg says, "Religious liberty is merely endured until the opposite can be carried into effect without peril to the Catholic world." The Archbishop of St. Louis said, "If the Catholics ever gain, which they surely will, an immense numerical majority, religious freedom in this country will be at an end." "The Catholic Review" (January, 1852) said, "Protestantism of every form has not, and never can have, any rights where Catholicity is triumphant ; and we lose the breath we expend in declaiming against bigotry and intolerance, and in favor of religious liberty, or the right of every man to be of any religion, as best pleases him." Father Hecker, in 1869, in New York, said, "The Catholic Church numbers one-third of the American

---

[1] Priest and Huguenot, ii. 191.

population ; and, if its membership shall increase for the next thirty years as it has for the thirty years past, in 1900 Rome will have a majority, and be bound to take this country and keep it." He also predicts that "there is ere long to be a State religion in this country, and that State religion is to be Roman Catholic." Again he says, "We number seven millions ; and in fifteen years we will take this country, and build our institutions over the grave of Protestantism." This purpose to destroy American institutions is, then, clearly written ; "too fairly, Hubert, for so foul a deed."

It is also contained in the proposition that the Bible in the schools is the outmost and strongest fort, the best place to thwart Papal intentions. And this for two reasons among others. *First*, because the Bible is conspicuously connected with American institutions, since "free America is born of the Bible," and "all modern education owns the Bible as mother." It is peculiarly *American*, therefore, to retain this book, not only because the best book *about* God, but because intimately and vitally connected with the life of America. To give up the Bible in the schools is to renounce, in advance, the America born of the Bible, and our education born of the Bible. *In the second place*, the reading of the Bible is the best place to meet Papal attacks, because, if we give up that fort, *they propose to build one on the very same foundation*. They do not want secular schools, which we are hastening to concede : they anathematize them. They say, Put your Bible out or not ; we care not : we shall put our religion in just as soon as we have power.

"The Tablet" (Nov. 30, 1869) says, "Exclude every sectarian exercise, and wholly secularize the schools ; let them teach nothing of religion, but be confined solely to secular education : what is the result? The system is even more objectionable than before. It has always been a cardinal doctrine in the economy of the Catholic Church to incorporate religious instruction with the daily secular teaching of its scholars."

What, then, are we to do? Simply to make that fortress invincible ; and this can be done in only one way, — by establishing religious exercises absolutely unsectarian, by unsectarian devotions, and reading, without explanation, of the "English" Bible, with permission to read simultaneously from any other. Settle the thought of America for twenty years upon the *idea of an entirely unsectarian religious exercise,* and Protestants and Catholics, whatever Romanists might say, would defend that idea for a hundred years. But put out *all* religion from the school, and, as soon as Catholics have power, they *must* put *theirs* in. Therefore make the fight here, on the Bible unsectarianly used, and unsectarian prayer and praise: there you will carry and anchor the best judgment of the Catholic world; there you will be invincible, if anywhere, in resisting the attack of Jesuits upon the liberty of America.

Surely it cannot be wise to weaken before God and man our public-school system, by destroying the religious side of it, when by wisdom we can make it absolutely unsectarian, and so make our system impregnable to the assaults to be made upon it; while, if we reject the religious side, we make it "*even more objectionable*" (and justly so) to Catholics, — make them more determined to destroy it, and us less whole-hearted to defend it. And the weakest side, and that on which Catholicism will assail and finally destroy it, is to be that it is an "atheistic, godless education," "a system which ought to go where it came from, — to the Devil." If we cannot defend education with God in it, we certainly, as before Catholics, cannot defend an educational system which leaves God out.

The state of things is this: *Both Protestants and Catholics believe in religion as a part of education.* Protestants, who now have the majority, say, "We are willing to compromise by leaving religion out." Catholics, who will, perhaps, have the majority, say, "Never, never, will *we* compromise on secular schools;" and they never will. Therefore the compromise must be on the other side, — *how much religion both shall agree to as proper to a public school.* The only wise way, therefore, is, while we have the power, to have *unsectarian religion in the schools,* with which neither Protestants nor Catholics can find *just* fault. To strengthen the fortress by making it unsectarian, and not to abandon it, is, therefore, our wisdom.

III. The exile of God and righteousness from the school introduces this false and pernicious idea, that education is merely intellectual training.

We have already reaped some tares from this sowing. The true, the salutary idea of education is, that it is the complete development of man. Pestalozzi says, — and his word stands in all European schools, — "Education is the development of mind, heart, hands." This, however, is not a new idea in the world. Plato, in Protagoras, says that the Athenians, "sending their son to the schoolmaster, are more urgent in requiring him to look after the manners and morals of the youth than after his letters and music." Felton says, "All being necessary to the education of the citizen, who should be able, in the language of Milton, 'to perform, justly, wisely, and magnanimously, all the duties both of peace and war.'"

This idea of a complete public education, that it includes moral as well as mental training, is as old as Cyrus. "Persia," says Xenophon, "did not content herself with legislating against crime : she moulded the minds of her citizens from childhood by a public educational system to virtue." "In the boys' quarter the time appears to have been chiefly occupied in trying, under the president, all cases of crime and misdemeanor which had arisen among the boys themselves. Theft, deceit, calumny, and ingratitude were thus brought to punishment ; and it is commonly said that the Persian boys went to school to learn justice, as elsewhere boys go to school to learn to read." Hence the saying of Herodotus, that "the Persian was taught to ride, to shoot the bow, and to speak the truth." Cyrus gives this incident of his boyhood : "I have often been appointed to decide cases, and I made only one mistake. That was in the case of the boys and the coats. There was a big boy who had a little coat, quite too small for him ; and there was a little boy who had a large coat, very loose upon him. So the big boy made the little boy exchange coats with him ; and I decided that he was right in doing so, and that each boy should keep the coat which best fitted him. But the master beat me for giving this decision ; for he said that it was against the law to force a person to give up his property, and that justice consisted in obeying the law. So now I know what justice is." Pestalozzi has expressed the true idea of education thus: "I consider early physical and intellectual education as merely leading to a higher aim, to qualify the human being for the free and full use of all the faculties implanted by the Creator, and to direct all these faculties towards the perfection of the whole being of man, that he may be enabled to act in his peculiar station as an instrument of the all-wise and almighty Power that has called him into life."

An education without a moral aim may make for our State an Alcibiades, a Machiavel, a Borgia, a Tweed, but not a Washington, an Alfred, a Wilberforce, a Howard. Prof. Tholuck says, "That word 'smart' will break America's neck, unless America breaks its neck;" which is only saying in epigram, that an education of intellect, apart from education of conscience, will ruin America.

IV. THE EXILE OF GOD AND RIGHTEOUSNESS FROM THE PUBLIC SCHOOL INTRODUCES A STRANGE INCONGRUITY BETWEEN THE DRIFT OF MODERN THOUGHT AND THE SCHOOL INSTRUCTION.

This will sooner or later breed contempt of our system of education, and of those who conduct it. Cook said, in one of his fine outbursts of eloquence at Tremont Temple, "I look up to the highest summits of science, and I reverence properly, I hope, all that is established by the scientific method: but, when I lift my gaze to the uppermost pinnacles of the mount of established truth, I find standing there, not Haeckel, nor Spencer, but Helmholtz of Berlin, and Wundt of Heidelberg, and Herman Lotze of Göttingen, physiologists as well as metaphysicians all; and they, as free investigators of the relations between matter and mind, are all on their knees before a living God."

Is this, then, a time to banish the thought of God and the best Occidental book about him, and the saying to him, "Our Father," in the place of public education?

The age of materialism is passing. Mr. Cook remarks, "Prof. Tholuck said to me repeatedly, 'If a man is a materialist, we Germans think he is not educated.'" While the foremost naturalist of the age stands with his scholars at Penikese in reverent silent prayer before the God of Nature, was it the day for the State to say to our youth within the places of education, It is now time to desist from saying "Our Father"?

It is as if Mr. Cook, who commenced his lectures with prayers, should say, as the proof of the living God grew stronger from week to week, *Now*, gentlemen, we will omit the address to God. So a father, who should talk as never before, to his children at the table, of the wonderful provision for man's wants made by the Father Almighty in the cereals and animals, but should add, My daughter, you may *now* remove these mottoes which have adorned the dining-room so long, " Give us our daily bread," and "The Lord will provide."

Especially will this harsh incongruity appear if we consider this new arrangement in contrast with educational systems which we are pleased to consider altogether inferior. "What is the secret of your prosperity?" asked the Chinese embassy at the Revere House dinner. "Our educational system," was the reply. "They should have told them," said Dr. Neale, "that it was the knowledge that ' God so loved the world that he gave his only-begotten Son, that whosoever believeth in him might not perish, but have everlasting life.' "

But let the answer pass, "Our education." Its newest development, they might have said, is, that the name of God, which has always been mentioned, is now thrust out. Ah! says the Chinese, I must adopt that. I, in my pagan, ignorant boyhood, made my most reverent bow, as I entered school, before the name of Confucius on a tablet; and I, says the Japanese, in my folly and heathen blindness, believed that education should acknowledge God, and in my boyhood made my salutation to Tenjin, god of learning. And they depart from America, *instructed;* and they say to their countrymen, In America educated men more and more believe in God; but — why we know not — in the *place* of education the name of God is not to be spoken.

V. IN THE EXILE OF THE THINGS OF GOD THE STATE RE-NOUNCES THE PREROGATIVE OF FORMING THE CHARACTER OF HER FUTURE CITIZENS.

. The State, in that case, says in effect that she has the prerogative to form the intellectual character of her citizens ; but she has no authority to teach them to be virtuous, honest, temperate, reverent. She has absolutely no power for an hour, for a minute, anywhere to teach the boy Tweed that he is not to make the man Tweed.

We need not adduce the sayings of our statesmen on this point ; for every one knows that this assertion reverses the opinion of all whose names and whose words have been revered in modern history. Since our government reposes on the virtue as well as intelligence of her citizens, since all nations have declined and fallen through lack of public virtue, it is universally recognized, except by some narrow minds, — which think that music and art and science make *men*, — that the State should secure the virtue of her citizens. She has the right to form the moral character of her future citizens in the school.

VI. THE STATE AND EDUCATION WILL BE IN THE INCONSISTENCY OF REPUDIATING THE BOOK TO WHICH THEY BOTH OWE THEIR EXISTENCE.

There is a story of a slave-mother, who, by hard labor, had earned her daughter's freedom ; and, having bought her a pair of shoes, she came into the room and sat down to view with great satisfaction her emancipated child. But the daughter rose, and ordered her mother out of the room, saying that she was a slave, and not fit to sit with free folks.

Some one pertinently inquires, "whether the Bible, if thrust ‹ forth, will allow the *school* to live." We may add, and whether it will allow the *nation* to live.

VII. THE STATE WILL GIVE UP MORAL TRAINING AS NECESSARY TO ECONOMIZE AND UTILIZE THE TALENT OF HER SONS.

Had not the State a right to give such a training, if that had been possible, to Edgar A. Poe, as would have given her seventy years of his wonderful imaginative powers directed to higher ends ?

We do not hold the Spartan theory of the State, that she· is the supreme unit, and that every man is to be trained, even contrary to all his normal powers, to subserve the purposes of the State. Nor is the Egyptian theory respectable, — of holding every man in the caste and occupation of his fathers. But this is the thought: The State has a right to give every man a full development of his powers, and by instruction furnish moral safeguards to him, leaving the direction of those cultured powers to the man himself, yet fairly expecting that those powers, in some sphere, will in some way advance, and not mar, the general welfare. This is the principle at the root of those many addresses to graduating classes, reminding youth that their country and their state have a right to expect a return in worthy and valuable lives. "Every virtuous youth formed for the public is a blessing to it," says an old writer.[1] There are, *by statistics, one million drunkards, of whom sixty thousand die annually, and five hundred thousand drunkard-makers, in the United States.* By certain instructions given at the proper time to her youth on temperance and on the sin of wicked gain, the State might save half the number, and turn their talent into valuable channels. This modern school-arrangement says the State has no right to do it. On the contrary, we affirm, that if the State, by proper instructions, could have saved Poe's life and talents to herself and humanity, she was derelict in duty in not doing it. There are, we will suppose, thirty every month (which is nearly the number), whose dripping, lifeless bodies are laid in the Morgue in Paris. In ten years there were 2,807 of these suicides, most of them taken from the Seine. But in 1872 there were 567 ; in 1873, 660 ; and in 1874, the immense number of 1,000, or nearly three every day. The State could have saved half of them by reading to them in the Scripture the story of God's care for oppressed and desolate Hagar. But you say, France has no right to read them this salutary story ; for you say, The State has no right to save the lives of her citizens, and economize and utilize the talents of her sons, by throwing around them the safeguard of a moral training. That must be left to the possible or chance action of religious bodies ; but the State, though the sufferer, has no duty, and no protection

[1] Dodd: Sermons.

VIII. ᴇᴅᴜᴄᴀᴛɪᴏɴ ᴀɴᴅ ᴛʜᴇ Sᴛᴀᴛᴇ ᴡɪʟʟ ʀᴇᴘᴜᴅɪᴀᴛᴇ ᴛʜᴇɪʀ ᴘᴀsᴛ.

No nation, without great cause, — as the Japanese, on the introduction of great light, — should repudiate the great features of its past. We say to the fathers who founded our system of education and set the Bible in it, we say to Gov. Tompkins of New York and to Benjamin Franklin, " Your ideas are obsolete, and we inaugurate a new system."

Nay, rather, we say of our public-school system, with the Bible and moral instruction in it, the heritage received from the venerated fathers, —

> " Woodman, spare that tree ;
>   Touch not a single bough :
> In youth it sheltered me,
>   And I'll protect it now.
> 'Twas my forefather's hand
>   That placed it near his cot :
> There, woodman, let it stand ;
>   Thy axe shall harm it not.
>
> That old familiar tree,
>   Whose glory and renown
> Are spread o'er land and sea, —
>   And wouldst thou hew it down ?
> Woodman, forbear thy stroke ;
>   Cut not its earth-bound ties :
> Oh ! spare that aged oak,
>   Now towering to the skies."

IX. Fɪɴᴀʟʟʏ, ᴛʜᴇ ᴇxɪʟᴇ ᴏꜰ ᴛʜɪs ʙᴏᴏᴋ ᴀɴᴅ ᴛʜᴇ ʀᴇᴠᴇʀᴇɴᴛ ᴘʀᴀʏᴇʀ ᴡɪʟʟ ᴇʀᴇ ʟᴏɴɢ ᴄʀᴇᴀᴛᴇ ᴛʜɪs sᴛʀᴀɴɢᴇ ɪɴᴄᴏɴɢʀᴜɪᴛʏ, ᴛʜᴀᴛ ᴛʜᴇ ᴘᴀʀᴛʏ ᴏᴘᴘᴏsᴇᴅ ᴛᴏ ᴘᴜʙʟɪᴄ sᴄʜᴏᴏʟs ᴀɴᴅ ᴅᴇᴠᴏᴛɪᴏɴᴀʟ ᴇxᴇʀᴄɪsᴇs ɪɴ ᴛʜᴇᴍ ᴡɪʟʟ ʙᴇ ᴍᴀᴅᴇ ᴛᴏ ᴀᴘᴘᴇᴀʀ ᴛʜᴇ ᴍᴏsᴛ ʀᴇʟɪɢɪᴏᴜs ᴀɴᴅ ᴅᴇᴠᴏᴜᴛ ᴘᴀʀᴛʏ.

They say, "We do not want the Bible read in the school where we are, nor the Lord's Prayer uttered ;" and when you concede, and cast God's things out, they say, — the phrase is theirs, — " Atheistic Protestantism." Protestantism has prevailed two centuries and a half in America, has been leader in State and education ; and its crowning glory, its consummate

flower, the proud plume on its helmet, was, in the summer of
the Centennial year, to banish the Lord's Prayer from the
school. We say, SHAME!

The time may come when such sentences as these which
follow may seem refreshing; when, in drinking in their noble
words, we shall half forget that they mean the "Catholic" religion, which the State has no right to teach in her schools, and
not the "catholic religion," "that which is everywhere and always religion," as Brownson so well defines it, which is the real
meaning to fill out these words, and which it is the State's duty
to teach, — these noble words of the Davenport Catholics, "We
believe and hold, and all history sustains us, that *all education
not based on religion is heathenish, and must prove destructive to the
State in the end;* that the safety of the republic depends on the
intelligence and virtue of its citizens; that the downfall of nations has always been caused by irreligion and immorality;" or
these words of McQuaid, "The new-fangled scheme of education without God;" or these words of Archbishop Purcell, "We
Catholics are of the conviction that children are sent to school
not only to be formed into citizens, but also, and especially, to
be educated into good men and good Christians; and our
church believes in all earnestness with Guizot, the celebrated
Protestant statesman of France, that education can by no
means be separated from religious influence."

And these men are right, while we are wrong, if you limit
their utterances to their *prima facie* meaning, — in which the
Protestant Guizot and the Catholic Purcell might agree, — the
unsectarian recognition of God and his righteousness in education. Such is the incongruity to which an atheistic Protestantism will bring us, that the men whom we consider, some of
them, the enemies of good institutions, shall appear more wise,
more advanced in their thinking, more devout and regardful of
the welfare of the republic, than the unworthy descendants of
those who crossed the seas to find a place to establish a State
with God in it. Nay, more, *the time may come when disgust may
be so keen at a Protestantism that put God out of public education,
that thoughtful men — that the State — may make suit to Catholi-*

*cism to take the helm of education, and give us a school that will
at least have God in it.*

If " Our Father " is for the next century not to be murmured
in our schools, if morality is not to be explicitly inculcated there
as preparation for citizenship, if God's name and the best
thoughts about him are to be banished from the State's instructions to her youth, we say with Webster, as we think of what
would be the logical result, " May my eyes never be opened to
what lies behind ! "

THE BIBLE AND THE MANUAL OF MORALS.

THIS concluding essay will aim to sum up as *recapitulation*, and perhaps add to by way of further corroboration, the grounds on which there should be a service to God in the public schools, and that service should include reading the best book about him ; and also, further, to show how these ideas can be realized in a satisfactory and effective and — it is believed, to candid and devout minds in every religious sect — an approved and desirable service.

FIRST, THE PROPER MATERIAL OF THE DEVOTIONAL EXERCISE SHOULD BE CONSIDERED.

It has been made plain, it is believed, that,

I. GOD AND HIS RIGHTEOUSNESS SHOULD HAVE PLACE IN THE SCHOOL.

It would seem that this had been sufficiently argued. It remains only to sum up the principal reasons, that we may have them distinctly before us as a proper preparation for seeing and stating clearly what kind of a service will be effective and acceptable, and will answer all the requirements of the case, as in the broadest and best sense a catholic and not a sectarian service.

(1.) GOD *should have place in the school.*

1. God, as the God of all sciences and knowledges, should be recognized in the place of public education. The argument is sufficiently drawn out in the first paper, All natural science conducts to the one, — to God. Zoölogy, botany, the " star-eyed

300

science," geology, physiology, — all lead to a great Being. "The undevout astronomer is mad." Agassiz requesting his students, at the opening of the Penikese School, to pause in silent prayer, is suggestive and delightful. Whittier has set the noble fact in the gilded frame of his poem. "God geometrizes," says Plato. "History requires the hand of God." "No one is educated who fails to see God in history." "Ethics, as the science of duties, runs as on a sunbeam up to God." "The science of government traces back to God."

Atheistic scholarship is crude ; even the most splendid minds of atheists showing a fault in reasoning which in the *forum scientiæ* is indefensible, and which works like a flaw in a carpenter's plane, or a break in the thread which spoils the web through the whole piece. Education is sound and full only when Copernican, with God in the centre.

2. God, as the great moral Being, should be recognized in the school. The true education, according to Pestalozzi, is that of the whole man, — heart, mind, head. In the school, the teacher, impressing truth and honesty and self-sacrifice, mentions Washington, Colbert, Florence Nightingale. Is she not to mention God ? Whoever and whatever this Being, we all ascribe to him all goodness. He is the pleroma of every excellence. An educator who proposes to carry out Pestalozzi's idea, to cultivate the heart, will find no better way than daily reverent calling on the Supreme Excellence before the pupils, and choice words read descriptive of his attributes and imitable perfections.

We believe nothing will so calm yet exhilarate the mind for the studies and duties of school as a devotional exercise, properly conducted. Reinhard says,[1] "It was a matter of no small difficulty to preserve order among several thousand men, some days, in a retired place, without any form of police or civil power, as the Lord evidently maintained by the authority he then enjoyed. It shows us, in general, the silent influence always exerted by the presence of virtue upon mankind."

Dr. Arnold of Rugby, Mary Lyon of Mount Holyoke, and whatsoever other teacher characterized by moral seriousness,

[1] Twelfth Sermon, on Mark viii. 1-9.

have, by their conduct of the devotional service at the opening
of school, made

> " His morning smile cheer all the day."

3. God as the God of all life, and as the moral Governor over
the world, should be recognized in the school.   The school is a
preparation for the State.   The State is to teach in the school
whatever she wishes should appear in the life, order, and welfare
of her citizens.   In a composite nation like ours, made up of
streams from diverse nations, and destined to be, as Sumner
has so finely said, the " *aurichalcum* " of the world, there will
doubtless be many strange and pernicious ideas in the mass as
yet heterogeneous, which the State, regardful of the temporal
good of her citizens, and her own general good growing out of
that, is bound to counteract.   The State is to deal with moral
subjects so far as they concern the temporal welfare of her people, as bound to her, and as connected with each other.   She
regards their welfare only as they live in a mortal sphere.   As
immortals, the State takes no cognizance of men, or as beings
responsible to God for their secret character and relations to
him.   Yet she cannot be insensible to those views of God which
on the one hand cherish the sense of duty to the State and to
fellow-citizens, and those on the other which diffuse cheerful,
salutary, and elevated views of life.   Now, the State doubtless
finds an ally in the Church, in giving salutary moral instruction
to the people ; but among a free people, who may, if they choose,
absent themselves and keep their children from all such instructions, or who may hold and teach their children baneful ideas
without State interference, it is extremely unwise to relegate the
moral instruction of the people to religious or irreligious sects,
or to parents avowedly criminal or voluntarily aloof from every
moral influence.   Even if all the citizens were church-goers, and
the children all received Sabbath-school instruction, this would
not be adequate : for there are some religious topics which it
is incumbent on the State to teach decidedly, which churches
may not chance to teach ; those topics being more necessary
when viewed in connection with the State than in their connec-

tion with a small community or a particular church. Take, for instance, suicide. We never heard Sabbath-school instructions touch on this point ; yet the State sees so many of her brilliant and of her wealthiest citizens, male and female, destroy themselves, that it were well for her to read to all her pupils the story of Hagar. The gracious view of God there would counteract the morbid state of mind of Goethe's "Sorrows of Werther," which has made, it is said, more suicides than any other book ever written.[1] The spirit of communism needs a glimpse of the early Pentecostal community ; for, as one has well said, the difference between the two is this: "Communism says, ' All thine is mine ; ' Christianity, ' All mine is thine.' " So the whole matter of drunkenness and " drunkard-making," and defence of nefarious business, would be checked, if the State were to teach her children, from five to fifteen, that there is a God in heaven who sees and will punish. So the matter of the oppressions of capital and the oppressions of "strikes" and trades-unions should be viewed as if all such oppressions would meet a "just recompense of reward." To accomplish this end of which we speak, the child is to be taught, that during all his life, watching, controlling, rewarding him, there is One who is on the one hand Father, on the other hand moral Governor and Judge, who holds both sceptre and shield. All this, of course, without regard to eternity, but simply in temporal relations to State and fellow-citizens, just as Bishop Warburton, in the " Divine Legation," has it that Moses' state had no support from eternal, but only temporal rewards and sanctions of the Almighty. Taking no account of a future world, it is the clear way for the State to diminish its crime, and diffuse cheerful and elevated sentiments, by imprinting on her children, while she has them in the school, — and, be it remembered, she holds them nowhere else under her authoritative instructions, — that, in all their lives, the regard of One who is both Father and King is upon them.

---

[1] " A great many cases of self-murder came to Goethe's notice, in which the victims attributed their rash act to the influence of Werther. He was overwhelmed with letters from persons meditating suicide." — J. MANNING : *Half-Truths and the Truth*, p. 207.

4. God, as the God of the nation, should be recognized in the school. The Prussian maxim is the correct one, "Whatever we would have in the State we must have in the schoolroom." Our grand centennial utterances, it is cheering to see, are full of devout remembrance that "to Him all the shields of the earth belong." Winthrop told the people of Boston, in his fine peroration, that "If that second century of self-government is to go on safely to its close, or is to go on safely and prosperously at all, there must be some renewal of that old spirit of subordination and obedience to divine as well as human laws which has been our security in the past. There must be faith in something higher and better than ourselves. There must be a reverent acknowledgment of an unseen, but all-seeing, all-controlling Ruler of the universe. His word, his day, his house, his worship, must be sacred to our children, as they have been to their fathers; and his blessing must never fail to be invoked upon our land and upon our liberties. The patriot voice which cried from the balcony of yonder old State House, when the Declaration had been originally proclaimed, ' Stability and perpetuity to American independence!' did not fail to add, 'God save our American States!' I would prolong that ancestral prayer. And the last phrase to pass my lips at this hour, and to take its chance for remembrance or oblivion in years to come, as the conclusion of this centennial oration, and the sum and summing-up of all I can say to the present or the future, shall be, There is, there can be, no independence of God: in him as a nation, no less than in him as individuals, 'we live and move, and have our being.' ' GOD SAVE OUR AMERICAN STATES!'"

Whittier's magnificent Centennial Hymn, sublime and American as Yosemite, and which seems like the lofty, leaping, crystal, rainbowed fall of Yosemite's waters from the verges of heaven, is full of recognition of God : —

> "Our fathers' God! from out whose hand
> The centuries fall like grains of sand,
> We meet to-day, united, free,
> And loyal to our land and thee,
> To thank thee for the era done,
> And trust thee for the opening one.

Oh! make thou us, through centuries long,
In peace secure, and justice strong ;
Around our gifts of freedom draw
The safeguard of thy righteous law ;
And, cast in some diviner mould,
Let the new cycle shame the old."

(2.) *God's* RIGHTEOUSNESS *should also have place in the school.*
By this expression is meant true righteousness, according to
eternal standards of right and wrong, — righteousness in God's
sight, righteousness as noticed and rewarded by him.   It includes morality, but as seen in the clearest divine light, as well
as reverence and worship of the Supreme Being.

Every one, of course, recognizes that morality is necessary
in the State.   Every reader of history knows that the old nations
went to decay because the days of their incorruptible simplicity
passed away, and because of their subsequent moral corruption.
Every one knows how morals had declined in the time of the
later Cæsars, and Rome's imperial purple was sold to the highest bidder.   Every one is aware of the reason for the "decline
and fall " of the universal empires.

But it is taken for granted — most unwisely as we think —
that sufficient morality will be absorbed or imbibed from some
source, — from churches, from lectures, from the atmosphere of
general moral excellence.

It may be asked, But how is it that you lay such stress on
the necessity of the *State saving itself,* when you, perchance,
believe that it is *religion and the Church which saves the State?*
It is as "the befriending power," and as infusing virtue into
individuals who then act as righteous citizens, that the Church
saves the State.   Then, as to why the State as well as the
Church should strive for the State's salvation, is it not written,
" Let every man *bear his own burden,*" as well as " Bear ye one
another's burdens " ?

To us, we repeat, it is exceedingly unwise, and one of the
unwisdoms into which this age seems tending to fall, and in
some degree has already fallen, — and that, too, with the history of corrupt and dead nations before us, — to leave so

momentous a matter as the morality of the State, on which, if there be a God, her *life* as a State depends, to the chance instructions of parties outside of her own authority, even though they be on so grand a scale, and of so potent an influence, as those of the Christian Church. *This, perhaps, is the deepest point of divergence now between men who study this subject.* Some think that the State is bound to secure that moral instruction in her schools, where only she is authoritative in this matter, which alone will keep her righteous and prosperous. Others fancy that the State can safely allow this morality in part to be farmed out to the churches, and in part to be totally neglected. Need it be said, that all these articles have been written on the first ground, which seems to us the only wise course, the only view to be entertained for a moment, that, as the State is to stand or fall by her morality or immorality, she must herself be strenuous that she secure morality enough to preserve her from destruction. Recklessness here is suicidal. This view is urgently commended to the profoundest thought of those who are reflecting on this important matter, or who are addressing the public ear or eye upon it.

Some considerations are added, enforcing this point, which, it is hoped, may be pondered most deeply, and considered in the whole breadth and extent of the injurious effects hinted at, not only such as are now visible, but such as will result to the nation from the sowing and reaping of these tares for a hundred years.

1. Some religious corporations — and fullest liberty, be it remembered, is given, in its sphere, to the religious society to teach almost any thing — may teach what the State will consider false and destructive morality. Will the Jesuit, the Mormon, the Freelover, the Chinese, prove good farmers of the morality of the State? History makes us hesitant. On the 24th of August, 1572, says Tytler, "one-half of the French nation, with the sword in one hand and the crucifix in the other, fell with the fury of wild beasts upon their unarmed and defenceless brethren." "The plot was laid with a dissimulation equal to the atrociousness of the design." "Thirty thousand fell by the sword," says the best authority.

"We thought of Seine's empurpled flood,
And good Coligni's hoary hair all dabbled with his blood."

"The Pope," says Father Daniel, "highly commended the zeal of this monarch, and the exemplary punishment which he had inflicted on the heretics. The parliament of Paris decreed an annual procession on St. Bartholomew's Day to offer up thanks to God." Lingard attempts in vain to explain away this massacre while the medal remains, — on one side the face and name, "Gregorius XIII. ;" on the other, "Ugonotorum strages," and an angel with crucifix and sword urging upon the fallen Frenchmen. Plainer it could not be that it was a religious massacre. I know not whether the Papacy of to-day defends this plot; but it is the boast and creed of this hierarchy that Rome never does wrong, and Rome never changes. Is this morality of "no faith with those of another creed" to enter into the State unchecked? Is the morality of Ravaillac to be taught this side the Atlantic? Is that treacherous slaughter which once occurred on American soil to be repeated on American soil, when Ribaut and his band were cut down in cool blood, and Menendez hung their bodies to the trees of Florida, with this justification, "Not because they are Frenchmen, but because they are heretics, and enemies of God." The violation of the safe-conduct of Huss at the command of priests — is it to occur again? These sad pages of history are not recalled to inflame American against American, but to show that the question may well arise, whether it is wise to commit the moral teaching of the State to Rome, which plots such things, and justifies them; Rome, which never does wrong; Rome, which never changes. Is language unjust in making the word Jesuitism a synonyme for "lubricity of morals," as De Quincey might say? Is there a candid American Catholic, however disposed to venerate his "holy Church," who does not see that the *State must teach her own morality*, and not leave to Machiavellian Italy to sow seeds of perfidy which will bear fruitage in some future "*Strages Ungonotorum*"? Chimerical the thought will be considered, that such things may be on the scroll of American history in 1976, and by a good Providence they may not be. But is the *State* in any way guaranteeing *herself* against an American Saint Bartholomew within a hundred years? And — for this is the point — shall the State forego the neutralizing effect of her own public instructions in morality, and give up the entire moral instruction of millions of her citizens to an Italian monarch across the seas? Furthermore, shall there be added to Jesuits the Freelovers, Mormons, and Chinese, as the chosen farmers of the morality of the republic?

2. Some youth are outcasts, not in any religious society. The writer has no statistics before him; but by high authority he is informed that from one-fourth to one-third of the people of Massachusetts are by constant habit absent from church. Larger is the proportion elsewhere. One would not underrate the religious influences in the very air of a Christian community; but many children evidently receive no systematic moral instruction. The State has no right to force them to Church to receive moral training. *There is one place, however, where, between five and fifteen years of age, she has them under her special control for purposes of intellectual and moral discipline.* There she can train these gamins and outcasts to become good citizens.

3. Some heads of families teach no morality, or they teach, substantially, immorality.

This anecdote is more than a *jeu d'esprit.* "Father," said a boy, "do you believe in reading the Bible in schools?" — "Certainly, my son: why do you ask?" — "Because I knew you didn't believe in reading the Bible at home."

Positively, on the other hand, immorality is taught.

I do not need to speak of the teaching in low cellars, of thieving and pocket-picking, and gambling and drinking. But, in many refined homes, the whole drift of conversation and living is an instruction and incentive to the child in "sinful gain and sinful spending." "Covetousness and luxury" are the moral lessons day after day reiterated. "One of the meanest men," says Tenney, "that has lately walked the earth, said, 'Why do you wonder? My father never praised me for any thing but saving half a penny.'"[1] One would be curious to learn in what

[1] Jubilee Essays.

early home atmosphere Tweed breathed. He is proof enough that the State cannot afford to dispense with sound practical instruction on righteous ways of getting and spending money. The State suffers : States have crumbled by "covetousness and luxury." "No man doth dissemble, lie, oppress, defraud, for love of poverty; but thousands do it for love of riches." "He that maketh haste to be rich shall not be innocent." Shall not the State remember that "we belong not so much to an age as to a race loving money, and for it ready to commit all crimes"? Yet this avarice is taught and imbibed in thousands of homes. Shall not the State, with the view of "whiskey rings" and "Indian rings," and bribed legislators, feel that it rests directly on her to give the boys at her knee instructions on righteousness in money-concerns?

Murder is rife, and no wonder. Revenge is taught in some homes ; and, in some, passion is encouraged by example. Has the State, which suffers, no lessons to give on the ruling of the passions?

How can the State find fault with peculation if she did not instruct the boy against it? Tweed might say, A moral sense I had, it is true, which I offended; the law I disregarded, and I suffer by it justly: but why does the *State* complain of what I am, and what I have done, when she never opened her lips in my childhood days to teach me and train me, nor made it her care whether anybody else taught me strict righteousness in acquiring wealth? Does one hazard much in conjecturing that New York lost that six millions, and many a million beside, because the State did not impress upon the boy Tweed, and the boys who grew up with him, that he must acquire wealth lawfully?

4. Some topics are not taught systematically by churches or parents. Moralities important, some of them most important, to the State, are neglected. Suicide, the spirit of communism, fair play between capital and labor, have received mention. It is natural that some moralities should be neglected ; for it would seem almost impertinent for father or church to suppose it possible that any in their circle should traffic in rum and opium and prostitution. But the State cannot be unaware that in the

wide circle of her future citizens, in every large school, there are those who are germinating for this crime of nefarious trafficking, the parent of crimes and untold misery to the State. If every child were taught by the State, from his fifth to fifteenth year, that to drink and to sell intoxicating liquors are iniquitous, would there be in our land nearly *one million habitual drunkards*, sixty thousand of which die annually, and nearly *five hundred thousand drunkard-makers*? At least, in that case, might the State applaud herself as a careful and resolute mother; while now she weakly looks aghast, and wrings her hands over crimes which she never trained her youth to abhor.

Still, men are willing to run the fearful risks that the friction of morality neglected and immorality inculcated shall not finally stop the machine. The American people, part of them, have an unbounded presumption, and do not shrink from casting themselves down from pinnacles, even where they see bones below. Bushnell, thirty years ago, gave a discourse, "Barbarism our great danger." One memorable example he adduces: "If it seems extravagant to speak of any such result, let it not be forgotten that one emigrant family of the Saxon race has already sunk into barbarism since our history began. I speak of the Dutch Boers in South Africa. They are Calvinistic Protestants: they began the settlement at Cape Town in the year 1651; and now they are virtually barbarians, for they are scarcely less wild in their habits than the Hottentots themselves." "A standing proof that Protestants, and they, too, of Saxon blood, may drop out of civilization, and take their place on the same level of ignorance and social brutality with the barbarous tribes of the earth. Let no American who loves his country refuse to heed the example." Wendell Phillips says, "It requires great faith to believe that we shall celebrate our second Centennial; but I believe it, because I believe in God."

It is not auspicious of a happy second Centennial that we commenced our second century with a monsoon of mobs in nine of our large cities, — and that in the temperate North, — some of which would have disgraced Paris.

"*Esto perpetua* will not save us," says Anderson.

In this recapitulatory essay we advance to say, that,

II. GOD AND HIS RIGHTEOUSNESS SHOULD HAVE PLACE IN THE SCHOOL BY THE BIBLE.

Here we need do little more than to give an intelligible *résumé.* A few arguments additional are interpolated.

1. The Bible should be employed in recognizing God and fostering righteousness in the school, because it is now used for that purpose. This is on the logical ground, that, unless there is reason for a change, things should remain as they are. So far as the Bible has been used, its influence has been beneficent. Great names have borne witness to this. Arguments must be of exceeding weight and cogency to persuade to such a revolution.

2. The fathers of the republic instituted the present order of things. For more than two hundred years, the use of the Bible in schools has been sanctioned by our great statesmen. It is unwise to make a change in State polity, and disregard the wisdom of the succession of statesmen, without prevailing reasons.

3. Some book is needful in stimulating to reverential worship. If the object be really to compass this end, the best thoughts of men in their highest moods should be chosen to awaken the mind to its best thoughts and feelings. Prof. Phelps says much to this point in the chapter of his unprinted lectures on "Study of Models." He reminds us that modern literature and art were born by the revival of the study of the ancient models, in composition, painting, and sculpture, of Greece and Rome. He dwells instructively on the "stimulus of a suggestive model." "It has become a standard among the expedients of self-culture. Wirt mentions a friend who made such a daily use of Bolingbroke. Voltaire made a similar use of Massillon; a suggestive fact, the infidel resorting to the noblest of the French preachers. Bossuet was accustomed to prepare his mind for any great effort by the study of Homer, lighting, as he said, his candle at the sun. Gray always read Spenser. Milton used a variety; but his favorites were Homer and Euripides. Pope used Dryden as his constant aid to composition." These

all "chose models as immediate aids to their own labors." "The devout and contemplative East" has one book *greatly calculated to stir devotion.*

4. Some book should be used which may suggest, and by distinct and well-known examples illustrate, the lessons of righteousness to be taught. These, by well-nigh universal consent, are found in the Scriptures. They are "profitable for instruction in righteousness," even if, as we are about to propose, the Scriptures be not *taught*, but only be *read* as the groundwork of moral teaching and the fountain of moral sentiments.

5. This book is acknowledged to be the most successful attempt to describe the divine and the human in themselves and in their relations to each other. "They are revealed in comparison ; they are revealed in contrast; in things similar, and in things dissimilar; the fountains of the great deep of human thought, of human action, are broken up ; and man, inward and outward, is contemplated, not in the dim taper-light of time, but the broad light of eternity."

This book, therefore, contains vital, educating forces.

6. The Bible should be used because it constantly suggests God as the great moral Being, and the great Rewarder of moral actions. Whether this book is infallible in its declarations of the ways in which God will reward good and punish evil, it is not needful to our argument to inquire ; but of this much, which is pertinent to our purpose, every one is aware, that the book makes impressive appeal to the universal sense that God is King and Judge of all.

Other reasons for the use of the Bible are these : —

7. The Bible is the mother of modern education. For the child not only to ignore the benefactions of the one who gave birth and nurture, but to cast her out of doors, is shameful. Modern education should set *a golden throne for its venerable mother*, its truly *Alma Mater*, the Scriptures.

8. This book is intimately connected with the liberty of the State. From it sprung the idea of "a church without a bishop, and a state without a king." For though this book says, "Honor the king," "Put them in mind to be subject to prin-

cipalities and .powers, to obey magistrates," yet it also says[1] that a kingdom is an inferior, worldly, oppressive, and burdensome form of government. "Howbeit," says God to Samuel, "solemnly protest unto them, and show them the manner of the king that shall reign over them."

To this book is due the Sabbath,[2] — "the holy day of freedom, the holiday of despotism," says the wise observer before quoted. Pres. Hopkins's two propositions are, "First, A religious observance of the Sabbath will secure the permanence of free institutions. Second, Without the Sabbath religiously observed, the permanence of free institutions cannot be secured."

9. All the nations of Europe, the languages of Western civilization, hold this book, the Bible, as containing the sublimest, most righteous, most gracious views of the Divine Being.

10. The Bible, early translated into all the languages of Europe, is that book whose language and diction in regard to God permeate all our literatures.

11. The Bible is the book of the founders of our nation's institutions, — the book of Bradford, Carver, Winthrop, of Washington, Sherman, and Ames.

12. This book, of all religious volumes, in all climes, gives the truest cosmogony, the only one which is not open to ridicule, and a view of God throughout which is sublime, and in no way below the teachings of advanced science. Such a literary cosmopolitan as Edward Everett, referring to the religious volumes of other climes and races, speaks of "the extreme repulsiveness of those books." He says, that, with the scholar's literary thirst, he has several times tried to read the Koran. "Any thing more repulsive and uninviting than the Koran I have seldom attempted to peruse, even when taken up with these kindly feelings." "With such portions of the sacred books of the Hindoos as have fallen in my way the case is far worse." "The mythological system contained in them is .a tissue of monstrosities and absurdities, by turns so revolting and nauseous as to defy perusal." "Few things would do more to raise

---

[1] 1 Sam. viii.   [2] Refer back to the Sabbath discussion.

the Scriptures in our estimation than to compare the Bible with the Koran and the Vedas."[1]

13. This book deserves the preference in the recognition of God in the school, because it contains the one, unique, perfect man, Jesus Christ, whose character enters widely and deeply into all modern philanthropy and ethics.

Premising that the next point is secondary, we nevertheless add, that,

III. THE TRANSLATION OF THE BIBLE MADE BY KING JAMES, THE ENGLISH VERSION, SHOULD GENERALLY BE THE VERSION WHICH IS ADOPTED AS THE STANDARD VERSION IN READING THIS BOOK IN THE SCHOOLS.

This, indeed, is a minor point; and it is not necessary to press it. A fair mind will be willing to concede that other versions may be simultaneously used, — simultaneously even as to the utterance of reading; and that, where the majority shall prefer, another version should be used. For what are they but versions of the same book? But, in general, the English version is to be preferred on these entirely unsectarian grounds.

1. The English version is a direct translation, made with great care from the original languages.

2. The English version is the translation which is used by scholars, orators, poets.

3. The English version is the State version. It was made by the State, for the State.

4. The English version is that generally used in the State, in legislature, courts, and State benevolent institutions.

IV. A MANUAL OF MORALITY SHOULD ALSO BE PREPARED FOR USE IN SCHOOLS.

For the INSTRUCTION IN MORALS, a *manual* is necessary.

1. Some would say that the instruction should be scriptural, — explanations of the Scripture utterances on the various duties. In this method, the Bible being read, certain verses or sections of the reading would then be taken as the basis of comment and application by the teacher.

ANSWER 1. — While all admit that the Bible is a fountain of

[1] Works, ii. 672.

morality, few desire the exposition of the Scriptures in the school.

ANS. 2. — The instructions in morals should be prepared by the State, and as little of instruction as possible be left to the discretion of the teacher. Thus only will the State secure the imparting of the moral lessons she deems needful for her welfare, without addition or subtraction; thus she will secure uniformity in the subjects presented. Ample scope can be allowed the teacher in illustrating and enforcing the duties taught.

2. Some would say, Let there be a manual prepared in two parts; Part I. containing in full the Bible-readings for the year, and Part II. containing moral instructions. In this way, it might be averred, the prejudices of some against the appearance of the Bible itself in the school might be allayed, while substantially the same reverence and righteousness would be inculcated.

ANSWER 1. — The very Book, the Bible itself, the parent of modern education, the fosterer of republics, *should appear in the schoolroom. The Bible should have an honored place in the school as on the church pulpit, or in the " holy ark " of the synagogue.* I would have the very desk on which the Bible is placed suggestive of the honor due to it. I would not have the Bible laid or thrown about on the teacher's desk among miscellaneous books. Somewhere on the platform I would have a choice little piece of furniture, with pedestal, column, and table, about eighteen inches square. On that, as in a place of honor before the school, the Bible should rest, to be suggestive of its place in Occidental worship, in modern literature, in American history.

Edward Everett, in one of his great orations, raised in his hand, high above his head, a copy of Homer, as an emblem of the power of letters. The Bible itself, quite apart from its containing the gospel of salvation, but on account of its paramount and indispensable power in morals, literature, politics, art, education, should be *displayed* in the schoolroom as it is *displayed* at the monarch's coronation.

ANS. 2. — Any thing that would pave the way for the withdrawal of this book from the schoolroom should be avoided.

ANS. 3. — There would be no serious objection to such a manual for convenience of use, provided it were designated a *Bible Manual,* and provided that the Bible itself were retained in its place of honor at the desk.

3. By far the preferable way seems to be, *to use the Bible, without note or comment, for readings;* and to have a MANUAL, *separate and distinct, which shall contain instructions in morals.* There should be, every year if desirable to change so often, a printed card of selected sections from the Bible for daily reading.

The selections from the Scriptures can be made of great value. Though the writer has not spent much time on this part of the subject, a few selections are here indicated as specimens of what a more skilful hand could do in this department. Readings should generally not exceed twenty or thirty verses. Gen. i., Creation. Gen. viii., Deluge. Gen. ix., Reason for the Death Penalty. Gen. x., Peopling of the Earth. "History has its beginning in this ethnological table," says Johannes von Müller. Exod. xx., The Ten Commandments. Joshua i., Courage and Obedience. 1 Kings viii., Solomon's Prayer at the Temple. 1 Sam. xv., Disobedience and Rejection of Saul. 1 Sam. xx., Friendship of David and Jonathan. Neh. vi., Esther (selections). Daniel, most of it, especially ii. 31–49, The Image of Gold; vii., The Beasts; vii., Alexander's Empire. Matt. v., vi., vii., Sermon on the Mount. Matt. xxiii. 1–12, Humility. 1 Cor. xiii., Charity. John's Epistle 1 (many parts), Revelation, Descriptions of Heaven. These are only a few chance specimens.

Job, Isaiah, and the Psalms will furnish abundant selections of a liturgical and devotional character. Proverbs and Ecclesiastes are of course, of themselves, almost a manual of wise conduct. A book of carefully collected and unsectarian hymns should be compiled.

The manual should consist of lessons, forty perhaps in number, one for every week in the year, on the various moral duties. Each duty should be explained, enforced, and illustrated by standard and effective examples from ancient and modern history and biography. The manual should, of course, be prepared with the greatest care and moral earnestness by some of the best men in the State, yet with circumspection in excluding every thing sectarian.

This committee should consist of the most earnest moral men, yet the broadest-minded and most catholic in the State. We take the liberty to suggest a few names, not to give a complete list, but to show the *kind* of men whom the State should employ in so important a work. Of course we omit a great many names as good as those which we give : —

Rev. Phillips Brooks ; A. P. Peabody, D.D. ; James Freeman Clarke, D.D. ; E. K. Alden, D.D. ; George E. Lorimer, D.D. ; B. K. Peirce, D.D. ; A. A. Miner, D.D. ; Archbishop Williams ; Father Robert Fulton ; Rabbi Lasker ; Rev. Charles B. Rice ; Rev. E. P. Tenney (now President of Colorado College) ; Rev. George L. Chaney ; Miss Jane H. Stickney ; Miss Annie E. Johnson of Bradford Seminary ; Miss E. P. Peabody ; Mrs. Cowles of Ipswich Seminary ; the Misses McKeen of Andover Seminary, and others ; Hon. John D. Philbrick ; John W. Dickinson Esq. ; the principals of the several normal schools ; the Presidents of colleges, past and present, not forgetting Thomas Hill, D.D., and Mark Hopkins, D.D. ; Hon. Alexander H. Rice, Hon. Henry L. Pierce, Hon. Edward L. Pierce, Hon. E. R. Hoar, Hon. George F. Hoar, Hon. George S. Boutwell, Hon. A. H. Bullock, &c.

This committee, of course, must have a sub-committee. That sub-committee would have such important duties as these : —

1. To decide upon the forty or more topics.

2. To study them as to the proper moral view of them, with limitations, &c.

3. To prepare the didactic matter.

4. To prepare the illustrative matter. This, of course, is one of the most important duties of the preparation, and will require wide and patient research in the field of moral anecdote and of history, and great judgment in selection.

5. To prepare the interrogatory matter.

6. To prepare all this matter with reference to its simultaneous use by scholars of all ages, from five to fifteen, perhaps in three series.

The field is comparatively a new one. Yet there have been a few manuals of morals, not so many nor so established in public regard as one would suppose would have been the case, considering these words of Horace Mann : " Some work on morals for common schools, which shall excite the sympathies as well as the intellect, which shall make children love virtue as well as understand what it is, is the greatest desideratum of our schools."

One of the best manuals is a little book by Miss A. Hall, published by John P. Jewett, 1850, entitled, "A Manual of Morals for Common Schools." On the titlepage are these lines, which fairly indicate the high purpose of the author : — .

> " 'Tis a fond yet a fearful thing to rule
> O'er the opening mind in the village school :
> Like wax ye can mould it in the form ye will ;
> What ye write on the tablet remains there still ;
> *And an angel's work is not more high*
> *Than aiding to form one's destiny.*"

There is much valuable material in the "Moral Instructor," by Jesse Torrey, Jr., which received the commendation of Pres. John Adams in 1820.

There are books which should be consulted as containing valuable didactic or illustrative material, such as Dr. Wayland's "Moral Science," Dymond's "Essays on Morality," Whewell's "Elements of Morality," Peabody's "Manual of Moral Philosophy," Whately's "Lessons on Morals," Sullivan's "Moral Class-Book," Paley's "Moral and Political Philosophy," Henry Owgan's "Manual of Ethics" (the chapter on "The Cardinal Virtues"), Silvio Pellico's "The Duties of Men" (a choice little volume from the Italian prisoner), with some of the books used in Kindergartens, such as "Sandford and Merton." Nor should one forget to glean whole "handfuls" from ancient works, — Plutarch's "Moral Writings," and Anecdotes from Plutarch's Lives, if there is such a book ; Cicero's De Officiis, Seneca's Morals, and the writings of Orientals, — Confucius and others. One should not neglect Emerson, his superlative "Essays on the Conduct of Life," and, in the other volumes, the series of Essays, History, Self-Reliance, &c. Carlyle and others who have striven to stir men should not escape the glance of this committee. Charles Sumner, with his grand moral nature, said grand moral things. Nor should we forget the poets; since one has well said, "Poetry is *beautiful truth;*" and a poet has said of some poems, that they are

> "Thoughts that enrich the life-blood of the world."

Our own poets, Lowell, Bryant, Longfellow, should be in the minds of that committee. We are grateful that our best poets have written what is sweet with moral goodness. Milton, Shakspeare, Mrs. Browning, and others might give some beams of their glory to such a book, intended to quicken youth to higher views of duty.

The writer, though not ambitious to do more than roughly sketch this part of his work, has thrown together a sufficient number of topics to show what this manual should attempt to accomplish, — Reverence and Worship of God; Benevolence (Howard, Clarkson); Respect for Aged, Superiors, Parents, Teachers (Spartans in Athenian Theatre, Napoleon's Mother, Teacher's Father and School Sleighride); Friendship (Damon and Pythias); Kindness to Animals (Stories from "Our Dumb Animals"); Care of Body; Temperance; Chastity; Self-Control; Self-Respect; Docility (Agassiz); Modesty (Isaac Newton); Self-Improvement; Industry; Order; Punctuality (Washington); Self-Knowledge; Reciprocity; Deference; Honesty (Colbert and the Merchant); Use of Public Money (John Quincy Adams, Charles Sumner); Discharge of Trusts; Righteous Business; Righteous Trading; Legitimate Business Sagacity with God's Blessing (Jacob and Laban); Reciprocal Duties of Capital and Labor; Promise-Keeping; Payment of Debts; Sabbath Observance; Sacredness of Life; Penalties of Crime; Choosing of Magistrates; Duties of Magistrates to God and the People; Filial Duties; Parental Duties; Peace and War; Reciprocal Duties of Nations; Patriotism; &c.

We believe we say only what is right and fitting and graceful in suggesting — entirely unprompted, and at our own thought — that the excellent publishing-house which gives to the public this *idea* of a manual of morals should have given to it by the State the *publication* of the manual itself. It is a kind of justice in accordance with Gen. xli. 38–40.

Having considered at such length the *material* of the devotional and ethical exercise, we need to spend but few words upon,

SECOND, THE MANNER OF THE DEVOTIONAL AND MORAL EXERCISE. This has been foreshadowed and almost stated in the account of the devotional and instructive material.

A preliminary remark, however, is of great importance. *The devotional exercise should no longer skulk : it ought to stand forth and erect in its full manhood stature.* This exercise is now like Charles Edward, having the name of king, yet his title disputed, and he called by his enemies the " Pretender," hiding in forests and ravines : it should be like a monarch on his rightful throne. It is a common remark among school committees and teachers, that the exercise now amounts to little. This is for two reasons. First, because the educationalists seem not to have thought themselves clear as to whether they have a right to recognize God, and teach righteousness in the school, and they therefore proceed with the timidity and half-heartedness of the undecided ; and, second, because they have never set themselves to estimate how much can be made of this exercise for the benefit of the State. At one of the schools which the writer attended, the honored principal, who conducted the devotions with sufficient reverence, seemed, however, hardly to observe, in his mechanical reading of the Scripture, how often he informed us that "at that season there were some who told him of the Galileans, whose blood Pilate had mingled with their sacrifices." All this should be changed. Alfred should leave the herdsman's hut and the umbrageous rendezvous, and take his regal place in the palace of the metropolis. The devotional exercise should take its place openly, firmly, fully, and decidedly, not only as one who has a right to occupy a place, but of one who is conscious of being on a throne of power, — *Dei gratia Rex,* — and a seat of usefulness, direct and instant in its benefactions, yet which are also so far reaching and potent and divine, that they are likely to be the very salvation of the State. The devotional exercise is to come to the youth in our schools quietly yet authoritatively, like *some angel,* like some Sandalphon, *intrusted with extraordinary power,* — *the mission to bring this nation forward to its second Centennial.*

The daily exercise should occupy about fifteen minutes. It should consist of the Scripture-reading for the day, and prayer, and, if possible, a hymn. The Scripture-reading may consist, following the table of sections, of a selection of considerable length (thirty verses), either didactic, historical, or devotional; or it may consist of a brief section for instruction, and a brief psalm. The table is to regulate this. There may be a golden text or passage for the day.

The reading may be conducted variously. The teacher alone may read ; or the teachers and scholars may read alternately, in which case the child may *simultaneously* (in utterance we mean : there will be not so much indistinctness as in the pleasant jargon of an Episcopal service) read the Douai version if he choose; or the children may read, in rotation, each a verse, in which case also, each, unblamed, should read his own version ; or the reading may be responsive, — the boys, for example, in a mixed school, reading one verse, and the girls reading the next, or one part of the school reading in response to the other. In all these, each should freely use his own version.

The hymn, of course, should be unsectarian, patriotic, or religious, such as "Nearer, my God, to Thee," and "My Country, 'tis of thee." Vinet is hardly correct when he says, " It would be impossible to unite, even once in a century, Christians and Deists in a common worship. Such a worship would, in truth, be only that of Deism, into which Christians would be constrained to descend, without the possibility of elevating their companions."

On the contrary, the heart can truly worship with the Deist, and then dilate to worship the God of revelation, almost as easily as the pupil of the eye dilates according to the degree of light. We worship in " Nearer, my God, to Thee," with the Deist, although we can readily expand the soul to sing the new stanza, "Christ alone beareth me." Allusions to Christ, especially

,where Jews are present, should be in the nature of recognition, and not of worship. The Lord's Prayer may be the usual prayer. There may be special prayers for occasions, as for exhibition, first and last days, death of scholars or teachers. The Israelites, in their liturgy, have some prayers which are religious and patriotic, which would be admirable for school use. The Episcopal liturgy would furnish choice extracts in the composition of prayers.

The exercise in the manual of morals should be as frequent as once a week. An hour might profitably be given to it. The text of the lesson should be well studied, and carefully recited; after which scholars might discuss the topic freely, under their teacher's direction. Much interest and effectiveness would be added to this moral study from the fact that all the scholars in a commonwealth might be studying the same topic together, such as Lawful Business, Use of Public Money; while the newspapers of the day, as in the case of the International Biblical Lessons, might strive which should furnish the most valuable discussion of the topic, and the most interesting illustrative materials. Such a devotional service would no longer seem unimportant, or unworthy the striving to maintain; but a few years would place it among the permanent American institutions; God would be honored, and his blessing invoked; righteousness would flourish, — "instead of the thorn, the fir-tree; instead of the brier, the myrtle;" the tone of public morality would be immeasurably elevated; "whatsoever things are true, honest, just, pure, lovely, of good report, whatever virtue, whatever praise," would be more in the thought and the life; we should have a "nationality with a quickened conscience;"

"AND, CAST IN SOME DIVINER MOULD,
WILL THE NEW CYCLE SHAME THE OLD."

. THE STATE INSTITUTIONS AND RELIGION.

THE STATE INSTITUTIONS AND RE-
LIGION.

IN the year 1755, John Howard, having recently laid his wife in her last resting-place, set out from England to make a tour of the Continent. It was the year of the Lisbon earthquake. For that city he sailed. "The ship was taken by a French privateer. Howard was made prisoner. The treatment he met was inhuman. For forty hours he was kept with the other prisoners on board the French vessel, without water, and with hardly a morsel of food. They were then carried into Brest, and committed to the castle. They were flung into a dungeon; and, after a further period of starvation, 'a joint of mutton was at length thrown into the midst of them, which, for the want of accommodation of so much as a solitary knife, they were obliged to tear to pieces, and gnaw like dogs.' There was nothing in the dungeon to sleep on, except some straw; and in such a place, and with such treatment, he and his fellow-prisoners remained a week." He was then removed to Morlaix. "But," says Bayne,[1] "he did not remain idle. The sufferings he had witnessed while inmate of a French prison would not let him rest. He had seen something amiss, something unjust, something which pained his heart as a feeling man. His English sense of order and of work was outraged. There was something to be done, and he set himself to do it. He collected information respecting the state of English prisoners of war in France. He

---

[1] Peter Bayne, Christian Life, 102: Howard and the Rise of Philanthropy.

found that his own treatment was part, and nowise a remarkable part, of a system ; that many hundreds of these prisoners had perished through sheer ill-usage, and that thirty-six had been buried in a hole at Dinan in one day.   In fact, he discovered that he had come upon an abomination and iniquity on the face of the earth, which, strangely enough, had been permitted to go on unheeded until it had reached that frightful excess.   He learned its extent, and departed with his information for England.   He was permitted to cross the Channel on pledging his word to return if a French officer was not exchanged for him."   By his exertions, the inmates of the three prisons soon put their feet on the soil of their native land.   "Howard modestly remarks, that perhaps his sufferings on this occasion increased his sympathy with the inhabitants of prisons."

Returned to England, Howard married again, felicitously. After a delightful seven years spent in Cardington, which, under their fostering care, blossomed like the rose, his beloved wife died (1765).   "Not long after her death, he heard the call which bade him leave the wells and the palm-trees of rest to take his road along the burning sand of duty."

In 1773 he was appointed sheriff of Bedford.   He was struck and amazed at the condition of the jails.   In his plain, direct, penetrating way, he sought information ; then began to go beyond the county in search of prison abuses ; next crossed over to the Continent, and made wide researches ; and in 1777 he published his first book on the "State of Prisons in England and Wales."   That has been called "*the beginning of prison science.*"   Again and again he visited Europe, even to Constantinople and distant Russia.   Invited by the Empress Catherine to visit the palace, he declined, saying that he had come to the capital to visit, not palaces, but prisons.   "I cannot name this gentleman," says Burke,[1] "without remarking that his labors and writings have done much to open the eyes and hearts of mankind.   He has visited all Europe, not to survey the sumptuousness of palaces or the stateliness of temples ; not to make accurate measurements of the remains of ancient grandeur, nor

---

[1] Speech at Guildhall in Bristol, 1780.

to form a scale of the curiosity of modern art; not to collect medals or collate manuscripts; but to dive into the depths of dungeons; to plunge into the infection of hospitals; to survey the mansions of sorrow and pain; to take the gauge and dimensions of misery, depression, and contempt; to remember the forgotten, to attend to the neglected, to visit the forsaken, and to compare and collate the distresses of all men in all countries. His plan is original, and it is as full of genius as it is of humanity. It was a voyage of discovery, a circumnavigation of charity. Already the benefit of his labor is felt more or less in every country."

In seventeen years — he was sixty years old when he declined Catherine's invitation — he travelled fifty thousand miles, and spent one hundred and twenty-five thousand dollars from his own purse. It was John Howard's strong sense of the call of God to this mission, and his strong faith as a disciple of his divine Master, which connected his name immortally with prisons. For his epitaph he wished the simple words, "My hope is in Christ."

Religion and *Prisons:* there was a still older connection, in the words of him whom Christendom recognizes as Master, "Sick and in prison, and ye came unto me." He thus indicated that it was natural for a religion which should be the outflow of his spirit to go into prisons to find and relieve sickness and distress.

Religion, too, has established hospitals. Arvine tells us that "the first hospital for the reception of the diseased and infirm' was founded at Edessa, in Syria, by the sagacious and provident humanity of a Christian Father. The history of this memorable foundation is given by Sozomen in his life of Ephrem Syrus." By the venerable deacon of that city, and at his expense, three hundred beds were set in the porticoes of the city for the reception of the fever patients. The poor, also, she has ever cared for. "Only they would," said Paul, "that we should remember the poor; which thing I also was forward to do." The blind, the inebriate, the paupers, the bereft of reason, and the idiotic, she has ever deemed it a part of her vocation to relieve, whether single, or collected in establishments. "Pure religion before God and the Father is to visit the widows and the fatherless in their affliction."

Unofficial, as thus far considered, is this connection of religion with the afflicted and criminal. But now we find that the State — and that, too, among a people jealous of every thing like the connection of State and Church — has given this "befriending power," as Coleridge might call it, an *official place* in the person of a chaplain, and religious opportunity in a "divine service," and has instructed this power to take general and particular measures promotive of its ends and purposes.

The history of chaplaincies remains still to be written. The materials accessible are not abundant. The main lessons which such a history would force home upon us are these: the earnestness with which the best men, who, like Howard, have understood prisons, ships, regiments, &c., have advocated the religious chaplaincy; *second,* the great value in experience of such a chaplaincy, whether on sea or on land; *third,* the general idea of the chaplaincy, that the office should be governmental; and, *fourth,* the general, though not universal, idea of the chaplaincy, that the office should be held by one only. Perhaps for Americans it should be added, as the historic lesson, that the *unsectarian chaplaincy is American,* rooted among the institutions by the fathers, Madison and Sherman, and fostered by our great statesmen; by Webster, for example.

The materials are sufficient to show these historic lessons, though not enough, perhaps, to illustrate them in an interesting manner.

The proper history of *prison chaplaincies* is very recent. Latimer, as early as Edward Sixth's time, encouraged them, as something not yet realized. Philanthropic ministers, like Kilpin in Queen Elizabeth's time, had a chance visit and godly exhortation for the prison. The early Methodists exhibited their love by "remembering those in bonds." About 1700 there were few ministers in prisons, and these generally inferior, not to say unworthy men. They were appointed by the prison-officers, or were called in by the jailer. Dr. Bray, in 1702, has an "Essay towards the Reformation of Prisons, Newgate, &c.:" he refers to "ministers of prisons."

Chaplaincies became an institution of government by statute,

13th of George III., or 1773, and have continued uninterrupted since that time. This, we believe, is the oldest statute extant on the subject: "Whereas there is no provision made by law for the appointment of proper ministers to officiate in the several county gaols within that part of Great Britain called England and the principality of Wales; and whereas the appointment of ministers to such gaols with a proper salary, for the due execution of their duty as clergymen, would alleviate the distress of the persons under confinement, and would greatly contribute to the purposes of morality and religion." Observe in this earliest statute, under a State, too, which had a State religion, how broad and unsectarian are the purposes of the proposed chaplaincy under government. The pay of chaplains was £50. Howard's first report was in 1777. He expresses in the most emphatic words that there should be a chapel in a prison, and a chaplain who should be a man of living and active piety. "Hanway, Howard, and Paul," says Clay, "all insisted on the necessity of able, earnest, and constant religious ministrations in prisons."[1] All chaplains, we believe, agree with Chaplain Kingsmill, "That which is reformatory in the highest degree, Christian instruction in the hands of Christian men." Before 1830 there were few chaplains' reports. The character of the chaplaincies has been greatly improved, and the chaplaincy has received more of the honor which is due to it. 56th of Geo. III., an act was passed increasing the duties and pay of chaplains. In 1823 by a new act, the salary of Clay, for example, was raised from £100 to £250. At the time of Clay's appointment (1821), there was as yet no school in the prison. "The prison-parson, at that period, still ranked rather low in the scale of clerical gradations. Half a century earlier, any needy priest of damaged character was thought good enough to minister among rogues."[2] "On a week-day he was ready to crack a bottle or shuffle a pack with his flock; on a Sunday he mumbled a service and sermon to them in one of the day-rooms."[3]

"In our time," says Kingsmill, "probably no part of the Church is served by more excellent, faithful, and painstaking

---

[1] Clay's Memoir, 101.   [2] Ibid., 101.   [3] Ibid., 17.

clergymen than the prisons of England." It was said of Chaplain Clay, that he knew more of the working-classes than any other man living. It is a mistake that any minister can make a chaplain. Thomas Starr King says, "To deal with criminals for the purpose of reformation is a task requiring special aptitude. You may make soldiers, you may make administrators, you may make clergymen, you may even, to a great extent, make schoolmasters, out of the materials of ordinary humanity : but chaplains or governors of jails, and conductors of reformatory schools, are like poets, — you must find them ; you cannot manufacture them. Their original endowments and qualities must be peculiar, or they will not succeed."

In 1853 Mr. Lucas in Parliament advocated Roman-Catholic chaplains, as they had for a long time acted in Ireland, and in the penal colonies since Lord Derby's administration of the colonial government. He was not successful in changing the ancient policy of one govermental chaplain. We are not aware that any change has since taken place in England from this traditional policy. At that time the law read as, we believe, now : "*If any prisoner shall be of a religious persuasion differing from that of the Established Church, a minister of such persuasion,* AT THE SPECIAL REQUEST OF SUCH PRISONER, *shall be allowed to visit him,*" &c.[1] It would be interesting to penetrate the history of the penal colonies, and see what *wonderful transformations* had there, or on the transport-ships, been effected by chaplains, such as Dr. Vanderkemp in "The Hillsborough," Dr. Browning, and Rev. Thomas Rogers.[2] So marked were these, that the lieutenant-governor of Botany Bay said, in 1839, "I am convinced that were £2,000 per annum expended by her Majesty's Government in supporting ten pious and zealous ministers, to be employed in the interior of this colony, in preaching daily, not in churches, but to the *convicts in the houses of the settlers*, the benefit to be derived from such a measure would be very great."[3] We commend to the reader the excellent memoir of John Clay, as illustrating the possible usefulness of a chaplain.

Chaplaincies in legislative bodies have existed from the earliest

---

[1] Kingsmill, 202.   [2] Kingsmill, chap. vii.   [3] Ibid., 156.

period of our national life. The Continental Congress met on the 5th of September, 1774, in Carpenters' Hall, Philadelphia. Peyton Randolph of Virginia was speaker. "It was proposed to open the sessions with prayer. Some of the members thought this might be inexpedient, as all the delegates might not be able to join in the same form of worship. Up rose Samuel Adams, in whose great soul there was not a grain of sham. He was a strict Congregationalist. 'I am no bigot,' he said: '*I can hear a prayer from a man of piety and virtue, whatever may be his cloth, provided he is at the same time a friend to his country.*' On his motion, Rev. Mr. Duché, an Episcopal clergyman of Philadelphia, was invited to act as chaplain. Mr. Duché accepted the invitation." "He appeared next morning, with his clerk and in his pontifical, and read several prayers in the established form ; and then read the collect for the seventh day of September, which was the thirty-fifth psalm. You must remember this was the morning after we heard the horrible rumor of the cannonade of Boston. I never saw greater effect upon an audience. It seemed as if Heaven had ordained that psalm to be read on that morning.

"After that, Mr. Duché, very unexpectedly to everybody, struck out into an extemporary prayer, which filled the bosom of every man present. I must confess I never heard a better prayer, or one so well pronounced. Episcopalian as he is, Dr. Cooper never prayed with such fervor, such ardor, such earnestness and pathos, and in language so elegant and sublime, for America, for Congress, for the Province of Massachusetts Bay, and especially the town of Boston. It had an excellent effect upon everybody here. I must beg you to read that psalm." [1]

That same clergyman was afterwards appointed chaplain of the American Congress. He had such an appointment five days after the declaration of independence.

Dec. 22, 1776, Dec. 13, 1784, chaplains were chosen ; and on Feb. 29, 1788, it was resolved that two chaplains should be appointed. So far the old Congress. [2]

---

[1] Letter from John Adams to Mrs. Adams, Sept. 16, 1774.
[2] Lorenzo D. Johnson: Government Chaplains, New York, 1856.

Samuel Adams struck the true key-note for all time, in America, of *unsectarian chaplaincies;* and in Congress there have been chaplains, "Methodist, Baptist, Episcopalian, Presbyterian, Congregationalist, Catholic, Unitarian, and others."

The first Congress under the Constitution began March 4, 1789. Almost as soon as a quorum was obtained, on the 9th of April, a committee on chaplains was appointed. It was decided to have two, of different denominations, each alternating between House and Senate. Washington's first speech was read to the House May 1; and the *first* business after that speech was the appointment of Dr. Linn as chaplain. Three out of six of that committee — Madison, Ellsworth, and Sherman — had been on the Constitutional Committee, and *understood perfectly the American ideas.* The law of 1789 was passed in compliance with their plan. The chaplaincy is *American,* according to the fathers. This law was re-enacted in 1816.

It is interesting to reflect that the first *public prayer on board ship* was probably made by Noah, and the first *service in camp* conducted by Abraham. Moses praying, with Aaron and Hur (Miriam's husband) holding up his hands, is probably the oldest extant example of prayer during battle. An interesting service of encouragement to battle is commanded in Deut. xx. 2–4: "And it shall be, when ye are come nigh unto the battle, that the priest shall approach and speak unto the people, and shall say unto them, Hear, O Israel! ye approach this day unto battle against your enemies: let not your hearts faint, fear not, and do not tremble, neither be ye terrified because of them; for the Lord your God is he that goeth with you, to fight for you against your enemies, to save you." Prayer and hymn have often been raised to God before battle, notably by the army of Gustavus Adolphus, and by the Scotch army at Bannockburn. McDonnough also read service previous to the naval engagement on Lake Champlain.

Of the necessity for chaplains in army and navy there can be no doubt. Our naval chaplain friend says, "After an experience of ten years, I cannot understand how a ship" (carrying, as they do, from six hundred to one thousand men of all nationalities, and apart from restraints of society) "can be much better than a hell, without a chaplain. Of about one-eighth of the crew he makes a nucleus, and through them exercises influence upon the rest." "A chaplain can be useful every minute of his time."

Movements are on foot for great improvements in our naval chaplaincies, which will gladden many hearts.

In England, "Chambers' Journal" informs us, there have been chaplains for many generations; but the system was re-organized and improved in 1795. "*In recent years,*" — observe, this was not the original policy, — "Roman-Catholic and Presbyterian chaplains have been also appointed." "The chaplains belong, not to the regiments, but to the staff, so as to be readily available. At home they are attached to military stations; in the field they are located at headquarters, at the hospitals, and with divisions." "They visit the sick at the hospitals, and examine and encourage the regimental schools. Among the wooden huts of Aldershott camp a church has been built, which is rendered available for chaplains of different religious denominations in succession." In 1796 there was a chaplaincy-general, which was abolished by the Duke of Wellington, but revived in 1846. It is one of the eight departments under the new organization of the War Office. He assists the War Office in selecting chaplains. There are seventy-eight chaplains on staff. In the navy, every ship in commission, down to and including fifth-rates, has a chaplain (1873–74). There are eighty-three commissioned chaplains. "Chaplains perform divine service at stated times on shipboard, visit the sick sailors, and assist in maintaining moral discipline among the crew."

"Napoleon," it is said, "was obliged to establish chaplains for his army, in order to their quiet, while making his winter quarters in the heart of an enemy's country, and that army had been drenched in the infidelity of the French Revolution."

As to American chaplaincies, the only book we have found is "Chaplains of the General Government," by Lorenzo D. Johnson (1856). He quotes the report of Hon. James Meacham, which recites facts showing the *national policy* of *America:* "Chaplains were appointed for the Revolutionary army on its organization.   Congress ordered, May 27, 1777, that there should be one chaplain for each brigade of the army, nominated by the brigadier-general, and appointed by Congress, with the same pay as colonel ; and, on the 18th of September following, ordered chaplains to be appointed to the hospitals in the several departments."   We find provision for chaplains in the acts of 1791, 1812, and 1838.   "By the last, one chaplain was appointed to each brigade in the army."   There are also chaplains for forts and military stations.   These also act as schoolmasters, — "preaching schoolmasters" they have been called. In our late war, each regiment had a chaplain commissioned. How useful they were, many can recall from their recollections of several years, and all can read in the life of *Arthur Fuller*, who was killed at Fredericksburg, after crossing on the pontoons.   It was of Fuller that one wrote, what might apply to many a chaplain : —

> "Hero and saint ! enrolled upon the page of history,
>   Telling of deeds sublime to future ages,
>   Thy name shall be ;
> And, better still, the Lamb's resplendent volume
>   Thy name shall bear,
> Heading perchance a long and brilliant column
>   Of heroes there."

One is not surprised to find that chaplains have done incidental services of no inconsiderable importance.   It was an army-chaplain (Rev. William Burnett, Fort Columbus, Governor's Island, near New-York City, 1838), eminently successful in drawing soldiers from intemperance, who obtained from Gen. Cass, secretary of war, the order that spirit-rations should be abolished, and tea and coffee rations should be substituted. Rev. Walter Colton wrote several books which awaken interest in the sailor, — "Ship and Shore," "Deck and Port," "Three Years in California."   He built the first schoolhouse in California, and was the first (through "The North American," Philadelphia) to make known to the residents of the Atlantic States the gold discovery of that country.   Rev. George Jones, while on leave of absence, made a tour of discovery in South America.

These few facts will suffice as to the history of chaplaincies.

This measure, the appointment of chaplains, no doubt approves itself to the inner sense of all men as right and excellent, for the advantage of all, and in no way infringing the conscience of any. But the grounds for this inner sense of approval are elusive to many: they cannot tell why they have a quiet conviction of the rightness of things. Those who are able to give reasons, duly set in order, for the inner sense of well-balanced minds, furnish strong foundations for right and permanent opinions among men. One great way of gaining eternally right views of subjects is, after the landscape of facts is before the mind, to consult the innermost sense in regard to them, note its affirmations and negations, and then seek to find and to expound the reasons for the affirmations of the inner sense. Bring your compass to a level, mark where it points, — that is infallibly north, — and from that direction you can make true research into the whole domain of magnetic geography. Ask your Ruskin to give you his sense of Turner's "Slave Ship;" and that sense, though opposing the first impressions of many, is right and defensible.

We believe there has been, in the whole history of appointed chaplains, but one single attempt to oppose them on principle. This was at the memorable time when the clergy of New York, and the more than three thousand clergy of New England, solemnly memorialized the Thirty-third Congress against the repeal of the Missouri Compromise. "Never," says Lorenzo Johnson,[1] "since that memorable proceeding in Congress relating to running the mail on the Sabbath, had there been such an uprising of the clergy, speaking in tones of such remonstrance, as on this occasion; and never before did members of Congress take it upon themselves to say so much in the way of defining the position of a Christian minister as at that time." From the hostile spirit then excited came an attack upon government chaplaincies, which seemed for a time likely to be successful, but which was nobly met by Meacham's Report (1853), and within a few years sub-

[1] Government Chaplains, p. 5.

sided.   There is something so intrinsically fit, and so certainly
beneficial, in chaplaincies, that such an attack will probably
never be made again.   Johnson says, writing at about that time,
referring to those large crews of eight hundred or a thousand
men, amongst whom he had been one, "We have seen many a
youthful sailor, who in his waywárdness had wandered from
home, and ere long found himself shipped into the naval service.
After long and tedious duty had sobered him down to the reflecting point, or the sudden change from easy to hard labor, as well
as that of an unhealthy climate, had brought him upon the 'sick
list,' — there on the high seas, or in a foreign port, on coming
thoroughly to himself, he welcomes with true cordiality the man
who in a quiet manner goes to his couch to speak of his mother's
counsels, his father's advice, of Sabbath privileges perhaps neglected, and of a sin-pardoning God.   How shall we calculate
the importance, the worth, of this timely visitation of a chaplain
charged with duties of this nature ?   If the objectors to the
employment of chaplains were to receive the last message of a
dying son or brother from the hand of one of these ambassadors
of Christ, — to whom such words are usually uttered, — would
they feel any regret that the government provides for the suste-
nance of such men, while accompanying these hundreds of sea-
men through their perilous voyages around the world ?   We
cannot believe they would." [1]   This is the one main attack on
chaplaincies in all their history, European and American, due
to the irritation consequent on the faithful dealing of the clergy
in an excited hour, and that attack brief, and we believe never
to be repeated.   There is an inner, invincible sense that chaplaincies are right.

   This paper will seek to find and to explain the relation of
Religion to the *State Institutions.*

   The relation of the State to those in her various institutions
has been admirably described by Chaplain Speare in his earnest
and manly report of 1876, to which we may make frequent reference, in these words : "Constitutional immunities are for *citizens :* and convicts, who are only the *wards* of the State, cannot

---

[1] Johnson, 25.

claim them ; otherwise civil liberty would be claimed, and followed by a jail delivery *en masse.*" [1]

"The *wards* of the State ; " that is, they are as minors or children, who are subject to control, and are allowed liberty only according to the mind of those who control them, to secure results which are in the purpose of those who control them. Those, also, who are inmates of other State institutions, are also wards of the State ; and even those who have of their free will entered such an institution as a poorhouse thereby voluntarily surrender their liberty to such a degree as the State conceives is necessary for uniformity and for the general good.

It is plain then, without further argument, that whatever is fitting for the State to do towards children in her public schools in preparation for noble lives and good citizenship, *mutatis mutandis* the State has right and duty to do for her wards in her institutions.

To these institutions, therefore, applies all which has been said, in the preceding discussion, on the daily public reading of the Bible, the singing of the hymn, the offering of prayer, and the weekly exercises and studies in a *manual of morals.* Especially in prisons and reformatory institutions is teaching of morals even more obligatory on the State. While instructing in the virtues in schools, there may be a question, in some individual cases, whether the scholar has not, perchance, received more advanced teaching at home. But, in case of criminals and the unruly, their moral training is visibly a failure : parents and churches have failed; and the State has duty to do what others have failed to do, — give the lacking culture in morals.

So far we are on sure ground, already tried and found firm.

But now the question comes, Why do we all, in a State cut aloof so decidedly and held aloof so jealously from Church and from personal religion, instinctively feel that the State is right in the provision in General Statutes which reads as follows? —
" The chaplain of the State Prison shall perform divine service in the chapel of the prison, instruct the convicts in their moral

---

[1] Rev. S. Lewis B. Speare, Chaplain of Charlestown State Prison : Report for 1876.

and religious duties, visit the sick on suitable occasions, and have charge of the school and library of the prison."

From this point this paper will aim to discover the true reasons and basis on which a State institution can legitimately have a " *divine service,*" and a *chaplain,* and *but one chaplain.*

It will perhaps be best to clear the ground of confused ideas and misconceptions before we commence to build. We shall first, therefore, inquire

WHAT CANNOT BE THE REASONS FOR THE APPOINTMENT OF A CHAPLAIN AND THE HOLDING OF A RELIGIOUS SERVICE IN A STATE PRISON.

1. IT CANNOT BE THE REASON WHY THE STATE APPOINTS A CHAPLAIN AND DIVINE SERVICE, THAT ANY PRISONER, OR ANY NUMBER OF PRISONERS, THINK AND ASSERT THAT THIS PROVISION WILL BE FOR THEIR GOOD. The State, in making all provisions for prisoners, looks on matters from her own standpoint. She acts entirely *proprio motu,* not by individual solicitation, least of all by solicitation of the convicts or wards themselves. Their *wants,* indeed, affect her, but not their *requests as such.* The State is affected by their condition, but is not *constrained* by their petitions. Even where there is great plausibility, or even reality, of good, she gives to her wards as much or as little as she thinks best, not as much as they think desirable. She constantly bears in mind her own purposes and views in relation to them and their welfare. A notable example is this. One would surely think that frequent correspondence with home were desirable and beneficial. But the prisoner does not obtain his plea beyond that meagre limit which the State has thought best for his good, as her ward ; for, while he may receive letters daily, he is limited for reasons, some of which are obvious on reflection, to the sending home of but one letter in three months. The same restrictions are put upon the prisoner in what would seem so salutary an allowance as visits. "Every convict," says an English chaplain, "is allowed to see his friends once in six months for twenty minutes, unless deprived of the privilege by misconduct."[1]   In such a matter as

---

[1] Kingsmill, 256.

a *divine service*, therefore, the prisoner's representations that it is desired, and even his view, which may be perfectly correct, that it would *benefit him*, is not the consideration which moves and constrains the State to make this provision. His needs may affect the State, but not his mere representations, as the expression of his wishes or demands; and, if she grants such a service, it will be, not to the extent the prisoner would like, but to the extent which will subserve the purposes of the State.

2. IT CANNOT BE THE REASON FOR THE APPOINTMENT OF A CHAPLAIN AND A DIVINE SERVICE IN STATE INSTITUTIONS, THAT ANY ORGANIZATION, SOCIAL, LITERARY, RELIGIOUS, OR POLITICAL, THINKS IT BEST TO HAVE SUCH A MAN THERE AS ITS AGENT, TO CARRY OUT ITS ENDS, AND SECURE BENEFITS WHICH IT SUPPOSES, AND EVEN WHICH IT CAN SHOW, WOULD FOLLOW.

The Handel and Haydn Society cannot say, Music, as we conceive, would be greatly beneficial to these men: therefore, as those who desire the good of these men, we will put a man there to carry out our purposes of good. The Mount-Vernon Literary Club would not deem it proper, in view of the great benefits and pleasures of literature which they enjoy, to vote that one of its members should be established in the State prison to carry out their good intentions to awaken all men to literature. The Republican party could not, from the supposed merits of its political creed, maintain that it had a right to send a speaker into the prison at Charlestown who would foster their political ideas. Nor can the Mormon Church maintain, that, as their principles are the salvation of mankind, they are therefore entitled to appoint and station a man to represent and propound their doctrines there.

The truth is, all organized societies, of whatever name or nature, stop their visible and corporate connection with men at the prison-walls. They may claim that their field is the world; but their *external* field does not embrace the prison, which is emphatically, what it is sometimes called, the *State's* prison. If any of these organizations, whether church or other, claims that it has a right to universal dominion, and that to it there is no State wall which it is bound to respect, through which it has not right by a visible messenger and agent to pass, the State repels such organization as a false claimant, seeking to effect a usurpation over the State, whether this be the Mormon or the Romish or the Mohammedan Church, or the literary, political, or musical society. They have no more right to enter the *State's* prison by an agent to reside and act therein, at their own option, than they have to enter a citizen's residence at their own will and pleasure.

3. IT CANNOT BE THE REASON WHY THE STATE APPOINTS A CHAPLAIN AND A DIVINE SERVICE, THAT ANY ORGANIZATION, POLITICAL, RELIGIOUS, OR LITERARY, HAS A CONSIDERABLE CON-STITUENCY THERE. We have been considering that such organizations have no right to station men in State institutions, to promulgate their views and gain adherents, because they believe their principles salutary. We are now saying, that, even if they have a constituency there, that does not entitle them to appoint an agent there to care for the wants, supposed or real, temporal or spiritual, of their constituency. Suppose that such respectable bodies as the musical, political, and literary societies which we have mentioned should be so unfortunate as to have each ten members incarcerated there : would that entitle them to establish in the prison such an agency to look after their ten musical men, or their ten members of the Republican party? No one would seriously assert their right to pass the prison-walls for that purpose, or assert the obligation of the State to permit them. Nor could the Mormon Church successfully claim, that, because it had five or fifty members there, therefore the State is under obligation to establish a Mormon chaplain there in her behalf or in their behalf.

Especially is this true when the society is a *religious* society which claims right to have agent or minister in the institution to reform the erring. In case of the various societies mentioned, the State could not interpose bar to their further claim over the prisoner, that it was in their sphere he had failed. His delinquency was in morals. They had not been inefficient in *their* education of him. He did not fail in his literary, musical, or political career. Therefore, since our ministrations were successful, permit us to continue them. When, on the other hand, a *religious* body claims further domain, as to its previous constituency, in matters of *character*, the State interposes, Precisely in *character* has his career failed. Your religious body had in charge the moral character of this man: you have failed to secure the morals of this criminal: he has, *therefore*, become my ward. I have taken in hand to teach him morality: I will call in such aid as seems to *me*, the *State*, best likely to supply the lack. Besides all this, the State has not, by *explicit law*, debarred other societies from entering; but she has, by positive regulations, debarred any particular *religious society* from entering her institutions.

Least of all is the claim valid, that, because a religious organization has a *large* constituency in prison, therefore they should be entitled to send an agent there to reform and care for them. *Precisely the contrary* should be the argument of the State. If the Mormon Church has three-fourths of the criminals in the State institutions, when she has but a small portion of the population, that should be an argument, rather, why she should *not* be allowed to have, and why the State should be unwilling that she should have, an established teacher there. The argument is, If you have had these men under your charge from their childhood, and your teachings have had no restraining power to prevent them from becoming criminals, the State prefers to select a moral teacher who will make a new attempt. If, indeed, a church were but just entering into a parish work, and had accomplished in a degraded population such magnificent results as did Chalmers in Glasgow, it would be no discredit if the parish still contained so many degraded as to have a large proportion of the criminals in prison: but if, on the contrary, a church has had the training, not only of children, but of the fathers and mothers of those children, and has failed to prevent them from being the most criminal of all classes, such a church should be a little modest about insisting upon further power of instruction over them; and the State, if it did not ignore churches altogether, — *as it does,* — certainly would not seek for a chaplain to the church which had the most criminals in her institutions.

Rather it would be thought that the preference should be given to that church, which, taking all things into account, the numbers, the locations, city or country, had been most successful in instilling morality, and had inflicted the least percentage of criminals upon the State.

It was unfortunate, therefore, for Mr. Lucas, in Parliament, seeking to establish Romish chaplains in English prisons, to quote Dr. Wilson, Roman-Catholic Bishop of Tasmania, who remarks, "In the convicts transported to this island from Ireland, he had found not more than ten in the hundred who were Protestants; but in those who came from England, from fifteen to twenty were Catholics."[1]   The significancy of these figures is this: Since three-fourths of the Irish are Catholic, three-fourths of the Irish people give nine-tenths of the crimes, and one-fourth of the people (Protestant) give only one-tenth of the crimes; while in England, since "five per cent by accredited returns are Romanists,"[2] one-twentieth of the population (Catholic) gives three-twentieths of the crimes.

Kingsmill also informs us, that "in Ulster, the northern province of Ireland, although it has the poorest soil and densest population, but is about two-thirds Protestant, the proportion of criminals to the population is only one in six hundred; whereas in Munster, the southern province, although the most fertile, but intensely Romanist, the proportion is one in two hundred and seventy-three."[3]

An Episcopal clergyman in Boston, with whom I was conversing, said somewhat gravely, "Perhaps you do not know their *strongest argument* for the appointment of their own chaplains. Bishop Lynch of Toronto said, '*Most of those in the jails are my people.*'"   I saw a twinkle in his eye, and a smile on his face, as he uttered, in effect, that this was "a kind of *Boyle-Roach joke.*"

Such statistics as those above, even were the State — which it is not — searching among the *churches* for moral teachers for her institutions, should not make any church bold to compete for the chaplaincy.

4. ONCE MORE: THE REASON WHY THE STATE INSTITUTES

---

[1] Kingsmill, 200, 482.   [2] Ibid., 483.   [3] Ibid., 481.

CHAPLAINCIES AND "DIVINE SERVICE" IN PRISON IS NOT BECAUSE SHE UNDERTAKES THERE TO "SAVE SOULS," TO TEACH PERSONAL RELIGION, THE MEANS OF ACCEPTANCE WITH GOD. Whatever right she has to take cognizance of "spiritual life," as an exercise averred to be experienced by her citizens, or "salvation" as a private possession belonging to them, and whatever right she has to satisfy general cravings which are credibly represented to her of an invisible soul or spirit, she does not, as the natural man, know, nor will she, remaining in her due sphere, undertake to formulate, dogma, and present it to men through a chaplain. The State does not, once and exceptionally, become, in her institutions, the Church, to promulgate doctrines and institute worship. So far as the service is "divine," the direct worship of each spirit with God, the State merely furnishes one general channel in which certain feelings, unknown to her ken, yet not unuseful in their observed effects, can find an exercise satisfying and gratifying to her wards, and by them said to be important in securing some good which they claim will be immortal. There are, as we shall see, other uses to this service. We are here simply observing the relation of the State to it as a "*divine*" service of personal worship, — that it undertakes to make *one general channel for the exercise of religious feeling so far as it is common to all.* So far, because so far it may be beneficial ; no further, *because she cannot do so without such discord and friction in her institutions, and in regard to them, as will defeat or mar many of her cherished purposes in regard to her wards.*

The State, then, does not, *proprio motu, command* "divine service" in her institutions, — so far, that is, as it is *divine,* the exercise of *personal* religion ; she *permits ;* and *commands,* to give shape and effect to her permission.

If, now, the ground is quite clear from all misconceptions that the State appoints its chaplains as having a right to *teach* religion, or because individuals within claim that it would be for their good, or because organizations claim a right to extend their benevolent operations to inmates of her institutions, or because they have a large constituency there, which have gone there notwithstanding their care, we are prepared to inquire, positively, —

WHAT MUST BE THE REASONS FOR THE APPOINTMENT OF A
CHAPLAIN AND THE HOLDING OF A RELIGIOUS SERVICE IN THE
PRISON?

Since the State views all things from her own standpoint, the
general statement is that her reason for a chaplaincy and a
divine service is, because *she deems it for the State's interest, and
in her view, for the good of the inmates, regarded as her wards;
and in her view, also, an allowable liberty granted and made effective to them as desiring it for their satisfaction and gratification.*

The State, regarding the efforts of philanthropists and religious preachers in connection with prisons, studies their effects.
The names and labors of Howard, Elizabeth Fry, Sarah Martin, Whitefield, Wesley, are known to her. The thought of a
permanent ministry of this sort is suggested to her. Always
viewing matters from her own standpoint, let us see what the
State observes, which is inducement to establish chaplaincies
and "divine service."

THE DIVINE SERVICE.

1. THE STATE OBSERVES THE EFFECT UPON MEN OF GATHER-
ING THEM STATEDLY ONCE A WEEK, in due order and repose and
cleanliness, on a rest day, when they are free from labor. 'Tis
a genial and useful exhilaration. In rural New England
the church became "the *meeting-house.*" Ik Marvel, in his
"Dream Life," brings up a pleasant picture of "the country
church." "After the morning service they have an hour's 'in-
termission,' as the preacher calls it, during which the old men
gather on the sunny side of the building; and after shaking
hands all around, and asking after the folks at home, they enjoy a quiet talk about the crops." The prison-chapel, indeed,
affords no such free opportunities for prolonged social chat and
friendly intercourse; but it is an influence which the State may
fairly take account of, that the prisoner on that day shall *meet*
with all his fellows and superiors. It is even possible that five
or ten minutes might be allowed for social intercourse after a
"divine service." It is something to have seen human faces.
This "holy *convocation*" is felt to have its uses.

"Their meeting in chapel," says Clay,[1] chaplain of Preston Gaol,[2] "is a privilege, and I know it is highly esteemed." "As a congregation, the behavior of the prisoners is not only decorous, but exemplary." "It is a proof, that, when gathered together to worship God, they may be freed from almost all restraint but that of their reverence for him."[3] "The chapel brings the acceptable hour, the welcome and interesting occupation, which relieves the severe monotony of the prisoner's daily life."[4]

2. THE STATE CAN TAKE ACCOUNT OF THE POWER OF THOUGHTS APPROPRIATE TO THE SABBATH in connection with divine service on the day of rest. It is true indeed, unfortunately, that a large proportion of criminals have been regardless of the Sabbath. The chaplain of Clerkenwell said, that, out of a hundred thousand inmates, "the usual process has been impatience of parental restraint, violation of the Sabbath, and the neglect of religious ordinances. I do not recollect a single case of capital offence where the party has not been a Sabbath-breaker. Indeed, I may say, in reference to prisoners of all classes, that in nineteen cases out of twenty they are persons who have not only neglected the Sabbath, but all religious ordinances."[5]

Yet these same men are not insensible to the idea of the Sabbath; of one day set apart as holy time; of what it means; of the truths usually taught on that day; of the bells which they hear chiming, or calling to each other from the church-towers. A chaplain can make this idea alone very effective upon a prisoner for good.

If Sabbath-keeping is intimately connected with all virtues, we can even, without difficulty, conceive of the valuable effect of the enforced Sabbath-keeping during two or three years as pro-

---

[1] The Prison Chaplain: Memoir of Rev. John Clay, B.D., Chaplain of Preston Gaol. By his Son, Rev. Walter Lowe Clay. With Portrait. London, 1861, pp. 621.

[2] "Gaol (pronounced jāl.): Lat. gayola, gabiola, as if from caveola, diminutive of cavea, cavity, cage. Hence, It., gabbiuola; Sp., gayola, jaula; Pg., gaiola; N. French, geôle; Norm. Fr., geaule, geole; O. Fr., gaole, gaiole, jaiole." "Written also, and preferably, jail," says Webster.

[3] Clay, 276.　　　[4] Ibid., 280.　　　[5] Kingsmill, 53.

ducing a *habit* which shall follow the man in his after-life, of desisting from labor, and going where good tidings are spoken on that day.

"I wish the chapel service — and especially that of the Sabbath — to be so consolatory, so agreeable, so necessary to the prisoners, that participation in divine worship, begun under compulsion, may be continued ever after from choice and affection. I would, therefore, have the chapel present, as far as practicable, — even in the minutest particulars, — the appearance of a well-ordered church, so that some who enter it may be beneficially reminded of the Sundays of a more innocent and happier time; and that many may be so trained, during imprisonment, to the observance of Sabbath duties, that they may resort, when at liberty, to their own house of prayer, with hearts still grateful for the comfort received in a similar place, and at a time when almost every thing else spoke sorrow and disgrace."[1] "It is not in my power to express all that I feel and think on the subject of prison-chapel service. That it ought, as far as possible, to be instrumental in creating reverence and love for the Lord's Day and for divine worship in those who so much need every incentive to true religion, all nourishment in goodness, no one will venture to dispute. It is well worth considering, by every one who feels an interest in the treatment of our criminals, that one hundred thousand offenders are discharged from our prisons every year; and that it cannot but be of the highest moment to themselves, to their families, and to the community, that they should return into the world with a grateful and abiding remembrance of Sabbath rest and instruction."[2]

3. THE STATE CAN TAKE ACCOUNT OF THIS DAY, AND A SERVICE ON THIS DAY, AS A REMEMBRANCER OF HOME AND THE FAMILY. Though the prisoner was no church-goer in his late years, yet in his childhood he used to go with his father and mother, brothers and sisters. "He walked to the house of God in company, with the multitude that kept holy day." He is now separated by his crimes from that home. "If I had followed your advice," is written by many a criminal to his parents, "I

---

[1] Clay, 280, 281: Report of 1847.   [2] Clay, 337: Report of 1854.

should not have been here." Probably, in the free world at large, there are more thoughts of home and loved ones and the departed on the Sabbath than on all the hurrying six days of care and labor. As a device to make home memories potent and salutary, nothing could be more effective than a Sabbath religious service. Says Kingsmill, chaplain of Pentonville Prison, London, "The last thing forgotten, in all the recklessness of dissolute profligacy, is the prayer and hymn taught by the mother's lips, or uttered at a father's knee ; and the most poignant sting of conscience, in solitude and adversity, is that which the recollection of filial disobedience and ingratitude inflicts." [1]

"There is a well-authenticated story," says George Macdonald, " of a convict's having been greatly reformed for a time by going, in one of the English colonies, into a church where the matting along the aisle was of the same pattern as that in the church to which he had gone, when a boy, with his mother." [2]

When the call comes to the " chapel," how potent the chaplain can make the thought, in his prayer or sermon, that the families to which those belong who are gathered there are going to the house of God at this very hour, and perhaps are speaking of their absent prodigal child! Nothing, one would say, except the home letters, could so keep alive and effective the tender and hallowed memories of home.

4. THE STATE CAN OBSERVE THE SOFTENING, REFINING INFLUENCES OF A RELIGIOUS SERVICE. " David took a harp, and played with his hand : so Saul was refreshed and was well, and the evil spirit departed from him." The organ-peal, the three or four hymns, the prayer of the good man, the presence of the interested stranger, the stories and kindly thoughts of the sermon, the cheering words of the Scriptures, — all these are calculated to win the heart from its solitary, despairing, brutal, selfish mood, and humanize and affect it, not only for a moment, but for all time. They melt the wax for the stamp ; they break up matted turf, and soften the soil for the seed.

---

[1] Joseph Kingsmill, Chaplain of Pentonville Prison, London: Chapters on Prisons and Prisoners, London, 1854, pp. 508. — P. 40.

[2] Robert Falconer, 489.

5. THE STATE CAN OBSERVE, AS PROMPTING HER TO INSTI-
TUTE A DIVINE SERVICE, THAT THE SERMONS OR DISCOURSES OR
TALKS CONTAIN A VAST AMOUNT OF USEFUL MORAL INSTRUC-
TION.   From the instructions of a faithful chaplain, in a series
of years, one might almost prepare a book of lessons and illustrations and appeals on the duties.   " The next day being Sunday, Mr. Eden preached two sermons that many will remember
all their lives.   The first was against *theft* and all the shades
of *dishonesty.*"   "In the afternoon, Mr. Eden preached against
cruelty." [1]

6. THE STATE CAN TAKE NOTE, AS REASON FOR A DIVINE SER-
VICE, THAT THE MAIN VIEW BEFORE THE PREACHER IS EFFICA-
CIOUS FOR GOOD ON THE PRISONER, — NAMELY, THE VIEW OF
GOD AS KING AND JUDGE ; as just, yet merciful ; as one to whom
men are responsible ; one who, for proper reasons, will pardon
offenders.

First, all these subjects are analogous to those which have
reference to the State's relation to the prisoner.   Law, government, responsibility, punishment, reward, pardon, ill-desert, good-
desert, — these are ideas which are constantly in the preacher's
mouth ; and there is an analogy by which the mind naturally
refers what the preacher says to the State, as a governmental
power ordained of God, as well as to the divine government.

Then, again, the State can take note that the impression made
of the solemnity of responsibility to divine government will be
radical and generic, and that one specific form of that responsibility will be responsibility to God in the State and in the social
order.

7. THE STATE CAN OBSERVE THE INTENTION OF A "DIVINE
SERVICE" TO MAKE A NEW MAN, A RESTORED HUMANITY.   It
is quite within her ken to see that, externally, the convict is
fallen from the state of rectitude, and is in many respects a ruin.
Whether there be a future world, whether there be a spiritual
life, she knows not, as a State ; but she can see before her
humanity in ruins.   She is competent, in her sphere, to have a
service which shall say, *Manhood, —* "*a new creature.*"   Rev.

---

[1] Charles Reade: Never Too Late to Mend, chap. xv.

C. C. Foote, chaplain of the Detroit House of Correction, read at the National Congress, 1870, a paper, "The Importance and Power of Religious Forces in Prisons." He exclaims, "Towering above all else, and inclusive of all else, he should know but that one comprehensive condition, — *humanity in ruins* to be saved." "Like the Good Shepherd, the chaplain's mission is to find and restore the lost."

8. THE STATE IS COMPETENT, WITHIN HER SPHERE, TO OB-SERVE THE EFFECT OF THE PREACHING OF CERTAIN STRANGE, GRAND DOCTRINES, WHICH EXCITE IN A MARVELLOUS MANNER THE DEEPEST EMOTIONS OF HER WARDS. It is not for her to inquire into their truth. She notes only their melting, exhilarating, forming, and transforming power as motives. So far as the *State* is concerned, this "old, old story" might as well be the history of Washington's boyhood, or the story of Arnold Winkelried; so far as the *State* is concerned, it may be truth, or it may be fanaticism: but she sees the marvellous transforming effects of this story of the cross. True or false, it affects men.

The Man of Calvary was right: "I, if I be lifted up, will draw all men unto me." "By this sign conquer" is still written on the heavens, as before Constantine's eyes. Shelley was esteemed no Christian; but he wrote the beautiful lines, —

> "The moon of Mahomet
> Arose, and it shall set;
> While, blazoned as on heaven's immortal noon,
> The cross leads generations on."[1]

De Quincey, looking back in fond and pensive reminiscence into his childhood,

> "Pictured in memory's mellowing glass,"

recalls to us, "It had happened, that amongst our vast nursery collection of books was the Bible, illustrated with many pictures; and in long, dark evenings, as my three sisters and myself sat by firelight round the *guard* (fender) of our nursery, no book was so much in request amongst us. It ruled us and swayed us as mysteriously as music." "Above all, the story of a just

---

[1] Hellas, Chorus.

man, — man, and yet *not* man, — real above all things, and yet shadowy above all things, who had suffered the passion of death in Palestine, slept upon our minds like early dawn upon the waters."[1]

"The Cross in the Cell" is the true story of the power of the "Lamb of God" to "take away the sins of the world."[2]

> "Still thy love, O Christ arisen !
> Yearns to reach these souls in prison :
> Through all depths of sin and loss
> Drops the plummet of thy cross :
> Never yet abyss was found
> Deeper than thy cross can sound."

This moves men. Speaking of John Clay, chaplain for forty years, " one, whose frequent attendance in the chapel of Preston Gaol had qualified him for forming an opinion not quite worthless, delivers himself thus : ' Now and then you have a chance of preaching God's gospel to men in prison chapels and such places. Did you ever see it done, and mark how it was done successfully ? The preacher may speak of heaven ; but those men cannot understand him. Spiritual pleasure is a thing utterly beyond their comprehension. They know of no happiness except gross, foul, animal indulgence. The preacher may speak of hell, and they will wince. But is it true ? They harden themselves, and won't believe it. But now let him preach Christ crucified, and mark the effects of his preaching, as, in vivid, strong words, he tells the story of that life and death, — the story of that Friday morning. As he speaks thus, and tells the tale in living language, watch those men's faces, — faces stupefied, marred, brutalized by years of selfishness and lust and gross ignorance. Here and there you will see one on which the look of sullen defiance and stolid stupidity is beginning to change. It changes and softens : a gleam of intelligence and better feeling passes athwart their features. That strange, novel idea of God having actually suffered to save them from suffering astounds and bewilders them. Unwonted feelings and thoughts begin to

---

[1] Autobiographic Sketches, 13.

[2] N. Adams, D.D. : The Cross in the Cell; Conversations with a Prisoner awaiting Execution.

stir in their hearts. Vaguely and dimly they begin to feel that they ought, they must, they will, love this Jesus, who has so loved them. They feel that they should like to do, to suffer, something to prove their love. The old self-love is shaken; the new life from God is stirring within them; and, when those men go back to their cells, they will kneel down, and, in their half-dumb, inarticulate fashion, they will gasp out a prayer.

"'I speak that I do know; I testify that which I have seen.'"[1]

And the State can take account of such testimony as to external results following from the strange and solemn enchantment upon men of the story of the Crucified One, and she may suffer and use that enchantment in a religious service.

Passing now to a sphere where the State may not observe, but may gain rational evidence, —

9. THE STATE CAN TAKE ACCOUNT OF A CERTAIN SOMETHING WHICH IS REPRESENTED TO HER, CALLED "PERSONAL RELIGION;" OF CERTAIN GREAT BENEFITS WHICH THE WARDS ALLEGE THEY WOULD RECEIVE, — benefits which go under different names, — "salvation," a "hope of glory," "the immortal good," "eternal life." To the State, which is only the *natural man*, all this is of the nature of *invisible riches, "mansions in the skies;"* but she can receive testimony which is credible about it, that it is something which the prisoner considers unspeakably precious. Now, were the prisoners their "own men," — free in society, — the State would have no more to do with their religion, even if asked, than to furnish them with milk or honey. Moreover, were this *somewhat* of an injurious tendency, usually producing madness or other evil results, or interfering with prison discipline, the State would be under no obligation to gratify this *craving*.

But as this *somewhat*, this "salvation," this "*religion*," this "hope of glory," is accompanied, so far as she can observe, with fruits of good; as it is connected with the preacher of righteousness, with that best book about God, as all her statesmen call it, — she feels not only at liberty to allow this divine service,

[1] Clay's Memoir, 202, 203.

so called, but also a kind of obligation to prepare and command one general channel for its exercise.

Be it observed, the chaplain and the religious do not take this cool view of religion. They view it from within ; the State, from without. They view it as, to them, *the great reality* of existence ; the State, as a gratification and satisfaction to her wards. While the State, therefore, with cool calculation, appoints divine service, she does not, therefore, mean that that service shall be a cold one. From the religious side, it must be fervent to be anything. The State might as coolly allow music in an Independence celebration ; but your Zerrahn and your Tourjée must not, therefore, furnish lifeless music.

Moreover, it must be observed, that, in the *chapel*, the Bible takes on a different use from that which it has in the public schools. There it is the *prescribed* book *about* God for general devotion : in the *chapel* it is the book by law *permitted* to be used as the general book of *personal religion*.

For all the preceding reasons, so briefly stated, the State still maintaining strict separation from church and personal religion, the State appoints "a divine service."

THE CHAPLAIN.

The next point is the appointment of a minister for the chapel, — a chaplain.

1. THE STATE, HAVING OBSERVED THE VALUE OF A DIVINE SERVICE, OBSERVES ALSO THE NECESSITY OF HAVING A PERSON TO CONDUCT IT. Every reason leads to the appointment of *one* person *permanently* to do this.

The history of prison services shows, that, without appointment, only the most earnest and philanthropic preachers have sought to minister the gospel in the prison. "In the life of Bernard Gilpin, in Queen Elizabeth's time, the author (speaking of his labors) informs us, that, wherever he came, he used to visit all the gaols and places of confinement, few in the kingdom having at that time any appointed minister ; and, by his affectionate address, he is said to have reformed many very abandoned persons in those places." "In 1700," writes Clay, "chaplains and chaplaincies were seldom part of the prison establishment. Some loose parson of insolvent tendencies was commonly hired at a cheap rate for the office of ordinary." "The act for appointing chaplains to gaols was passed just before the commencement of Howard's labors."[1]

On the other hand, there is liability of the exclusion of good men who desire to minister in prison "In accordance with the traditions of English piety," Clay tells us, "when the 'Godly Club' was first formed at Oxford, the Wesleys and other members offered their first ministrations to the prisoners in the castle. The good work, once begun, was not lightly abandoned. For some years, Whitefield, Wesley, and their most zealous followers, prayed, preached, and distributed alms in all the gaols, bride-wells, and bedlams that came within their circuits ; and it was only under compulsion that they at length forsook this portion of their mission. When the storm of unpopularity was at its height, they found the doors even of prisons and madhouses shut against them. 'So,' said John Wesley, 'we are forbid to go to Newgate for fear of making them wicked, and to Bedlam for fear of making them mad ;' and, from that time, he and his brother Charles discontinued their prison visitations." But Sarah Peters continued.[2]

It is manifestly unwise to leave the religious service to chance-comers. Latimer, in a sermon preached before Edward VI., exclaimed, "I would there were curates of prisons, that we might say, 'The curate of Newgate,' 'The curate of the Fleet ;' and I would have them waged for their labor. It is holiday work to visit the prisoners ; for they be kept from sermons."[3]

In 1826, according to the Report of the Boston Prison Discipline Society, "there was not a resident chaplain in any State prison in the United States ; and the religious instruction imparted was, for the most part, reduced down to the merest modicum."[4]

John Howard, in his first report on prisons, 1777, writes, "A chaplain is necessary in a gaol. I had the pleasure to find a

[1] Clay, 101.   [2] Clay, 35.   [3] Clay's Memoir, 24.

[4] Report on Prisons and Reformatories in the United States and Canada: E. C. Wines, D.D., and Theod. W. Dwight, LL.D. 1867. — Sect. 6, Mor. and Relig. Agencies, 184-220.

chaplain appointed to most of the county gaols, in consequence of the act made the 13th of his present Majesty. When their office is vacant, it behooves magistrates not to take the first clergyman who offers his services, without regarding his real character. They should choose one who is in principle a Christian; who will not content himself with officiating in public, but will converse with the prisoners, admonish the profligate, exhort the thoughtless, comfort the sick, and make known to the condemned that *mercy* which is revealed in the *gospel.*"[1]

. *The same reasons which make a pastor more efficient than a transient preacher apply as well to a prison chapel as to a local church.* The chaplain is the *prisoners' pastor.*

2. THE STATE DISCERNS THE BENEFIT OF HAVING WITHIN HER INSTITUTIONS ONE WHO REPRESENTS GOODNESS. What is congregated in prisons is *badness* of all sorts. The State chooses a man pre-eminent in living goodness, and sends him, like a pure and vital flood of sunbeams, into the darkness. Go in and out before them, and encourage virtue and repress vice. It was said of a certain minister, by a sea-captain not professedly religious, " He does more good by walking the streets than most men do by preaching."

My chaplain friend of the flagship said to me, " The wickedest officer I have known said, as I chanced to hear him, — and he commenced and ended with a round oath, — 'We must have a chaplain to keep down the fearful demoralization on board ship.' A Christian officer, on the other hand, advocated the chaplaincy from expediency, because it diminished greatly the number of punishments among the men."

The chaplain represents *goodness* in its stern purity, in its gentle benignity. It does not detract from the force of this consideration to remember, that, from 1844–54, " nearly a million and a half passed through the prisons of the United Kingdom, and 90,000 annually enter our prisons for the first time."[2]

3 THE STATE OBSERVES THAT IT IS USEFUL TO HAVE ONE IN THE PRISON WHO REPRESENTS AND EMBODIES THE IDEA OF PHILANTHROPY AND THE BENEVOLENT THOUGHTS OF THE OUTSIDE

---

[a] Prisons in England and Wales, 28.   [2] Clay, 338, 395.

WORLD. The government of the prison may be mild in firmness; yet it represents, as it ought, law and authority. The chaplaincy represents benevolence, — the unspoken benevolence of thousands who wish well to the unhappy and criminal. Sometimes the world expresses its kindness in ways which affect prisoners' hearts deeply. In the Portland Prison are a Bible and a Prayer-Book, the gift of Prince Albert, who was himself present at the prison dedication in 1849, in which are these cheering words: "Presented to the chapel of the convicts at Portland as token of interest, and in hope of their amendment. ALBERT." [1]

Of that outside interest in the prisoner, expressing itself occasionally in one form or other, the chaplain's presence is a constant living remembrance and exponent. He is felt to sustain a relation to them of good-will, rather than an official relation.

4. THE STATE CAN SEE THAT IT IS WELL THAT THERE SHOULD BE ONE WHO, FREED AS MUCH AS POSSIBLE FROM OFFICIAL TIES, WILL BE, AND WILL BE CONSIDERED, THEIR PERSONAL FRIEND. Noble portraiture and picture is that where a chaplain, — who, I sometimes imagine, was sketched from Frederick W. Robertson, sometimes I imagine from Newman Hall, — a man of culture, taste, choiceness, fitted to move in any society and to adorn it, crouching, at half an hour after midnight, outside the iron door of the subterranean cell, where was confined a criminal who had spurned what this visitant had already done for him, and, filled with madness and despair, was meditating self-destruction, — Francis Eden, crouching after midnight outside his cell, tapping on the iron door, and uttering, in the silence and darkness, the amazing word, "BROTHER!" [2]

"The first thing," John Clay used to remark, "for a chaplain to aim at, is to make his poor fellows believe that he is their friend; that he simply wants to do them good. All his preaching and teaching will, otherwise, go for very little." "There is abundant evidence of the success of his plan. 'The prisoners generally listened to him' was the account given by an infidel socialist, who had himself been in the gaol for a Chartist irregu-

---

[1] Kingsmill, 180.   [2] Charles Reade: Never Too Late to Mend, chap. xv.

larity; 'but they wouldn't have minded any thing that he either read or said to them, if they hadn't thought he was willing to befriend them. When they were abusing the parsons, they commonly made an exception in his favor.'"[1] When, in 1850, the chapel was repaired, he got the *prisoners* to paint the panels in the roof blue, spangled with yellow stars, and to inscribe various devices; and he made the chapel a gift of his own handiwork, — a large altar-piece representing the Crucifixion, on which he had spent his leisure for some months.[2]

A prisoner in the terrible hulks at the Bermudas wrote, "Dr. King was more than a father to all who came under him." Of Mr. Kingston, chaplain at Gibraltar, one writes, "Now I don't think but that any of the prisoners would have gone through fire if he had wished." "So it is," writes John Clay, — for this is from his report for 1851, — "what these poor creatures chiefly need, in order to restore in them the image of humanity, is consideration and sympathy. It is not the mere chaplain, but the earnest and pitying Christian, who, while armed with authority to repress all tendencies to evil, can at the same time touch the chord in the convict's heart, which is still capable of vibrating in harmony with what is good."[3] "In my own experience, I believe myself to have been successful in proportion as I have been able to persuade the prisoner that his temporal and religious good was our earnest desire and prayer, — the great end aimed at by our discipline. I conceive that Capt. Maconochie's remarkable success among the outcasts of Norfolk Island was chiefly owing to their conviction of his deep interest in their amendment."

The story of Capt. Maconochie is among the most inspiring in the history of convicts. Capt. Alexander Maconochie had a plan called the "mark system," which commended itself; and, in 1840, this convict island was given into his charge. He objected against such a place for a fair experiment; "but 'fiat experimentum in corpore vili' was the only answer he could obtain from the government." In 1834 a mutiny had been quelled; twenty-nine ringleaders sentenced. Thirteen were called to be

---

[1] Clay's Memoir, 118.   [2] Ibid., 204.   [3] Ibid., 314.

hanged : the other sixteen were reprieved. The reprieved remained sadly mute ; the ones allotted to the gallows fell on their knees, one by one, and thanked God. It was a mercy, they thought, to escape from the tyranny. " When Capt. Maconochie took command, there were two thousand convicts on the island, — one part, the worst felonry of England ; the rest, the reconvict villains of New South Wales and Tasmania, — the dregs of criminality. For trifling offences they were flogged, ironed, or locked up in a dark den for a term of days." " In all this, Capt. Maconochie wrought a speedy change. He threw himself heart and soul into the work of regenerating these degraded brutes. He built churches, established schools, imported a catechist, and, on Sunday, toiled as ministering deacon himself. Day after day his brain was incessantly busy, elaborating new expedients with which to raise his fallen charge out of bestial lust and demoniacal malignity into self-respect, loyalty, and human affection. And his success was great." " Capt. Maconochie was four years in Norfolk Island. ' I found it,' he says, ' a turbulent, brutal hell ; and I left it a well-ordered community.' " Studious of allurements to tempt to effort for self-restoration, he incurred odium at Australia because he gave the convicts the Queen's birthday as a holiday ; allowed tea, coffee, and tobacco ; and wanted seraphines in the churches. " You must remember," was his own defence of the indulgences he permitted, "that I was dragging up two thousand of my fellow-men almost by the hair of the head from perdition." [1]

5. THE STATE CAN SEE THE BENEFIT OF HAVING ONE PERSON IN THE INSTITUTION WHO SHALL REPRESENT HOPE. The officers of a prison, as kind as the chaplain, nevertheless represent law in its strictness. Contact with wily convicts has put officers on their guard. They wear the watchful look on their faces. Underneath they may have the kindest hearts. We do not mean to imply that officers are really hopeless of prisoners : on the contrary, Gideon Haynes says,[2] " I have no doubt that at least

---

[1] Clay's Memoir, 251 ; Maconochie, Norfolk Island (1849), of which six pages are given in Carpenter's Our Convicts. There is, I find, a copy in Boston Public Library.

[2] Pictures from Prison Life, 264.

eighty per cent of all convicted of crime may be reclaimed, and made useful members of society, by proper discipline." Gen. Samuel E. Chamberlain, the present warden at Charlestown, wrote recently in the same hopeful tone : " A happy combination of useful trades—religious, moral, and educational teachings — would, I believe, produce wonderful results on the future of our criminals." [1]

A chaplain, on the other hand, may " be wise as a serpent ; " but his whole religious experience, the transactions between his soul and God, have given him boundless ideas of God's mercy to the repentant. He is accustomed to think of the thief on the cross. To John Newton some one observed, " If God can convert such a one, he can convert anybody." "I never doubted that," was the reply, "since he converted me." 'Tis the chaplain who remembers that " He layeth the beams of His chambers in the *waters.*" Says John Clay's biographer, "To the charge of being sanguine he would angrily plead guilty. ' Sanguine ! ' was the usual reply ; ' why, of course, I am sanguine ; I should have no business to be the chaplain of a gaol if I wasn't sanguine : and I am sure of this, that a firm, obstinate, enthusiastic belief in the possibility of saving even the worst of the poor fellows committed to his charge, is a prison chaplain's most necessary qualification. I wonder what some of the knowing gentlemen who criticise my simplicity would make of it, if they had to minister in this place. It would be barren work, I think, going from cell to cell to let the prisoner know how acute and wide-awake you were yourself, and what hypocritical scoundrels you thought them. It is hard enough, I can tell you, working in such a place, hoping against hope ; and our gratitude, therefore, is not very profound to the kind monitors who think us a pack of fools for our pains." [2]

This was written, not by a sentimentalist, but by one who was chaplain nearly forty years ; who is described as "a man confessedly practical and sagacious, and gifted with a keen insight into human nature, with the experience of a lifetime." He writes again, " When religious teachers were called to minister

[1] Report, 1876.   [2] Clay's Memoir, 231, 232.

in gaols, the proceeding at once admitted the duty of society to attempt the recovery of its outcasts, and implied a hope that such attempts might be sometimes successful." [1] "Having seen what our system *was* for more than twenty years, I am as much astonished at, as I am deeply grateful for, the results accomplished in a few years of more wholesome rule, — results which show that the work has not been unblessed by Him who '*is not willing that any should perish, but that all should come to repentance.*' " [2] "If a clergyman," he would sometimes say, "is willing to put all ambition and hope of advancement on one side, and make the salvation of souls the great end and aim of his ministry, he could choose no field for work so fruitful as a prison." [8]

The very presence of a chaplain in a prison says HOPE! The longer one muses on the chaplain, in thought of *whom he represents*, the *more* his presence says HOPE!

The chaplain, as the messenger of hope, finds beautiful emblem in the Angel of the Lord who came to the Galilean fisherman in prison, in night's darkness, sleeping between two soldiers, bound with two chains, under doom of certain death on the morrow. Fair and exhilarating picture, worthy to be set on the chapel-wall, — the Angel appearing; a "light shining in the prison;" the prisoner awakened; "Arise up quickly;" the chains falling off; "Gird thyself, and bind on thy sandals;" "Cast thy garment about thee, and follow me;" the celestial Conductor leading him past the first and second ward, through the iron gate, opening to them of its own accord, into the city; and the amazed yet thankful Peter, "Now know I that the Lord hath sent his Angel, and hath delivered me."

That "light shines in a prison," that hope, present and eternal, when the gospel enters, in the person of a consecrated chaplain.

6. THE STATE CAN OBSERVE THE BENEFIT OF HAVING ONE WHO, WHILE HONORING OFFICERS, AND STRICTLY OBSERVING HIS OWN SPHERE, WILL BE, IN THINGS CONCERNING THE PRISONERS, THE REPRESENTATIVE OF HUMANITY. To a judicious extent, when necessary, the chaplain should strive to mitigate the severities

---

[1] Clay's Memoir, 288; Circular Letter, 1849. [2] Ibid., 287. [8] Ibid., 231.

of discipline; and time was when it was necessary for him to protest against cruelties which were inflicted by thoughtless and brutal officers.

On the other hand, he has a work to do, at proper times, to arouse the public interest in those under his charge. This was done by Howard. To make us "remember those who are in bonds as bound with them" is one of his duties. Clay's Memoir says of him, " His Reports helped, in no slight degree, to force the special question of prison-discipline and the general question of the cure of crime upon public notice." [1]

" I consider that a gaol chaplain's opportunities for research into these things, sad and disheartening as the case may be, should not be neglected, nor the result of his investigations be suppressed. I believe it to be a momentous necessity, that the public, especially the Christian public, should be kept fully informed of the progress made by the malign powers leagued against the happiness and charácter of the industrious classes, and of the condition of *millions* in the country whom I have, on former occasions, spoken of as our *home heathens*." [2]

"I have felt it my duty to publish what you call 'Annual Warnings' of the state of debasement of our gaol inmates. Longer imprisonment and harder labor would be repaid by the gratifying consciousness that our wisest legislators have occasionally found matter in my Reports which has conduced to the progress of prison-discipline and popular education." [3]

These " Reports " began in 1824. " The first scarcely filled one column of a newspaper: the last was a thick octavo pamphlet." " Latterly he aimed at helping on the amendment of prison-discipline and the repression of crime throughout the kingdom. At the time the earliest were written, the general ignorance and unconcern about prisons and criminals were little short of profound." [4] " He set himself to study, through the prisons, the habits, characters, wants, temptations, and vices of the masses from which they were drawn." " It was from the constant watching of the stream of criminality which flowed through the prison that he drew his main conclusions. The

---

[1] Clay's Memoir, 125.   [2] Ibid., 519, 520.   [3] Ibid., 560.   [4] Ibid., 124.

prison, in fact, was his crime-gauge, by means of which, after endless observations year after year, taken and registered, he gradually detected curious phenomena about the fluctuations of crime generally, the waxing and waning of particular species, the effect of good and bad times, the power of various trades to foster vicious propensities, the results of legislation," &c. "His gaol studies were, of course, supplemented in various ways. He systematically read right through both the extinct and the current literature of crime." "Every book or report connected with prison-management that was published in England he carefully studied." "By degrees he established special correspondents all over the country."[1] "'I wish,' was his constant remark, 'that I could persuade people to notice and believe and think about these things : it is my business, therefore, to make my language not only lucid, but pellucid, so that people may understand it at once.' To this end, the text was profusely illustrated with 'maps showing the localities of crime,' 'diagrams to explain the effects of drunkenness,'" &c. "It is not easy to estimate the effects which he produced by these reports and otherwise ; but that he exercised a very appreciable influence in stirring up the present crusade against crime is beyond denial. He was, undoubtedly, one of the first who fathomed and understood, in any adequate degree, the nature of crime in England. The compliment repeatedly paid to him in Parliament, that 'he knew more of the working-classes than any other man living,' was probably hardly an exaggeration."[2]

"In 1838 the Central Society on Education circulated an epitome of his educational investigations. During the great debates on education in 1839, Lord John Russell quoted the description he had given the year before of the ignorance of prisoners. From this time, when education, prison-discipline, or any subject connected with crime, was under discussion, in Parliament or elsewhere, he was almost invariably quoted as a noteworthy authority."[3]

"*You have kept me awake half the night,*" wrote Lord Brougham to Clay, in acknowledgment of one of his chaplain Reports.

---

[1] Clay's Memoir, 128, 129, 119.   [2] Ibid., 130, 131.   [3] Ibid., 126.

7. THE STATE CAN TAKE COGNIZANCE OF THE INSPIRATION AND GUIDANCE WHICH THE CHAPLAIN, AN EDUCATED MAN, CAN GIVE TO THE EDUCATION OF THE PRISONERS, to the library, and other means for their improvement.

"Out of 1,000 as they stood on the registry," writes Kingsmill of Pentonville Prison, London, "15 were liberally educated." "845 had attended some sort of school, as children, for periods averaging about four years. Of these, 347 had received education in schools kept by private persons, 221 in national schools, 20 in grammar schools, 92 in Sabbath schools, and 160 in other kinds. The attainments of these men were not equal to their opportunities. More than half could not read with *understanding*, or write their own letters; and 758 had no knowledge of any rule in arithmetic beyond addition." [1] "The convicts who could read with intelligence were readers only of the light and trifling productions of the day. Their minds were, therefore, like an unweeded garden, in which the useless predominated." "There was no thirst for wholesome knowledge." [2] As to religious education, "children of nine or ten years of age in a well-ordered Christian family knew as much as the very best informed, with very few exceptions."

In his Report for 1854, Clay says, "During two years I have conversed with 1,088 male prisoners incapable of reading, 41.7 per cent of the whole number of male prisoners committed; 938 male prisoners unable to repeat the Lord's Prayer with any approach to accuracy in the words, or a proper comprehension of their meaning, 36.3 per cent; 1,836 male prisoners who could not understand the import of the plainest language necessary to convey instruction in moral and religious truth, 72.4 per cent." [3] What he means by "plainest language" is shown in the lamentable ignorance described in Clay's letter to Sir. J. S. Packington." [4]

Now, "*Ignorance is the mother of Vice.*"

---

[1] American prisoners, in education, would rank vastly higher. Most of them have had more schooling. Yet, no doubt, prisoners are below the average in good learning and good reading. The above statistics, in comparison, suggest the superiority of our common-school system, and the benefit of separation of State and Church. It is significant that Chaplain Clay's prison observations made him an earnest advocate of national education.

[2] Kingsmill, 39, 40.   [3] Clay's Memoir, 554.   [4] Ibid., 559.

The chaplain represents and urges forward education of the prisoners, secular and religious.

"Cutting through jungles of difficulties," Clay early (1826) established a school and a Sunday school.[1]

Chaplain Speare of Charlestown devotes a section of his Report to the "day school," in which he says, —

"The demand for convict labor, and our straitened accommodations, have caused a suspension of this prosperous feature of my department. When men sign the temperance pledge, saying that they learned to write at that school," "I regret its discontinuance. For the past two years I have urged legislative requirements of a small school, whatever may be the demand for labor."

The Seventh Section of the Report of Wines and Dwight[2] on Secular Instruction contains interesting statements as to the benefits of good books and good reading in a prison. The section is prefaced with this anecdote: "A person passing through a prison as a visitor was shocked at the profane speech of one of the convicts. 'Why do you not have better thoughts?' he inquired. 'Better thoughts!' was the forlorn response: 'where shall I get them?' In that startling question, coming to us from the dungeon, coming to us from a felon and an outcast, we have the whole philosophy of crime and reformation. 'Better thoughts' are what society should have supplied to criminals before they became such, and so have prevented their fall. 'Better thoughts' now that they have fallen, and are suffering the punishment she has imposed for the breach of her laws, are what, by a double bond, she is required to supply them, to the end, that, when released from the stern grasp of justice, they may go and sin no more." These "better thoughts" are found in good books. A good library in prison is a fountain of life to thousands.

An interesting story is given of the foundation of the Prison Library at Alton, Ill. "Their chaplain, in 1846, congratulated the prisoners in the Massachusetts State Prison on their excellent library. The next day a prisoner told him he and some of

---

[1] Clay's Memoir, 112.   [2] Pp. 221-239.

his mates had some books to spare for the prisoners at Alton. Public request was made by the warden for any such books. The chaplain came next day with a large silk handkerchief to take away the books. What was his astonishment to find a present of more than four hundred bound volumes! The silk handkerchief would not do; and the prisoners requested permission to make boxes to pack the books in."[1]

The chaplain is Teacher as well as Preacher in the prison.

These reasons make the appointment of chaplains in our State institutions not only a legitimate procedure, but a matter of exceeding importance to the State and to her wards.

We now proceed to the third important point: —

ONLY ONE CHAPLAIN.

By this we mean that one person alone, or one person with assistants, should hold and exercise the functions which we have designated. "You have no curate?" asked Lord Brougham's committee of Clay. "No," was the reply. "I may venture to say, that, if the separate system is carried more generally into effect, a prison calculated to hold two hundred or three hundred prisoners will find work for two or three chaplains." "His meaning was simply this, that, in his own prison, there was about three times as much work [ministrations in the cells] as he could get through." It is not said that a chaplain should never have assistants; though, in our American prisons, they are probably unnecessary. What is intended is, that *only one man should represent, as the head, those interests of which we have spoken.* There should be one chaplain, as there is one warden and one surgeon. There should not be a second man who holds a chaplaincy or *quasi* chaplaincy, anything which may be called a chaplaincy, apart from the one appointed chaplain; least of all, one in any way antagonistic to that one, or who is seeking to neutralize his work, or, in the face of all, do a rival work in the same line, yet in different fashion, intended to be at variance with the first. This is what we think the State, through eyes of wisdom, always has discerned, and through eyes of wisdom is

[1] Report of Wines and Dwight, 229.

competent to discern, from the following reasons, why only one chaplain is allowable in each institution: —

1. THE STATE CAN DISCERN THAT THE ANALOGY OF OFFICIAL FUNCTIONS IN A PRISON ALLOWS BUT ONE CHAPLAIN.

The idea of prison official life is, that the various work in the institution is divided into departments, with a responsible head over each department. The warden, the surgeon, are heads of their departments. They were directly appointed by the State. They make annual reports to the State. It would not be an interference to give them subordinate assistants; but it would be to give them rivals, — a rival warden with other ideas of prison-discipline, a rival surgeon of another school of medicine.

The chaplain is likewise an *official* of the institution. He is appointed by the Executive. He reports to him. Analogy requires, that, in his department, he shall be sole and responsible head.

2. THE STATE TAKES NOTE, THAT, IN ALL THE GENERAL PLAN OF GOOD FOR THE PRISONERS, — "RELIGIOUS INSTRUCTION, EDUCATION, AND IMPROVEMENT OF THE PRISONERS," — THERE MUST BE BUT ONE CHAPLAIN.

After appointing Napoleon to the command of the army of Italy, the Directory were alarmed at their step, and proposed to associate with him a colleague. "If you do," said Bonaparte, "recall me. One poor commander is better than two good ones." In the olden time, the Athenian generals were wise enough not to attempt to command together, but in rotation; and so Miltiades was commander at Marathon. One head is enough for one body. Considered as a system for the religious and educational improvement of prisoners conducted on a *plan* covering, perhaps, years, one chaplain is best. Two chaplains means *two plans*, which cannot be wise within a prison's limits.

3. THE STATE CAN TAKE NOTE THAT ONE CHAPLAIN CAN DO ALL WHICH THE TRUE OFFICE OF CHAPLAIN DEMANDS. For all the purposes designated, to conduct a divine service, to be a father or personal friend, to represent humanity, to represent and encourage education, one person is sufficient and satisfactory to the State: therefore the *State*, the only party which has any-

thing to do with a chaplain, has no reason to appoint or allow a second, or twelve, or twenty.

4. THE STATE CAN OBSERVE, THAT, UNTIL THE PRESENT LAW IS REPEALED, THE STATE MAKES AN IMPLIED PROMISE TO THE CHAPLAIN THAT HE IS TO BE THE ONLY CHAPLAIN, UNIMPEDED IN HIS PLANS. "*The* chàplain shall devote *his whole time* to the religious instruction, education, and improvement of the convicts." Any man appointed under such laws and regulations would consider them an implied promise that he should have free scope, and should be unhindered in every thing necessary to effect "the religious instruction, education, and improvement of the convicts," while alone held responsible for that work.

5. THE STATE CAN RECALL TO HERSELF THAT THE NATURAL IDEA OF A CHAPLAIN, THE TRADITIONAL IDEA, THE LEGAL IDEA, SHOWS THAT THERE SHALL BE BUT ONE. The General Statutes embody the time-honored as well as the legal conception of this office. "The chaplain of the State prison," &c., are the words of the statute. "*The* chaplain," — only one is contemplated. Again : "The chaplain shall devote his whole time to the religious instruction, education, and improvement of the convicts." All through this enumeration of duties the word is "*he.*" Evidently, therefore, the State and the civil community have from time immemorial felt that all which they had in mind as belonging to that office required that it should be performed by one. The State, doubtless, has understood its own idea of a chaplain and his work ; and this traditional idea and this legal enactment *ought not to be set aside except by direct, specific, unequivocal enactment of law, that there shall be a rival chaplain.*

6. THE STATE CAN OBSERVE, THAT SO FAR AS SHE' PROPOSES, AND IT IS ALLOWABLE TO HER, TO TOUCH THE RELATIONS OF THE SOUL TO GOD, THE ENDS OF THE STATE, AND THE PEACE AND DISCIPLINE OF THE PRISON, REQUIRE AND PERMIT THAT SHE SHALL SIMPLY ALLOW A SERVICE, WHICH, AS A GENERAL EXERCISE, SHALL' AROUSE ALL SOULS, and awaken general ideas of the divine mercy and divine life, but leave to the communings of the prisoner's own spirit, or to his private intercourse with some spiritual confidant, clerical or lay, to answer definitely the question which

‚personal religion puts, "*What* must *I* do to be saved?" The State can consistently stop nowhere between these two positions, — to have one public divine service, which shall, in a general way, exhort, arouse, awaken, comfort all souls, and afford one general channel for the spiritual emotions of all ; or to conduct twelve different services to gratify twelve different constituencies. Is it not clear as light that the *one general appeal to the spiritual nature,* the one general channel for religious worship, is all which a chaplaincy contemplates, or has ever contemplated? May we not go further, and say that the allowing a particular denomination to be named in the statutes, to have a *separate denominational officer* in State institutions, is as glaring a disregard of American ideas as to the separation of State and Church as can be perpetrated? nay, more, is an *invasion of the rights of all denominations,* who accept, in good faith, the separation of State and Church?

The State allows the presentation of the general view of God, his judgment, his mercy, hope, fear, invitation, illustrated and pressed home by the particular mode and manner and secondary opinions of the person whom the State has chosen as wise and earnest enough to do it. The State proposes wisely to attempt no more than this in a public service. She leaves to each man to meet the *personal* question to which that *general appeal* awakens him, by private recourse to those whom he desires as spiritual confidants.

Bayard Taylor tells us in pleasant rhyme an incident of Balaklava. It was evening, and the men were in camp around their fires. Home had been the theme. Perhaps the mail had just arrived from distant England. In the glow of that home-feeling some one struck up "Annie Laurie," and all, owning the feeling that prompted it, joined at once ; and Taylor says, reading from the act to the thought, —

> "Each heart recalled a different name ;
> But all sang Annie Laurie."

The *general appeal to the spiritual nature* is all which the State proposes to give channel for in her public divine service in her institutions: she leaves to "each heart" to "recall" all that is suggested of its own personal needs and hopes, fears and joys. As the State proposes to give opportunity only to this general appeal to the soul, but one chaplain is necessary.

7. THE STATE CAN ALSO OBSERVE, THAT ANY GROUND ON WHICH THERE SHOULD BE MORE THAN ONE CHAPLAIN IN AN INSTITUTION WOULD CONTRAVENE HER NECESSARY AND TRADI- TIONARY IDEAS OF A CHAPLAIN, AND HER EXPRESS REGULA- TIONS.

On what ground is it imagined there can be two or twelve chaplains? There can be no other ground than difference of faith. We claim, is the demand, a chaplain, because we do not agree in the worship of the chapel. That claim is counter to the State's idea of a chaplain, — that he is one who is to hold a general religious service ; counter to the regulations, which read, " *No attempt shall be made to teach any sectarian belief to the convicts.*" Therefore a sectarian chaplain, *under law*, is an impos- sibility. If the chapel service is fairly conforming to the State's idea of a general service, and an ecclesiastic makes objection that that service does not suit him, and therefore claims a chap- laincy, *the ground of the claim kills the petition.* "No sectarian preaching," says the State. "My petition is on the ground that my services are denominational." That claim bars your en- trance, until the State shall go down to the foundations, change her traditional idea — the only one congruous in a free State — of a general chaplain, and with a revolutionary pen write her statutes over again.

The State knows nothing of sects.

A second chaplain, unless petitioning to be an assistant of the first, must claim his place on *illegal grounds*, and against the State's historic idea of the chaplaincy.

8. THE STATE TAKES NOTE THAT ANY GROUND ON WHICH THERE SHOULD BE MORE THAN ONE CHAPLAIN WOULD NECESSI- TATE A DOZEN CHAPLAINS OR MORE.

If the ground for appointing a chaplain and divine service were the *churches* represented in a State institution, then must there be as many chaplains as churches. "Then," to use the words of Chaplain Speare's report, "our Jews must" "have a synagogue furnished them; then the High Church Episcopalian must have a Sabbath service performed by some one in the true apostolic descent, and clad in all becoming vestments; then the Chinese must have a joss-house set up within prison-walls, duly appointed, and fragrant with burning incense."[1] Is it true that twelve chaplains and twelve services comport with the *State's* idea and need of a chaplain? Is not all this claim on the *erroneous notion* that a prison is a place with all the liberty and privilege of the outside world?

If the ground on which a chaplain is appointed were the religious preferences of the individual, fifty chaplains would hardly suffice. Indeed, to meet the demands of an ever-fluctuating community like a prison, the balloting for chaplains must be a common occurrence within the walls. No! "Positive provision," says the same report, "to gratify every man's religious preferences, has not been made, and *never can be.* The prison is not administered for that purpose."

It is indeed customary in State institutions on both sides of the Atlantic to allow individuals, at proper times, to see privately such religious advisers as they may designate; but this is very different from a chaplain and a public service. There must be, therefore, either one chaplain or twelve, unless you say, One general chaplain; *but,* considering the *political importance* of one *particular church,* the State must yield to their pertinacious demand. Has it come to that? Do we live in America, a free State? or in Spain? "*Ubi gentium sumus?*" The State is no respecter of persons; knows no church, no party; knows, therefore, no ground of favoring one or another, no ground between appointing one chaplain or twenty. Any call for more than one chaplain proceeds on an entire misconception of what a *State* chaplain is.

9. THE STATE CAN OBSERVE THE PROBABLE COLLISION BETWEEN TWO CHAPLAINS sooner or later, even were both legally appointed; the *certain* collision, if the State chaplain is a man of proper self-respect, and has true sense of his office, as long

[1] Report of 1876.

as another, without law, attempts to enter the prison, to interfere with his department, to act as *quasi*-chaplain.

10. THE STATE CAN OBSERVE THE PROBABLE EFFECT ON THE
PRISON-OFFICERS OF TWO RIVAL CHAPLAINS. They will hold
either with the one or the other. They may be tempted to do
things for the *quasi*-chaplain, representing a large religious and
political constituency, which they ought not to do, which would
irritate a State chaplain representing only the State.

11. THE STATE CAN FORECAST THE PROBABLE AND NECESSARY
ANTAGONISM AMONG THE PRISONERS from the presence of two
religious parties led by two chaplains.

"I am thankful," writes John Clay, "that my isolated position
as a gaol-chaplain saves me from the danger of religious parti-
sanship." "If the energy which is wasted on these miserable
controversies were combined into one great crusade against
vice and ignorance, it would change the fate of England and
the world."[1]

12. THE STATE CAN NOTE AND DEPRECATE THE PROBABLE
EFFECT, ON ALL THE OBJECTS WHICH SHE HOLDS OF VALUE CON-
CERNING THE PRISONERS CONSIDERED AS HER WARDS, OF THAT
CONSTANT EXCITEMENT AND IRRITATION AMONG THE PRISONERS
which must arise at the spectacle of two hostile religious teachers. It is believed no one can fail to see that this must be injurious to the formation of such a moral character as the State
desires to form in her wards before sending them out again into
the world.

> "The Spirit, like a peaceful dove,
> Flies from the realms of noise and strife."

Need we further multiply considerations, patent to the State,
why only one chaplain is possible in each institution?

We gather up the results of this discussion in these few final
words : —

1. *The State appoints chaplain and divine service from her own
stand-point.* Nor does she do it *constrained*, but of her own option. She can abolish the chaplaincy, if her ends demand :
she can have one, and only one, if that subserves her purposes.

[1] Clay's Memoir, 577.

2. *The State does not appoint a chaplain and divine service at the request of her wards* that she will satisfy and gratify their religious preferences.

3. *The State does not appoint a chaplain to gratify what is called a church,* or organization of any kind.

4. *So far as a chaplain and divine services are for spiritual purposes, the State, according to her historic and legal idea, attempts only a general channel for religious appeal and worship.* She never has gone further. A new departure, revolutionary indeed, could alone change her traditional idea. The State furnishes a spiritual "commons," not a *table d'hôte.* Accordingly, such men have always been recognized as model chaplains who stirred the religious nature of all. Such men as Father Taylor, Bridaine, Father Mathew, Francis Eden as sketched by Charles Reade, Mr. Moody, Father Mason, Phineas Stowe, — these large catholic men, who could not pause to be polemic on a small point, — these would be chaplains indeed.

Spontaneously and earnestly my chaplain friend of the flagship exclaimed to me, "For the sake of all that's good, say, if you write on chaplaincies, that *a chaplain who is denominational cuts off his fingers,* so far as good work is concerned. For a year, they didn't know what was my denomination."

Just as soon as any man puts any particular name in place of "Annie Laurie," the charm of the song is gone to all.

One of the most amusing things in the literature of chaplaincies is the resignation of Rev. Walter Balfour, quoted by Gideon Haynes in his interesting "Prison Incidents." Mr. Balfour, it seems, in 1808, had changed his views on a comparatively insignificant article of faith ; and he hastens to write this note, yielding up his office : —

"GENTLEMEN, — As a change of sentiment has taken place with me on the subject of infant-baptism, and not knowing but this may form some objection to the continuance of my services at the State prison, I think it my duty to intimate to you my desire to discontinue them. If desired, I have no objection to supply for a Sabbath or two, until you may conveniently provide yourselves with some other person.

"WALTER BALFOUR."

In the slightly slang expression sometimes used by a lady-friend, " This is too funny for anything." Had this gentleman, then, supposed, that, in the eye of the State, his fitness for the chaplaincy had consisted in his views on the minor point to which he refers? If so, he never had been a *chaplain* of that prison in any large, true idea of that office, or in the State idea of that office.

5. *Ecclesiastics who ask for additional chaplaincies,* on the ground that they belong to a particular church not reached by the State-appointed chaplain, show *on the face of their petition* cause *why they cannot be allowed,* legally or by civil right, to enter a State institution as recognized chaplains ; ecclesiastics who claim entrance to State institutions on the ground that they have a large constituency there, give reason to the State, on the face of their petition, for questioning their fitness to be shepherds of souls ; ecclesiastics who claim that their church has supreme visible jurisdiction, *divino jure,* everywhere, and has a divine right to pass, visibly and by ministers, all State barriers and walls, by the face of that claim cut themselves off from *chaplaincies,* which are of the *State's* commission for purposes allowed and permitted of the State, within its sovereign sphere. " He that climbeth up some other way, the same is a thief and a robber."

" HE WHO WOULD SCALE A WALL TO GO WHERE HE HAS NO RIGHT WOULD LAY FLAT THAT WALL IF HIS POWER WERE EQUAL TO HIS WILL."

6. *Any law regarding State Institutions and Religion,* to be permanently satisfactory, must be, first of all, EXPLICIT; its terms not permitting quarrel or subingression.[1] It must, further, provide for an unsectarian " divine service," a chaplain, and only one chaplain ; it should not only not allow any thing detrimental to discipline, but should not depart from the analogy of official functions, *one officer of a kind to an institution,* unhindered in his department, and responsible for its success ; it must, a least in *all penal, corrective, and reformatory institutions,* whose inmates have become *the wards of the State through default of*

---

[1] Vernacular, Sneaking in. Subingression is historical in Massachusetts.

character, require the presence of all inmates at divine service, though none should be compelled to take active part in the same ; it should, as in the past, make full provision for private visits, and *private visits only*, at proper times, of other religious friends, lay or clerical, at the request of the prisoner himself.

7. The State should exercise the largest wisdom and the greatest care in the selection of chaplains for her institutions.

The large number and the great moral needs of her wards, and the beneficent purposes she has towards them, exact this.

The State should select chaplains on the same principles on which men of large common sense select agents, the merchant his clerk, the corporation its foreman ; namely, one the least objectionable, one heartily entering into the employer's plans, one eminently fitted for the work, one who is likely to improve in efficiency by experience.

It is evident, then, that, at the outset, the State must rule out of the candidacy all who cannot enter the chaplaincy with a sufficient sympathy with her view of the ends to be secured. She cannot admit a Jesuit, who will not recognize the State as "independent" and "sovereign," who will not take oath of allegiance to the State ; nor can she allow as chaplains those whose thoughts are mainly bent on bringing the religious life which may be awakened within the prison into connection with, and subjection to, a particular church-system without. All this is implied in the idea of a *State* chaplain and a "divine service," "unsectarian."

The candidacy of good men earnestly attached to particular religious systems is by no means, therefore, excluded. It is interesting, however, to observe how one who is appointed chaplain is recognized as set apart for an unsectarian work. My naval chaplain friend said, as if lamenting the separation of the chaplain from the sympathy of religious bodies, "As soon as a man becomes a chaplain, his church forgets him." This remark is significant of the peculiarly unsectarian popular idea of the chaplaincy. Yet, as we have said, men earnestly attached to particular religious systems are not excluded from candidacy. There are Catholics who are catholic. Father Mathew, the great Apostle of Temperance, was catholic enough for a chaplain. Bridaine, as described by both Carron and Bungener, had that largeness of heart which would have admirably fitted him for such a sphere. Indeed, even in those early days (1725), half a century before Howard, we find this noble man thoughtful of prisoners, preaching sermons in their behalf.[1] He went more than once to comfort Protestants condemned to death for religion's sake. His biographer says, "How many prisoners in detention for debt, quarrels, or for other misdemeanors, who seemed to him to merit clemency, have found in Brydayne a father and a savior!"[2] The late Father Dougherty of Cambridge, if private report and public encomium are true, had that catholicity, sympathy, and efficiency which would have made him a worthy chaplain.

If one thinks that the Catholic Church would not allow one of her ministers to continue a course of unsectarian ministrations for a term of years, he does not reckon so great as we the adaptability of the Romish Church, which would gladly have its ministers in places of influence, even if shorn of some of their activities. The Jesuits have always acted thus, and in China, as we have seen, even allowed external idolatry in order to secure and hold converts. But we see no reason why, in all honesty, Père Bridaine and Father Mathew should refuse to conduct a service in which they should be limited to prayer, praise, reading of the Scriptures, and the sermon. But should ministers of this church insist, We are NOTHING IF NOT SECTARIAN, then the State has no parley with them, but, whatever their abounding merits, must summarily bar them out. If one cannot conform to the rules of the arena, he must keep out of it. For the State knows nothing of sects, nor of sectarian teachings, except so far as they thrust themselves upon her notice as an *inseparable* part of a man, and so excluding him from the office.

---

[1] Carron, Vie de Brydayne, 47. All English authorities spell Bridaine, Bungener also; his biographer, the abbé Carron, Brydayne; his epitaph, as quoted by him, "Hic jacet Jacobus Erydayne," &c.

[2] Vie de Brydayne, 184.

But it may be thought that all ministers are sectarian. Not in the popular, nor, indeed, in any true philosophical sense. The catholic is he who holds the truths held by all (*καθ' ὅλον*). In unrevealed truth, a man is catholic who holds the great truths as held by devout thinkers all the world over. As a believer in a special revelation, he is catholic who holds the great truths taught by the Founder of that religion in the way they are held by the body universal, and in such a spirit that he can hold them with all ; namely, in St. Augustine's noble words, " In necessariis, unitas ; in dubiis, libertas ; in omnibus, caritas," — " In essentials, unity ; in doubtful, liberty ; in all, charity." A sectarian, on the contrary, is one of a *sect*, or *cut-off* (*seco*, to cut). He belongs to a *section* of the great body of believers. Disregarding the great truths which are believed " semper, ubique, et ab omnibus," — " always, everywhere, and by all," — he foists into prominence the *dubia*, or " doubtful " things, and, with others who agree to cut off from the main body on those secondary matters, he becomes a sectarist. He thinks with a sect, acts with a sect, and largely, as a partisan, for a sect. In dealing with men, he meets them primarily with his special doctrines, which, nevertheless, are not the essential doctrines. That is a sectarian.

We do not account it sectarian for one in special time and place and company to explain and expound special doctrines, if this is done with catholic distinction between the *necessaria* and the *dubia*.

Nor, which bears on our present subject, do we account a man sectarian who forces home catholic truths with appeals drawn from special ideas believed by himself alone. Were Archbishop Williams invited to preach before the Evangelical Alliance a sermon on Persuasives to the Lord's Supper, we would not deem it sectarian to name as one head, one persuasive, that the Lord Jesus' body was actually before us, at the Table. *But if,* on the other hand, he were invited to deliver an address before the assembled ministry, without any understanding that he was to present his own peculiar doctrines, we should consider it sectarian were he to present a *discussion* of the doctrine of Transubstantiation. In the first case, the purpose was catholic, — to induce to come to the Lord's Supper. That catholic purpose governed all the special arguments which he might · present. In the latter case, his aim would be sectarian, — to make us believe as a *section* of the Church on a minor tenet. One would not necessarily be a sectarian who preached of " temperance, righteousness, and judgment," because, in appeal, he used his own peculiar beliefs of the near approach of judgment at a specified time. But to *teach* that doctrine as opposed to the prevailing idea would be sectarian. No minister or chaplain is sectarian who presents the general truths of judgment, mercy, righteousness, brotherly kindness, " the love of God, the grace of the Lord Jesus Christ, and the communion of the Holy Spirit," although he may enforce his appeals by doctrines held by only a section. If his *purpose* is catholic, his *preaching* is *catholic.* In this sense, — and we believe we have only explained the popular thought of the meaning of the word, — there are hundreds, thousands, of men earnestly attached to particular doctrines who are catholic, and whose preaching is catholic. It matters not that their incidental utterances, and the manner of their appeal, show them to be Methodist, Episcopal, Papist : if their purpose is predominant, to *save souls* by presenting the justice and mercy of God, men consider them unsectarian. A catholic purpose makes one a catholic preacher.

The State, then, is to select one for chaplain on the ground that he is a good man, and efficient in doing and securing good. From all the good men, of whatever religious order, who are before her view, she is to select one who is pre-eminently fitted to be such a chaplain as we have described him, — an eminent representative of goodness, hope, sympathy, and divine love. Thomas Starr King, we recall, said that not every minister could be a chaplain. The largest measure of vital goodness, the largest and most Christlike love, the most potent force to draw down upon men " the love of God, the grace of the Lord Jesus Christ, the communion of the Holy Spirit," and to move men with divine knowledge and motives and persuasives, and these joined with the most thorough understanding of men and the most roundabout common sense, the heartiest sympathy with men, are not too much to bring to this important office. He should be an Israel, "having power with God and with men;" one who is "prevailing."

The State should, moreover, select one for this office who possesses what Bushnell so happily called "the Talent of Growth." Entering the chaplaincy at thirty, with the crudity of youth gone, and somewhat of maturity gained, he should be one who, by more careful observation, wider reading, profounder insight and reflection concerning prisons and prisoners, criminals and crime, would gain, year by year, larger conceptions of his office, greater ability to meet his people's deepest needs, their sins and sorrows. He must be an enthusiast, one who loves to learn about prisoners, emphatically the Prisoner's Friend. "Nihil" carcerei "a me alienum esse puto,"—"Nothing concerning the prisoner count I foreign to myself." Advancing as rapidly in divine knowledge, and growth in personal goodness, as in knowledge of men, and how to meet them to do them good, retaining his early enthusiasm, and increasing in the love with which he began his career, he should be one who would ripen, not wither, and, valuable at thirty-five, should be indispensable at forty-five. Such a chaplaincy as that of John Clay, of forty years, is as blessed to the institution in its hallowed ministrations and maturing usefulness as it is beneficial to the State in the recorded results of his ripe experience. Choosing such a one, who is willing to become for a score of years the Prisoners' Pastor, to the exclusion of all other pastoral ambitions, the State should make it reasonably certain, that, unless he disappoint her hopes in his service, he should be guaranteed opportunity for a long and beneficent and uninterrupted career of ever-ripening usefulness.

Thus, in conclusion, the State, which has equal aversion, on the one hand, to connection with Church, and, on the other hand, to sects and the strife of sects, can yet, without transcending her sphere, open her prison-windows to permit that on her wards within may fall some of that glory which shone from the skies in the darkness of another night, when angelic visitants —

celestial, and not sectarian — brought the dawn of heaven to earth, and sang that hymn which is the harbinger of the universal Hope of sinners : "Glory to God in the highest, on earth peace, good-will toward men."

What *should* enter the prison is not the formulated dogma and the articulated creed, but that hope of the divine mercy. That cheering light can nowhere be more gladdening and efficient than in a prison. Even the most criminal and imbruted may prove in themselves "The Forces of a Sunbeam."

What *should* penetrate the prison-wall is the pure sunlight, unrefracted, undiscolored by painted glass of sect, — the simple, full ray, — "the Light that lighteth every man that cometh into the world," — "unto which" *all* "would do well to take heed, as unto a light that shineth in a dark place, *until the day dawn, and the daystar arise in their hearts."*

"The ivy in a dungeon grew,
Unfed by rain, uncheered by dew :
The pallid leaflets only drank
Cave-moistures foul and odors dank.

But through the dungeon's grating high
There fell a sunbeam from the sky :
It slept upon the grateful floor
In silent gladness evermore.

The ivy felt a tremor shoot
Through all its fibres to the root ;
It felt the light ; it saw the ray ;
It strove to blossom into day ;

It grew, it crept, it pushed, it clomb :
Long had the darkness been its home ;
But well it knew, though veiled in night,
The goodness and the joy of light.

It reached the beam, it thrilled, it curled ;
It blessed the warmth that cheers the world ;
It rose towards the dungeon-bars ;
It looked upon the light and stars ;